这是一本绝对不可错过的"英语学习+人生励志"双

每天30分钟轻松
听懂读懂
名家访谈

创业
领袖
面对面

In Conversation with
Entrepreneurial Leaders

主　编

编　委

芳　刘傅曹孙万包么高阜叶李
晶　丹雪芳晨举亮隃奇梅
婷　姜富王佳李刘蔡曹蔡佟姜吴
宁　霞焱进杰亮琳琦姜菲衡
黄乐军石岩徐怀陈黄庄王王包乔
香伟亮伟继武哲志君哲
田东婷王甜甜徐伟高韩李王
权健生丹蕊一雷
杨晶文王虹斌孟亚王亚范俊吴沈甘程玉培
佟团结宙黄振潇浩张雨吴春牛治程常张
钱晓辉季君苏士姜卞亭张婷徐越牛庆毛勤
房立伟丁小英李宁代学于方彬彬张明明沈吴春维刘

大连理工大学出版社

图书在版编目（CIP）数据

创业领袖面对面 / 刘芳主编. —大连：大连理工大学
出版社，2012.10
（每天30分钟轻松听懂读懂名家访谈）
ISBN 978-7-5611-7353-4

Ⅰ.①创… Ⅱ.①刘… Ⅲ.①英语—汉语—对照读物
②企业家—访问记—世界 Ⅳ.①H319.4：K

中国版本图书馆CIP数据核字（2012）第232751号

大连理工大学出版社出版
地址：大连市软件园路80号　邮政编码：116023
发行：0411-84708842　邮购：0411-84703636　传真：0411-84701466
E-mail:dutp@dutp.cn　URL:http://www.dutp.cn
辽宁星海彩色印刷有限公司印刷　大连理工大学出版社发行

幅面尺寸：168mm×235mm	印张：17.75	字数：504千字
附件：光盘1张		印数：1~8000
2012年10月第1版		2012年10月第1次印刷

责任编辑：高颖　　　　　　　　　　　　　　　　　责任校对：王丽丽
封面设计：嘉美和

ISBN 978-7-5611-7353-4　　　　　　　　　　　　　定价：30.00元

前 言 *Preface*

英语的学习不仅是脑力活，也是体力活，它不光需要用脑筋去"攻读"，更需要花时间去"熟练"。英语听力和阅读的输入训练是英语学习的关键环节，这是很多成功的英语学习者的亲身体会。有效地进行输入环节听和读的学习和积累，有助于我们对英语单词、句型及习惯用法的积累，有助于我们提高英语口语的流利程度，提高听、说、读、写、译多方面的能力。每天拿出来30分钟，走近名人，亲历访谈，与各界精英面对面，感悟他们的智慧，领略他们的风采。

本系列丛书《每天30分钟轻松听懂读懂名家访谈》，是精选自国外报刊、杂志、电视等权威媒体对各界精英的访谈实录选编而成，是您不可错过的具有"英语学习+人生励志"双重功用的英汉对照读物。

我们将这些名人访谈分为四册：

《每天30分钟轻松听懂读懂名家访谈：财经名人面对面》：这里的每个人都是足以影响世界经济的财经领袖。他们中，有戴尔、谷歌、通用、宝洁、沃尔玛这些世界500强公司的CEO，也有美国财政部长、美联储主席、股神巴菲特这样对世界金融界举足轻重的人物。阅读他们睿智理性的分析，我们将经历一场头脑风暴。

《每天30分钟轻松听懂读懂名家访谈：大牌明星面对面》：这里星光熠熠，既有汤姆•克鲁斯、妮可•基德曼、安吉丽娜•朱莉、布拉德•皮特、尼古拉斯•凯奇等影视明星，也有里奥•梅西、大卫•贝克汉姆、林书豪、迈克尔•乔丹、科比•布兰恩特这样的体坛巨星。带您走进25位全球顶级明星的内心世界。

《每天30分钟轻松听懂读懂名家访谈：政界精英面对面》：这里是英美政坛精英的聚集地，17位英国和美国政界精英各自为您阐述对于全球政治的独特见解。

《每天30分钟轻松听懂读懂名家访谈：创业领袖面对面》：创业者是这个时代最闪耀的潮流引领者。24位举世公认的杰出创业成功人士，讲述他们创业中的艰辛，分享成功的经验教训。站在巨人的肩膀上，这是您不可错过的人生一课。

本套丛书具有以下特色：

1. 榜样的力量

本书所选的访谈对象世界知名、形象健康，都是大家公认的某一领域的精英人士，中国读者非常熟悉。阅读他们的访谈，读者会有更多的亲切感和认同感，学习兴趣自然高涨。

2. 内容的力量

本书编选的访谈内容，尽量避免过于生僻的专业领域知识，着重选择体现被访者智慧、人生理念、社会价值观等方面的信息。另外，对于某些过于晦涩难懂的内容，也做了适当调整。更加便于广大读者进行英语学习。

3. 知识的力量

编者将访谈的内容详细梳理加工，精准控制每篇访谈的篇幅，便于读者更有计划地学习。同时把每篇访谈的英文都做了全文翻译，并将重点词汇标注于中、英文旁边。在正文后，还辅以本文内应知应会的知识点睛，使广大读者能学有所获。

4. 方法的力量

按照编者设置的学习时间段使用本书，学习效果将更好。

• 轻松输入十分钟：在仅有关键词（页面左栏）提示下，尽量不借助其他工具边阅读英文边听音频，了解文章大致主题思想（8分钟左右）。复习单词（2分钟左右）。

• 有效学习十分钟：对照中文译文和关键英文单词（页面右栏），边看中文译文，边听英文音频。可以根据自己的英文水平，以句子、句群甚至段落为单位停顿15～30秒。通过巩固和强化，听懂和读懂文章的意思（8分钟左右）。复习单词（2分钟左右）。

• 自由输出十分钟：每篇访谈之后都有关键知识点的提炼，编者以数十年的英语学习经历、海外见闻、教学经验针对每一个话题倾囊而出，这是全书的精华所在（10分钟左右）。即使前面环节未能达到我们预期的效果，只要认真学习本环节，都会有所收获。

5. 科技的力量

编者投入大量的资金、时间和精力，开发了iPhone、iPad平台的配套学习APP。相比纸质图书，APP可以更便捷地查询、记忆；有更丰富的内容和更生动的互动学习形式。有iPhone、iTouch、iPad的读者可以到APP Store搜索"名人访谈录"下载本书配备的互动APP应用，随时随地学习。

我们不希望您仅仅成为某个成功者的粉丝去了解他们，而是为了将他们身上独特的闪光点挖掘出来。他们的睿智、勇敢、持之以恒和敬业精神是广大读者学习的榜样。对比成功者，再对照自己，每个读者都会在人生的成长中获得更多的感悟。

祝大家每天都有新收获！

编者

2012年9月

目 录
Contents

苹果创始人之一：
史蒂夫·乔布斯
Co-founder of Apple: Steve Jobs

　　史蒂夫·乔布斯（1955~2011），1955年2月出生于美国加利福尼亚州的旧金山。他是发明家、企业家、美国苹果公司联合创办人、前行政总裁，同时也是前皮克斯动画工作室的董事长兼行政总裁。1976年，乔布斯和朋友成立苹果电脑公司，他陪伴了苹果公司数十年的衰落与复兴，先后领导和推出了麦金塔计算机、iMac、iPod、iPhone等风靡全球的电子产品，深刻地改变了现代通讯、娱乐乃至生活的方式。2011年10月5日，他因病逝世，享年56岁。

　　乔布斯是改变世界的天才，他凭着敏锐的触觉和过人的智慧，勇于变革，不断创新，引领全球资讯科技和电子产品的潮流，把电脑和电子产品变得简约化、平民化，使曾经是昂贵稀罕的电子产品成为现代人生活的一部分。

Apple Has Lots of Capable People

轻松输入十分钟

Reporter: Let's start with the birth of the iPhone. How did you get the idea to create it?

Jobs: We all had cellphones. We just hated them, they were so awful to use. The software was terrible. The hardware wasn't very good. We talked to our friends, and they all hated their cellphones too. Everybody seemed to hate their phones. And we saw that these things really could become much more powerful and interesting to license. It's a huge market. I mean a billion phones get shipped every year, and that's almost an order of magnitude greater than the number of music players. It's four times the number of PCs that ship every year. It was a great challenge. Let's make a great phone that we fall in love with. And we've got the technology. We've got the miniaturization from the iPod. We've got the sophisticated operating system from Mac. Nobody had ever thought about putting operating systems as sophisticated as OSX inside a phone, so that was a real question. We had a big debate inside the company whether we could do that or not. And that was one where I had to adjudicate it and just say, "We're going to do it. Let's try." The smartest software guys were saying they can do it, so let's give them a shot. And they did.

Reporter: How did Apple connect with its customers?

Jobs: We did iTunes because we all love music. We made what we thought was the best jukebox in iTunes. Then we all wanted to carry our whole music libraries around with us. The team worked really hard. And the reason that they worked so hard is because we all wanted one. You know? I mean, the first few hundred customers were us. It's not about pop culture, and it's not about fooling people, and it's not about convincing people that they want something they don't. We figure out what we want. And I think we're pretty good at having the right discipline to think through whether a lot of other people are going to want it, too. That's what we get paid to do. So you can't go out and ask people, you know, what the next big thing is.

awful *adj.*
糟糕的，可怕的

hardware *n.*
硬件，装备

magnitude *n.*
大小，量级

miniaturization *n.*
（尤指电子装置）
微型化，小型化

sophisticated *adj.*
精密的，富有经验的

adjudicate *v.*
决定，判决

jukebox *n.*
自动点唱机，媒体柜

discipline *n.*
方法，准则

苹果公司人才辈出

有效学习十分钟

记者： 我们先从iPhone的起源谈起吧，您是怎么想到发明它的？

乔布斯： 我们都用过手机。我们都不喜欢用手机，因为它们并不好用。<u>软件[1]</u>烂得一塌糊涂，<u>硬件[2]</u>也不怎么样。我们和朋友聊天，他们也都非常痛恨自己的手机。似乎每个人都痛恨自己的手机。于是我们觉得，这些东西完全可以变得更加<u>强大[3]</u>，摆出来也会很有意思。这是一个巨大的市场，我是说每年有10亿部手机被卖掉，这单生意在数量上可比音乐播放器庞大多了，是每年<u>个人电脑[4]</u>销量的四倍。这是个巨大的挑战。我们要做出一款可以让我们自己都<u>一见钟情[5]</u>的手机。我们手中有技术，有源于iPod的<u>微型制造工艺[6]</u>，还有来自Mac电脑的<u>精密操作系统[7]</u>。从未有人想过往手机里放进一个如OSX般精密的<u>操作系统[8]</u>，这看来确实是个问题。关于我们能否做到这点，我们公司内部进行过激烈的<u>讨论[9]</u>。我不得不当机立断地做出决定："我们可以做到的。让我们试试看吧。"那些最聪明的<u>软件工程师[10]</u>说他们可以做得到，那么我们给他们这个机会。他们果然做到了。

记者： 苹果和<u>消费者[11]</u>之间的联系是怎样的？

乔布斯： 我们之所以去做iTunes，是因为我们都热爱音乐。我们在iTunes里做出了自认为是最好的<u>自动唱片点唱机[12]</u>。然后我们又都希望随身携带全部的<u>音乐资料库[13]</u>。研发团队展开了非常艰辛的工作。他们之所以这么卖命，就是因为我们都需要一个这样的产品。你知道吗？我是说我们自己就是最早的那几百个用户。这事儿和<u>流行文化[14]</u>无关，和<u>坑蒙拐骗[15]</u>无关，和说服人们接受一件他们压根儿不需要的东西也无关。我们只是在搞明白我们自己需要什么而已。而且我认为，我们已经建立了一套良好的<u>思维体系[16]</u>，其他许多人都会需要。我们收了钱就是来做这件事的。所以你没法走上大街去问别人下一件大事会是什么。亨利·福特曾经有过一句<u>名言[17]</u>，"如果我当年去问顾客他们想

1. software *n.*
2. hardware *n.*
3. powerful *adj.*
4. PC (personal computer)
5. fall in love with
6. miniaturization *n.*
7. sophisticated operating system
8. operating system
9. debate *n.*
10. software guy
11. customer *n.*
12. jukebox *n.*
13. music library
14. pop culture
15. fool people
16. discipline to think
17. quote *n.*

3

There's a great quote by Henry Ford, [right]? He said, "If I'd have asked my customers what they wanted, they would have told me 'A faster horse'."

Reporter: What will affect your decision? How do you make your strategy?

Jobs: We do no market research. We don't hire consultants. The only consultants I've ever hired in my 10 years is one firm to analyze Gateway's retail strategy so I would not make some of the same mistakes they made (when launching Apple's retail stores). But we never hire consultants, per se. We just want to make great products. When we created the iTunes Music Store, we did that because we thought it would be great to be able to buy music electronically, not because we had plans to redefine the music industry. I mean, it just seemed like writing on the wall, that eventually all music would be distributed electronically. That seemed obvious. The music industry has huge returns. Why have all this overhead when you can just send electrons around easily?

Reporter: What drives Apple employees? What kind of motivation do they have?

Jobs: We don't get a chance to do that many things, and everyone should be really excellent. Because this is our life. Life is brief, and then you die, you know? So this is what we've chosen to do with our life. We could be sitting in a monastery somewhere in Japan. We could be out sailing. Some of the executive team could be playing golf. They could be running other companies. And we've all chosen to do this with our lives. So it better be damn good. It better be worth it. And we think it is.

Reporter: Why do people want to work at Apple?

Jobs: The reason is, is because you can't do what you can do at Apple anywhere else. The engineering is long gone in most PC companies. In the consumer electronics companies, they don't understand the software parts of it. And so you really can't make the products that you can make at Apple anywhere else right now. Apple's the only company that has everything under one roof. There's no other company that could make a MacBook Air and the reason is that not only do we control the hardware, but we control the operating system. And it is the intimate interaction between the operating system and the hardware that allows us to do that. There is no intimate interaction between Windows and a Dell notebook. Our DNA is as a consumer company—for that individual customer who's voting thumbs up or thumbs down. That's who we think about. And we think that our job is to take responsibility for the complete user experience. And if it's not up to par, it's our fault, plain and simply.

Reporter: Do you think that Apple could live without you?

Jobs: We've got really capable people at Apple. I made Tim [Cook] COO and gave him the Mac division and he's done brilliantly. I mean, some people say, "Oh, God, if Jobs got run over by a bus, Apple would be in trouble."

strategy n.
策略，计谋

consultant n.
顾问，咨询者

electronically adv.
通过电子方式，电子地

distribute v.
将商品推销（到特定市场）

overhead n.
经费，天花板

motivation n.
动机，刺激

monastery n.
寺院，全体修道士

executive adj.
管理的，行政上的

damn adv.
非常，完全地

intimate adj.
紧密的，舒适的

interaction n.
互动，互相影响

thumbs up 赞成

complete adj.
完整的，完全的

plain adj.
清楚的，朴素的

capable adj.
有能力的，有可能的

brilliantly adv.
出色地，灿烂地

要什么，他们肯定会告诉我'一匹更快的马'。"

记者：　您根据什么做出决定，怎样制定发展战略[18]？

乔布斯：我们从不做市场调研[19]，我们不雇佣顾问[20]。这十年来我只请过一家公司帮忙
　　　　分析Gateway的零售策略[21]，以免犯下与他们一样的错误(在开设苹果零售店
　　　　时)。但是，我们本身是不招顾问的。我们只是想制造出伟大的产品。我们之
　　　　所以开发iTunes音乐商店，是因为我们觉得，能够以电子方式购买音乐将会
　　　　相当了不起，而不是因为我们计划去重新定义音乐产业[22]。我的意思是，就
　　　　像在墙上写字，音乐最终还是要通过电子化[23]来发行，这很明显。音乐产业
　　　　拥有巨大回报[24]。如果你可以简单地通过电子进行传播，为什么还要多花那
　　　　些冤枉钱呢？

记者：　是什么在驱使苹果的员工进步？他们的动力[25]是什么？

乔布斯：人这一生没法做太多事情，所以每一件都要做到精彩绝伦[26]。这就是生活。
　　　　人生苦短，你知道吗？所以这是我们为人生做出的选择。我们本可以在日本
　　　　某地的某座寺庙里打坐，或扬帆远航。管理层[27]本可以去打高尔夫，或掌管
　　　　其他公司，而我们全都选择了用一辈子来做这件事。所以这件事情最好能够
　　　　做得好一点。它最好能够物有所值[28]。我们觉得它的确还不错。

记者：　人们为什么希望在苹果公司工作？

乔布斯：因为你在其他任何地方都做不了你在苹果公司可以做的事情。在那些电脑公
　　　　司里，工程师早就没影儿了。在消费类电子产品公司里，他们根本不了解软
　　　　件层面的事情。所以，现在苹果能做出的产品，在其他公司你根本做不出
　　　　来。苹果是惟一一家将方方面面全盘掌控的公司。没有其他公司能够造一台
　　　　MacBook Air出来，因为我们不仅控制了硬件，我们还控制了操作系统。而这
　　　　些得益于操作系统和硬件之间的紧密互动。Windows和戴尔笔记本之间就没
　　　　有什么紧密互动可言。我们骨子里就是一家消费品公司[29]，你的生死存亡掌
　　　　握在消费者的手中。他们才是我们关注的对象。我们觉得自己的工作就是对
　　　　整个用户体验负责。如果表现不及格，那就是我们的错，就这么简单。

记者：　您认为如果没有您，苹果还能继续存活吗？

乔布斯：苹果公司人才辈出。我把蒂姆（库克）提拔成了首席运营官[30]并将Mac部门交
　　　　到他手上，确实成绩斐然。我的意思是，
　　　　有人说："哦，老天，如果乔布斯被公交
　　　　车给碾死了，苹果就'歇菜了'。"你知
　　　　道，虽然这不是什么值得高兴的事儿，而
　　　　正因苹果公司人才济济，董事会肯定会选
　　　　出一位合适的CEO。我的任务就是将整个
　　　　管理团队都培养成优秀的继任者[31]，这也是

18. strategy *n.*
19. market research
20. consultant *n.*
21. retail strategy
22. music industry
23. electronically *adv.*
24. huge return
25. motivation *n.*
26. excellent *adj.*
27. executive team
28. be worth it
29. consumer company
30. COO (chief operating officer)
31. successor *n.*

And, you know, I think it wouldn't be a party, but there are really capable people at Apple. And the board would have some good choices about who to pick as CEO. My job is to make the whole executive team good enough to be successors, so that's what I try to do.

Reporter: What do you think of your demanding reputation?

Jobs: My job is to not be easy on people. My job is to make them better. My job is to pull things together from different parts of the company and clear the ways and get the resources for the key projects. And to take these great people we have and to push them and make them even better, coming up with more aggressive visions of how it could be.

Reporter: OK, I'm wondering that what Apple really focuses on?

Jobs: Apple is a $30 billion company, yet we've got less than 30 major products. I don't know if that's ever been done before. Certainly the great consumer electronics companies of the past had thousands of products. We tend to focus much more. People think focus means saying yes to the thing you've got to focus on. But that's not what it means at all. It means saying no to the hundred other good ideas that there are. You have to pick carefully. I'm actually as proud of many of the things we haven't done as the things we have done. The clearest example was when we were pressured for years to do a PDA, and I realized one day that 90% of the people who use a PDA only take information out of it on the road. They don't put information into it. Pretty soon cellphones are going to do that, so the PDA market's going to get reduced to a fraction of its current size, and it won't really be sustainable. So we decided not to get into it. If we had gotten into it, we wouldn't have had the resources to do the iPod. We probably wouldn't have seen it coming.

Reporter: What's your management style?

Jobs: We've got 25,000 people at Apple. About 10,000 of them are in the stores. And my job is to work with sort of the top 100 people, that's what I do. That doesn't mean they're all vice presidents. Some of them are just key individual contributors. So when a good idea comes, you know, part of my job is to move it around, just see what different people think, get people talking about it, argue with people about it, get ideas moving among that group of 100 people, get different people together to explore different aspects of it quietly, and, you know—just explore things.

Reporter: What do you think of the operating system? Do you think it's beneficial?

Jobs: That allows us to innovate at a much faster rate than if we had to wait for Microsoft, like Dell and HP and everybody else does. Because Microsoft has their own timetable, for probably good reasons. I mean Vista took what—seven or eight years? It's hard to get your new feature that you need for your new hardware if it has to wait eight years. So we can set our own priorities and look at things in a more holistic way from the point of view of the customer. It

---

successor *n.*
继任者，后续事物

reputation *n.*
名誉，名声

aggressive *adj.*
极端的，侵犯的

pressure *v.*
迫使，施压

sustainable *adj.*
可持续的，能维持的

quietly *adv.*
秘密地，安静地

beneficial *adj.*
有益的，有帮助的

innovate *v.*
创新，改变

priority *n.*
优势，优先

holistic *adj.*
全部的，整体的

我在努力的目标。

记者： 有人说您很苛刻[32]，您怎么看？

乔布斯： 我的工作不是对人表现得和蔼可亲。我的工作是让他们做得更好。我的工作是把公司里的各种资源聚拢到一起，清除路障，然后把资源投放到最关键的项目上。我要把我们手下这些天才们召集起来并督促他们，让他们更上一层楼。怎么做呢？只好采取更为极端的方法。

记者： 好的，我想知道苹果公司究竟专注于[33]什么？

乔布斯： 苹果是一家价值300亿美元的公司，但主要产品却不到30种。我不知道这种状况是否曾经存在过。毫无疑问，过去那些有上千种产品的消费电子公司，我们专注得多。人们以为"专注"的意思就是对你必须关注的事情点头称是。但这并不是"专注"的全部内涵。"专注"意味着必须对另外100个好点子说不，谨慎小心地做出选择。事实上，任何事情，做或不做，我都引以为傲。有一个再贴切不过的例子：多年以来，我们都迫切地需要一款PDA产品，而终于有一天我意识到，90%的PDA用户只是在路上把信息从里头调出来而已，而不放进去。不久，手机就实现了这样的功能，于是PDA市场就萎缩到了今天的规模，而且也没有可持续性[34]。所以我们决定不进入这个领域。如果我们选择跟进，我们就没有资源去开发iPod了。我们基本上会连它的影子都见不着。

记者： 您的管理风格[35]是怎样的？

乔布斯： 在苹果公司，我们有2.5万人。差不多1万人在专卖店里工作。而我的工作是和最顶端的大约100个人协作，这就是我的工作内容。这并不意味着他们都是副总裁之类的领导，他们中的一些人只是贡献卓越的关键性个体[36]。所以如果有好点子出现，我的一部分工作就是把它传播开来，看看不同的人怎么想，让人们围绕着它展开讨论，让想法在这个由100人组成的群体里充分循环，让不同的人从不同的层面悄悄地对它展开摸索，你知道的，就是深入摸索。

记者： 您对操作系统怎么看？您认为它有好处吗？

乔布斯： 它使我们更快地创新，而不像戴尔、惠普和其他所有公司那样看着微软干着急。因为微软或许是出于好意，有自己的时间安排。我说的是，Vista好像让人等了七八年，如果你需要等上八年，那为新硬件添加新功能就更无从谈起了。而我们则可以自行决定孰轻孰重，从消费者的角度出发，更全面地看问题。这也意味着我们不但可以把系统玩弄于股掌之间，还可以为iPhone和iPod制作特别的版本。你知道，如果没有操作系统，我们什么都实现不了。

记者： 跟我们说说你们苹果公司周一马拉松似的例会吧。

乔布斯： 当你招到了真正的人才时，你就必须让他们分担一部分业务，并且充分放权。当然这并不意味着我就不能发表意见了。可是你招他们进来就是为了把

32. demanding *adj.*
33. focus on
34. sustainable *adj.*
35. management style
36. key individual
    contributor

also means that we can take it and we can make a version of it to fit in the iPhone and the iPod. And, you know, we certainly couldn't do that if we didn't own it.

Reporter: Then tell us something about your marathon Monday meetings.

Jobs: When you hire really good people you have to give them a piece of the business and let them run with it. That doesn't mean I don't get to kibitz a lot. But the reason you're hiring them is because you're going to give them the reins. I want them making as good or better decisions than I would. So the way to do that is to have them know everything, not just in their part of the business, but in every part of the business. So what we do every Monday is we review the whole business. We look at what we sold the week before. We look at every single product under development, products we're having trouble with, products where the demand is larger than we can make. All the stuff in development, we review. And we do it every single week. I put out an agenda—80% is the same as it was the last week, and we just walk down it every single week. We don't have a lot of process at Apple, but that's one of the few things we do just to all stay on the same page.

接力棒交到他们手里。我希望他们能够做到青出于蓝而胜于蓝。所以要实现这个目标，就必须让他们了解所有事情，而不是停留于自身的业务范围之内。所以我们每周一做的事情就是回顾整个公司的运营情况。我们着眼于之前一周的销售项目，每一件正在开发的产品，以及那些麻烦的产品，那些供不应求的产品。我们检查所有开发中的产品，每周一次。我们做了一份日程——80%是与上周相同的，我们每周都重新做。在苹果公司，我们没有太多的繁文缛节，但这是为数不多的雷打不动的惯例之一。

version *n.* 版本，译文

marathon *n.* 马拉松，耐力比赛

kibitz *v.* 乱插嘴，发表意见

review *v.* 回顾，评论

single *adj.* 单一的，孤单的

agenda *n.* 日程，议程

自由输出十分钟

1. 渐进（climax）是英语修辞手法之一，是指将一些词语按照意念的大小、轻重、深浅、高低等逐层渐进，最后达到顶点。这种修辞方法可以增强语势，逐渐加深读者的印象。例如：I am sorry, I am so sorry, I am so extremely sorry. 通过so和so extremely加深了道歉的诚意。

2. 英语中一些形容词可以通过添加后缀"-ization"变成相应的名词，表示"……化"，例如：globalization（全球化）；industrialization（工业化）；miniaturization（微型化）等。

3. 词组give sb. a shot意为"试一试，给某人一个机会"，例如：I'm not sure if I'll be able to help you with your homework, but I'll give it a shot.（我不确定我是否能够帮你做作业，不过我会试试看。）

4. drive一词的应用非常广泛，"促进，激励"便是从其本意"开车"中引申出来的，例如：Her pride drove her to complete this job.（她的自尊心促使她完成了这项工作。）

5. thumbs up是"拇指向上"的意思，表示赞许；thumbs down是"拇指向下"，表示责备。这两个肢体语言所表示的意义与汉语中的相同。

6. 一些动词可以通过在词尾添加后缀-or变为相应的名词，表示"……人"，例如：contributor（贡献者，投稿者，捐助者）；visitor（参观者）；actor（演员）等。

7. kibitz是"乱出主意，多管闲事"的意思，可以作不及物动词用，例如：He never stopped kibitzing when we played cards.（我们玩牌时，他一直多嘴多舌，乱出主意。）

8. 英语中，破折号可以表示在说话时有意地中断一下，以便强调或引起他人注意破折号后面要说的话。例如：In a word, the spirit of the whole country may be described as—self-reliance and arduous struggle.（总而言之，整个国家的精神可以说是——自力更生，艰苦奋斗。）

9. 表语从句就是用一个句子作为表语。修饰说明主语，由名词、形容词或相当于名词或形容词的词或短语充当，和系动词一起构成谓语。例如：The problem is when we can get a pay rise.（问题是什么时候我们可以得到加薪。）when引导的句子即为表语从句。

10. business可构成不同的词组，例如词组get down to business意为"言归正传"，例如：OK, at least we know now. Let's just get down to business.（好的，至少我们现在知道怎么回事了，让我们切入主题吧。）

1.2 Apple's Innovation, Engineering and Design Are Important

轻松输入十分钟

Reporter: How do you deal with roadblocks?

Jobs: At Pixar when we were making *Toy Story*, there came a time when we were forced to admit that the story wasn't great. It just wasn't great. We stopped production for five months... We paid them all to twiddle their thumbs while the team perfected the story into what became *Toy Story*. And if they hadn't had the courage to stop, there would have never been a *Toy Story* the way it is, and there probably would have never been a Pixar. We called that "the story crisis", and we never expected to have another one. But you know what? There's been one on every film. We don't stop production for five months. We've gotten a little smarter about it. But there always seems to come a moment where it's just not working, and it's so easy to fool yourself—to convince yourself that it is when you know in your heart that it isn't. Well, you know what? It's been that way with almost every major project at Apple, too... Take the iPhone. We had a different enclosure design for this iPhone until way too close to the introduction to ever change it. And I came in one Monday morning, I said, "I just don't love this. I can't convince myself to fall in love with this. And this is the most important product we've ever done." And we pushed the reset button. We went through all of the zillions of models we'd made and ideas we'd had. And we ended up creating what you see here as the iPhone, which is dramatically better. It was hell because we had to go to the team and say, "All this work you've done for the last year, we're going to have to throw it away and start over, and we're going to have to work twice as hard now because we don't have enough time." And you know what everybody said? "Sign us up." That happens more than you think, because this is not just engineering and science. There is art, too. Sometimes when you're in the middle of one of these crises, you're not sure you're going to make it to the other end. But we've always made it, and so we have a certain degree of confidence, although sometimes you wonder. I think the key thing is that we're not all terrified at the same time. I mean, we do put our heart and soul into these things.

Reporter: What's the iPod's tipping point?

Jobs: It was difficult for a while because for various reasons the Mac had not been accepted by a lot of people, who went with Windows. And we were

---

roadblock *n.*
障碍，路障

twiddle their thumbs
打发时间

convince *v.*
使信服，说服

enclosure design
封装设计

dramatically *adv.*
出人意料地，引人注目地

hell *n.* 地狱，训斥

engineering *n.*
工程学，工程

tipping pot 引爆点

苹果的创新、策划和设计至关重要

有效学习十分钟

记者：　你们是如何排除万难[1]的？

乔布斯：当我们在皮克斯公司制作《玩具总动员》的时候，曾经有一次，我们不得不
　　　　承认剧本实在不行。它就是不过关。我们一度暂停了五个月……当团队着手
　　　　完善剧本时，我们让每个人都拿着工资放大假去了。后来才做出你所看到的
　　　　《玩具总动员》。假如当时他们没有停下来的勇气，那也不会有最终的《玩
　　　　具总动员》，甚至也不会有皮克斯的今天。我们曾称之为"危机总动员"，
　　　　谁也不希望这种事情再发生。可你知道吗？每部电影都是这样。但我们找到
　　　　了更聪明的解决办法，不再停工五个月。总会有些山穷水尽的时刻，要蒙骗
　　　　自己其实并不难——说服自己[2]：其实你心里清楚，事情并不是这样的。那
　　　　么，你知道吗？在苹果公司，几乎每个大项目也都会遇到这种情况……以
　　　　iPhone为例，我们曾经有过一个迥异的iPhone封装设计[3]，那时候离面世已经
　　　　为时不远，甚至没有时间再做改动了。在某个周一的早晨，我走进公司说：
　　　　"我真没法爱上这个玩意儿。我说服不了自己。而这是我们做过的最重要的
　　　　产品。"然后我们就按下了重启键[4]。我们重新回顾了曾经做出来的无数款模
　　　　型机[5]以及曾经有过的想法。最终，我们做出了你今天看到的iPhone，好得出
　　　　人意料[6]。那个过程简直如同去地狱里走了一圈，因为你不得不当着整个团队
　　　　的面说："你们在过去一年里做出的所有东西，我们都要全盘否定[7]并且从头
　　　　再来[8]。而且我们必须加倍努力，因为我们已经没时间了。"而你知道他们说
　　　　了什么吗？"算我一个。"这种情况比你想象的频繁得多，因为这不仅仅是
　　　　策划[9]和科学，这也是艺术。有些时候，当你置身于危机时，你并不能保证你
　　　　能走到终点。但我们总能挺过来，我想我们有着一定程度的自信，尽管有些
　　　　时候你会质疑。我认为关键在于，我们在这种时候不会被完全吓倒。我指的
　　　　是，我们全身心地投入到了这些事情之中。

记者：　iPod的引爆点[10]是什么？

乔布斯：有段时间我们很艰难。Mac因为各种各样的原因不被众人接受，这些人选择
　　　　了Windows。即便我们全力以赴，市场份额[11]仍没有增长。有时你会想是不是
　　　　你真的做错了。或许尽管我们认为自己做得很好，但我们的产品仍不够好。或

1. roadblock *n.*
2. convince yourself
3. enclosure design
4. reset button
5. model *n.*
6. dramatically *adv.*
7. throw away
8. start over
9. engineering *n.*
10. tipping point
11. market share

just working really hard, and our market share wasn't going up. It makes you wonder sometimes whether you're wrong. Maybe our stuff isn't better, although we thought it was. Or maybe people don't care, which is even more depressing. It turns out with the iPod we kind of got out from that operating-system glass ceiling and it was great because it showed that Apple innovation, Apple engineering, Apple design did matter. The iPod captured 70% market share. I cannot tell you how important that was after so many years of laboring and seeing a 4% to 5% market share on the Mac. To see something like that happen with the iPod was a great shot in the arm for everybody.

Reporter: Then, what did you do next?

Jobs: We made more. We worked harder. We said: "This is great. Let's do more." I mean, the Mac market share is going up every single quarter. We're growing four times faster than the industry. People are starting to pay a little more attention. We've helped it along. We put Intel processors in and we can run PC apps alongside Mac apps. We helped it along. But I think a lot of it is people have finally started to realize that they don't have to put up with Windows—that there is an alternative. I think nobody really thought about it that way before.

Reporter: Why did you get the idea to launch the Apple store?

Jobs: It was very simple. The Mac faithful will drive to a destination, right? They'll drive somewhere special just to do that. But people who own Windows—we want to convert them to Mac. They will not drive somewhere special. They don't think they want a Mac. They will not take the risk of a 20-minute drive in case they don't like it. But if we put our store in a mall or on a street that they're walking by, and we reduce that risk from a 20-minute drive to 20 footsteps, then they're more likely to go in because there's really no risk. So we decided to put our stores in high-traffic locations. And it works.

Reporter: Will you catch tech's next wave?

Jobs: Things happen fairly slowly, you know. They do. These waves of technology, you can see them way before they happen, and you just have to choose wisely which ones you're going to surf. If you choose unwisely, then you can waste a lot of energy, but if you choose wisely it actually unfolds fairly slowly. It takes years. One of our biggest insights years ago was that we didn't want to get into any business where we didn't own or control the primary technology because you'll get your head handed to you. We realized that almost all—maybe all—of future consumer electronics, the primary technology was going to be software. And we were pretty good at software. We could do the operating system software. We could write applications on the Mac or even PC, like iTunes. We could write the software in the device, like you might put in an iPod or an iPhone or something. And we could write the back-end software that runs on a cloud, like iTunes. So we could write all these different kinds of software and make it work seamlessly. And you ask yourself, what other companies can do that? It's a pretty short list. The reason that we were very excited about the

---

depressing *adj.*
令人沮丧的，压抑的

innovation *n.*
创新，革新

capture *v.*
获得，占领

quarter *n.*
地区，四分之一

alongside *prep.*
与……并存

alternative *n.*
选择，二选一

launch *v.*
开设，发射

destination *n.*
目的地，终点

convert *v.*
转变，改变信仰

footstep *n.*
足迹，脚步

unfold *v.*
呈现，显露

insight *n.*
洞察力，洞悉

primary *adj.*
基本的，主要的

software *n.*
软件

application *n.*
应用程序，申请

device *n.*
设备，装置

back-end *adj.*
后期的，后端的

者人们对此根本漠不关心，那就更令人难过了。iPod的出现让我们突破了操作系统[12]的瓶颈[13]。事情的美妙之处在于，它证明了苹果式的创新[14]、苹果式的策划[15]以及苹果式的设计[16]都是至关重要的。iPod占据了70%的市场份额。在打拼多年并见证了Mac电脑4%至5%的市场份额之后，我简直无法告诉你这是多么的重要。看到iPod惊人的表现，这仿佛给我们每个人打了一针药效惊人的强心针[17]。

记者：　那么，接下来你们怎么做的？

乔布斯：我们干劲倍增[18]，并且更加努力。我们曾经说过："这事儿挺不错，让我们做得更棒些。"我的意思是，Mac的市场份额每个季度都有增长。我们的增长速度比整个行业快四倍。人们开始关注我们。而且我们正保持着这个势头。我们把英特尔处理器[19]放了进来，于是我们不仅可以运行Mac软件，还可以运行PC上的应用程序。我认为这件事情最重要的一点在于，人们终于意识到，他们没必要再忍受Windows了——其实还有另一个选择。我认为在此之前，从来没有人这样想过。

记者：　您为什么会想开设苹果专卖店[20]？

乔布斯：很简单。苹果的信徒们将会驾车驶向一个目的地，对吧？他们会开车去一个特别的地方做喜欢做的事。但是对于Windows用户来说——我们想要他们转而使用Mac。他们不会开车去特别的地方。他们觉得自己不需要Mac电脑。他们甚至不愿意花上20分钟开车来瞅瞅，他们担心自己压根儿就不喜欢苹果果。但是如果我们把店面开在大商场里或者大街上，人们会经常走过路过，而我们就可以将20分钟的车程缩短为20步的距离。他们进来参观的可能性就大大增加了，因为不用付出什么成本。所以我们决定将苹果专卖店开到车流密集的区域[21]。它确实奏效了。

记者：　你们会赶上下一波技术热潮[22]吗？

乔布斯：事情的发展速度其实十分缓慢，这你也是知道的。确实如此。这些一波接一波的技术热潮，都是可预见的。你要做的，只是精明地选择站在哪儿。如果你站错队，那么你就会浪费许多精力。但是如果你走对方向，它呈现的速度也是相当之缓慢。可能要花上几年。多年前，我们最具前瞻性[23]的观点之一，就是不要涉足[24]任何我们不具备或不能掌控核心技术[25]的领域，因为你会被杀得片甲不留[26]。我们意识到，对于全部的——或许是全部，未来的消费类电子产品[27]而言，软件都将是核心技术。而我们在软件领域实在是得心应手。我们会做操作系统软件。我们可以在Mac甚至PC上编写像iTunes一样的各种程序。我们可以编写设备软件，就像你可以放在iPod或者iPhone或者其他设备中的程序。同样我们也可以编写像iTunes一样的后台软件[28]。因此，我们可以编写多种软件，让它们交织在一起严丝合缝地协同工作。试问还有哪些其他公司可以做

handset n.
手机，电话听筒

manufacturer n.
制造商，厂商

competence n.
能力，胜任

ante n.
赌注，预付款

recruiting n.
招聘，招募

haystack n.
干草堆

participate v.
参与，分享

ultimately adv.
最后，根本

metadata n.
元数据

bunch n.
群，串

wireless n.
无线电

frost v.
冷冻，结霜

Hollywood studio
好莱坞影城

license v.
许可，特许

ingest v.
摄取，吸收

resonate v.
共鸣，共振

downturn n.
衰退，低迷时期

dot-com n.
网络公司，商业
域名

bubble n.
泡沫，气泡

tremendous adj.
巨大的，极大的

phone, beyond that fact that we all hated our phones, was that we didn't see anyone else who could make that kind of contribution. None of the handset manufacturers really are strong in software.

Reporter: How do you find talented people? Do you have a special way?

Jobs: When I hire somebody really senior, competence is the ante. They have to be really smart. But the real issue for me is, are they going to fall in love with Apple? Because if they fall in love with Apple, everything else will take care of itself. They'll want to do what's best for Apple, not what's best for them, what's best for Steve, or anybody else. Recruiting is hard. It's just finding the needles in the haystack. We do it ourselves and we spend a lot of time on it. I've participated in the hiring of maybe 5,000-plus people in my life. So I take it very seriously. You can't know enough in a one hour interview. So, in the end, it's ultimately based on your gut. How do I feel about this person? What are they like when they're challenged? Why are they here? I ask everybody that: "Why are you here?" The answers themselves are not what you're looking for. It's the metadata.

Reporter: So far, Apple TV's failing, what do you think of this?

Jobs: Here's how I look at it. Everybody's tried to make a great product for the living room. Microsoft's tried, we've tried—everybody's tried. And everybody's failed. We failed, so far. So there's a whole bunch of people that have tried, and every single one of them's failed, including us. And that's why I call it a hobby. It's not a business yet, it's a hobby. We've come out with our second try—"Apple TV, Take 2" is what we call it internally. We realized that the first product we did was about helping you view the content of whatever you had in iTunes on your Mac or PC, and wireless sending it to your widescreen TV. Well, it turns out that's not what people really wanted to do. I mean, yeah, it's nice to see your photos up on the big screen. That's frosting on the cake, but it's not the cake. What everybody really wanted, it turned out, was movies. So we began the process of talking to Hollywood studios and were able to get all the major studios to license their movies for rental. And we only have about 600 movies so far ingested on iTunes, but we'll have thousands later this year. We lowered the price to $229. And we'll see how it does. Will this resonate and be something that you just can't live without and love? We'll see. I think it's got a shot.

Reporter: Does the economic downturn have any influence on Apple? How do you manage through this period?

Jobs: We've had one of these before, when the dot-com bubble burst. What I told our company was that we were just going to invest our way through the downturn, that we weren't going to lay off people, that we'd taken a tremendous amount of effort to get them into Apple in the first place—the last thing we were going to do is laying them off. And we were going to keep funding. In fact we were going to up our R&D budget so that we would be ahead of our competitors when the downturn was over. And that's exactly what we did. And it worked. And that's exactly what we'll do this time.

到这点？寥寥无几。在发现了人们厌倦自己手机的事实之后，我们对自己的手机产品变得极端兴奋，另一个原因在于，我们发现除了我们没人能为此做出贡献。没有任何一个掌上设备制造商[29]在软件领域有实力。

记者：　苹果公司怎样寻找人才？有没有什么特殊渠道？

乔布斯：　我要招一名高级员工的时候，能力是我所看重的。他们必须够聪明。但对于我来说，问题则在于：他们是否会爱上苹果公司？因为如果会，那么其他所有事情就会迎刃而解。他们的工作会以苹果公司的最大利益为出发点，而非个人利益[30]、史蒂夫的利益或者其他某个人的利益。招聘[31]绝非易事，就像是大海捞针[32]一般。我们自己去招聘，我们在这方面花费了大量的精力。我一生中面试过5000多人。我对待此事的态度非常严肃。你无法在一个小时的面试里了解足够多的信息。所以最后，你只能凭借直觉做出选择。我对这人的感觉是怎样的？他们面临挑战时，会是什么样的呢？他们为什么会在这里？我问所有人："你为什么来这里？"答案本身并不是你想要的东西。这只是元数据[33]。

记者：　到目前为止，Apple TV做得并不成功，您怎么看？

乔布斯：　我来说说我的看法。每个人都曾经尝试过为客厅开发一个了不起的产品。微软试过了，我们也试过了——每个人都试过了。但每个人都失败了，我们目前也失败了。有很多人都在尝试，然后所有人都以失败告终，包括我们。这就是为什么我将其称作一个"爱好"。它还不可以称作一门生意，它只是一个爱好。我们已经作了第二次尝试——"Apple TV, Take 2"是我们在公司内部的称呼。我们意识到，我们的第一款产品只是在帮助你从Mac或电脑上的iTunes中获得内容，并且通过无线网络[34]发送到宽屏电视[35]。嗯，事实证明这并不是人们想要的。我的意思是，没错，能在大屏幕上看到你的照片也不错——但那是蛋糕上面的糖霜而不是蛋糕。事实证明，人们真正需要的是电影。所以我们开始和好莱坞制片商进行对话，并且尽可能地取得所有好莱坞大片的租赁授权。现在iTunes里面只能找到大约600部电影，但是在今年晚些时候，我们就会有上千种选择。我们把价格降到了229美元，准备看看效果如何。至于这会不会引发你的共鸣，并且成为你愿意与之共度余生的钟情之物？等着瞧吧。我看行。

记者：　经济衰退期会对苹果公司造成影响吗？在这个时期你如何管理？

乔布斯：　我们之前已经经历了一次，就是在dot-com泡沫破灭的时候。我告诉公司员工的是，我们会在经济衰退期里继续坚持自己的投资思路。我们不会裁员，我们会付出巨大的努力将员工放在苹果各项工作的首位，最后一步才是裁员。而且我们还将持续拨款。实际上，我们当时计划调高研发预算，这样在度过经济衰退期之后，我们才可以领先于竞争对手。我们确实这样做了，而且行之有效。这次我们还会这样做的。

29. handset manufacturer
30. what's best for them
31. recruiting *n.*
32. find the needles in the haystack
33. metadata *n.*
34. wireless *n.*
35. widescreen TV

自由输出十分钟

1. 完全倒装是将整个谓语提到主语之前。例如在以here、there、now、then等副词开头的句子里：Now comes your turn.（现在该你了。）将谓语动词comes完全提到了主语之前。

2. 词组twiddle one's thumbs意为"玩弄手指"，其引申义为"无聊地消磨时间；游手好闲"。例如：You're not being paid to twiddle your thumbs all day.（给你工钱不是让你整天游手好闲的。）

3. 《玩具总动员》（*Toy Story*）是皮克斯的动画系列电影，共制作了三部，由华特·迪士尼影片公司和皮克斯动画工作室合作推出。而《玩具总动员3》是皮克斯的首部IMAX影片，于2010年6月18日在北美上映。

4. 词组sign up意为"选课，报名参加"。例如：So where do I sign up for the time machine?（那么我到哪里报名参加时光旅游呢？）；We highly recommend that you sign up for this course.（我们强烈推荐您选修这门课程。）

5. 苹果公司旗下的主要产品有iPod系列，iPhone，Apple TV，Macbook，Macbook pro，iMac，Mac mini，Mac pro，Mac OS等。

6. 明喻（simile）是最常见的修辞方法，是将具有共性的不同事物作对比。这种共性存在于人们的心里，而不是事物的自然属性。常见的标志词有：as, like, seem, as if, similar to等。例如：I wandered alone as a cloud.（我如同一朵云一样，孤独游荡。）

7. 合成法是英语构词方法之一，是指将两个或两个以上的单词合成在一起形成新词，例如：downtown（市中心区），downturn（经济低迷时期），income（收入），afternoon（下午）等。

8. 英语中表示数量的单词有：hundred，thousand，million（百万），billion（十亿），trillion（万亿），zillion（不计其数的）等。

9. risk "风险"作动词时后面接动名词形式，例如：The skipper was not willing to risk taking his ship through the straits until he could see where he was going.（这位船长不愿意冒险在看不见方向之前将船开过海峡。）

10. "大学一年级学生"为freshman，"大学二年级学生"为sophomore，"大学三年级学生"为junior，"大学四年级学生"为senior。

2

微软公司董事长：
比尔·盖茨
Chairman of Microsoft: Bill Gates

　　比尔·盖茨（Bill Gates），全名威廉·亨利·盖茨，美国微软公司的董事长。他于1955年10月28日出生在美国西海岸华盛顿州的西雅图。他是一名出色的学生，毕业于哈佛大学。13岁时就开始了电脑程式设计，17岁时卖掉了第一个电脑编程作品，时间表格系统。

　　他与保罗·艾伦一起创建了微软公司，曾任微软CEO和首席软件设计师，并持有公司超过8％的普通股，也是公司最大的个人股东。1995年至2007年的《福布斯》全球亿万富翁排行榜中，比尔·盖茨连续13年蝉联世界首富。2008年6月27日正式退出微软公司，并把580亿美元个人财产尽数捐给比尔与美琳达·盖茨基金会。2012年3月，福布斯全球富豪榜发布，比尔·盖茨以610亿美元位列第二。

2.1 Self-exploration Is Great and Important

轻松输入十分钟

Reporter: Were other of your contemporaries equally interested in the business, or did you find yourself unusual among the groups?

Gates: Well, when I went to Lakeside School, I was about 12 years old. I started there in seventh grade. That was kind of a change for me. It is a private boys' school. Very strict. At first I really didn't like the environment. I did eventually find some friends there, some of who had the same sort of interest, like reading business magazines and *Fortune*. We were always creating funny company names and having people send us their product literature.[laughs] Trying to think about how business worked. And in particular, looking at computer companies and what was going on with them.

Reporter: What companies, in particular, did you like to follow?

Gates: The first computer we used was a GE time-sharing system. It was connected over a phone line. Actually, the school couldn't afford a full phone line, so someone in the offices had a switch where you could take over the phone line. It was an ASR-33 Teletype with paper tape connected up to a GE computer. But, very quickly, we found out about PDP-8s, and eventually got one loaned to us. And then eventually, Data General Nova got loaned to us. So, these companies making smaller computers were very fascinating to us. Joining all the user groups. DEC had one called the DECUS User Group. Getting on every mailing list. In Datamation they had these bingo cards where you could check everything you were interested in. So, we just put our names down and checked everything there and tried to learn about the world of computing.

Reporter: How did the faculty respond to your interest outside of your curriculum compared to your interest in your own studies?

Gates: Well, I was relieved from some classes, Maths in particular, because I'd read ahead. So, I had quite a bit of free time. When the Mother's Club which did this rummage sale, got the money for this Teletype and a certain amount of time to buy computer time, it was a question of who was going to figure this thing out? Now, I was very young. I was in eighth grade and some of the older students kind of barged in and thought they could figure it out. And very quickly, the

contemporary *n.*
同龄人，同辈人

eventually *adv.*
后来，最终

particular *adj.*
特别的，详细的

switch *n.*
转换器，开关

fascinating *adj.*
吸引人的，迷人的

curriculum *n.*
课程

rummage *n.*
杂物，翻找

barge *v.*
闯入

自我探索很重要

有效学习十分钟

记者：您周围的同龄人也同样对商业感兴趣吗？还是您与众不同？

盖茨：嗯，我12岁的时候进入湖滨中学学习。我从七年级开始读。那对我来说是一种改变。湖滨中学是一所<u>私立男校</u>[1]，管理非常严格。开始的时候，我真的不喜欢那种环境。后来，我交到了一些好朋友，其中的一些跟我有同样的爱好，比如阅读商业杂志或者《财富》。我们经常起一些有趣的公司名字，让别人给我们发他们的<u>产品资料</u>[2]（笑声）。我们总是思考商业是如何运行的，而且特别关注一些电脑公司的发展经营状况。

记者：你们会<u>特别</u>[3]关注哪些公司？

盖茨：我们用的第一台电脑采用的是<u>GE分时系统</u>[4]。它通过一条电话线连接。事实上，学校并不能给我们提供一根独立的电话线，因此需要在办公室里通过终端机<u>转换</u>[5]。那是一台ASR-33型号的终端机，通过纸带接到一台GE电脑上。但是，很快我们发现了PDP-8，并且最终租到了一台。最终我们租用了通用数据公司的新星开发操作系统。所以，主要是这些制造小型计算机的公司吸引了我们。我们加入到使用者的行列中。DEC有一个叫DECUS的用户群。把自己的电子邮件地址加入到他们的电邮数据库中。他们会通过数据库自动发送各种<u>宾戈卡片</u>[6]，你可以由此找到自己感兴趣的东西。因此，我们填上姓名，选择全部选项，想了解整个计算机世界。

记者：相比您的学习生活而言，老师们对您的课余爱好怎么看？

盖茨：嗯，有一些课我可以不去上，尤其是数学，因为我之前已经学过了。所以我有很多时间可以自己支配。当母亲俱乐部通过<u>义卖</u>[7]筹集到钱来支付终端机和电脑使用时间的费用时，这时出现问题该由谁来<u>解决</u>[8]呢？那时候我很小，才读八年级。一些高年级的学生介入并认为他们可以解决。很快，老师们的地位受到了威胁。一群学生读了手册，又进行了试验。你可以离线在这个黄色纸带<u>上编程</u>[9]，之后把它放在<u>读带机</u>[10]上，用电脑拨号，很快就可以输入纸带上的程序并运行。这个过程中，不仅仅有连接的时间，同时还需要储存单元和中央处理器运行的时间。因此，如果你开发了这样一个程序，它将很快消耗掉大笔费用。母亲俱乐部不断

1. private boys' school
2. product literature
3. in particular
4. GE time-sharing system
5. switch *v.*
6. bingo cards
7. rummage sale
8. figure out
9. type the program
10. tape reader

teachers were intimidated. So, it was sort of a group of students reading the manuals and trying things out. You would type the programs off-line on this yellow paper tape and then put it into the tape reader, dial up the computer, and very quickly feed in the paper tape and run your program. They charged you not only for the connect time, but also for storage units and CPU time. So, if you had a program that had a loop in it of some type you could spend a lot of money very quickly. And so we went through the money that the Mother's Club had given very rapidly. It was a little awkward for the teachers, because it was just students sitting there and zoom—the money was gone. I wrote a tic-tactoe program and a couple of other base conversion programs. It was the BASIC language running on this GE system. So, people didn't know what to think because teachers were fairly dignified in those days and usually were supposed to know what was going on. They were okay about it, but then when the money was gone, they had to start billing us for all of our usage. We had these kinds of funny student checking accounts so my friends and I still stayed very active. We were kind of desperate to get free computer time one way or another. The amount of time we'd spend in this particular room that had the Teletype was quite extreme. We sort of took over the room, myself and two other people. They called it the Teletype Room. We were always coming up with schemes to get free computer time, and eventually did with a local company. Convinced them that because they had a deal with DEC for this big computer, an early PDP-10, serial number 36, that if they could find problems with it they wouldn't have to pay their rent. Having a few of the students, including me, bang on it and try to find bugs seemed like a good idea. And particularly, let us do that mostly at night. So, we were going down to this... it was called Computer Center Corporation, C-Cubed, in the University District, staffed by some old people from the University of Washington Academic Computing Center had gone over there. So, for a few years that is where I spent my time. I'd skip out on athletics and go down to this computer center. We were moving ahead very rapidly: BASIC, FORTRAN, LISP, PDP-10 machine language, digging out the operating system listings from the trash and studying those. Really not just banging away to find bugs like monkeys[laughs], but actually studying the code to see what was wrong. The teachers thought we were quite unusual. And pretty quickly there were four of us who got more addicted, more involved, and understood it better than the others. And those were myself, Paul Allen, who later founded Microsoft with me, Ric Weiland, who actually worked at Microsoft in the early days, and Kent Evans, who was my closest friend, and most my age, was killed in a mountain climbing accident when I was in 11th grade in high school. So, the four of us became the Lakeside Programming Group.

Reporter: Clearly, your extracurricular activity was probably more important in your later development than what you did in class, or at least equally important [Gates laughs]. How do you feel as we look at problems in education, that students that

intimidated adj.
受到威胁的

manual n.
手册，指南

storage n.
存储，仓库

awkward adj.
尴尬的，笨拙的

conversion n.
变换，转换

dignified adj.
庄严的

desperate adj.
极度渴望的，不顾
一切的

extreme adj.
极度的；最大的

scheme n.
方案，计划

serial adj.
序列的，连续的

staff v.
给……配备职员，
供给人员

athletic n.
体育运动，竞技

trash n.
废物，杂物

addict v.
使上瘾，使沉迷

extracurricular adj.
业余的，课外的

给我们运作经费。这样的局面让老师们或多或少有一些尴尬，因为只是一群学生坐在那里不断地发出嗡嗡声，钱就花没了。我写过一个"一字棋"的游戏程序，还有两个其他的基础转换程序[11]。在GE系统里运行BASIC语言。因为那时老师毫无疑问是高高在上[12]的，通常情况下，大家都认为他们应该知道接下来应该发生什么，但那时他们都不知该如何打算。他们并不反对我们的行为，但是当钱很快被花光的时候，他们开始要求我们付费。有趣的是，我们认识一些对账[13]的学生，所以我和伙伴们总还是能找到电脑用的。我们总是想尽各种办法免费使用电脑。我们在有终端机的机房里度过了很多时间。我和另外两个人几乎接管了这个房间。他们称这个房间为终端机房。我们经常想办法免费使用计算机，最终找到了一家当地的公司。他们与DEC签订了一个关于大型计算机的合约，早期的PDP-10，序列号36。协议中说如果这个公司可以找到电脑中存在的一些问题，则无需付租金。对一些学生，包括我来说，真是正中下怀。努力找出电脑中的程序错误看起来是个不错的想法。并且我们的工作时间多集中在晚上。于是我们达成了协议……那家公司名叫计算机中心股份公司，C的立方，就在大学区，工作人员是一些华盛顿学术计算机中心的老员工。可以说，我在那儿度过了几年时间。我放弃[14]了各种运动，专注于这个计算机中心。我们进步很快：BASIC、FORTRAN、LISP、PDP-10计算机语言[15]，从一堆"杂物"[16]中找出[17]有用的操作系统表格[18]并学习。真的，我们做的不仅仅是像猴子一样努力地找出那些漏洞（笑声），我们通常会研究代码[19]，看看到底是哪些地方出了问题。老师们觉得我们与众不同。很快，我们中的四个人更加投入，更加痴迷于此，并且比别人理解得更透彻。这四个人是：我，保罗•艾伦（后来我们一起创立了微软），里克•韦兰德（开始的时候他也在微软工作）和肯特•伊万斯（他是我最亲密的好朋友，我们年纪相仿，我在高中读11年级的时候，他在一次爬山时遇到意外去世了）。因此，是我们四个建立了湖滨程序小组。

记者：显然，与课上学到的知识相比，您的这些课外活动[20]对您日后的发展更有帮助，至少是一样重要的（盖茨笑）。现在的教育中也存在一些问题，很多学生对技术方面的东西更感兴趣，认为应将其与课堂上的知识平衡[21]，您对此怎么看？您觉得自我探索[22]对于那个年龄段的人来说很重要吗？

盖茨：自我探索很重要，因为在这个过程中你可以培养自信心[23]和一种自我认同感[24]："嘿，我很擅长这个。对于这个问题我比老师懂得还多。我要试试我是不是

11. base conversion program
12. dignified *adj.*
13. check accounts
14. skip out
15. machine language
16. trash *n.*
17. dig out
18. operating system listing
19. code *n.*
20. extracurricular activity
21. balance *n.*
22. explore things on one's own/ self-exploration
23. self-confidence
24. identity *n.*

are coming up interested in technical things should balance those. Do you think it is important to explore things on your own at that age?

Gates: Self-exploration is great, because you develop a sense of self-confidence and an identity of "Hey, I know this pretty well. I know this better than the teachers. Let me try and see if I can understand at the next level. Maybe I'm pretty good at this stuff." And particularly with the computer where if your program is wrong, you know you try it and if it doesn't work and then you fix it and try it again. It is kind of a feedback loop, which because the classroom has a lot of people, and maybe there is not a subject that you think you are good at or interested in. It is just fascinating to try and figure out the computer. I remember at Computer Center Corporation they had hired in some of the great people of early computer days, including Bob Gruen, Dick Russell, a guy named Weir who was a Stanford guy. Anyway, these guys would kind of loan us deep manuals on the system, just for a few hours and then take them away. So, we'd spend those few hours just reading carefully. It was so exciting to get a little glimpse and begin to figure out how computers were built, and why they were expensive. I certainly think that having some dimension, when you're young, that you feel a mastery of, versus the other people around you is a very positive thing. And for me that came in several ways: the reading I was doing non-computer related in Maths. But computers, timewise, for many years was a key center of excitement.

Reporter: We are going to talk a little bit about your transition into Harvard before you got to the Altair. You mentioned that even though you worked in computing, that it wasn't your goal when you went to college. Do you want to say what your goal was?

Gates: That's right. I finished up at TRW, went back, and graduated from Lakeside School. I picked out of the schools I'd been accepted to, to go back to Harvard. They seemed to have a lot of different things. I knew that if I wanted to be a lawyer or a mathematician, Harvard had good courses for these things. Once I got there, I thought economics was pretty interesting. And I felt that I understood computers well enough, that I really didn't need to hang out with a computer crowd there, because they weren't as interesting. I did end up taking a few computer courses. But most of what I did was not related to computers. And meanwhile, Paul Allen, who had worked with me on everything, basically[chuckles], and who shared this idea that we should go to do a company —he actually tried to convince me after TRW that we should start a company then, and try to build PDP-8- like systems around 8080 chips. But it just was too vague and my parents wanted me to go back to school. So, I went back there. But Paul was there and we were always talking about, "Could we stick a lot of microprocessors together to do something powerful? Could we do a 360 emulator using micro controllers? Could we do a time-sharing system where lots of people could dial-in and get consumer information?" A lot of different ideas.

explore *v.*
探索，探险

identity *n.*
认同，身份

feedback *n.*
反馈，成果

glimpse *n.*
一瞥，一看

dimension *n.*
特点，特征

mastery *n.*
精通，优势

computing *n.*
从事电脑工作，计算

hang *v.*
中止，悬挂

basically *adv.*
主要地，基本上

convince *v.*
说服，使确信

vague *adj.*
不明确的，模糊的

microprocessor *n.*
微处理器，微处理机

emulator *n.*
模拟器，仿真器

可以做得更进一步。或许我有这方面的天赋。"对于计算机来讲，如果你的程序出现了错误，你尝试了之后就会发现是哪里错了，为什么不能正常运行，然后你就可以进行修复，再运行。这就类似于一个反馈的过程[25]，一个教室里有很多

人，或许你对任何一门科目都不擅长，或是不感兴趣。只有计算机才对你充满吸引力。我记得在计算机中心股份公司的时候，他们雇用[26]了早期一些很有名的人，包括鲍博·格伦，迪克·罗素，还有一个斯坦福大学的威尔。总而言之，这些人只把系统的详细操作手册借给我们看几个小时，然后便拿走了。因此，在这几个小时，我们就仔细地读。这惊鸿一瞥[27]很让人兴奋，看了这些知识让我们知道了计算机是如何建立起来的，为什么那么贵。当然，我肯定地认为年轻人跟其他人相比，在某方面是有一定的竞争优势的。对于我而言，这体现在很多方面：我曾经一直研读数学。但是，这么多年来，计算机一直是我最感兴趣的东西。

记者：在谈"牛郎星"之前，我们先来谈谈您在哈佛大学的经历。您之前提到，即使在计算机行业工作，也并不是您进入大学时的目标。可以说说您那时的目标吗？

盖茨：是的。我结束了在TRW的工作回去之后，从湖滨中学毕业。我没有去录取我的学校，而是回到了哈佛大学，他们似乎有很多与众不同的地方。我知道，如果我想做一名律师或者数学家[28]，哈佛大学的课程再好不过了。我一到那儿，就觉得经济学[29]很有趣。并且，我觉得自己的计算机已经学得很好了，完全不需要和那里的一群人在一起研究，因为没什么意思。最终我只选了几门计算机课程。但是，我所选的大部分与计算机无关。同时还有保罗·艾伦，我们基本上做什么都在一起（轻声笑），他建议我们一起创办一个公司——事实上，离开TRW以后他就这样说服[30]我，希望建立一个像PDP-8一样包含大约8080个芯片的系统。但那只是一个很模糊的[31]概念，并且我的父母要求我回去上学。所以，我就回去了。但是，保罗在那儿，我们还经常一起讨论："我们是不是可以把许多微处理器[32]集中起来，让它的功能更强大？我们是不是可以用微控制器[33]做一个360仿真器[34]？我们能不能做一个分时系统，让很多用户可以同时拨号[35]并获取信息？"等很多新奇的想法。

25. feedback loop
26. hire in
27. glimpse n.
28. mathematician n.
29. economics n.
30. convince v.
31. vague adj.
32. microprocessor n.
33. micro controller n.
34. emulator n.
35. dial-in

1. 《财富》（*Fortune*）是一本由美国人亨利·鲁斯于1930年创办，主要刊登经济问题研究文章的杂志。《财富》杂志自1954年推出全球500强排行榜，历来都是经济界关注的焦点，影响巨大。

2. rummage sale是一个固定词组，意为"清仓大甩卖，义卖会"。例如：The students are holding a rummage sale tomorrow to raise money for a schoolmate who needs an operation.（学生们明天将要办一场义卖会，为一位需要开刀的同学筹款。）

3. 英语中有一些与speaking连用的具有副词性质的词组，可做插入语，例如：generally speaking（一般来说），frankly speaking（坦白地说），strictly speaking（严格来说）等。

4. 中英文中的颜色词不能完全等同，例如：红茶（black tea），在中文中通常用"黄色"表示"下流的"，而英文中则用blue。

5. 由self组成的合成词有：self-confidence（自信），self-dignified（自重），self-esteem（自负）等。

6. 头韵法（alliteration）是常用的英语修辞手法之一，是指在文章中有两个以上连在一起的词或词组，其开头的音节有同样的字母或声音，以增强语言的节奏感。例如：How and why he had come to Princeton, New Jersey is a story of struggle, success and sadness.（他如何来以及为什么来到新泽西州的普林斯顿是一个充满奋斗、成功和悲伤的一段经历。）句中的story of struggle和success and sadness即体现了此手法。

7. pick out是"选出，挑选"的意思。例如：If they need to pick out your skills and experience for you, then you have failed.（如果他们需要来帮你挑选出你的技能和经历，那你肯定会落选。）

8. 在句子中，将do或did提到谓语动词之前可表强调，例如：I did end up taking a few computer courses.（我就只选了几门计算机课程），强调选的只有几门计算机课程，没有其他课程。

9. 词组"pick up"有"结识某人"的意思。例如：I picked him up ten years ago.（我是十年前认识他的。）

10. 独立主格结构主要用于描绘性文字中，其作用相当于一个状语从句，常用来表示时间、原因、条件、行为方式或伴随情况等。例如：The condition being favourable, he may succeed.（若条件有利，他或许能成功。）

2.2 / Different Groups Have Different Enterprise Cultures
不同的团队有不同的企业文化

轻松输入十分钟

Reporter: Bill, what led to your decision to build your own site, your own corporate campus?

Gates: Well, I was always thinking that environment that we did product development in should be a fun environment, a lot like a college campus. And this idea of using small teams means you want to give them all the tools, all the computers, an individual office, whatever it takes so that they feel like they can concentrate on their jobs and be very creative. And, in the Northwest, having a lot of trees around, you know, one, two, and three story buildings where offices are very good sized. That made sense to me. And we had been looking ever since we moved up to Seattle for a piece of land that wasn't too far away and yet

有效学习十分钟

记者： 比尔，是什么使你决定建立自己的网站及自己的公司园区[1]呢？

盖茨： 嗯，我一直认为我们生产产品的环境应该是一个很有趣的环境，像大学校园一样。用一个小团队来工作的概念就意味着你要给他们所有的工具、所有的计算机、一间个人办公室和他们需要的任何东西，这样他们才能感觉到自己可以将精力集中在工作上并且富有创造性[2]。你知道，在西北地区，树林环绕，一、二、三层的楼房内的办公室空间很棒。我觉得不错。自从我们搬到了西雅图之后，就一直在寻找一块离市区不远却可以让我们成长为一个

---

concentrate *v.* 集中，浓缩

1. corporate campus   2. creative *adj.*

that would let us grow as a company. And in 1986 we actually got to move into our corporate campus. This kind of shows you one of the buildings here. Initially, there were four buildings like this clustered around the lake you see here, and each of the main Development groups got their own building. And that meant that we really had the best of all worlds. People felt that it was a fun environment, but yet we were really close to each other as far as working together. Things like people juggling or riding unicycles around, having barbecues outside, having company meetings where everybody would stand around. This was the original ground breaking. And these are two of the developers, but here we see Jon Shirley who started with the company in 1983 . He came from Radio Shack and played a very critical role, because, although I had Steve Ballmer helping me think through business issues and a lot of other people like Kazuhiko Nishi on the product side, or Paul Allen, it was Jon who helped us really grow; what kind of systems did we have to have in place. And Jon had been my good friend when he worked at Radio Shack, so we were excited to have him come on board. Actually, he was the second president of Microsoft. We hired another gentleman[chuckles] who was with us for a little less than a year where it wasn't a good match. A gentleman from Tektronix. And then brought in Jon after that. There was a week in 1986 that was pretty exciting because that was the week we moved into the campus. But that same week we moved in, we went public as a company, this is our offering prospectus. And that was also the week of Microsoft's first CD-ROM Conference where we were pushing the idea of multimedia back in 1986 that didn't really catch on, you could say, until 1994 so before it was in the mainstream. But this kind of shows you the pace of activity at that time. We felt fine to have all those things happen all at once. And I know that next Monday I flew down to Australia to be part of a big software show down there.

Reporter: Let's talk a little about going public and whether that was something that everybody accepted that you needed to do, whether it was a controversial issue, and what difference it made.

Gates: Well, Microsoft had started giving out stock options to people as early as 1981. So we were sharing in the success we thought we'd have. As we did that, they had about a five-year vesting period. And so as some people were starting to vest on quite a bit of their stock, there was the question of how would they get liquidity. Now you could just let it be traded privately, but then the price would fluctuate a lot because the supply would be so short. And I was quite reluctant to go public because of the overhead.

initially *adv.*
起初，开头

cluster *v.*
聚集，丛生

juggling *n.*
杂耍，欺骗

unicycle *n.*
独轮脚踏车

original *adj.*
原始的，最初的

critical *adj.*
决定性的，关键的

prospectus *n.*
计划书，说明书

multimedia *n.*
多媒体

mainstream *n.*
主流

controversial *adj.*
有争议的，有争论的

vesting *n.*
保留财产的权利，背心料子

liquidity *n.*
流动资产，流动性

fluctuate *v.*
波动，动摇

reluctant *adj.*
不情愿的，勉强的

overhead *n.*
经费问题，间接费用

公司的地方。1986年，我们搬进了我们的公司园区。类似于现在你看到的其中一个楼房。起初[3]，我们有四个环湖办公楼，每一个主要开发团队[4]都有自己的办公楼。那意味着我们有世界上最好的一切。大家都觉得那是一个有趣的环境，我们在一起工作，彼此感情很好。外边有杂耍[5]和独轮车表演[6]，人们在室外烧烤[7]，所有人站成一圈开公司会议。这是一种全新的尝试。这是其中两位开发者。乔•雪莉1983年开始在公司工作。他之前在Radio Shack公司担任重要职位[8]，尽管我让史蒂夫•鲍尔默帮我处理一些商务问题[9]，还有很多其他人比如彦西和保罗•艾伦分管产品[10]，但是乔真正做到了让公司壮大，他知道我们在什么位置需要怎样的系统。乔在Radio Shack公司工作的时候就是我的好朋友，所以我们很高兴他能加入。事实上，他是微软的第二任总裁。之前我们聘请了另外一位绅士（轻声笑），他感觉这里不合适，在公司待了不到一年。他来自Tektronix公司。之后乔就入职了。1986年我们搬入这个园区的那个星期，我们都非常兴奋。也就在同一周，我们正式宣布公司成立，这是我们的招股说明[11]。同时，那一周我们召开了微软的第一次CD-ROM会议，我们把多媒体[12]的概念推回到1986年，那时并没有真正流行起来，可以说，直到1994年之前都是主流之一。但是你可以看到那时活动的速度。所有事情都来得很快，我们觉得很好。并且我知道，下个星期一我要飞到澳大利亚去参加一个大型的软件展览会[13]。

记者： 我们来谈一谈上市[14]，你们做的事情是不是所有人都认可，有没有争议[15]，上市带来什么变化？

盖茨： 嗯，微软早在1981年就开始对外出售股票。所以我们分享的是我们觉得理应有的成功。这样做，我们大概有五年的财产保留期[16]。当有些人开始对他们的股票实行保留权的时候，问题来了，他们如何进行资产流动？现在，你可以直接私下交易[17]，但当时价格会浮动得很大，因为供应不足。由于经费问题，我不愿意上市。我们可以直接内部跟踪我们的股价。而在股票市场上可能对未来期望过高[18]，或变得动荡——你知道股票是变幻无常的。但我确信它有意义。

3. initially *adv.*
4. development group
5. juggling *n.*
6. riding unicycle
7. barbecue *v.*
8. critical role
9. business issue
10. on the product side
11. offering prospectus
12. multimedia *n.*
13. software show
14. going public
15. controversial issue
16. vesting period
17. trade privately
18. over-anticipating

We had been able to track our stock price internally up in a very linear way. And with the market sort of maybe over-anticipating the future, or getting paranoid—you know the stock would be very volatile. But I was convinced that it made sense. And as long as we were going to do it, it was an opportunity to really expose the company broadly. Talk about our vision where we had done well, where we were taking the industry. And it did become something that was covered very, very broadly by a lot of people. And it was extremely successful. The stock took off after this offering at $21.00 and it just zoomed up from there for many, many years.

Reporter: There was no regret about going public?

Gates: Going public is not without its complexities in terms of dealing with analysts and all the reports. It is a little convoluted about when you can keep things secret versus having to go out and talk about those things. So, it is not totally simple. But the benefit of having the stock be very liquid for everyone was very positive. We didn't use any of the money that we raised. We just put that money in the bank and it sat there with all of the money that we had earned, because we were very profitable and had plenty of cash by this time. So our reason for going public was very different than any other company that was going public.

Reporter: You have a couple of charts there, Bill, that kind of track your growth that you might want to pick up. I'm curious to know whether it was more satisfying for you to add your first 100, 1,000, or 10,000 employees? And, how did you feel about the incredible growth in your company in this time period?

Gates: Well, the growth in sales was pretty rapid. We were doubling every two years. It just looks like an exponential curve. It is unusual because there are a lot of products that are coming and going, and products that are doing incredibly well and yet it looks very well ordered. The profits went up the same way. Actually, the profitability percentage rose a little bit as we moved up here. So it was very tightly managed. The thing that really changes the company isn't the sales growth, though, it is the number of people. This shows you the total here. We are now well over 15 ,000 employees. And yet, until we moved to Seattle we were about sixteen employees. Then we got up to a little over 30 when Steve came. Then right after Steve Ballmer comes then you see these periods of 40 to 129, 220— 476 increasing at a very rapid rate. It is swelling because you can have all these other product groups. You can sell around the world and you can do better product support. You can lavish on the developers a great library. You can start a research group that is looking way out into the future. And your recruiting department can be the best at going out to all of those universities. So

volatile *adj.*
不稳定的，爆炸性的

zoom *v.*
急速上升，摄像机移动

complexity *n.*
复杂性，错综复杂的事物

convolute *v.*
盘旋，回旋

profitable *adj.*
有利的，赚钱的

chart *n.*
图表，图纸

exponential *adj.*
指数的

tightly *adv.*
紧紧地，坚固地

swell *v.*
膨胀

lavish on
大肆花费

recruiting *n.*
招聘，招募

并且只要我们着
手去做，这就是
一次公司广泛曝
光[19]的机会。谈
论我们的梦想，
我们做得好的地
方，我们将这个
产业带向何方。
确实，有许多人
参与进来。确实
办得很成功。股票
发行时的价格是21美金，这么多年一直在直线上涨[20]。

记者： 所以上市并没有什么遗憾了？

盖茨： 上市并不容易，需要和分析家讨论并处理所有的报告。什么时候应该保密，什
么时候对外公布，这并不好控制。所以并不简单。但股票可以随时流通[21]对每个
人来说是有很明显的好处的。我们没有花一分筹到的钱。我们把这些钱存入银
行，和我们赚到的钱放在一起，因为我们的利润空间很大，并且现金充裕。所
以我们上市的原因与其他上市公司完全不同。

记者： 您那儿有两个表格[22]，比尔，您期望的公司发展轨迹。我很好奇[23]，当您在雇
用第100名、1000名、10,000名员工的时候，这种公司规模的扩张是不是让您
感觉更满意？您对公司这个时期令人难以置信的[24]发展怎么看？

盖茨： 嗯，销售的发展很快。每两年就会翻一番[25]。就像一条指数曲线[26]。这很不寻
常，因为不断有新产品被开发出来，并且都做得好到令人难以置信的程度，看
起来订单不少。利润同样也在上升。事实上，我们搬到这里以后，利润率[27]又
有所上升。因此，管理很紧凑。真正改变公司的不是销售额[28]的增长，而是员
工人数。你可以在这表上看到。我们现在有超过1.5万名员工。但是，在搬到
西雅图之前，我们差不多只有16名员工。Steve来了之后，我们的员工数目增
加到30多人。之后，从40到129、220再到476，增长非常迅速。迅速膨胀[29]是
因为你可以拥有其他所有这些产品组[30]。你可以在全世界销售产品并可以提供
更好的支持。可以斥巨资[31]为开发人员建一座图书馆。可以组建一个前景规划[32]
研究团队。你的人力资源团队可以找到大学里最好的毕业生。所以，我们雇用
的很多精力充沛且聪明的员工，可以帮助我们做许多优秀的事情。但这也就意

19. expose *n.*
20. zoom up
21. liquid *n.*
22. chart *n.*
23. curious *adj.*
24. incredible *adj.*
25. double
26. exponential curve
27. profitability
    percentage
28. sale *n.*
29. swell *v.*
30. product group
31. lavish on
32. look way out into
    the future

many excellent things that the energetic, smart people we hired empowered us to do. But it does mean that I got to the point where I couldn't look at all of the code, which I had done in the early years. At 100 people, I knew everybody. I even knew their license plates when they came and went. I knew really what everyone was up to. By the time it got to 1,000 that was no longer the case. I was hiring the managers and knew all of the managers, but there was a level of indirection. And, certainly, as you go up over 10,000 then there are several levels indirect. There are some managers you don't know. There are some products that you certainly know how they fit in if you are setting the overall strategy. Now electronic mail has been a huge phenomena for us. And it keeps a little bit of a closer feel even if somebody's office is in another building, you're always sending them messages. Or, even if they're off in another country it makes that easy. So, we are not as big as our size suggests. But, it certainly has a bit of a different feel than the small company.

Reporter: At the same time, has your culture changed? Or has it been pretty stable?

Gates: Well, the culture, of course, varies by group. The sales force has great sales people and has the same enthusiasm for software, but their day-to-day activity and measurement is quite different. In the product groups it is pretty similar today. The developers like writing great code. They like collaborating with the team, they like getting things out every eighteen months. They like watching the competition. If somebody is very smart and contributing a lot, then it is fun. If they don't match that kind of level of energy, then it is really not the right place for them. It is an exciting thing. It is still a little bit different. People can't come and talk to me every day [laughs]. And so they have to look to their Business Unit Manager, which is how we have it set up. Certainly, we are trying to preserve all of that culture, and get the advantages of being a large company with a broad product line, with stability, worldwide presence, great support, and yet have the advantages that a small software company has.

Reporter: Is there anything else you want to add?

Gates: I'd say that my job, throughout all this, has been, I think, the most fun job I can imagine having. And partly the people I've gotten to work with outside the company. Certainly there are great people inside the company. And certainly, for at least a decade or [laughs], that will just continue to be the case.

energetic *adj.*
精力充沛的，积极的

empower *v.*
授权，使能够，使可能

indirection *n.*
间接，迂回

phenomenon *n.*
（复数 phenomena）
现象，奇迹

enthusiasm *n.*
热情，热心

collaborating *n.*
合作，协作

set up
建立，安排

preserve *v.*
保护，维持

stability *n.*
稳定，坚定

throughout *prep.*
贯穿，遍及

味着，我不再像早先一样可以了解到一切。100个人的时候，我认识所有的人。上下班时，我甚至可以认出他们的车牌。我知道每个人到底是做什么的。员工数量达到1000人的时候，事情就不是这样了。我雇用了管理人员[33]，并且了解所有的管理层，这样就有了间接的层级[34]。

当然，当人数增加到1万的时候，间接的层级就更多了。有一些管理者我根本不认识。如果你做市场的整体战略[35]的话，你当然会知道一些产品应该是怎样的。现在使用电子邮件已是普遍现象了。即使是跟在另外一个办公楼的人，你们也可以经常传信息，让人感觉很近。或者，即使他们是在国外，你们沟通起来也很方便。所以，我们看起来并不像公司规模那样大，但是感觉当然会和小公司不一样。

记者：同时，您的企业文化改变了吗？还是一直保持原有的？

盖茨：嗯，企业文化，当然，不同的团队有不同的文化。销售团队有很好的销售人员，软件团队也很有工作热情，但是他们每天的工作和衡量尺码[36]却是不一样的。现在，产品部门的文化都很相似。开发人员喜欢编写好的程序。他们喜欢与团队合作，喜欢每18个月都拿出成果。他们乐于看到竞赛。如果有人很聪明并乐于奉献，那么这里就会很有趣。如果他们达不到那样的精力水平，那么这里并不适合他们。这是一件令人兴奋的事情。但是也有不同于其他公司的地方。大家不能每天都来找我谈话（笑声）。所以，他们要去找他们的部门经理，这是我们建立的管理模式。当然，我们希望保持所有这些企业文化，保持大企业的优势，有一条很广泛的生产线，有稳定性，在全球有广阔的市场，强大的支持，同时也拥有小软件公司的优势。

记者：您还有什么其他想补充的吗？

盖茨：我想说，我的工作，通过这一切来看，我想是我可以想象得到的最有趣的工作了。部分原因是与公司外部一些优秀人才的合作。当然，公司里也有很多出色的人才。当然，在未来至少10年的时间里（笑声），都会是这样。

33. manager *n.*
34. level of indirection
35. overall strategy
36. measurement

1. 非限制性定语从句起补充说明作用，其前面往往用逗号隔开，例如：The sun heats the earth, which makes it possible for plants to grow.（太阳给予大地热量，这就使植物的生长成为可能。）

2. whatever相当于no matter what，意为"无论什么"，例如：No matter what happened, he would not mind. =Whatever happened, he would not mind.（不管发生什么事，他都不在意。）

3. 与汉语相比，英语多用被动句，例如："你不能在这儿吸烟。"应该翻译成："You are not allowed smoking here."而不是"You can't smoke here."。

4. president除了有"总统"的意思外，还有"公司董事长"的意思。例如：His father is the president of that corporation.（他爸爸是那家大企业的董事长。）

5. 词组catch on表示"明白，理解"的意思。例如：Please repeat what you said, I didn't quite catch on.（请把你的话再重复一遍，我没太听明白。）

6. 修饰可数名词表示"很多的"的词组有：a lot of，lots of，many，a number of，numbers of，dozens of，scores of等。

7. 动词后可以通过添加er变成相应的表示人的名词，例如：developer（开发商），explorer（探险家），debater（辩论家），interviewer（面试者）等。

8. 词组forget to do sth.与forget doing sth.意义上是有差别的。forget to do sth.意为"忘记要做某事"，而forget doing sth.是"忘记已经做了某事了"。例如：I forgot to close the door.（我忘记关门了。）I forgot closing the door.（我忘记已经关了门了。）

9. pretty一词除了有"漂亮的"的意思外，还可做程度副词，表示"相当"，例如：You speak English pretty well.（你英语讲得相当好。）

10. 英语中有一些名词的复数形式是不规则的，不只是在词尾添加s或es，例如单词phenomenon的复数形式是phenomena而并非phenomenons。

3 脸谱网创始人：
马克·扎克伯格
Founder of Facebook: Mark Zuckerberg

　　马克·扎克伯格，美国社交网站脸谱网的创办人，被人们冠以"盖茨第二"的美誉。他于1984年5月出生在纽约的一个犹太人家庭，从小就是个电脑神童。他10岁时得到了第一台电脑，从此将大量时间花在上面。高中时，为学校设计了一款MP3播放机。20岁的扎克伯格虽然考入了知名的哈佛大学，但却是该校计算机和心理学系的辍学生。在哈佛时代，扎克伯格被誉为"程序神人"，开发出了多种不同的程序。

　　2004年，扎克伯格在哈佛大学的宿舍里创办了脸谱网。短短数年，这一网站风靡全世界，如今，它已成为世界上最重要的社交网站之一，就连美国总统奥巴马、英国女王伊丽莎白二世等政界要人都成了脸谱网的用户。据《福布斯》杂志保守估计，马克·扎克伯格拥有135亿美元身价，是2008年全球最年轻的单身巨富，也是历来全球最年轻的自行创业亿万富豪。

3.1 Zuckerberg Has Enough Confidence in Facebook's Future

轻松输入十分钟

Reporter: What is your vision for Facebook?

Zuckerberg: When I started Facebook from my dorm room in 2004, the idea that my roommates and I talked about all the time was a world that was more open. We believed that people being able to share the information they wanted and having access to the information they wanted is just a better world: People can connect better with the people around them, understand more of what's going on with the people around them, and understand more in general. Also, openness fundamentally affects a lot of the core institutions in society—the media, the economy, how people relate to the government and just their leadership. We thought that stuff was really interesting to pursue. I think it turns out that the best way to do that is to build a company and an organization. We've learned a lot along the way about how to do that. One of the things we learned was that there were two ways to get to this place of more information access. There was the top-down way, right—you can kind of characterize that by the Google, or search approach—where you have a bunch of machines and algorithms going out and crawling the web and bringing information into them. But we figured that over time that wouldn't actually be the best approach. We figured it wouldn't get the most information. It would only get stuff that was publicly available to everyone, and it wouldn't give people the control that they needed to be really comfortable. No one wants to live in a surveillance society, which, if you take that to its extreme, could be where that's going. And there's (Facebook) where people choose to share all this information themselves. It's a slower approach, right, because what it means is that people need to move through this process of realizing that sharing information is good, and slowly sharing more and more information over time. But by doing that you get a lot richer information; you get information that people don't want to share with everyone, but they just want to share with some

vision *n.*
展望，视野

fundamentally *adv.*
根本地，基础地

pursue *v.*
追求，从事

top-down *adj.*
自上而下的，组织
管理严密的

characterize *v.*
具有……的特征，
塑造人物

algorithm *n.*
算法，运算法则

surveillance *n.*
监督，监视

approach *n.*
方法，途径

扎克伯格对脸谱网的
未来信心十足

有效学习十分钟

记者：　您对脸谱网的展望[1]是什么？

扎克伯格：当我于2004年在自己的宿舍推出脸谱网时，我和我的室友谈及的理念一直是建立一个更为开放的世界。我们认为，人们可以按照自己的想法共享或访问信息[2]，那将是一个更为完美的世界。在这个世界里，人们可以更好地与周围的人联系、更多地了解周围的人、更多地了解一切。同时，开放性[3]从根本上影响了社会中的许多核心体系[4]，包括媒体[5]、经济[6]、人们与政府如何联系等等。我们认为这些都是确实值得去追求的方向。我认为实现上述目标的最佳方式是创建一家公司和一个组织，我们在这个过程中学习到了许多如何去做的东西，其中一件是，有两种方式可以获得更多信息，其中之一是自上而下[7]的方式，即通过谷歌或搜索的方法，这需要大量的设备和运算[8]，到处检索网页并将信息带给用户。但久而久之我们发现这实际上并非最佳方法，因为该方法并不能获得最大的信息量，这只能提供给每个人都可以看到的公开内容，并不会为用户提供真正感觉舒适的控制权，因为没有人希望生活在一个处于监督[9]下的社会中。而如果将其发挥到极致，就会走入这样一个社会。而脸谱网则可以让用户选择共享所有此类信息，这是一种较为缓慢的办法，对，因为这需要一个过程，让人们认识到分享信息是一件好事，并随着时间的推移分享越来越多的信息，而这种方法同时可以积累丰富的信息。你获得的信息并非是

1. vision *n.*
2. have access to the information
3. openness *n.*
4. core institution
5. media *n.*
6. economy *n.*
7. top-down
8. algorithm *n.*
9. surveillance *n.*

people around them. You get personal information, like photos from my vacation, or a trip that I want to share with people. And it just ends up being a richer web, and it's more democratically controlled by the people who are sharing stuff, as opposed to by some central entity that's going out and indexing all this information, right? And that's the path we've been on, and it's really interesting just watching the rate of information production change. I think at this point there are probably more people who are sharing stuff either privately or semi-privately on social networks (than just letting it be crawled by search engines). When I use that word, I mean sharing with 100 or 1,000 or 10,000 people. It's not e-mail that you're sending to one or two people, but it's also not something that you're making available to everyone. I think there's a lot of information that people are sharing like that now, and that's probably growing a lot more quickly than the volume of blogs, or other completely open sites on the web. There's something like a billion new photos a month (on Facebook), and that's just one type of media on the site (Facebook) where there is over a billion new pieces of information shared each week.

Reporter: Let's be a little bit more specific. You just gave us a 30,000-foot view. Maybe we should do it now from 5,000 or 10,000 feet.

Zuckerberg: So I think there are two big themes: One is just the trend that Facebook is taking for the next couple years, and then there's more structural stuff that's underlying that in terms of the platform that we're building. First, think about how the Facebook platform has evolved. We started off as this platform inside Facebook; and we were pretty clear from the beginning that that wasn't where it was going to end up. A lot of people saw it and asked, "Why is Facebook trying to get all these applications inside Facebook when the web is clearly the platform?" And we actually agreed with that. It's just that we were just getting started. And now as time goes on, we're shifting away from Platform inside Facebook and shifting more towards Connect (outside of Facebook). And Connect has just a lot of advantages that I think developers will gravitate towards. So, the ability for developers to have their own website with all the same functionality in it that they could've built inside Facebook allows them to build their own brand, allows them to have their own users more than just getting Facebook users inside the site. So, I just think it ends up being a stronger system than the first Facebook platform we had. The structural change comes from this point of openness. We talk about this concept of openness

---

vacation n.
假期，搬出

democratically adv.
民主地，民主主义
地

index v.
指出，编入索引

privately adv.
私下地，秘密地

available adj.
可得的，有效的

volume n.
量，体积

platform n.
平台，站台

application n.
应用，申请

shift v.
转移，改变

gravitate v.
被吸引，受引力作
用

functionality n.
功能，函数性

人们想与所有人分享的，而是仅仅希望与周围人分享的。你可以得到度假照片、一段希望与他人分享的旅行等个人信息[10]。这将会是一个十分丰富的页面，由那些共享资源的人来管理，而不是像那些网站一样列出资讯目录[11]，是吧？这就是我们正在走的路，仅是看到信息飞速的变化就会让我们觉得很有趣。我认为，在这种情况下，人们可能正在秘密地或半秘密地[12]在社会网络上共享大量的此类信息（而不只是把它放到那里等着被搜索引擎索引）。当我用到那个词的时候，我的意思是说与100个、1000个或者10000个人共享信息。这并不是你发给一两个人的邮件，但也不是那些你允许所有人都能看到的东西。我想现在有很多信息都是通过这种方式共享的，这比博客或者其他网络上完全公开的网站的发展速度要快。（脸谱网上）差不多每个月都有10亿张新照片，这仅仅是其中的一种媒体形式[13]而已，每个星期都有10亿多条新的共享资讯[14]。

记者：　能不能更具体[15]一些？您仅仅是让我们在3万英尺以外看。或许现在我们应该走近点，到5000或者1万英尺的地方。

扎克伯格：我认为有两大主题[16]，其一是脸谱网未来几年的趋势[17]，另外就是为构建平台[18]建造基础性的结构。首先，考虑一下脸谱网平台的演变过程。我们开始时是在脸谱网内部推出了该平台，但我们一开始就很清楚这并不是终点。有许多人看到了并问："为什么在网络显然已成为平台的时候，脸谱网还试图将所有的应用程序[19]放在脸谱网内部？"事实上我们完全同意这个说法，但我们那时才刚刚起步。现在随着时间的推移，我们正将平台从脸谱网内部拓展到连接服务[20]，即脸谱网的外部。连接服务有许多吸引开发人员[21]的优势，该服务可以让他们在自己的网站上建立与脸谱网同样的功能[22]，以打造自己的品牌，允许开发人员拥有自己的用户，而不仅仅是脸谱网网站的用户。所以，我认为连接服务

10. personal information
11. index all information
12. semi-privately
13. type of media
14. information shared
15. specific *adj.*
16. theme *n.*
17. trend *n.*
18. platform *n.*
19. application *n.*
20. connect *v.*
21. developer *n.*
22. functionality *n.*

and transparency as the high level ideal that we're moving towards at Facebook. The way that we get there is by empowering people to share and connect. The combination of those two things leads the world to become more open. And so as time has gone on, we've actually shifted a bit more of a focus not just on directly making it so people can use Facebook and share and be open on Facebook, but instead on making it so that the systems themselves have open properties. So, one analogy that we think about is a government or a nation. If you want to be free, or you want to preserve freedom for people, you both need to have laws that make it so people have freedom of speech and all the freedoms that they need. You also need to have an open governance system where people can vote and people have representation. And we think that over the longterm the way that we actually create the most openness and transparency in the world (at Facebook) is both by creating the most powerful applications ourselves and creating a platform that is fundamentally moving more in the direction of being an open platform itself, right? So we're aiming for openness on two levels: One on the fact that there's more sharing, and another on the fact that by having these open standards, you're constantly moving towards a place in the industry where there will be more and more sharing, right? So people can bring their information anywhere they want. Anyone can use the platform.

Reporter: Does that mean every Facebook user will have control over how public his/her information is and be able to decide whether or not it can be crawled by search engines?

Zuckerberg: We've already started moving in that direction. Just a couple of weeks ago we announced this open privacy setting where prior to that it was impossible for someone to take their profile and say that they wanted it to be open. Now they can do that. They can say it's open to everyone. And what I would just expect is that as time goes on, we're just going to keep on moving more and more in that direction.

Reporter: In just five years, Facebook has attracted 250 million members and become a huge cultural phenomenon. Could you ever have imagined this when you were starting out in your dorm room at Harvard?

Zuckerberg: Well, no. It was a really interesting time. Like a lot of college kids, we spent a lot of time talking about abstract things that interested us and how things in the world would play out, about trends in technology. We were looking at all this over late-night pizza, while we were

---

transparency *n.*
透明性，幻灯片

empower *v.*
授权，允许

property *n.*
性能，财产

analogy *n.*
类比，类推

representation *n.*
代表，表现

constantly *adv.*
不断地，时常地

crawl *v.*
（网页）抓取

profile *n.*
轮廓，侧面

attract *v.*
吸引，引起

abstract *adj.*
抽象的，深奥的

late-night *adj.*
深夜的，午夜的

最终将成为一个强大的系统，超出脸谱网最初的平台概念范围。这种结构性的转变正是来自于开放性。我们所谈论的开放性和透明性[23]是脸谱网所追求的高层次理想[24]。我们实现这个目标的方式是为用户的共享和连接提供更多便利。开放性和透明度的结合将使这个世界变得更为开放，随着时间的推移，我们不但可以让用户直接利用脸谱网共享和公开信息，同时也为这个系统本身赋予了开放属性。所以，我们由此想到了政府或者国家。如果你想自由，或者想为人民争取自由，你就需要健全立法以保障公民的言论自由[25]和其他所需要的自由权利。同时，你需要为公众提供一个公开的管理系统，人们可以投票，可以陈述。所以，从长远来看，我们通过自己开发功能最强大的应用程序和逐渐走向公开化的平台，我们建立了世界上最公开和最透明的系统，不是吗？所以我们正在争取达到两个层面上的开放，其中一个就是更多地共享，另外一个就是通过开放的标准，让这个行业变得越来越具有共享性。因此，用户可以将信息放到他们希望的任何地方，任何人都可以使用该平台。

记者：　这是否意味着每个脸谱网的用户都可以控制其信息如何公开，并且能决定是否让搜索引擎[26]对其信息进行索引？

扎克伯格：我们已经在朝着这个方向努力了。就在几周前我们宣布了这个公开隐私设置[27]，若是有人拿着他们的资料并表示他们想要公开这些资料，这在之前是不可能的，但是，他们现在可以这样做了。他们可以说，这些对所有人公开。我预期，随着时间的推移，我们以后将更多地往这个方向转变。

记者：　仅仅用了5年时间，脸谱网全球用户就达到了2.5亿，脸谱网也成为全球范围内的一种文化现象[28]。您当年在哈佛大学学生宿舍创办脸谱网时，是否已预见到脸谱网今日的局面？

扎克伯格：应该说是没有。那真是一段很有趣的时光。与大多数大学生一样，我们经常在一起谈论那些让我们感兴趣的抽象事物[29]以及世界上的事物如何结束，例如技术的发展趋势。当我们在外面闲逛时，我们会去午夜比萨店

23. transparency n.
24. high level ideal
25. freedom of speech
26. search engine
27. open privacy setting
28. cultural phenomenon
29. abstract thing

negotiate *v.*
商议，谈判

irony *n.*
讽刺，反语

impact *n.*
影响，效果

evolve *v.*
发展，进展

stuff *n.*
东西，材料

underlying *adj.*
潜在的，根本的

launch *v.*
开设，发射

hanging out. We thought that during our lifetimes the way people negotiated their identity and their privacy would be changed. There would be a lot more information, and a lot more transparency. That was really interesting to us. At the same time we had no idea that we would build a business that would shape that in any way. I was just building something that would let me and the people around me stay in touch. But then it just kind of grew and grew. The cool irony is that now we are able to have an impact on some of those lofty things we used to discuss in our college dorm room.

Reporter: Has Facebook changed our ideas about privacy?

Zuckerberg: I think social norms have evolved a bit. When we were just getting started five years ago, people were not sure whether they wanted to put anything about themselves on the Internet at all. It was more about control. People want to feel that they can put something up and can control who sees it and if they want to take it down, they can do that. By giving people that control, we enable them to share more stuff. The debate about privacy is really a debate about control. The system we're building is one that strives to give people more control over their information.

Reporter: What will Facebook look like five years from now?

Zuckerberg: Facebook will be less about *Facebook.com* and more about this underlying system and platform that we're building. What we're trying to do is be more about letting people use their information on any site or platform they want. We launched Facebook Connect last year, and we now have more than 15,000 sites using it, and that's just a start. Within five years we hope to have hundreds of millions of [more] people using Facebook. But it's more about using the system to make other sites more social.

讨论这些。我们当时觉得，在我们有生之年，人们谈论自己身份和隐私的方式将得以大幅度改变。世界将有更大的信息量，而且也会越来越透明化。我们对此很感兴趣，但当时我们根本不知道这还能做成事业。我只是为了方便本人同好友保持联系。随后它的规模越来越大。而最出乎意料的事情是：当年我们在大学宿舍谈论过的一些崇高的事物，我们现在已经有能力对它们造成影响了。

记者：　脸谱网是不是改变了我们对于隐私[30]的观念?

扎克伯格：我觉得社会准则[31]已发生了改变。5年前脸谱网刚刚推出时，当时网民还不清楚是否应把个人信息发布到网上。当时网民更关注如何控制自己的个人信息。换句话说，网民一方面愿意发布个人信息，另一方面又希望能控制让谁看到这些信息，当他们想要取消时，他们也可以做到。在我们给予用户这种控制权后，他们就愿意共享更多的信息。所有同隐私保护相关的讨论，其实是在谈论由谁来控制这些个人信息。脸谱网正在建造的系统，也是为了让用户更容易控制个人信息。

记者：　您觉得5年后脸谱网将会是什么样子?

扎克伯格：估计脸谱网届时将不再过于强调*Facebook.com*网站的业务，而是更专注于我们正在组建的基本系统[32]和平台。我们希望网民能够在任何网站和平台中共享个人信息。去年我们推出[33]了脸谱网连接服务，目前使用该服务的外部网站已超过1.5万家，这还只是个开始。今后5年内，我们希望数以亿计（更多）的网民使用脸谱网服务。但更重要的是利用系统[34]使得其他网站更加社会化[35]。

30. privacy *n.*
31. social norm
32. underlying system
33. launch *v.*
34. system *n.*
35. social *adj.*

自由输出十分钟

1. 主语从句是在复合句中充当主语成分的句子，其时态不受主句时态的影响。例如：Whether we will go for an outing tomorrow remains unknown.（我们明天是否要去郊游还不知道呢。）从句用了将来时，而主句则用了现在时。

2. 词组have access to有"接触，使用"的意思，例如：If students do not have access to weapons, then they are less likely to use them in school.（如果学生们没有接触过武器，那么他们在学校里使用它们的可能性就小一些。）

3. 词组on the path的意思是"在……的道路上"，例如：Whether this means China is on the path to global dominance, or just a more balanced growth, remains to be seen.（这是否表明中国正在成为全球经济的主导力量，还是仅仅表明中国只不过取得了更加均衡的经济增长，仍有待观察。）

4. 集合名词意指一种可用来指称一组对象的词，而这些对象可以是人、动物，或是一组概念等事物。英语中的集合名词有很多，例如：family，people，cattle，police，fruit等。

5. Facebook是一个社交网络服务网站，于2004年2月4日上线。网站的名字Facebook来自于传统的纸质"花名册"。通常美国的大学和预科学校把这种印有学校社区所有成员的"花名册"发放给新来的学生和教职员工，帮助大家认识学校的其他成员。在2008年年初，Facebook的全球访问量已经超过MySpace，成为全球第一大社交网站。

6. 表示"优点，长处"的词有：advantage，merit，strength，virtue等。例如：To be sure, each of these proposals has merit—laying off teachers is bad both for children and the economy.（诚然，每个法案都有可取之处——解雇教师无论对孩子还是经济而言都是不利的。）

7. as是连词，后面要加句子，而with是介词，后加名词短语，例如：As time passed quickly, we found it time to say goodbye to each other.=With time passing quickly, we found it time to say goodbye to each other.

8. 反语（irony）是英语修辞手法之一，指用相反意义的词来表达意思的修辞方式，如在职责产生过失时用赞同过失的说法，而在表扬时，则用近乎责难的说法。例如：Well, of course, I knew that gentleman like you carry only large notes.（啊，当然，我知道像你这样的人只带大票子。）

9. 现在进行时有时可表将来，例如：I'm coming.（我来了。）将要来，但还没来。

10. 词组put up可表示"张贴"的意思，例如：They're putting new street signs up.（他们正在张贴新路标。）

3.2 / Facebook Is A "Social Utility" Rather Than A "Social Network"
脸谱网是"社交工具"，而非"社交网络"

轻松输入十分钟

Reporter: Facebook is undergoing a huge period of growth. With more than 150,000 new users signing up daily, it is growing three times as fast as rival MySpace. What do you attribute that spike to?

Zuckerberg: For a while we actually constrained our growth. We made it so that only people in college could sign up. Initially it was only available to people at Harvard, where I was at college. We rolled it out to all the colleges, all the high schools, then a bunch of companies could sign up, and now everyone can sign up. It may seem like the growth is really accelerating at a crazy rate, but it's actually been growing and doubling about once every six months

有效学习十分钟

记者：　脸谱网正在经历一个高速发展期[1]，每天新注册用户多达15万人，增长速度是聚友网的3倍，如此迅猛增长的原因是什么？

扎克伯格：有一段时间，我们实际上抑制[2]了用户的增长。最初只有大学生才可以注册[3]。最早的时候，只有我就读的哈佛大学的同学才能注册，后来面向所有大学开放，所有高中、许多公司人士也可以注册，现在任何人都可以注册了。现在

---

undergo v. 经历，经受

constrain v. 限制，束缚

initially adv. 起初，最初

accelerate v. 增加，促进

1. huge period of growth
2. constrain v.
3. sign up

for quite a while.

Reporter: Is Facebook's popularity connected to its focus on authenticity? On your site, misrepresentation of your real self is a violation of company policy.

Zuckerberg: That's the critical part of it. Our whole theory is that people have real connections in the world. People communicate most naturally and effectively with their friends and the people around them. What we figured is that if we could model what those connections were, we could provide that information to a set of applications through which people want to share information, photos or videos or events. But that only works if those relationships are real. That's a really big difference between Facebook and a lot of other sites. We're not thinking about ourselves as a community—we're not trying to build a community—we're not trying to make new connections.

Reporter: Why do you describe Facebook as a "social utility" rather than a "social network?"

Zuckerberg: I think there's confusion around what the point of social network is. A lot of different companies characterized as social networks have different goals—some serve the function of business networking, some are media portals. What we're trying to do is to just make it really efficient for people to communicate, get information and share information. We always try to emphasize the utility component.

Reporter: In September you rebuffed Yahoo's offer to buy Facebook for nearly $1 billion. Before that, Viacom put up a $750 million bid. And about two months ago you clearly said Facebook would stay independent. Is that still the plan?

Zuckerberg: That has always been the plan. As a company we're very focused on what we're building and not as focused on the exit. We just believe that we're adding a certain amount of value to people's lives if we build a very good product. That's the reason why more than half of our users use the product every day—it's a more efficient way for them to communicate with their friends and get information about the people around them than anything else they can do. We're not really looking to sell the company. We're not looking to IPO anytime soon. It's just not the core focus of the company.

Reporter: So, if Facebook isn't for sale and there's no IPO in the works, how do you intend to satisfy your investors who put a total of $38 million into the company?

Zuckerberg: Well, they're actually really supportive of this. What they want is to build a really great company, too. And if you think about the timeframe over which this has happened—we took our venture round from Accel Partners just about two years ago—they're not in a rush. We have plenty of time to build

authenticity *n.*
真实性，确定性

misrepresentation *n.*
失实的陈述

violation *n.*
违背，妨碍

naturally *adv.*
自然地

figure *v.*
设想，描绘

community *n.*
社区

utility *n.*
工具，实用

confusion *n.*
困惑，混乱

portal *n.*
门户网站

component *n.*
组件，成分

rebuff *v.*
断然拒绝

bid *n.*
出价，叫牌

core *n.*
核心，要点

supportive *adj.*
支持的，赞助的

timeframe *n.*
时间表

venture *n.*
风险投资，商业冒险

的增长速度正在以一种疯狂的速率增加[4]，不过过去的速度事实上是每半年用户增加1倍。

记者：　脸谱网的流行和它注重[5]真实身份有关吗？在你们的网站上，用户资料如果与现实有偏差[6]是违反公司政策[7]的。

扎克伯格：这正是最重要的部分。我们所有的整体理念是，人们在世界上存在真实的人际关系。人们最自然、最有效的沟通是和他们周围的朋友之间的沟通。我们没想，如果脸谱网能够在网络上模拟这种人际连接，那么我们就可以通过各种应用软件让人们分享信息、照片、视频或者活动。这一切的基础是真实的人际关系[8]。这也是脸谱网和许多网站的不同之处。我们并没有把自己当做一个网络社区，我们也不准备建设社区[9]，也不要建立新的人际关系。

记者：　您为什么要把脸谱网称作"社交工具[10]"，而不是"社交网络"？

扎克伯格：我认为人们在"社交网络是什么"上有一些误解。许多不同的公司把自己叫做社交网络，但是都有其目的。一些是为了维护商业网络，一些网站其实是媒体门

户[11]。脸谱网想做的是让人们更高效地沟通[12]，获得信息和分享信息。我们始终强调脸谱网的工具属性[13]。

记者：　9月份，您拒绝了雅虎公司10亿美元的收购邀约。之前，维亚康姆公司给出了7.5亿美元的邀约。两个月前，您表示脸谱网要保持独立，现在还是这么想吗？

扎克伯格：一直都会这样想。作为一个公司，我们聚焦于我们正在做的事情，而不是退出[14]。我们认为，如果能够做出一个好产品，我们将会给人们的生活带来极大的价值[15]。这就是为什么有超过一半的用户每天都登录网站——与其他途径相比，脸谱网让他们能够更加高效地和朋友沟通，并且获悉周围人的信息。我们并不想出售公司，在短期之内我们也不会考虑募股

4. accelerate *v.*
5. focus on
6. misrepresentation *n.*
7. company policy
8. relationship *n.*
9. community *n.*
10. social utility
11. media portal
12. communicate *v.*
13. component *n.*
14. exit *v.*
15. value *n.*

something good.

Reporter: Facebook is looking to hire a stock administrator, isn't that a signal you're preparing for an IPO?

Zuckerberg: Well, no. [pause] I mean, we grant options to all of our employees. At this point we have more than 250. It's a core part of compensation, so you want to make sure you get it right for people. At some point in the future, if we get a chance to go down that [IPO] path, it will be valuable to have that—it's a part of building out the company. I think it's funny that people are paying so much attention to that.

Reporter: The frenzy surrounding Facebook seems to have intensified quite dramatically over the past several months. What do you think is behind the company's newfound cachet?

Zuckerberg: I think the most recent surge, at least in the press, is around the launch of Facebook Platform. For the first time we're allowing developers who don't work at Facebook to develop applications just as if they were. That's a big deal because it means that all developers have a new way of doing business if they choose to take advantage of it. There are whole companies that are forming whose only product is a Facebook Platform application. That provides an opportunity for them, it provides an opportunity for people who want to make money by investing in those companies, and I think that's something that's pretty exciting to the business community. It's also really exciting to our users because it means that a whole new variety of services are going to be made available.

Reporter: What's your grand plan for the company? How do you see it evolving over the next three to five years?

Zuckerberg: It's tough to say, exactly, what things will look like in three to five years, but there's a lot of work to do in just moving along the path that we've already set out. Right now we have 30 million active users on Facebook. There's a lot more to go. And there are a lot of different applications that are going to be developed to allow people to share information in different ways. I would expect the user base will grow and there will be more ways for advertisers to reach people and communicate in a very natural way, just like users communicate with each other. All these things will just get more and more evolved.

Reporter: Beyond Facebook's exclusive advertising deal with Microsoft, which gives the software giant the right to sell ads on the site, what are some of your ideas about monetizing your 30 million users?

Zuckerberg: Advertising works most effectively when it's in line with what people are already trying to do. And people are trying to communicate in a certain way

compensation *n.*
报酬，补偿

frenzy *n.*
狂热，狂怒

intensify *v.*
加强，使……变激烈

newfound *adj.*
新发现的，新得到的

deal *n.*
交易，待遇

application *n.*
应用程序，申请

tough *adj.*
困难的，坚强的

evolve *v.*
发展，进化

exclusive *adj.*
独有的，专一的

monetize *v.*
将……换成现金，赚钱

上市[16]，这不是公司目前的核心。

记者：　如果脸谱网不转让，也不考虑上市，那么您打算怎么回报那些为公司投入了3800万美元的投资者[17]呢？

扎克伯格：事实上他们非常支持我们的决定。他们也希望建设一个卓越的公司。如果你看看我们的发展历程[18]——两年前我们才从阿克赛尔合伙公司获得了风险投资[19]，就会知道，他们并不着急获得回报。我们有充足的时间建设好产品。

记者：　脸谱网正在招募一名股票专员[20]，这是不是公司即将上市的征兆[21]？

扎克伯格：嗯，不是的。［停顿］我的意思是，我们已经开始进行股票期权[22]的奖励，而我们有250多名员工，这是补偿金的核心部分[23]，我们希望确保每个人都能正确地拿到它们。有朝一日，如果我们有机会上市，股票期权是一件好事，也是公司发展的一个组成部分。许多人非常关注这件事，我感觉很有趣。

记者：　在过去几个月时间里，围绕脸谱网的狂热氛围正在升级，您觉得公司新发现的特征背后是什么呢？

扎克伯格：最近的关注，尤其是媒体[24]领域，我认为和脸谱网平台的发布[25]有关。我们第一次可以让不在脸谱网工作的开发人员[26]开发各种应用软件[27]，这是一件大事，所有开发商通过脸谱网平台获得了一个新的发展机会。有许多公司，他们的全部产品就是脸谱网平台上的一个应用。这给他们提供了一个机会，也给他们背后想要通过投资赚钱的人提供了机会，对于商界来说这是一个令人激动的消息。同样，我们的用户可以获得更多的服务，他们也很激动。

记者：　您对公司有着怎样的宏大计划？未来3~5年，脸谱网将会怎样发展？

扎克伯格：很难确切地说未来3~5年将会是什么样子。不过，我们有很多工作要做，只有这样才能按照之前的部署[28]走下去。现在我们有了3000万活跃用户[29]，而且还会有更多。有许多不同的应用程序可以开发，让人们通过不同方式分享信息。我希望用户基数能够继续增长，一些广告客

16. IPO (Initial public offerings)
17. investor *v.*
18. timeframe *n.*
19. venture *n.*
20. stock administrator
21. signal *n.*
22. option *n.*
23. core part
24. the press
25. launch *v.*
26. developer *n.*
27. application *n.*
28. set out
29. active user

on Facebook—they share information with their friends; they learn about what their friends are doing —so there's really a whole new opportunity for a new type of advertising model within that. And I think we'll see more in the next couple months or years on that.

Reporter: With more than 40 billion page views every month, Facebook is the sixth most trafficked site in the US, and the top photo-sharing site. What are your international expansion plans?

Zuckerberg: Right now a lot of our growth is happening internationally. We have more than 10% or 15% of the population of Canada on the site. The U.K. has a huge user base. We haven't translated the site yet, but that's something we're working on and it should be done soon. What we're doing is pretty broadly applicable to people in all different age groups and demographics and places around the world.

Reporter: You recently took off for a summer vacation, what did you do?

Zuckerberg: Hang out with my family.

Reporter: What's a typical day like for the guy who founded Facebook in his Harvard dorm room just three years ago before becoming a full-time entrepreneur?

Zuckerberg: I wake up in the morning, I walk to work because I live four blocks from one of our offices, and I work, meet with people, and discuss things all day, and then I go home and go to sleep. I don't have an alarm clock. If someone needs to wake me up, then I have my BlackBerry next to me.

Reporter: You're a 23-year-old Silicon Valley CEO. How do you deal with all pressures that come along with running a hyper-fast paced, high-profile technology company?

Zuckerberg: I was watching an interview with Steve Jobs the other day, in which he said that "In order to be doing something like this, you have to really, really like what you're doing, because otherwise it just doesn't make sense". The demands and the amount of work that it takes to put something like Facebook into place, it's just so much that if you weren't completely into what you were doing and you didn't think it was an important thing, then it would be irrational to spend that much time on it. Part of the reason why this is fun is because we've managed to build a team of really smart people who come from different backgrounds and have different experiences and think in different ways. People constantly try to put us in a bucket: Are we trying to sell the company? What are we trying to do? What is the business strategy? People are often more interested in why we're hiring a stock-options administrator. Whereas for me and a lot of people around me, that's not really what we focus on. We're just focused on building things.

---

couple *n.*
数个，对

expansion *n.*
扩张，膨胀

demographics *n.*
人口统计资料

entrepreneur *n.*
企业家

high-profile *adj.*
备受瞩目的，高调的

completely *adv.*
完全地，彻底地

irrational *adj.*
不合理的，荒谬的

constantly *adv.*
不断地，时常地

bucket *n.*
桶

户也有机会以一种自然的方式沟通，就好像用户之间相互沟通一样。所有这些事情都会发展、都会完善[30]。

记者：　除了将独家广告[31]合作给了微软，使得这个软件巨人[32]有权在脸谱网网站上卖广告之外，你们还准备如何通过这3000万用户创收[33]？

扎克伯格：网络广告如果和人们的活动密切相关，才是最有效的。人们在脸谱网网站上尝试以特定的方式进行交流——他们和朋友分享信息，他们得知朋友们在做什么，这里存在一种全新的新型网络广告模式机会。在未来几个月或者几年里，我们将会看到更多的广告。

记者：　脸谱网每月的页面浏览量多达400亿，是美国第六大繁忙网站，也是最大的照片共享网站[34]。你们有什么样的国际化扩张计划？

扎克伯格：现在我们的很多增长来自国际市场。我们有10%～15%的用户来自加拿大，英国也有庞大的用户群。我们还没有把脸谱网翻译成其他语言版本，我们正在做这个工作，而且将会很快完成。我们目前所做的一切瞄准了不同年龄段及全世界不同地区的人们。

记者：　您最近度假，做了些什么？

扎克伯格：和我的家人出去转了转。

记者：　3年前，您在哈佛的宿舍里创建了脸谱网，现在已经是全职的企业家，您的一天是怎样度过的？

扎克伯格：早上起来，走路去上班，因为公司距离我住的地方只有4个街区。工作时，会见其他人，整天讨论事情，随后回家睡觉。我没有闹钟，如果有人需要叫醒我，我身旁有一部黑莓手机。

记者：　您是一位23岁的硅谷CEO，管理一个高速成长[35]、引人关注的技术公司，您如何应对各种压力？

扎克伯格：那天我看了对史蒂夫·乔布斯的一期访谈，他在里边说："如果要做成一些事，你必须对它十分热爱，否则就没有任何意义。"建立脸谱网需要付出大量的劳力，如果你不投入，如果你觉得不是很重要，那么可能会有点受不了，于是在这方面花大量的时间就显得太不合理了。脸谱网给我乐趣的一部分原因是，我们已经组建了一个团队，团队成员非常聪明，来自不同的背景，有着不同的经历，以不同的方式思考。许多人经常关注我们这些事：我们要卖掉公司吗？我们正在做什么？企业的战略是什么？许多人更关心我们为何要招募一名股票专员。然而对我或者是对于我周围的团队来说，那些根本不是我们关注的。我们所关心的事情只是建设脸谱网。

30. evolve v.
31. exclusive advertising
32. software giant
33. monetize v.
34. photo-sharing site
35. hyper-fast paced

1. 聚友网（MySpace），是以SNS为基础的娱乐平台，是全球最大的在线交友平台。MySpace的中国本地化网站，提供免费的微型博客、个人主页、个人空间、电子相册、博客空间、音乐和视频上传空间等服务。

2. 词组attribute to的意思是"归因于……"，例如：She attributes her great age to carefully planned diet.（她认为她的高寿是精心安排饮食的结果。）

3. 在英语中，破折号可用来表示反问，例如：It is clear—is it not? —that we must practice strict economy.（很清楚——不是吗？——我们必须厉行节俭。）

4. rather than表示"而不是……"的意思，例如：I, rather than you, should do the work.（该做这工作的是我，而不是你。）

5. 通感（synesthesia）是指在某个感官所产生的感觉，转到另一个感官的心理感受。例如：Taste the music of Mozart.（品尝莫扎特的音乐。）用味觉形容听觉。

6. 词组take advantage of意为"充分利用"，例如：Banks are still being stingy with credit but households are better positioned than they were to take advantage of cheaper homes.（各银行对信贷仍然非常严格，但是与以往相比，现在各家庭做好了更好利用较廉价住房的准备。）

7. 英语中很多单词是通过合成法构成的合成词，这些词的词意一般可以通过各个单词的意思进行推测，例如：newfound（新发现的），north-facing(朝北的)，hardworking（不辞辛苦的）等。

8. 夸张（hyperbole）是英语修辞方法之一，是运用丰富的想象、过激的言词来渲染和装饰客观事物，以达到强调的效果。例如：My blood froze.（我的血液都凝固了。）这里用凝固的血液表示震惊。

9. IPO是Initial Public Offerings的缩写，意为"首次公开募股"；CEO是Chief Executive Officer的缩写，意为"首席执行官"，两者均为经济学词汇。

10. available一词用法灵活，通常表示一种可能性，例如：Mr. Leach is on holiday and was not available for comment.（利奇先生在休假，没空作评论。）

4 推特网创始人：
埃文·威廉姆斯
Founder of Twitter: Evan Williams

埃文·威廉姆斯，于1972年3月31日出生于内布拉斯加州，是美国著名企业家，已建立了数家互联网公司。1999年，威廉姆斯和梅格·休利汉共同创立了Pyra实验室，专门开发项目管理软件，而后创建了一个名为Blogger的子项目——Web发行工具，用于创建和管理博客。最终在2003年2月17日被谷歌收购。

威廉姆斯于2004年10月离开谷歌，与他的一位朋友Noah Glass开办了一家播客公司Odeo，并在其内部开发了子项目Twitter。2006年年底，威廉姆斯与Biz Stone及其他前Odeo员工共同创立了Obvious Corp公司。2007年4月，埃文·威廉姆斯将Twitter剥离成一个独立的公司，而Sonic Mountain于2007年5月收购了Odeo。2008年10月他担任Twitter的CEO，并努力将其打造成通过手机和互联网向朋友发送短信的社交网络。

4.1 / Using Twitter Will Become An International Phenomenon

轻松输入十分钟

Reporter: Why do you think Twitter has had this extraordinary sort of not only growth, but popularity and visibility and talk?

Williams: It's something to tell you the truth that I can't fully explain. And I think the product is great. I think it's compelling. The level of attention has been a little surprising.

Reporter: All of us want—you're on our show, all magazines want to write about you, all newspapers want to profile you.

Williams: I think Twitter combines a lot—it distills a lot of what makes the Internet exciting into a very simple form. And it is about people connecting, and it really provides people with a new way to communicate that didn't exist. And as my co-founder Biz Stone likes to say, it gives us a way that we didn't know we needed.

Reporter: Exactly right.

Williams: Twitter is asynchronous relationship model. It looks a lot like a social network, but it is actually fundamentally different in how the relationship structures work. So a social network, like Facebook being the classic example, is about finding and encapsulating real-world connections, where if we know each other, we say we're friends on the social network, and then we can communicate. And it's two-way. So I can be interested in you and you are sending updates. You don't know who the heck I am, or you just don't care about my updates, and you ignore me. Whereas if I was on social networking and you wanted to be my friend, I would have to. You'd have to confirm. But here, I don't know who is getting it. Just the people who want it can get it.

Reporter: Yeah. But here, I don't know who is getting it. Just the people who want it can get it.

Williams: Right. So it's much more open. And it creates a different kind of dynamic. So what you are doing is you are just—you're kind of putting stuff out there, and sort of like you would put stuff out on the web or on a blog,

---

extraordinary *adj.*
特殊的，非凡的

visibility *n.*
能见度，可见性

compelling *adj.*
引人注目的

profile *v.*
报导，评论

distill *v.*
提取，蒸馏

co-founder *n.*
共同创立者

asynchronous *adj.*
异步的

encapsulate *v.*
压缩，封进内部

update *n.*
最新资料；最新知识

confirm *v.*
确定，证实

dynamic *n.*
动力，动态

使用推特网将成为一种国际现象

有效学习十分钟

记者：　您认为为什么推特网现在不仅发展很快，而且受欢迎程度[1]和知名度[2]也在快速提升？

威廉姆斯：说实话，我并不能解释得很清楚。我认为产品很好，对人们很有吸引力[3]。受关注的程度让人有点吃惊。

记者：　我们都想——您现在参加我们的节目，所有的报纸和杂志都想报道关于您的事迹。

威廉姆斯：我认为推特网结合了很多东西——它把互联网上令人兴奋的点都提取出来，做成一种很简单的模式。它给人们提供了一种从没有过的全新的沟通方式。和我一起创办推特网的比兹•斯通常说，它让我们找到了一条我们从未想过的自己需要的路。

记者：　没错。

威廉姆斯：推特网采用的是异步关系模式[4]，它非常像社交网站[5]，但它在构建人际关系结构时，却有着根本的不同。脸谱网是社交网站的"典型例子[6]"。脸谱网可以用来维持现实中的人际关系。两个在现实生活中彼此相识的人，在社交网站上成为好友，就可以通过脸谱网交流，这是双向的[7]。所以，我可以对你的页面进行关注，你不断地更新[8]。你不知道我是谁，或许你根本不关心我的更新，你完全忽视我。但是如果我在社交关系网络，你要成为我的好友，需要经过我的同意。你需要确认。但是在这里，我不知道谁会收到，只有想要的人才会得到。

记者：　是的，但是在这里，我不知道谁会收到。想要的人才会得到。

威廉姆斯：因此，推特网更为开放。它创造的是一种另类的动态[9]。你所做的就是对外发布信息，就像你通过网页或者博客发布信息一样，但是推特网更加"迅速"，也更具"约束性"。比如，你只能发送140字以内的信息，而且无法利用推特网发送图片，只是单纯的文字。这是推特网的一个现象，你可以通过第三方来传递图片。你可以发送一个网络链接，可以是一个网站[10]，也可以是一张图片。

1. popularity *n.*
2. visibility *n.*
3. compelling *adj.*
4. asynchronous relationship model
5. social network
6. classic example
7. two-way
8. update *v.*
9. dynamic *n.*
10. web site

but it's much faster and more constrained than that. Constrained because it's only 140 characters, and no pictures, nothing but pure text. That is one of the—the other phenomenon of Twitter is there—you can actually post pictures through a third party. What you do is you post a link. You post a link to anything, so it can be a web site; it can be a picture.

Reporter: Right. Right.

Williams: There is a service called TwitPic, which is one of many—there are at least 2,000 different programs that can send Twitter updates. And they use our—they are third-party developers who have completely on their own built software that plugs into Twitter. And they have done it for posting pictures, twittering from an iPhone or a BlackBerry or from a Windows or Mac or Linux computer. Almost anything you can imagine now has a Twitter interface and all built by third-party developers. So that's one of the phenomenon that Twitter has tapped into, I think because again, it's so simple, that people just build all kinds of things around it.

Reporter: What I love about it —is instant—it's instant. I mean, you had a senator twittering while the president was addressing the Congress.

Williams: Twitter, the real-time aspect is really one of the main benefits. And that partial—part of that is because the content is so short, it can both be written and sent instantly. And we use SMS and other technologies to really take advantage of that. And that's what makes it interesting even in the mundane stuff, when it's not the president, it's not a senator. But it's—it's your brother who lives across the country, you know, saying they are painting the garage. That's—it's not interesting to hear later that he painted the garage. But to hear in the moment that that is happening.

Reporter: The instant quality of it is the genius for me. And—and but at the same time, the president did use it when he won. Didn't he send out a tweet? How many people got it—he sent out a tweet that said, thank you all, this is a glorious day for all of us, and you deserve the credit, something to that effect.

Williams: Exactly.

Reporter: What's magical about 140 characters? You needed a number?

Williams: Well, the original reason it's 140 characters is because we wanted to support SMS, and we put a lot of focus on that at first. And SMS, text messages normally are limited to 160 characters, so we needed some room for the name, and we decided on 140.

Reporter: What is in your DNA that has enabled you to start blogger.com? And Twitter? I mean, what is it about you?

Williams: Well, first of all, I didn't invent the idea of Twitter. And I didn't really invent the idea of Blogger. I saw an opportunity. And in both cases, what

---

constrained *adj.*
束缚的，被强迫的

phenomenon *n.*
现象，奇迹

third-party *n.*
第三方

plug *v.*
插入，塞住

twittering *n.*
鸣声，呢喃

interface *n.*
界面，接口

instant *adj.*
瞬间的，立即的

senator *n.*
议员，理事

partial *adj.*
局部的，偏爱的

mundane *adj.*
平凡的，世俗的

garage *n.*
车库，飞机库

glorious *adj.*
辉煌的，极好的

normally *adv.*
通常地，一般地

记者： 是的，没错。

威廉姆斯： 有一项服务叫做TwitPic。现在已经有约2000个不同的程序可以帮助用户发送推特网更新。这都是由第三方开发的，他们在自己的软件中插入推特网。用户可以通过第三方程序[11]来发送图片，而且这些程序也遍及几乎所有平台，包括iPhone、黑莓、Windows、Mac或者Linux

等。几乎所有你可以想象得到的事情，现在都有推特网界面[12]，这些全部由第三方开发商来建立。这是推特网引发[13]的另一种现象[14]，我想这同样是因为推特网的界面很简洁，人们可以围绕它创建各种事物。

记者： 我喜欢的正是它的即时性。我是说，总统正在国会上演讲的时候，会有议员使用推特网。

威廉姆斯： 推特网的主要价值之一就在于即时性[15]。这只是一部分——还有一部分是因为内容很简短，可以即刻写并发送。我们吸收了短信息[16]和其他技术的优势。不仅仅是总统和议员，这让普通百姓也会觉得很有趣。但是如果你的兄弟住得很远，他跟你说他们正在给车库刷漆。如果你事后听说了他们给车库刷漆的事情并不会觉得好玩。但如果是当时听说，就很有趣了。

记者： 我太喜欢它的即时性了。但是同时，总统获选的时候他确实也用了推特网。他发了一条消息吧？有多少人收到了——他用推特网发了一条消息说，感谢所有的人，这是属于我们所有人的辉煌的一天，你们理应受到赞扬[17]，差不多是这样的效果。

威廉姆斯： 确实如此。

记者： 140个字有什么魔力[18]吗？您需要一个数字？

威廉姆斯： 嗯，最开始限定为140个字是因为我们想要支持短信息，首先就考虑到了这一点。短信息的字数一般限制为160字，我们需要为用户名预留一些空间，所以我们决定140字。

记者： 是什么原因让您创立了博客网和推特网？我的意思是您的初衷是什么？

威廉姆斯： 嗯，首先，推特网并不是我的创意。博客网也并不完全是我发明的。我看到了机会。在这两个例子中促使我去做的都是我想要自己先体验。我自出生以来就是一名企业家[19]，至少我自己是这样认为的。我喜欢创造新的事物。喜欢新颖的东西。我在创建博客网[20]和推特网时感觉到了类似的东

11. third-party developer
12. interface *n.*
13. tap into
14. phenomenon
15. real-time
16. SMS (Short Messaging Service)
17. credit *n.*
18. magical *adj.*
19. entrepreneur *n.*
20. blogger.com

drove me to pursue it was experiencing it myself. And I have been an entrepreneur since birth, at least in my mind. And I like creating things that are new. I like working things that are new. And I felt a similar thing when I created Blogger, and then was part of the team that created Twitter, that this is really fun. I don't know where it's going, but there is something very fundamental about what this can do. And of course, when Twitter came out, it had all the Blogger experience, so it was based on a lot more experience. And I thought, well, people will like this.

Reporter: Where is blogging today?

Williams: Blogging is an interesting place today, I think, because it's still actually a huge part of the web. There are millions of people who blog daily. But what it is, it's kind of morphing, I think. So it depends on how strict you define it.

Reporter: Morphing, yeah.

Williams: So, blogging has always been hard to define, which is why that question is a difficult one. Because it is what—a lot of the motivations to blog and the same acts are that people—what has started on Blogger. com for are tapped by people's participation in Facebook or MySpace or Twitter now. So I think as a—if you look at it generally, it's bigger than ever and pretty much growing, but it's definitely evolving.

Reporter: Is what we are talking about, in terms of social networking, in terms of Twitter and tweeting, is it at the essence of where sort of the Internet revolution is, the idea of community? The idea that you can take this remarkable tool and use it to create a community that brings you friendship, as well as information as well as something else?

Williams: I think it does all of that. And I think...

Reporter: But how powerful of a force is it, in terms of shaping the way the Internet is used today?

Williams: I think it's tremendously powerful. I think what the Internet—how the Internet has evolved over time is to more efficiently tap the most basic human desires. And there—they vary a lot, but the desire to connect with other people socially is a big one. And I think that is why social networks in general are very powerful. That's what people care about almost more than anything else.

Reporter: Project this forward five years. How will it be different, all of it?

Williams: Well, it's hard to imagine how the technology is going to be vastly different. I'm sure it will. I think a lot of it—that will be—the ways that it will be different is culturally. And so, people will be used to this mode of—I remember when blogging started, it seemed very strange to people that just anyone could write something on the web. How—how dare they

entrepreneur *n.*
企业家，主办者

fundamental *adj.*
基本的，根本的

blogging *n.*
博客，写网志

morphing *n.*
变异

participation *n.*
参与，分享

essence *n.*
本质，实质

remarkable *adj.*
非凡的，值得注意的

tremendously *adv.*
非常地，极大地

mode *n.*
方式，模式

西。我觉得这非常有趣。虽然我不知道它们将会如何发展，但这都是我基于经验[21]做出的判断。当然，当推特网诞生[22]之时，我已经有了博客网的相关经验，所以推特网是建立在经验之上的。我当时想，嗯，大家一定会喜欢。

记者：　　博客的现状怎样？

威廉姆斯：它现在处于一个很有意思的位置。我想是因为它仍然是互联网的很大一部分。数百万的人每天登录博客。但我想这是一种"变异[23]"，要看你怎样去定义[24]。

记者：　　变异，嗯。

威廉姆斯：是的，博客一直很难定义，所以这个问题很难回答。人们原先只在博客网这样纯粹的博客网站上写博客，但是现在却都通过脸谱网、聚友网和推特网来写博客。从总体上看，博客的规模的确比以往更大，确实也在发展，但博客的确处在变革[25]中。

记者：　　从社交网络和推特网以及使用推特网的角度来看，我们现在正在谈的可以说是互联网革命[26]的本质是——交往[27]的概念吗？是您可以使用这个不同寻常的工具去创造一种交友、获取信息或其他的沟通方式的概念吗？

威廉姆斯：我想它涵盖了所有，并且我认为……

记者：　　但是对于塑造[28]今天的互联网来说，它有多大的功效呢？

威廉姆斯：我认为它很强大[29]。互联网已经进化到能够更有效地满足人类最基本的[30]欲望，而与他人进行社会化联系就是其中一个很大的欲望。这也正是社交网站的力量所在，也是人们最关心的部分。

记者：　　展望未来5年的技术，会和现在有什么不同？

威廉姆斯：嗯，这很难说，我很难预料技术[31]上的变化，但我确信肯定会变。我认为更大的变化将在于文化上。因此，人们将会更加适应某些模式[32]。我记得当年我们创建博客网时，任何人都可以在网络上写些东西，很多人都觉得这非常奇怪，"他们怎么敢在网上写东西？谁会看啊？"如今，至少我还生活在旧金山泡沫[33]中，但人们逐渐接受了这种方式，变成了普通大众都在做的事。很明显，脸谱网和聚友网就是普通大众在做的事。

记者：　　互联网是一种国际现象，使用推

21. experience *n.*
22. come out
23. morphing *n.*
24. define *v.*
25. evolve *v.*
26. Internet revolution
27. community *n.*
28. shape *v.*
29. powerful *adj.*
30. basic *adj.*
31. technology *n.*
32. mode *n.*
33. San Francisco bubble

have the nerve to think that someone would want to read it? And now, at least I live in the San Francisco bubble, but it seems like people generally accept, sure, that's a thing that normal people do. Clearly Facebook and MySpace are things that normal people do.

Reporter: The Internet is an international pheno-menon. Is Tweeting an international phenomenon?

Williams: It is. Only about half our users are in the US right now. Japan is really big for us. Japanese is the one language we've translated the site to. But it was actually —we translated it because it got big in Japan first. The U.K. has actually exploded recently. The U.K. is the second biggest, and I think Canada and Germany and Brazil are creeping up.

Reporter: Some have suggested that for a while there, maybe still, you had a problem with crashing because there was so much usage.

Williams: We did. We had a terrible first year and a half, actually, where the site went down a lot and was slow a lot. And it took us a long time to get out of that. That almost killed us, I think.

特网也会成为一种国际现象吗？

威廉姆斯： 是的。现在只有半数推特网用户来自美国。日本对于我们而言是非常大的市场。我们推出了日文版的网站，事实上，我们将网站翻译成日语是因为我们首先是在日本市场得到壮大的。英国市场近期的增长也非常迅猛，并成为仅次于日本的推特网第二大海外市场。此外，加拿大、德国和巴西的增长[34]也相当不错。

记者： 有些人暗示，由于用户量太多，您或许曾存在崩溃[35]问题。

威廉姆斯： 确实有过。其实我们刚开始的一年半时间是非常艰苦的。那时网站非常慢，而且经常崩溃。我们花了很长时间才解决这个问题，这几乎让我们无法生存。

---

nerve n. 勇气，神经

bubble n. 泡沫，气泡

explode v. 激增，爆发

creep v. 蔓延，爬行

usage n. 使用，用法

34. creeping up

35. crashing n.

自由输出十分钟

1. Twitter（中文称：推特）是国外的一个社交网络及微博客服务网站。它利用无线网络、有线网络、通信技术进行即时通讯，是微博客的典型应用。它允许用户将自己的最新动态和想法以短信形式发送给手机和个性化网站群，而不仅仅是发送给个人。

2. 派生词是英语词汇的一大特点，派生词由词根通过添加词缀形成，例如：co-founder（共同创立者），enrich（使富裕），disadvantage（缺点）等。

3. 词组tap into的意思是"进入，参与"，例如：But fund managers are optimistic for the future, with a host of new products expected to tap into a market recovery.（但基金经理对未来持乐观态度，预计许多新产品将参与市场复苏。）

4. 地点状语从句是表示地点、方位等的从句，通常由where引导。例如：We must camp where we can get water.（我们必须在能找到水的地方露营。）

5. SMS是一种存储和转发服务。也就是说，短消息并不是直接从发送人发送到接收人，而始终通过SMS中心进行转发。如果接收人处于未连接状态（可能电话已关闭），则消息将在接收人再次连接时发送。

6. 表示"根据"的词组有：in terms of，according to，based on，on the basis of等。

7. 词组send out的意思是"发送"，例如：She had sent out well over four hundred invitations that afternoon.（那天下午她发出了远不止400份的请柬。）

8. 在名词后加后缀-ship表示一种关系，例如：relationship（关系），friendship（友谊），kinship（亲属关系）等。

9. 词组creep up的意思是"上升，爬上"，例如：One bad winter we watched the river creep up the lower meadows.（有一年冬天，情况糟透了，我们看见河水漫上低洼的草地。）

10. 对照（antithesis）是指将意义完全相反的语句排在一起对比的一种修辞方法，例如：Give me liberty，or give me death.（要么给我自由，要么让我死去。）

4.2 / Twitter Is User-driven

轻松输入十分钟

Reporter: Let's talk about the company as a business. It is—I know I am unlikely to get anywhere on this, but if Facebook wanted to buy you for anywhere between $300 and $500 million—was there an offer from Facebook?

Williams: We talked to Facebook, yeah.

Reporter: And is this valuation in the ballpark?

Williams: I can't comment on the valuation.

Reporter: Why did you make the decision not to sell?

Williams: Well, we thought about it carefully. And I can't say—you know, offers are in various forms of seriousness, and who knows if, you know, they would have done it, but our analysis was carefully considered. We're a for-profit company. We have outside investors that have to look at these deals. But I never felt like it was the best thing for Twitter. It really—it just seems way too early. We have a lot of momentum. There's tons of risk. We don't make money. Lots of things could go wrong. But the potential is so great that to stop now, even out of a big win financially, would just feel like a loss.

Reporter: Will the tremendous opportunity simply happen?

Williams: It is completely user-driven, for the most part. I mean, we are surprised daily by the types of things people do. And a lot of the evolution of the product has actually come from users themselves as well, just inventing things. As well as the developers, the third-party developers. So I feel like we're sort of at best just trying to keep it open and flexible and running for those people and trying to make it more valuable for them all the time, but we're not in charge of how it's used.

Reporter: Do you think it will have a form of journalism?

Williams: Yeah, I think there's certainly a form of journalism. And I think what's happened so far has been overblown a little bit. People are saying it's journalism. And it is. There are reporters who will use it to cover an event. Events are really interesting for Twitter, any sort of real-time, like. I think what could be really interesting is when you get the crowd and sort of have the collective intelligence. And you synthesize that and do more

valuation *n.*
估价，评价

ballpark *n.*
约略估计的数目

for-profit *adj.*
营利性的，牟利的

momentum *n.*
动力，势头

financially *adv.*
财政上地，金融上地

tremendous *adj.*
巨大的，惊人的

evolution *n.*
进展，演变

flexible *adj.*
灵活的

journalism *n.*
新闻业，新闻工作

overblow *v.*
过分渲染，用力吹

real-time *adj.*
实时的，接到指示立即执行的

synthesize *v.*
综合，合成

以客户为导向的推特网

有效学习十分钟

记者：　我们把公司当做生意来谈一下吧。我知道可能得不出什么结论，但是如果脸谱网愿意出3~5亿美金收购推特网的话——脸谱网是否提出过这样的条件？

威廉姆斯：是的，我们的确与脸谱网谈过。

记者：　那这是约略估计[1]的价值吗？

威廉姆斯：我不想对估值[2]发表任何看法。

记者：　为什么放弃出售？

威廉姆斯：嗯，我仔细考虑过。我不能说——你知道的，报价[3]有很多种不同的正式形式[4]，没人知道他们是否会那样做，但是我们的分析必须经过认真考虑。我们是盈利性公司[5]。我们外界的投资者会关注这些交易。但是我从不认为这是推特网最好的归宿。我觉得现在还为时尚早。我们动力[6]十足。这其中存在巨大的风险。我们没赚钱，也可能做错很多事，但是我们有着巨大的潜力，如果现在就停下来，就算拿到了一大笔资金，也会让我们感到非常失落[7]。

记者：　会有很多机会吗？

威廉姆斯：很大程度上，我们都是以用户为导向的[8]。我是说，我们每天都能从用户的使用方式中得到惊喜，其实很多具有革新性[9]的产品都是由用户自己创造的。当然，也包括第三方开发者。所以我希望平台能够更加开放且更具灵活性[10]，从而始终为用户提供更多的价值，但我们并不管怎么用。

记者：　您认为会被当做一种新闻报道[11]的方式吗？

威廉姆斯：是的，当然会。我想现在这些事情有过分渲染[12]的成分。人们都说这就是新闻报道。是的，有记者会用它报道新闻。推特网上报道的许多都是实时信息[13]，这也是推特网吸引人的地方。集中集体智慧[14]将是一种非常有趣的方式。你可以综合它们并做更多，我们有一个搜索功能[15]，现在很受欢迎。你只要输入一个地方，比如孟买，你就可以看到这里的每个人都在

1. in the ballpark
2. valuation *n.*
3. offer *n.*
4. form of seriousness
5. for-profit company
6. momentum *n.*
7. feel like a loss
8. user-driven
9. evolution *n.*
10. flexible *adj.*
11. journalism *n.*
12. overblow *v.*
13. real-time *adj.*
14. collective intelligence
15. search function

than—we have a search function that is very popular, where people—the Mumbai case, you could type in that and just see what everyone was saying. I think there is really interesting potential if we can synthesize more intelligence out of that.

Reporter: Is that an editing function or what?

Williams: No, I think it has to be algorithmic or crowd-source editing somehow. We can detect signals about what's interesting. We can—depending on how people react to the content and reputation systems that could say over time that this source is interesting. And we want to build more ways for the good stuff and the most interesting stuff to bubble to the top. Or at least bubble to the people who are interested in it.

Reporter: Exactly.

Williams: And I think that's kind of the—if I think of the ultimate version, what Twitter kind of does right now is it helps people figure out what's happening that's interesting to them. So—but I think if you take the ultimate version of that, then I should know—I don't necessarily know who to follow. So if there is something happening down the street, based on my past interests or how I have reacted or what my friends are saying, I may want to know about that, even if I didn't know I wanted to know about that.

Reporter: Monetizing is the question everybody asks. How do you monetize this?

Williams: We don't know for sure. But we have some ideas. It's going to, I think like the product itself, it is going to have to evolve over time. We are going to try things and see what works. But we're encouraged by a couple of things. One is that, I'd say three things. One is I don't think there is a question of can it make enough money to survive. Because I think there're a lot of people talk about how Twitter will ever make money, sort of this mentality still that Internet bubble, where things disappeared because they got hyped too much and then didn't make money. Now there is actually an economy built into the web that is much more real —so if something is popular, it probably won't go—it probably won't disappear because it can't make any money. That doesn't really happen anymore. So the question is, is there a killer business model there or just a survivable business model there? And what we're encouraged by is the fact that, as mentioned, there is a lot of commercial usage already. So if we could charge users at some point or charge for extra features, which a lot of companies do. We could obviously implement some sort of advertising, which we do none of right now. If we do that intelligently, it could be a win for users and make money for companies that pay for it, just like Google figured out how to do.

Reporter: On the other hand, Google has also figured out, I think, and have

---

intelligence *n.*
智慧，情报工作

editing *adj.*
编辑的

algorithmic *adj.*
算法的，规则系统的

detect *v.*
发现，察觉

bubble *v.*
沸腾，冒泡

version *n.*
版本，译文

monetize *v.*
盈利，定为货币

encourage *v.*
鼓励，怂恿

mentality *n.*
心态，智力

hyped *adj.*
兴奋的

survivable *adj.*
可生存的，可免于死亡的

implement *v.*
实施，使生效

说些什么。我想如果我们能从中综合出更多的智慧，这将是非常有趣的潜能。

记者： 是编辑功能[16]吗？还是其他的什么？

威廉姆斯： 不，我想应该算是"算法[17]和群体编辑[18]"。我们可以挖掘有趣的事情，同时了解人们对内容和声誉系统[19]的反应，看他们是否对资源感兴趣。我们将开发更多的途径，把那些好的、有趣的事情放在最顶端。或者至少是提供给[20]那些对此感兴趣的人。

记者： 一点儿不错。

威廉姆斯： 最终版本[21]的推特网可以帮助人们了解正在发生的他们感兴趣的新闻，但是我认为如果你用了最终版本的推特网，那么我应该知道——我没有必要知道谁在用。而如果在大街上发生了什么事情，推特网则可以根据用户以前的兴趣，对特定事件的反应或朋友的言论自动推送当前的信息，即使用户根本没有意识到自己想要去了解这些信息。

记者： 每个人都在关心盈利[22]的问题。你们如何盈利？

威廉姆斯： 我们还不十分肯定，但是我们已经有了一些想法。我认为，就像产品本身一样，假以时日会有的。我们会不断尝试并且确定什么才是有用的。有两件事情对我们鼓励[23]很大。其中一件事，应该说是三件事情。第一，我认为它是否可以帮我们赚到足够的钱以供生存，这不是问题。因为现在有很多人在谈论推特网怎样才能最终赚到钱，在互联网泡沫[24]中，一些网站被大肆宣传，但却因为赚不到钱而消失[25]了。事实上，现在的网络中也有经济，也更为真实。所以，如果什么东西很受欢迎的话，那么它将永远不会过时，不会因为赚不到钱而倒闭。但是这种情况已经一去不复返了。问题在于，到底这里存在致命的商业模式[26]还是能存活的商业模式[27]？值得欣慰的是，基于之前提到的事实，推特网已经有了许多商业用户。推特网有可能会就新的或者更多的功能向商业用户收费，很多公司都这么做。当然也可能开发独特的广告模式，目前我们还没有

任何广告。如果我们做得足够优秀[28]，那么不仅用户可以从中获益，企业同样可以利用推特网赚钱，像谷歌一样。

记者： 从另一方面来看，我认为，谷歌也指出，并且至少在我读到的某些资料里建议，社交网络并不是他们认为可行的广告手段[29]。

威廉姆斯： 是的。

记者： 这个地方不合适，社交网络中的人可能并

16. editing function
17. algorithmic *adj.*
18. crowd-source
    editing
19. reputation system
20. bubble to
21. ultimate version
22. monetize *v.*
23. encourage *v.*
24. Internet bubble
25. disappear *v.*
26. killer business
    model
27. survivable business
    model
28. intelligently
29. advertising vehicle

suggested at least in someplace that I've read, you know, that social networking is not the advertising vehicle they thought it might be.

Williams: Right.

Reporter: It's not a place—people who are engaged—who are on using social networking are not sort of likely to look at the ads.

Williams: Right. I think that's right. And you know, Twitter may be more like that. But there's this informational component to Twitter that makes it a little bit less like a pure social communication tool. I think social communications are really hard to monetize. Information seeking activities are much easier to monetize, Google being the ultimate example. Twitter is somewhere in between, because of the fact that I get my dad's tweets, but I also get—I also will do searches and find out what people are saying about the latest iPhone.

Reporter: Right. Suppose that this show, my with you, and I warn it is going to be on tonight, but I also wanted to tweet it to say to people, a group of people, and I'm not interested in numbers here, although there may be a bonanza of numbers—Evan was just on, we had this wonderful conversation, boom, here it is. How would that work?

Williams: How well would it work?

Reporter: How would it work and how well would it work?

Williams: It would work really well. I mean, one thing certainly people would want to follow Charlie Rose on Twitter.

Reporter: Right, right.

Williams: And they would want to hear who you are interviewing, when it's being taped, and what you are doing in between time...

Reporter: And I'm in San Francisco and what I am doing and where am I eating and all that stuff.

Williams: Exactly, yes, people love that. And it—when you get on, we'll point you out and you'll get hundreds of thousands of people. And then, any time you want, one of the benefits, obviously is you have this direct line to these people all the time. So you can ask questions. You can get feedback from them.

Reporter: Right.

Williams: You can send them links and they'll follow them.

Reporter: So we would send them a link to the show, so they go to *charlierose.com*, and there you go, they could watch the show.

Williams: Exactly. Exactly.

Reporter: All right. This is exciting to me. And it's also one of the reasons I love to come to San Francisco and come to the Silicon Valley and come to the West Coast, because all these interesting things are happening. And thank you for coming.

Williams: Thanks for having me.

vehicle *n.*
媒介，工具

engaged *adj.*
忙碌的，使用中的

informational *adj.*
新闻的，情报的

ultimate *adj.*
最终的，最后的

tweet *n.*
状况，叫声

bonanza *n.*
幸运，富矿带

tape *v.*
录制，录音

stuff *n.*
东西，材料

feedback *n.*
反馈，成果

exactly *adv.*
正是，完全地

不会去看那些广告。

威廉姆斯： 没错。我想这是对的。你知道，推特网可能就会那样。但是某些新闻元素也决定了推特网不会成为一种纯粹的社交工具[30]。我认为，想要利用社交网络赚钱并不容易，而利用人们搜寻信息的行为来赚钱就要

容易得多，谷歌就是很好的例子。推特网其实处于社交网站和信息搜寻网站[31]之间。因为事实上，我不仅会利用推特网得知老爸的近况，还可以通过搜索而得到大家对于最新款iPhone的评价。

记者： 是的。假设我们今天的对话，我预告说会在今晚播出，但是我同时又想用推特网跟一群人说，我对人数并不感兴趣，虽然可能会有很多人——我刚与埃文进行了非常完美的对话。效果会怎样？

威廉姆斯： 应该说效果会有多好？

记者： 会有什么效果，并且，效果会有多好？

威廉姆斯： 会有很好的效果。我的意思是说，人们当然愿意在推特网上了解到关于查理·罗斯的消息。

记者： 是的，没错。

威廉姆斯： 而且他们想知道你在和谁做访谈，什么时候录，这期间你做什么……

记者： 我在旧金山，我在做什么，我在哪儿吃东西等等。

威廉姆斯： 没错，人们喜欢这些。当你登录的时候我们会指出，然后就有成百上千的听众。然后，有一点好处就是，不论何时，你都可以直接跟这些人联系。你可以问问题，也可以从他们那里得到反馈[32]。

记者： 是的。

威廉姆斯： 你可以给他们发链接地址[33]，他们就可以点击查看。

记者： 所以我们要把今天的访谈链接发给他们，他们就会到 *charlierose.com* 看访谈。

威廉姆斯： 当然，肯定会。

记者： 很好，这太令我高兴了。这也是为什么我愿意来旧金山、硅谷、西海岸的原因，这里总有有趣的事情发生。感谢您参加我们的访谈。

威廉姆斯： 谢谢能邀请我过来。

30. social communication tool
31. Information seeking activity
32. feedback *n.*
33. link *n.*

1. 词组in the ballpark的意思是"差不多"，例如：I'd say that six to eight points would be in the ballpark.（我想差不多是六到八个点数。）

2. 插入语是在一个句子中间插入一个成分，它不作句子的何种成分，也不和句子的何种成分发生结构关系，同时既不起连接作用，也不表示语气。例如：He is, I think, a teacher.（我认为他是个老师。）其中，I think就是插入语。

3. 形容词加表示名词性质的后缀–ness可构成相应的名词，例如：seriousness（严重性）；sadness；kindness等。

4. 悖论（paradox）是一种貌似矛盾，但包含一定哲理的意味深长的说法，是一种矛盾修辞法。例如：More haste, less speed.（欲速则不达。）"速度快反而达不到目的"就是这样的修辞方法。

5. 词组in charge of sth.的意思是"负责做某事"，例如：He was in charge of overlooking prisoners.（他负责监视囚犯。）

6. 伴随状语是指状语从句的动作伴随主句发生，它的特点是：所表达的动作或状态是伴随着句子谓语动词的动作而发生或存在的。例如：He sat in the armchair，reading a newspaper.（他坐在扶手椅里读报。）

7. 夸张修辞方法在英语中非常常见，这种方法的运用可增强语气，引起共鸣。例如：When I told our father about this, his heart burst.（当我将这件事告诉我们的父亲时，他的心几乎要迸出来了。）"心要迸出来"就是一种夸张说法。

8. die一词是"死亡"的意思，但在口语中常常用来表示"没电了"，例如：The electric train stopped when the batteries died.（电池组一断电，电车就停了。）

9. 破折号在英语中可以用来补充说明，特别是在非正式文体中，例如：We'll be arriving on Monday morning—at least, I think so.（我们将在星期一上午抵达——至少我是这样想的。）

10. 词组be supposed to do的意思是"应该……"，例如：In this age of Facebook and Twitter, we are all supposed to have hundreds of friends.（在这个脸谱网和推特网盛行的时代，按理说我们每个人都应该有数百位朋友。）

5

腾讯公司创始人：
马化腾

Founder of Tencent:
Ma Huateng

　　马化腾，1971年10月出生于广东省汕头市，是腾讯主要创办人之一，现担任公司控股董事会主席兼首席执行官，被称为"QQ之父"。曾在深圳大学主修计算机及应用，于1993年取得深圳大学理学学士学位。1998年和好友张志东注册成立"深圳市腾讯计算机系统有限公司"。在创办腾讯之前，马化腾曾任职于深圳润迅通讯发展有限公司，从事寻呼软件研发工作。他在电信及互联网行业已拥有10多年的经验。

　　目前QQ在国内外(以国内为主)拥有注册用户9.349亿，并且在不断增加，可谓是国内网民使用最多的即时通讯工具。2009年马化腾当选中国经济十年商业领袖，腾讯入选《财富》"全球最受尊敬50家公司"。2011年福布斯中国富豪榜，马化腾以274.9亿元的身家位列第13位。

5.1 The Conflicts Between Tencent QQ and Qihoo 360

轻松输入十分钟

Reporter: Tencent's decision to stop providing services to QQ users running Qihoo's 360 antivirus software, is a decision that forces users to choose between the two software programs and has caused widespread dissatisfaction. Did Tencent consider that its decision might deprive web users of their right to choose which software they use?

Ma Huateng: It was a critical situation. If I had delayed the decision for another three days, QQ users may have been destroyed by 360. Tencent has complained to the government and the police ever since Qihoo 360 began spamming its users. We had hoped that this could be resolved through legal channels. But we also knew that the legal process would take a long time. From October 29 to November 1, more than 20 million QQ users had been attacked by Koukou Bodyguard (扣扣保镖) [a program developed by Qihoo 360 that is able to block QQ advertisements from popping up and that can also disable other QQ services] and this number was increasing by 10 million plus users every day. If we calculated the rate of infection according to the speed at which the Privacy Protector (隐私保护器) [another program developed by Qihoo 360 that was launched on September 27 and which claimed to protect the security of QQ users' private files and data] spread, 80 million QQ users would have been infected within three days. We had to address the problem on two fronts. We had been hijacked by a secretive and resistant virus that we had never encountered before. This kind of virus had only ever occured in the area of online games. It had the potential to be very damaging. If Tencent had done nothing, and every one of QQ users had been hurt by this attack, then it would have been too late. We had to contain the spread of the virus within two days, at the very least we had to ensure that most of our users would not be harmed.

Reporter: Tencent has long boasted of its technological prowess. Couldn't the problem be solved through technical means?

Ma Huateng: There was no way of doing that. Qihoo's 360 antivirus software is a

---

antivirus *n.*
反病毒程序

widespread *adj.*
普遍的，广泛的

deprive *v.*
剥夺，使丧失

delay *v.*
耽搁，延期

spam *v.*
发垃圾邮件

channel *n.*
手段

pop *v.*
突然行动，取出

calculate *v.*
计算

infection *n.*
影响，感染

hijack *v.*
劫持

resistant *adj.*
顽固的，抵抗的

encounter *v.*
遇到，遭遇

contain *v.*
控制

boast *v.*
夸口，自吹自擂

prowess *n.*
超凡技术，英勇

腾讯QQ与奇虎360之争

有效学习十分钟

记者：　腾讯宣布不再向装有奇虎360杀毒软件[1]的QQ用户[2]提供服务[3]。这使得用户不能同时使用QQ和360这两个软件[4]程序，为此用户普遍不满[5]。请问腾讯做出决策之前是否想到这会剥夺[6]网民选择自己所喜欢的软件的自主权？

马化腾：当时情况危急。如果我迟疑三天再做出决定，QQ用户恐怕早就受到奇虎360的危害了。其实从奇虎360向我们的用户发送垃圾邮件开始，腾讯就已经向政府部门和公安部门投诉了。我们原希望这件事可以通过法律手段[7]解决。但是我们也知道通过法律手段解决需要的时间较长。从10月29日到11月1日2000多万QQ用户被扣扣保镖[8]攻击【扣扣保镖是奇虎360开发的一种程序，该程序能阻止[9]页面突然冒出的QQ广告也可使用户无法使用QQ的其他服务】并且以每天超过1000万的速度增长。如果我们根据隐私保护器散布的速度计算，【隐私保护器也是奇虎360开发的一种程序，该程序于9月27日发行[10]，声称[11]可以保护QQ用户的个人文件和数据[12]的安全】三天内就会有8000万QQ用户受到感染[13]。我们不得不采用两种方法解决这个问题。我们被一种前所未有的隐蔽性极深、诱导性极强的病毒[14]劫持[15]。这种情况只有在打网络游戏[16]外挂时出现过。性质恶劣影响非常大。如果腾讯再不制止，等到所有QQ用户受到伤害就晚了。我们必须在两天内控制病毒的传播，至少我们要先保证大多数用户不会受到伤害。

记者：　腾讯一直自称[17]技术非常强大，难道不能通过技术手段解决问题吗？

马化腾：没办法那样做。奇虎360杀毒软件是一个电脑的底层软件，而QQ则只是一个应用层的工具软件，就好像要求一艘民用的[18]运货船去对一艘军用船[19]开火一样，即使军用船船小但火力都是军事化的。事实上除了直接对抗——强制删除之外别无他法，腾讯的技术是可以做到的，但是这是违法的[20]。他用违法的方式做，并不意味着我们也要用违法的方式对付他。如果我们真的那样做，他们肯定会投诉说我们在用户不知道的情况下删掉[21]了他们的商业软

1. antivirus software
2. user *n.*
3. service *n.*
4. software *n.*
5. dissatisfaction *n.*
6. deprive *v.*
7. legal channel
8. bodyguard *n.*
9. block *v.*
10. launch *v.*
11. claim *v.*
12. private files and data
13. infect *v.*
14. virus *n.*
15. hijack *v.*
16. online game
17. boast *v.*
18. civilian *adj.*
19. military vessel
20. illegal *adj.*
21. delete *v.*

basic underlying software while QQ is simply an application. It is like asking a civilian cargo boat to fire on a military vessel, though the military vessel may be small, it's still well armed. We had no choice aside from blocking it. Tencent could manage it technologically, but that would be illegal. Just because they are using illegal methods does not mean that we should follow suit. If we had done that, then they would have complained that we had broken the law by deleting a user's commercial software without the user's consent. Our last option was to ask users to delete QQ to avoid being attacked, and then reinstall the program. The situation was especially urgent on November 2. We saw the Qihoo 360 software update had been installed on more than 20 million computers, the update also asked users to import their lists of friends, which would have prompted a second wave of viral infections. Supposing that every user has about 40 friends, there would be more and more users being attacked. It was urgent and we had no choice but to pull the plug. It was impossible for users to know the whole story and it would have been too late when they did find out. Everyone knows we can't deny the users' right to choose. But it is hard for the outside world to understand the predicament that Tencent was in.

Reporter: How many PCs have installed both Tencent's QQ and Qihoo's 360 antivirus software?

Ma Huateng: Around 60 percent of QQ users have installed 360, so at least 100 million.

Reporter: When you made the decision, did you consider how many users would give up QQ?

Ma Huateng: I had no choice. If our users choose to avoid the viral attack by uninstalling QQ and reinstalling it at a later date, I accept that.

Reporter: Have you ever contacted Zhou Hongyi (the chairman of Qihoo)?

Ma Huateng: We met each other a long time ago. This year we didn't meet, but have sent each other short messages. We also exchanged messages in September when Zhou Hongyi felt threatened by the fact that we were developing Diannao Guanjia (电脑管家) [an antivirus software developed by Tencent].

Zhou Hongyi originally invited us to invest in Qihoo 360—he would sell us a small proportion of shares at a high price, just like Microsoft invested in Facebook. Then he invited us to attack Baidu together: he would sell the search flow to us and develop software to block many medical advertisements that appear on Baidu and which account for 30 percent of its income. To put it plainly, because I declined his offer, he decided to shift his target and attacked us instead, because we were developing our own antivirus software, and he would have been contained by Tencent when attacking Baidu. Finally he

vessel *n.*
船

delete *v.*
删除

consent *n.*
同意，答应

reinstall *v.*
重新安装，重新设置

urgent *adj.*
紧急的，急迫的

prompt *v.*
促进，提示

predicament *n.*
困境，状态

viral *adj.*
病毒的

uninstall *v.*
卸载软件

threatened *adj.*
受到威胁的

proportion *n.*
部分，比例

decline *v.*
婉拒，谢绝

件，这是违法行为。我们最终选择让用户先删除QQ，下网避开，或者等过一段时间再装回来。11月2日的情况尤其紧急[22]。我们看到奇虎360在2000多万台电脑上又更新[23]

模块，诱导用户把好友列表也拉进来，这会形成病毒式的二次传播。如果按每个用户40个好友计算，那么将会有越来越多的用户受到感染。当时的形势已经非常危急，其他办法已经来不及，除非紧急下网阻止传播。用户当时很难了解这些，等了解了也晚了。谁都知道不能剥夺用户的选择权，但外界很难了解腾讯的困境[24]。

记者：　腾讯这边统计有多少台电脑是同时装有腾讯QQ和奇虎360杀毒软件的？

马化腾：QQ用户中大约有60%装了奇虎360，所以至少一个亿以上的用户。

记者：　您做出这个决定的时候有没有预测过有多少用户会放弃QQ？

马化腾：没办法，如果说用户卸载[25]能避开这次病毒攻击，等过后再装回QQ，也行。

记者：　您跟周鸿祎之间有过沟通吗？【周鸿祎是奇虎公司总裁】

马化腾：很久之前见过面，今年没见过面，都是发短信[26]。9月还有一次，那时候周鸿祎看到我们做电脑管家，感到了很大的威胁【电脑管家是腾讯开发的一种杀毒软件】。

　　　　周鸿祎刚开始要我们给他投资，他想以高价卖给我们一小部分股份[27]，就像微软投资脸谱网一样。后来还曾说要联合我们打百度，说把搜索流量[28]卖给我们，他会开发一种软件拦截百度上出现的医疗广告打掉他们30%的收入。说实在的[29]，因为我不答应，所以他决定转变目标打我们，因为我们正在开发自己的杀毒软件，他认为他打百度会受到腾讯的牵制。他后来想清楚说还是一定要先打我们，便很快去做了隐私保护器。

记者：　奇虎攻打腾讯看起来是为了不被腾讯逐步吃掉[30]，是这样吗？

马化腾：保证大家生存的惟一方式就是公平竞争[31]。扣扣保镖绝不是短期之内就能研

22. urgent *adj.*
23. update *v.*
24. predicament *n.*
25. uninstall *v.*
26. short message
27. share *n.*
28. search flow
29. to put it plainly
30. swallow up
31. compete fairly

decided to attack us and developed Privacy Protector.

Reporter: It seems Qihoo is attacking Tencent in order to avoid being swallowed up. Is that the way it is?

Ma Huateng: The only way for each of us to survive is to compete fairly with each other. Qihoo did not develop the Koukou Bodyguard over night, even we don't fully understand many of its targets. We have noticed that Qihoo's 360 antivirus software first prohibited QQ users from upgrading, making it impossible for us to save it. Then it guided users to copy their list of friends which in fact, it was actually stealing users' information. It even replaced the TT browser with a 360 browser because that was an additional source of income. We thought that when its virus had attacked a large number of users' computers, it would ask users to copy their personal information, including their names, passwords, lists of friends. Then it would develop its own IM software and guide users to import the information. This is plainly an attempt to steal from us, and just like the actions of a Trojan malware, though it claims to be an antivirus software and is protected by the system drive. We have had all our evidence notarized.

Reporter: Do you have evidence to prove the final target of 360 is to promote its own IM software?

Ma Huateng: We have some screen shots along with inside information. We have known all along that 360 has been developing IM software and it has been contacting software companies some of which were our past competitors. It has even negotiated with Wang Zhidong to buy the "lavalava" [another instant messenger developed by Wang Zhidong].

Reporter: Did Tencent ever scan users' computers and upload their information? Are the private conversations and information of users safe?

Ma Huateng: QQ has been using a "safe module" to scan users' computers since 2006 when QQ IDs were frequently stolen and Trojan viruses were everywhere. Tencent had to protect users. The original design scanned before loading; now it loads and then scans. Now, Tencent can discover up to 1.7 million Trojan viruses every day. That is why I am determined to develop antivirus software. To be frank, I do not want to do it at all. If the antivirus manufacturers were able to do the job, we wouldn't continue to do it. But if I hadn't done it, all the QQ IDs would have been lost. As a listed company, for the past ten years or more, there've always been people out there looking to cause trouble for us. If Tencent was doing something dangerous, other companies would have figured out what we were up to. That's why Tencent would never do anything of the kind.

Reporter: Did Tencent ever upload users' files? Were those files, as claimed by 360,

---

swallow v.
吞下

compete v.
竞争，对抗

prohibit v.
阻止，禁止

upgrade v.
升级，提升

browser n.
浏览器

password n.
密码，口令

plainly adv.
明白地，坦率地

malware n.
恶意软件，恶意
程序

notarize v.
确认，证明

negotiate v.
商议，谈判

upload v.
上传，上载

module n.
模块，组件

scan v.
浏览，扫描

manufacturer n.
制造商，厂商

figure v.
计算

发出来的，里面的很多清理内容连我们自己平时都没有注意到。我们看到奇虎360杀毒软件通过诱导用户先<u>禁止</u>[32]QQ升级，断掉了后路，我们救也救不了了，再引导用户备份QQ好友列表，实际上是盗取用户的好友资料，还把TT<u>浏览器</u>[33]替换成360浏览器，因为这是他们收入的一个来源。最初我们就想到当感染率再高的时候他们就会让用户备份资料，包括用户名、<u>密码</u>[34]、好友列表都在360那里备份，再适时推出自己的IM软件，再让用户直接导入备份的好友。 这是明目张胆的盗取行为，就跟木马一样，一个外挂，而且它自称是杀毒软件，是由系统<u>驱动器</u>[35]来保护它的。所有这一切我们都在公证处做了证据保全。

记者：　　360的最终目标是为了推出自己的IM软件？这种判断有证据吗？

马化腾：我们看到了各种<u>截图</u>[36]，内部也有一些情况了解，也听说他们一直在开发IM软件，而且他们还在与一些我们过去打过的外挂厂商接触，招兵买马。甚至在跟王志东的lavalava【lavalava是由王志东开发的另一款<u>即时通讯工具</u>[37]】谈收购等等。

记者：　　腾讯究竟有没有扫描用户的电脑、<u>上传</u>[38]用户的信息？用户的聊天记录和信息是否真的安全？

马化腾：QQ扫描用户电脑的是一个安全<u>模块</u>[39]，从2006年开始，因为那个时候盗号猖獗，几乎是全民盗号，用户中木马的情况非常严重，腾讯必须保护用户的安全，因此增加了安全模块。原来是登陆前扫描的，后来因为耽误用户时间太长，就改为登陆后扫描。现在腾讯一天就能扫描出170万个木马。这也就是为什么我决心要腾讯自己来做安全软件。其实我真的不想做，要是杀毒厂商能挺住，我们就不做。但是如果不做的话，所有QQ账号将会丢失。 作为一个<u>上市公司</u>[40]，十几年来一直会有别人来找麻烦。假若腾讯有危险的动作，其他公司就能<u>分析出</u>[41]我们是怎么做的。所以这就是腾讯公司从不做那样的事情的原因。

记者：　　腾讯究竟有没有上传用户的文件？是否如360所说，腾讯上传的文件是加密的？

马化腾：怎么可能？加密的话他们肯定能

32. prohibit *v.*
33. browser *n.*
34. password *n.*
35. drive *n.*
36. screen shot
37. instant messager
38. upload *v.*
39. module *n.*
40. listed company
41. figure out

encrypted files?

Ma Huateng: How is that possible? If there were encrypted files then they certainly would have been decoded. Yes, we scan their computers, but we only do what all these kinds of antivirus software are supposed to do. The information QQ uploads are texts that contain Trojan viruses, and some data so we know there isn't an even larger virus somewhere, so Tencent will know how to respond. None of it contains the users' private information. If their computers are safe, QQ does not upload any information.

Reporter: Does Tencent scan users' computers to find out which software can be easily developed?

Ma Huateng: Would we need to? There are too many market surveys and consulting companies. What Tencent needs is only a market survey. We only need to know the general data—which software has occupied how much market quota. We would not need exact numbers; they are no use for developing software.

Reporter: Are you afraid that people will see Tencent as a monopoly?

Ma Huateng: Yes. But Tencent is not a monopoly. It is the largest company in many areas, such as web search and online commerce. It has the largest market shares in IM, but that doesn't make it a monopoly. A monopoly would not give users choices, but now users have choices. A company will prove to be a monopoly by using methods that hurts its users. Does 360 care more about our users than we do? This whole thing is caused by 360.

Reporter: But Tencent is powerful, and looks like a monopoly.

Ma Huateng: Ah, your rivals will always want to compete; they do not want you to be powerful. So they exaggerate every move you make. Our competitors are always saying "Tencent can't do everything." But if other companies are producing the products, why can't Tencent? That's not fair, either.

Reporter: The problem is that people believe Tencent's enormous user base makes your company too powerful.

Ma Huateng: Well, what are we supposed to do about that? Our users like our product. There's nothing we can do about that.

Reporter: The whole industry is worried that since Tencent is so big, it can force users to drop other products. What will happen when the next software or application company has a similar conflict with Tencent? Would you force users to make a decision again?

Ma Huateng: How can that be? This is an emergency. The truth is that we faced a do-or-die moment for our company. People refuse to believe us, even though we have explained it very clearly. Or they don't understand, either way, it's very upsetting.

encrypted *adj.*
加密码的

respond *v.*
回应，做出反应

consulting *adj.*
咨询的，顾问的

monopoly *n.*
垄断，垄断者

commerce *n.*
贸易，商业

exaggerate *v.*
夸大，夸张

suppose *v.*
假设，猜想

conflict *n.*
冲突，矛盾

emergency *n.*
紧急情况，突发事件

破解出来。是的，我们扫描了他们的电脑，但是我们做的都是杀毒软件应该做的事。QQ的程序上传用户的只是那些有木马的字段，以及统计数据，这样我们才能知道某个地区可能爆发了一个规模不大的木马病毒，这样腾讯才能知道如何对抗。上传的木马资料中也不包括用户的隐私资料。如果用户电脑安全，就不上传任何资料。

记者：　腾讯扫描用户的电脑是为了探查哪些软件好做吗？

马化腾：用得着那么麻烦吗？这件事很简单，有那么多市场调查、咨询公司，腾讯只要做个市场调查[42]就可以了，只要摸个市场的大概，这件事只需要定性就可以了——哪种软件占多少份额，我们不需要定量，绝对的量对开发是没有用的。

记者：　您怕不怕别人说腾讯垄断[43]？

马化腾：也怕。但腾讯没有垄断，腾讯在很多领域是最大的公司，例如网页搜索和在线商务[44]，在IM上也有很大的市场份额。但是市场份额大并不代表垄断，垄断是你不给用户其他的选择，但是现在用户有选择。伤害用户的公司被证明是垄断的公司。难道我自己的用户我不心疼，360倒比我们还心疼？这是有原因的嘛，而且这个原因就是旁边那个人（注：指360）造成的。

记者：　但腾讯的形象给人感觉就是很强大、很垄断。

马化腾：唉，竞争对手当然希望的就是竞争，不希望你强大。你做的任何事都会被夸大[45]。我们的竞争对手经常讲，腾讯不能什么都做。但是如果市场上的其他公司在做产品，为什么腾讯不能做？那也是不公平的。

记者：　问题是大家都认为腾讯的客户端太强大。

马化腾：那你说这个事情怎么办？我们的用户喜欢我们的产品。我们对此束手无策。

记者：　整个行业都在担心腾讯太强大了，它可以驱使用户放弃使用其他产品。如果以后再有哪家软件或应用程序公司与腾讯发生同样的激烈竞争，你还会迫使用户做出选择吗？

马化腾：怎么可能呢？这只是一个紧急情况[46]。事实上我们面临一个生死攸关的[47]时刻。即使我们解释得很清楚了，人们还是拒绝相信我们，或者还是不理解。我们也很苦恼[48]。

42. market survey
43. monopoly *n.*
44. online commerce
45. exaggerate *v.*
46. emergency *n.*
47. do-or-die
48. upsetting *adj.*

1. antivirus software意为"杀毒软件"，Privacy Protector意为"隐私保护器"，Koukou Bodyguard意为"扣扣保镖"，这些都是一些软件的表达方式。

2. 词组deprive of的意思是"剥夺，失去"，例如：If you do not drive carefully, I shall be obliged to deprive you of your license.（如果您不谨慎驾驶，我将不得不没收您的驾照。）

3. may作为动词，可以表示愿望，但后面需接动词原形，例如：Business has been thriving in the past year. Long may it continue to do so.（在过去的一年里生意蒸蒸日上。但愿这种情况能持续下去。）

4. 英语中有大量的词缀用来构成新词，例如后缀–ship表示一种状况、状态、身份或技能。例如：hardship（苦难），doctorship（博士学位），workmanship（手艺，工艺）等。

5. 倒装是一种语法手段，用于表示一定的句子结构或强调某一句子成分。完全倒装即把整个谓语放在主语之前，例如：The teacher came in and the class began. 这句话的倒装结构为：In came the teacher and the class began.

6. 词组boast of的意思为"吹牛；自夸"，例如：It has never been the boast of a modest person that he alone could accomplish such a hard task.（一个谦虚的人从来不会夸口说只有他才能够完成这样一件困难的任务。）

7. plug的意思是"塞子"，而由它组成的词组pull the plug则表示"终止，中断"，例如：It would be better to pull the plug on him than to keep his life in such a torture.（与其让他在这种折磨中苟且偷生，不如让他安乐死去。）

8. 反问（rhetorical question）是英语修辞方法之一，是以疑问为手段，取得修辞上的效果。其特点是肯定问句表示强烈否定，而否定问句表示强烈肯定，它的答案往往是不言而喻的。例如：Shall we allow those untruths to go unanswered?（我们不应该揭穿这些谎言吗？）这句话的言外之意就是谎言必须要揭穿，这是大家公认的，即使不回答也会得出结论。

9. 前缀mono–表示"单一，整体"，例如：monorail（单轨铁路），monogamy（一夫一妻制），monodrama（独角戏），monograph（专著），monologue（独白）等。

10. 在句子中起宾语作用的从句叫做宾语从句，大多数及物动词都可以带宾语从句。例如：We all expect that they will win, for members of their team are stronger.（我们都预料他们会赢，因为他们的队员更强壮。）这句话中that后面的即为宾语从句。

6

谷歌公司创始人之一：
拉里·佩吉
Co-founder of Google: Larry Page

　　拉里·佩吉（Larry Page）是搜索引擎谷歌的创始人之一，他是谷歌的首席执行官，带领公司发展成为了拥有 200 多名员工的盈利企业。在此之前，他曾担任密西根大学 Eta Kappa Nu 荣誉学会的会长。1996年年初，佩吉和布林开始合作研究一个名为"BackRub"的搜索引擎，到1998年上半年逐步完善了这项技术。1998年9月7日，谷歌公司在加利福尼亚州的曼罗帕克成立。短短几年谷歌就迅速发展成为了目前规模最大的搜索引擎，并向雅虎、美国在线等其他目录索引和搜索引擎提供后台网页查询服务。2001年4月，拉里·佩吉转任谷歌公司的产品总监。他目前仍与Eric Schmidt（埃里克·施密特）和Sergey Brin（塞尔吉·布林）共同负责谷歌的日常运作。

6.1 / The Growing Environment of Childhood Is Extremely Important

轻松输入十分钟

Reporter: Larry Page, what is responsible for your early progress in life? How did you get to where you are so quickly?

Larry Page: I think I was really lucky to have the environment I did when I was growing up. My dad was a professor; he happened to be a professor of computer science, and we had computers lying around the house from a really early age. I think I was the first kid in my elementary school to turn in a word-processed document. I just enjoyed using the stuff. It was sort of lying around, and I got to play with it. I had an older brother who was interested in it as well. So I think I had kind of a unique environment, that most people didn't have, because my dad was willing to spend all his available income on buying a computer or whatever. It was like 1978, when I was six. I don't think there're many people my age who've had that experience, or anyone in general. From a very early age, I also realized I wanted to invent things. So I became really interested in technology and also then, soon after, in business, because I figured that inventing things wasn't any good; you really had to get them out into the world and have people use them to have any effect. So probably from when I was 12, I knew I was going to start a company eventually.

Reporter: How do you think you knew at such an early age that you wanted to be an inventor?

Larry Page: I just sort of kept having ideas. We had a lot of magazines lying around our house. It was kind of messy. So you kind of read stuff all the time, and I would read *Popular Science* and things like that. I just got interested in stuff, I guess, technology and how devices work. My brother taught me how to take things apart, and I took apart everything in the house. So I just became interested in it, for whatever reason, and so I had lots of ideas about what things could be built and how to build them and all these kinds of things. I built like an electric go-cart at a pretty early age.

Reporter: It's as if computers were the toys of your childhood.

Larry Page: Yeah, basically, and electronics too.

Reporter: You mentioned reading magazines like *Popular Mechanics*. What else did you read that might have influenced or inspired you in some way?

---

responsible *adj.*
负责的，可靠的

elementary *adj.*
基础的，初级的

unique *adj.*
独特的，惟一的

available *adj.*
可支配的，有效的

realize *v.*
意识到，了解

eventually *adv.*
最终，终于

messy *adj.*
凌乱的

device *n.*
装置，设备

go-cart *n.*
手推车

electronics *n.*
电子设备，电子学

influence *v.*
影响，改变

童年的生长环境极其重要

有效学习十分钟

记者：拉里·佩吉，是什么使您在人生早期就取得了这么大的进展？您是如何这么快就做到这些的？

拉里·佩吉：我想我真的很幸运，能够有当年的生长环境。我的父亲是一名教授[1]，他正好是计算机科学系的教授。在我很小的时候，我们家就有电脑。我想我是我们小学[2]第一个提交[3]文字处理文档[4]的孩子。我只是喜欢用这东西。电脑一直悄无声息地摆在那里，渐渐地我开始和它一起玩。我有一个哥哥，他对它也很感兴趣。所以，我觉得我有一种大多数人没有的独特环境。因为我爸爸愿意将他所有的可支配收入[5]都用来购买一台计算机或诸如此类的东西，就像1978年，我六岁时那样。我认为很多跟我一样的同龄人都没有那种经历。从很小的时候起，我也意识到了我想发明东西。因此，我真的对科技很感兴趣。也是在那时，不久之后，我又对商业产生了兴趣，因为我意识到我发明的东西是没有任何用的。你真的必须将它们融入世界并且让人们使用它们，它们才会变得有用。因此，可能从我12岁的时候起，我就知道我最终要成立一家公司。

记者：您是如何看待您在那么小的年纪就知道自己想成为一名发明家[6]的？

拉里·佩吉：我只是有些想法不断涌现。我们家有很多杂志。它们放得有点凌乱[7]。所以你几乎随时随地都可以读到，我喜欢读《科普杂志》之类的东西。我想，那时我刚刚开始对一些事物——技术和设备[8]是如何工作的——感兴趣。我哥哥教我如何拆卸[9]东西，我拆了家里的所有东西。因此，我就对它产生了兴趣，不管出于何种原因，然后我就有了很多关于建造什么东西、如何建造东西和所有这类事情的很多想法。我在很小的时候，就建造了电动手推车。

记者：电脑似乎是你童年[10]时的玩具。

拉里·佩吉：基本上[11]是的，电子设备[12]也是。

记者：您提到了读杂志，像《大众机械》之类的杂志。除此之外，您还读了哪些在某种程度上可能会影响您或激发您的东西？

拉里·佩吉：我还读了所有的电脑杂志以及诸如此类的东西，我实际上对这些东西是如何工作的感兴趣——任何事物，内部都需要与力学打交道，要么力学[13]要么电子

1. professor *n.*
2. elementary school
3. turn in
4. document *n.*
5. available income
6. inventor *n.*
7. messy *adj.*
8. device *n.*
9. take apart
10. childhood *n.*
11. basically *n.*
12. electronics *n.*
13. mechanics *n.*

Larry Page: I read all the computer magazines and things like that, and I was sort of interested in how these things really work—anything having to do with the mechanics behind things, either the mechanics or the electronics. I wanted to be able to build things. Actually, in college I built an inkjet printer out of Legos, because I wanted to be able to print really big images. I figured you could print really big posters really cheaply using inkjet cartridges. So I reverse-engineered the cartridge, and I built all the electronics and mechanics to drive it. Just sort of fun projects. I like to be able to do those kinds of things.

Reporter: You certainly have an aptitude for it. Is this because of your early education or your parents? How do you explain that?

Larry Page: Actually, my brother was nine years older than me, and he went to Michigan as well. He brought home some of his labs for electronics and things like that, and sort of gave them to me. I learned how to do the stuff. I think there were a lot of lucky things like that.

Reporter: You seem to have had no fear of any of this. Where does this self-confidence come from?

Larry Page: I think that's true of kids today as well. If you have access to these things at a really young age, you just become used to it all, and it is natural to you. Kids certainly don't have fear of using computers now. It's the same kind of thing. If you grow up in environments where you have ICs (integrated circuits) lying around, you don't have fear of that either.

Reporter: And here you are now, a CEO at what age?

Larry Page: 27.

Reporter: Why is it that you perceived the need for Google before anyone else did?

Larry Page: Well, it's actually a great argument for pure research. We didn't start out to do a search engine at all. In late 1995, I started collecting the links on the web, because my advisor and I decided that would be a good thing to do. We didn't know exactly what I was going to do with it, but it seemed like no one was really looking at the links on the web—which pages link to which pages. In computer science, there're a lot of big graphs. Right now, (the web) has like 5 billion edges and 2 billion nodes. So it is a huge graph. I figured I could get a dissertation and do something fun and perhaps practical at the same time, which is really what motivates me. I started off by reversing the links, and then I wanted to find basically, say, who links to the Stanford home page, and there're 10,000 people who link to Stanford. Then the question is, which ones do you show? So you can only show 10, and we ended up with this way of ranking links, based on the links. Then we all said, "Wow, this is really good. It ranks things in the order you would expect to see them." Stanford would be the first. You can take universities and just rank them, and they come out in the order you'd expect. So we thought, "This is really interesting.

---

mechanics *n.*
力学

inkjet *n.*
喷墨

cartridge *n.*
墨盒，暗盒

aptitude *n.*
才能

stuff *n.*
东西，材料

access *n.*
使用权，进入

perceive *v.*
认识到，察觉

advisor *n.*
顾问，指导老师

graph *n.*
图表

node *n.*
节点，叉点

dissertation *n.*
论文，学术演讲

motivate *v.*
激励，使有动机

reverse *v.*
逆转，倒转

rank *v.*
排名，列队

学[14]。我希望能够创造东西。实际上，在大学时，我用乐高玩具制造了喷墨打印机，因为我想要打印出非常大的图像。我认为用墨盒就可以很廉价地打印出大海报。所以我反向设计了工程墨盒，为了驱动它，我建造了所有的电子设备和机械设备。这只是些有趣的项目。我愿意做这些事情。

记者：您必定是有这方面的才能[15]。这是因为您的早期教育还是您的父母呢？您如何解释这一点？

拉里·佩吉：事实上，我哥哥比我大九岁，而且他也去了芝加哥。他将实验室里的一些东西带回家，用于制造电子设备以及诸如此类的东西，并且偶尔他也会把它们给我。我学会了如何做这些东西。我觉得有很多像这样幸运的事情。

记者：您似乎没有任何恐惧。您的这种自信[16]是哪来的？

拉里·佩吉：我认为这对今天的孩子们来说也是一样的。如果你在很小的时候就接触到了这些事物，你就会习惯这一切，这对于你来说是很自然的。现在的孩子当然也不会对使用电脑产生恐惧。道理是一样的。如果你成长的环境里有集成电路[17]，你也不会对它产生恐惧。

记者：现在，您已经是首席执行官了，您是在多大的时候成为首席执行官的？

拉里·佩吉：27岁。

记者：您为什么会在其他人之前领会[18]到谷歌的必要性呢？

拉里·佩吉：嗯，对于纯粹的研究来说，它是一个伟大的论点。我们根本没有开始着手做搜索引擎[19]。在1995年年底，我开始在网络上收集链接[20]，因为我和我的顾问都认为这将是一件很好的事情。我们并不完全知道我们打算用它做什么，但似乎好像没有人会真的在网页上看链接——哪些页面链接到哪些页面。在计算机科学中，有很多大图[21]。眼下，（网络）好像也有50亿个边缘和20亿个节点。因此，它是一个巨大的图形。我想也许可以在获得一篇学士论文[22]的同时，做一些有趣且实际的[23]事情。这才是真正促使我创立谷歌的动力。我从扭转[24]链接开始，然后我想基本上找到，如，谁链接到了斯坦福主页，有10,000人链接到斯坦福主页[25]。接下来的问题是，要显示哪些？所以，你只能显示10个，基于链接，我们结束了这一排名的链接方式。然后我们都说："哇，这真的很好。它会根据你想要看到的顺序进行排名。"斯坦福大学将成为第一个。你可以写出大学名称，然后给它们排名，它们将按照你所期望的顺序出现。因此，我们认为："这是非常有趣的。这件事真的很有用。我们应该利用它进行搜索。"于是，我开始建立一个搜索引擎。塞尔吉也很早就来了，大概在1995年底或1996初，而且真的对数据挖掘这部分很感兴趣。基本

14. electronics *n.*
15. aptitude *n.*
16. self-confidence
17. integrated circuit
18. perceive *v.*
19. search engine
20. link *n.*
21. big graph
22. dissertation *n.*
23. practical *adj.*
24. reverse *v.*
25. home page

This thing really works. We should use it for search." So I started building a search engine. Sergey also came on very early, probably in late '95 or early '96, and was really interested in the data mining part. Basically, we thought, "Oh, we should be able to make a better search engine this way." Search engines didn't really understand the notion of which pages were more important. If you typed "Stanford", you got random pages that mentioned Stanford. This obviously wasn't going to work.

Reporter: Larry, you're a CEO at 27. What challenges or frustrations have you experienced at reaching this station at such a young age?

Larry Page: I think the age is a real issue. It's certainly a handicap in the sense of being able to manage people and to hire people and all these kinds of things, maybe more so than it should be. Certainly, I think, the things that I'm missing are more things that you acquire with time. If you manage people for 20 years, or something like that, you pick up things. So I certainly lack experience there, and that's an issue. But I sort of make up for that, I think, in terms of understanding where things are going to go, having a vision about the future, and really understanding the industry I am in, and what the company does, and also sort of the unique position of starting a company and working on it for three years before starting the company. Then working on it pretty hard, whatever, 24 hours a day. So I understand a lot of the aspects pretty well. I guess that compensates a little bit for lack of skills in other areas.

Reporter: Where do you go from here? What do you see yourself doing in ten or twenty years?

Larry Page: I think Google is great because, basically artificial intelligence would be the ultimate version of Google. So we have the ultimate search engine that would understand everything on the web. It would understand exactly what you wanted, and it would give you the right thing. That's obviously artificial intelligence, to be able to answer any question, basically, because almost everything is on the web, right? We're nowhere near doing that now. However, we can get incrementally closer to that, and that is basically what we work on. And that's tremendously interesting from an intellectual standpoint. We have all this data. If you printed out the index, it would be 70 miles high now. We have all this computation. We have about 6,000 computers. So we have a lot of resources available. We have enough space to store like 100 copies of the whole web. So you have a really interesting sort of confluence of a lot of different things: a lot of computation, a lot of data that used to be not available. From an engineering and scientific standpoint, building things to make use of this is a really interesting intellectual exercise. So I expect to be doing that for a while. On the other hand, I do have a lot of other interests as well. I am really interested in transportation and sustainable energy. For fun, I invent things on the side, but I don't really have time to follow up on them.

mine *v.*
挖掘，开采

random *adj.*
随机的，任意的

frustration *n.*
挫折

handicap *n.*
障碍，不利条件

acquire *v.*
获得，取得

vision *n.*
想象，美景

aspect *n.*
方面，方向

compensate *v.*
补偿，赔偿

artificial *adj.*
人工的，仿造的

ultimate *adj.*
最终的，极限的

intelligence *n.*
智能，智力

incrementally *adv.*
逐渐地，增值地

standpoint *n.*
立场，观点

computation *n.*
估计，计算

confluence *n.*
聚集，汇合

sustainable *adj.*
可持续的

上，我们是这样想的："哦，通过这种方式，我们应该能够做出更好的搜索引擎。"搜索引擎并不真正了解哪些页面更重要。如果你输入[26]"斯坦福大学"，你所得到的是随机页面[27]，是从提到斯坦福的所有页面中随机提取的。这显然是行不通的。

记者：拉里，您在27岁时就成了首席执行官。这么年纪轻轻就取得了这样的成绩，在这个过程中您经历过什么挑战和挫折[28]吗？

拉里•佩吉：我认为年龄就是一个问题。在管理人员和聘请人员及诸如此类的事情上，从某种意义上来说这是一个不利条件[29]，也许会超出它应有的影响。当然，我想，我缺少的东西更多的是人们随着时间而积累起来的东西。如果你已经管理人员或从事类似事业20年了，你学到了东西。那么，我当然缺乏经验了，这是一个问题。但我认为，在某些方面我正在逐渐弥补[30]，如理解事情的发展趋势、对未来的远见、真正理解自身行业及我们公司是做什么的，和创立公司[31]的独特地位并且在公司成立前对其进行三年的准备。然后开始相当艰苦的工作，每天24小时，不管结果如何。所以，我对很多方面都有相当不错的理解。我想这可以作为我在其他领域里所缺少技能的一点补偿[32]。

记者：接下来您会怎么做？在10年或20年以后您希望自己在做什么？

拉里•佩吉：我认为谷歌是了不起的，因为基本上，最终版本的谷歌将是人工智能[33]。因此，我们拥有最终的[34]搜索引擎，它将了解网上的一切事物。它会明白你想要什么，而且它会正确地提供给你情况。它可以回答任何问题，这显然是人工智能，因为基本上网上什么都有，对不对？我们已经离它不远了。但是，我们可以逐步接近这一目标，基本上，这是我们的工作。从知识产权的角度[35]来看，这是非常有趣的。我们拥有所有这些数据。现在，如果你将这些指数打印出来，将有70英里高。我们拥有所有的计算。我们拥有约6000台电脑。所以，我们有很多的可利用资源[36]。我们有足够的空间来存储100份完整的网页。所以，你汇

26. type *v.*
27. random page
28. frustration *n.*
29. handicap *n.*
30. make up
31. start a company
32. compensate *n.*
33. artificial intelligence
34. ultimate *adj.*
35. standpoint *n.*
36. resource *n.*
37. transportation *n.*

聚了各种有趣的资源，包括大量的计算，很多过去并不可用的数据。从工程和科学的角度来看，利用它来创造东西是一次很有趣的智力练习。因此，这项工作我希望做一段时间。另一方面，我也有很多其他的兴趣爱好。我对交通运输[37]和可持续性能源真的很感兴趣。为了乐趣，我将发明作为兼职，但我真的没有时间去一直做那些事情。

10 min

自由输出十分钟

1. happen一词做动词可以表示"恰巧，正好"的意思，后接动词不定式，也可以用it做形式主语，构成从句。例如：She happened to be out when we called.（我们打电话的时候她恰巧不在家。），这句话也可以改写成：It happened that she was out when we called.

2. 注意一些学校的表达方式：elementary school为"小学"，high school/secondary school为"中学"，senior high school为"高中"，university/college为"大学"。

3. 在由"for fear that/in case/lest"引导的目的状语从句中，若用虚拟语气，从句谓语为：should+do，并且should可以省略。例如：She examined the door again for fear that a thief (should) come in.（她又把门检查了一遍，以防盗贼的进入。）

4. 词组have an aptitude for的意思是"有……的才能，有……的倾向"，例如：They have an aptitude for making the simple complex, the easy hard, the minor issue a major drama and the painless painfull.（他们有把简单想得复杂，把容易想得困难，把一个小问题想成一个大悲剧，把十分轻松变成万分痛苦的潜能。）

5. 在英语口语中，sort of与kind of都有"有点，有几分"的意思，都可用于非正式的场合，例如：That makes me feel kind of stupid.（那使我感到有点愚蠢。）；I like him, sort of.（我有点喜欢他。）

6. 词组pick up有"得到，感染"的意思，例如：I seem to have picked up a terrible cold from somewhere.（我似乎从什么地方染上了重感冒。）；I picked up $30 in tips today.（我今天得到了30美元的小费。）

7. lack一词既可做动词也可做名词。做动词时为及物动词，做名词时后面需跟of，表示"缺乏，缺少"，例如：Some houses still lack basic amenities such as bathrooms.（有些住宅仍没有像卫生间这样的基本设施。）；The trip was cancelled because of the lack of interest.（因为缺乏兴趣，这次旅行被取消了。）

8. 词组follow up on的意思是"追踪，跟踪"，例如：They have also submitted requests for viewing time on big telescopes in order to follow up on some of the more unusual discoveries made by volunteers.（他们还提交了在天文望远镜上进行观看的时限请求，这样是为了跟踪志愿者们的一些更不同寻常的发现。）

9. 提喻（synecdoche）是英语修辞格之一，指用部分代替全体，或用全体代替部分，或特殊代替一般。例如：The fox goes very well with your cap.（这狐皮围脖与你的帽子很相配。）这句就是用整体"狐狸"代替部分的"狐皮围脖"。

10. 派生法是英语中重要的构词方法之一，主要是由词缀和词根相结合构成新词。大多数词缀都有一定的含义。例如：后缀–ese表示地方或国家的人或语言，Chinese，Japanese，Vietnamese（越南人）等；前缀fore–表示"预先，在前面"的意思，如：foretell（预言），forecast（预测）等。

7 谷歌公司创始人之一：
塞尔吉·布林
Co-founder of Google: Sergey Brin

　　塞尔吉·布林，谷歌创始人之一，出生于莫斯科，5岁那年，布林跟随父母一起移民美国，从而开始了他美国式的成功历程。塞尔吉·布林是马里兰大学的荣誉毕业生，拥有数学和计算机专业的理学学士学位。随后他考入斯坦福大学计算机专业就读。在大学时，布林就已经发明了一种超文本语言格式的搜索系统。1998年9月，布林和佩吉决定合伙开公司，公司提供的惟一服务就是搜索引擎。后来在斯坦福大学攻读博士的他选择了休学，并和佩吉一起创建了家喻户晓的互联网搜索引擎谷歌。目前，他正在全力发展谷歌公司。

7.1 Sergey Brin Is Always Curious About Science

轻松输入十分钟

Reporter:	Let's turn to your partner, Sergey Brin, for a moment. Sergey, how old are you now?
Sergey Brin:	Twenty-seven.
Reporter:	What do you think influenced or inspired you to do what you have at such a young age?
Sergey Brin:	I certainly like to think I'm young, but these days by Silicon Valley standards, I'm getting to be over the hill. If you look at Napster, for example, the founder is what? Twenty? I was really interested in computers ever since I got one, when I was in elementary school. Eventually, I went on to join the Ph.D. program in computer science at Stanford. Those purely, the interests of what can you do with all of the world's information—now that it's online—that interest spawned Google. And that was together with Larry Page, who is my co-founder and partner.
Reporter:	As a kid growing up, what or who has influenced you the most, Sergey?
Sergey Brin:	I think as a kid, I always had a kind of scientific curiosity. I was always interested in mathematics, and I always enjoyed doing math problems. In fact, my undergrad, I had a degree in both math and computer science. I think, eventually, I was really inspired by computers because of the amazing power that they give you. Today's PCs do a billion operations per second. It's almost inconceivable, and I think that was the most inspiring thing to me, how you could leverage that to actually produce something that was useful, beyond video games and things like that.
Reporter:	At what age would you say you had this realization?
Sergey Brin:	In middle school, I had a very good friend who I'm still in touch with, he had a Macintosh, one of the early ones, and he and I would just sit and play around and program. We had little programs for artificial

inspire v.
启发，鼓舞

elementary adj.
初级的，基本的

purely adv.
纯粹地，仅仅

spawn v.
催生，大量生产

curiosity n.
好奇心，好奇

mathematics n.
数学，算术

undergrad n.
大学生

amazing adj.
神奇的，令人吃惊的

inconceivable adj.
不可思议的，难以置信的

leverage v.
利用

realization n.
实现，领悟

artificial adj.
人工的，仿造的

对科学充满好奇的塞尔吉·布林

有效学习十分钟

记者： 现在轮到我们采访您的搭档[1]塞尔吉·布林了。塞尔吉，您多大了？

塞尔吉·布林： 27岁。

记者： 您认为是什么影响或启发了您在这么小的年龄就做了这些事情？

塞尔吉·布林： 当然，我认为我很年轻，但跟目前的硅谷[2]标准相比我已经是上了年纪了。举个例子，如果你关注纳普斯特（公司名称）的话，它的创始人多大年龄？20岁？自从我得到一台电脑时起，那时我在上小学，我就真的对电脑产生了兴趣。终于，我接着在斯坦福大学计算机科学系攻读博士学位。那些仅仅[3]是当你拥有全世界的信息后你对你能做什么的兴趣——现在，出现在了网上——那些兴趣催生了谷歌。拉里·佩吉是我的合作伙伴，也是谷歌的创立者。

记者： 塞尔吉，当您还是孩子的时候，在您的成长过程中，什么事情或什么人对您的影响最大？

塞尔吉·布林： 我觉得作为一个孩子，我总是有一种对科学的好奇心。我一直对数学[4]很感兴趣，我总是喜欢做数学题。事实上，大学时，我获得了数学和计算机科学的双学位。最后，我想，我真正受到电脑的启发是因为它们能给你神奇的[5]力量。今天的个人这个优势每秒[6]能做十亿次运算[7]。这几乎是不可思议的[8]，我认为，你究竟如何利用这个优势生产出超越视频游戏[9]之类的有用的东西，对我来说是最鼓舞人心的事情。

记者： 您在多大的时候，有这种认识[10]的？

塞尔吉·布林： 中学时，我有一个好朋友，我们现在仍然在联系，他有一个早期生产的苹果机，我和他坐在那台苹果机前玩耍并且编程。我们有很少的人工智能程序。我们有一个可以对话的程序。我们写了个程序来模仿[11]重力[12]。我记得我们写的程序是用来进行现在所谓的"光学[13]字符识别[14]"

1. partner n.
2. Silicon Valley
3. purely adv.
4. mathematics n.
5. amazing adj.
6. per second
7. operation n.
8. inconceivable adj.
9. video game
10. realization n.
11. simulate v.
12. gravity n.
13. optical adj.
14. recognition n.

intelligence. We'd have a program that would talk back to you. We wrote a program to simulate gravity. I remember we wrote a program to do what's called "OCR" now, optical character recognition. It was just for fun, purely out of intellectual curiosity. I think that's probably the first time I really experienced that.

Reporter: So this is what you did in your spare time. This is what you did for fun.

Sergey Brin: I have to admit I was a bit of a nerd. I still am.

Reporter: Do you have siblings?

Sergey Brin: I have a brother who is 13, and that's a big age difference, obviously. Maybe I've turned him away from computers and technical fields. He wants to be completely different. His interests are more in sports and languages these days.

Reporter: Were there any particular books that were especially important to you along the way?

Sergey Brin: I remember really enjoying (Richard) Feynman's books. He had several autobiographical books, and I read them. It seemed like a very great life he led. Aside from making really big contributions in his own field, he was pretty broad-minded. I remember he had an excerpt where he was explaining how he really wanted to be a Leonardo, an artist and scientist. I found that pretty inspiring. I think that leads to having a fulfilling life. Beyond that, just within the computer field, there are classical books I still find impressive, like *Snow Crash* by Neal Stephenson. That was really ten years ahead of its time. It kind of anticipated what's going to happen, and I find that really interesting.

Reporter: Sergey, how do you see Google as a company, and what do you hope to accomplish with it?

Sergey Brin: At Google, our mission is to make the world's information accessible and useful. And that means all of the world's information, which now, in our index, numbers over a billion documents, and it's an incredible resource. In history, you have never had access to just pretty much all of the world's information in seconds, and we have that now, and to make it really useful, you have to have a good way of finding whatever it is that you want. That's precisely what we work on at Google. My hope is to provide instant access to any information anybody ever wants in the future.

Reporter: Certainly, you weren't the only ones with that objective at the time, but you two did something about it. How do you account for that?

Sergey Brin: That's true. Certainly anyone can say, "Oh, I want to build a car that is

---

simulate v.
模仿

recognition n.
识别，认出

nerd n.
呆子，讨厌的人

sibling n.
兄弟姐妹

especially adv.
尤其，特别

autobiographical *adj.*
自传的，自传体的

broad-minded adj.
心胸开阔的，气量大的

excerpt n.
摘录，引用

anticipate v.
预料

accomplish v.
完成，实现

index n.
指标，索引

precisely adv.
精确地，恰恰

objective n.
目标，目的

account v.
解释

的"。这只是为了好玩，纯粹是出于求知欲。我想那可能是我第一次编程。

记者：　　　　所以，那就是您在空闲时间[15]所做的事情。您的一种消遣。

塞尔吉·布林：我不得不承认我是一个书呆子[16]，现在我仍然是这样。

记者：　　　　您有兄弟姐妹[17]吗？

塞尔吉·布林：我有一个13岁的弟弟。很显然，我们的年龄差距有点大。也许我已经使他远离了电脑和计算机领域。他想与我截然不同。目前，他对体育运动和语言更感兴趣。

记者：　　　　一路走来，有什么特别的书对您来说尤其重要吗？

塞尔吉·布林：我记得我真的很喜欢（理查德）费曼的书。我读过他的几本自传[18]。他的人生看上去非常伟大。除了在自己的领域做出了非常大的贡献外，他也相当心胸开阔[19]。我记得他有一个摘录[20]，在那里他解释到，他是如何想要成为莱昂纳多，一位艺术家和科学家的。我发现那非常鼓舞人心[21]。我认为那是令人满意的[22]生活。除此之外，仅仅在计算机领域，有些古典书籍，让我印象深刻，像尼尔·斯蒂芬森的《雪崩》。那本书的内容比他所生活的那个时期超前了十年。它是对未来将要发生什么的一种预测，我觉得真的很有趣。

记者：　　　　塞尔吉，您是怎么看待谷歌公司的，您希望通过它来完成[23]什么吗？

塞尔吉·布林：在谷歌，我们的任务[24]是获取全世界的信息并使其有用。这就意味着所有世界上的信息，现在都在我们的索引[25]中，字数超过10亿的文档，它是一个令人难以置信的资源。在历史上，从未有过在几秒钟内就可以访问大量世界信息的情况。而我们现在使它真的很有用，你必须要有一个好的查找方式去找到你想要的任何信息。这正是我们在谷歌要从事的工作。将来，我希望能够提供人们想要的任何信息的即时访问[26]。

记者：　　　　当然，在当时，有那个目标[27]的人不只是你们；但是你们真的做了一些事情。对此您如何解释[28]？

塞尔吉·布林：这是真的。当然，任何人都可以说："哦，我想用5美元制造一辆时速500英里的汽车，"那将棒极了。我很幸运能够在斯坦福

15. spare time
16. nerd *n.*
17. sibling *n.*
18. autobiographical book *n.*
19. broad-minded
20. excerpt *n.*
21. inspiring *adj.*
22. fulfilling *adj.*
23. accomplish *v.*
24. mission *n.*
25. index *n.*
26. instant access
27. objective *n.*
28. account *v.*

going to cost $5 and go 500 miles an hour," and that would be great.

I was fortunate to be at Stanford, and I was really interested in data mining, which means analyzing large amounts of data, discovering patterns and trends. And at the same time, Larry joined Stanford in '95, and he started downloading the web, which it turns out to be the most interesting data you can possibly mine. Our joint effort, just looking at the data out of curiosity, we found that we had technology to do a better job of search, and from that initial technology, we got really interested in the problem, and we realized how impactful having great search can be. So we built technology upon technology after that, to bring Google to where it is today, and we continue to develop lots of technology for tomorrow.

Reporter: Sergey, what challenges or obstacles have you had to deal with so far?

Sergey Brin: I will list several. One is providing a service that's going to serve millions of people. When we were at Stanford, we had about 10,000 searches per day. Now we serve over 50 million searches per day. That scaling of an infrastructure, that is pretty challenging. On a more personal level, I am now the President of Google, and we have about 170 people now. I think managing people, and being emotionally sensitive, and all the skills you learn in terms of communication and keeping people motivated, that has been a challenge. I have enjoyed learning that, but that's important, and a hard thing to learn.

Reporter: Are there any particular challenges you associate with being a son of immigrants who came to this country from Russia?

Sergey Brin: If anything, I think I benefit from it. I will say, as a child, I had an accent. I came to the U.S. at the age of six, and so I was teased and stuff in elementary school. I don't regard myself as being really popular going through school, but that was never that important to me, and I always had friends. I think, if anything, I feel like I have gotten a gift by being in the States rather than growing up in Russia. I know the hard times that my parents went through there, and I am very thankful that I was brought to the States. I think it just makes me appreciate my life much more.

---

download v.
下载

initial adj.
最初的

impactful adj.
有效的，有力的

obstacle n.
阻碍，干扰

infrastructure n.
基础设施，公共建设

sensitive adj.
敏感的，灵敏的

tease v.
取笑，戏弄

regard v.
认为，注重

大学读书，我对数据挖掘真的很感兴趣。数据挖掘指分析大量数据，发现模式[29]和趋势[30]。与此同时，拉里在1995年也来到了斯坦福大学，他开始下载网页，最后证明那是你可能挖掘的最有趣的数据。我们共同努力，着眼于数据仅仅是出于好奇。我们发现我们具有能使搜索工作做得更好的技术，并从最初技术那里，对问题产生了兴趣，我们意识到好的搜索是多么具有影响力。因此，在那之后，我们在技术的基础上创造技术，就有了今天的谷歌，为了明天，我们将继续开发更多的技术。

29. pattern *n.*
30. trend *n.*
31. obstacle *n.*
32. infrastructure *n.*
33. immigrant *n.*
34. particular *adj.*
35. accent *n.*
36. tease *v.*
37. appreciate *v.*

记者：　　　　塞尔吉，到目前为止，您需要处理的挑战和阻碍[31]是什么？

塞尔吉·布林：我将列举出几个。一是提供一个能够为数百万人服务的服务。当我们在斯坦福时，我们大约每天有一万个搜索。现在，我们每天提供五千万的搜索服务。这对基础架构[32]是个很大的挑战。从更私人的角度来说，我是谷歌的董事长，我们现在有170位员工。我认为管理员工、情绪敏感和在沟通方面及保持人的积极性方面学到的所有技能，对我来说都是一个挑战。我很喜欢学习那些东西，虽然很难学但是很重要。

记者：　　　　作为从俄罗斯移居至美国的移民[33]的孩子，您是否遇到过与此相关的特别的[34]挑战？

塞尔吉·布林：如果有的话，我想我是从中受益了。我会说，作为一个孩子，我有口音[35]。我六岁的时候来到了美国，所以在小学时，我遭到了嘲笑[36]和愚弄。我不认为自己在学校里很受欢迎，但我从不认为那很重要，我一直都有朋友。我认为，如果有什么区别的话，我觉得跟在俄国成长相比，我认为在美国成长像得到了一份礼物。我知道父母在那里生活得很艰辛，很庆幸我被带到了美国。我认为，它给我带来的更多的是对生活的感激[37]。

10 min

自由输出十分钟

1. 纳普斯特（Napster），是一种计算机程序，它允许用户在互联网上共享歌曲，而且全是免费的。在网络时代，第一个关于知识产权的伟大战争之一是巨型金属乐队Metallica对纳普斯特发起的版权起诉，因为该网站的共享文件用完了所有可用的宽带。2001年，美国34%的高校都已颁布对纳普斯特的禁止令，在2001年的暑假，免费的纳普斯特宣告结束。2008年数字千禧年版权法案禁止了所有的非法文件共享，并对下载的歌曲征收高达30,000美元的罚款。同时，学校安装了拦截软件，从此结束了长达10年的文件共享。

2. 拟人（personification）是将无生命的事物赋予生命的修辞方法，例如：The night gently laid her hand at my fevered heads.（夜轻轻地将她的手放在了我发烧的额头上。）句中将夜拟人化。

3. 词组have access to的意思是"使用，利用"，例如：You can have access to them via your public library.（你可以通过公共图书馆来使用它们。）

4. 人工智能（artificial intelligence）是研究、开发用于模拟、延伸和扩展人的智能的理论、方法、技术及应用系统的一门新的技术科学。人工智能是计算机科学的一个分支，它企图了解智能的实质，并生产出一种新的和人类智能相似的方式做出反应的智能机器，该领域的研究包括机器人、语言识别、图像识别、自然语言处理和专家系统等。

5. 理查德·费曼（Richard Feynman）是美国著名的物理学家。1965年诺贝尔物理学奖得主。他提出了费曼图、费曼规则和重正化的计算方法，是研究量子电动力学和粒子物理学不可缺少的工具。

6. kind of表示"种类"时，后面接单数名词或不可数名词，例如：This kind of question often appears in the exam.（这类问题在考试中经常出现。）；That kind of behavior is not acceptable.（那样的行为是不允许的。）

7. 词组account for表示"（尤指在事故之后）了解，查明"，例如：All passengers have now been accounted for.（现在所有乘客的情况均已查明。）

8. 表示"阻碍，挫折"的单词有：obstacle，barrier，frustration等，例如：The two parties have bargained out the remaining obstacles to an agreement.（双方经过协商扫除了达成协议的遗留障碍。）

9. gift一词作名词，既有"天赋"的意思，也有"礼物"的意思，例如：The watch was a gift from my mother.（这块表是妈妈送我的礼物。）；She has a great gift for music.（她极有音乐天赋。）

10. 倒装是英语中的重要语法之一，倒装分为完全倒装和部分倒装，部分倒装是只把谓语的一部分（如助动词、情态动词等）放在主语前，或把句子的强调成分提前。例如：Nor did he let the disease stop him from living the kind of life he has always dreamt about.（疾病没有使他放弃过梦想中的生活。）句中将否定词nor和助动词did提前。

8

雅虎公司创始人：
杨致远

Founder of Yahoo Corporation: Jerry Yang

杨致远，互联网公司雅虎（Yahoo!）的创始人，前首席执行官。1968年11月出生于中国台北市，是华裔美国人。1990年以优异的成绩进入斯坦福大学，主修电机工程，用了四年时间就获得了学士、硕士学位，并结识了戴维·费洛。

1994年4月，杨致远与戴维·费洛共同创立雅虎，因此杨致远被称为"世纪网络第一人"，开启了人类的网络时代。1998年上半年，每个月至少有3000万用户访问雅虎，每天的浏览下载量达到1亿页。1998年，《福布斯》杂志推出高科技百位富翁，杨致远以10亿美元的财富跃居第16位，超过了冠群CEO王嘉廉，成为高科技中的华人首富。2007年6月，他出任雅虎CEO一职。2012年1月18日，杨致远辞去了雅虎公司董事和所有其他职务。

8.1 Cutting Can Make Work More Effective

轻松输入十分钟

BT: How do you look at the last quarter?

Yang: What we said was that the quarter showed some strength in the U.S. search and performance display, but more weakness in branded, especially at the end in the U.S., and more so internationally. The U.S. started softening in Q2 and that continued into Q3. International was hit much harder, although display still grew double-digits there in Q3. Softness started in the U.K. early, and we knew when the French came back from vacation in September and did not buy ads at the same levels that those were trends we had to watch. Asia was more of a surprise, but the same trends were happening there too. Because we have such a big market share there, we are looking to every country for what is coming next.

BT: And what is your Q4 outlook?

Yang: Like everyone else, we are pretty much forced to formulate our views in an unprecedented set of circumstances because things are changing so quickly and the world looks a lot different than just three or four weeks ago. There has been some stability, and some business is being done still, but we don't know how bad it is going to get, and neither does anyone. Generally, of the spending that is done in the display advertising market online, we get our share. It is a little like 2001, when online usage continued to go up, but revenue drivers declined. And, even in times like this, the Internet continues to show more engagement. Obviously, no one knows when the market is going to bottom out, and I am certainly not an economist. You can talk yourself into a loop, but no one really knows where it is going yet. But when it does turn, people are going to ask where the audience is, and we have to be able to move fast when it turns. We also said that when advertisers are spending, they are spending with us, which is a good sign. Right now, we don't hear we are losing deals to social sites, for example. Of course, I can't imagine advertisers are going to say we're going to juice up spending soon, and so we're assuming a lengthy period of weakness. I don't think anyone is going to be immune, even though search performance ads are probably more able to withstand a downturn in spending. What was good for us was that our search and our performance display businesses were

performance n.
性能，表演

soften v.
变弱，缓和

double-digit adj.
两位数的

vacation n.
假期，搬出

formulate v.
表达，规划

unprecedented adj.
无前例的，空前的

stability n.
稳定性，坚定

revenue n.
收益，税收

engagement n.
使用，约会

loop n.
环，圈

assume v.
承担，假定

lengthy adj.
漫长的，啰嗦的

immune adj.
免于……的，免除的

withstand v.
反抗，抵挡

裁员可以使工作更有效率

有效学习十分钟

英国电信：您是如何看待上个季度[1]的？

杨致远：　我们认为上个季度表明在美国的搜索和性能[2]显示方面是有实力的，但是也表明了在品牌打造方面的弱势，特别是季度末，美国国内如此，国际[3]范围内更是如此。美国市场在第二季度开始变弱，第三季度持续走弱。国际市场受打击更大，尽管在第三季度，显示器的增长率仍为两位数。英国早前已开始软化，法国继9月的假期[4]后，便不再购买同级的广告。这些都是我们必须要观察的趋势[5]。亚洲的情况让人惊讶，但是也出现了同样的趋势。因为我们在亚洲有很大的市场份额[6]，所以我们现在观察每一个国家，看接下来会发生什么。

英国电信：那么您对第四季度的展望[7]是什么呢？

杨致远：　像其他人一样，我们必须在史无前例的[8]环境中形成[9]我们的看法，因为事情在迅速地发生变化，现在的世界与三、四周前相比，也有很大的不同。当今仍存在一些稳定性，仍然在完成一些业务，但是我们不知道，其他人也不知道，将来到底会变得多糟糕。总的来说，我们分担了在线显示广告市场的支出。这有点像2001年，虽然在线使用者持续增加，但是收益驱动因素却在下降。甚至在这种时候，互联网的使用仍持续增加。很明显，没有人知道市场什么时候会下降到最低点[10]，我也不是一名经济学家[11]。你可以不断地谈论它，但是没人知道它会到达哪儿。但是当它转向的时候，人们又会问观众去哪儿了。当它转向的时候，我们必须能够迅速移动。当广告商[12]支付的时候，我们与他们一起支付，这是一个好迹象。比如现在，我们还没听说我们与社会失去了交易[13]。当然，我不会去假想广告商对我们说要增加花费。我们现在假设了一个漫长的疲软期，即使搜索性能能禁得住[14]更少的花费[15]，我也不认为每个人都能免于其害。对我们有利的是，我们的搜索和性能显示业务在这个季度都上升了。

英国电信：可以透露关于裁员[16]和其他削减[17]方面的细节[18]吗？

杨致远：　在假期之前我们就想这么做了，这也是之所以我们让人们知道这会影响到

1. quarter *n.*
2. performance *n.*
3. international *adj.*
4. vacation *n.*
5. trend *n.*
6. market share
7. outlook *n.*
8. unprecedented *adj.*
9. formulate *v.*
10. bottom out
11. economist *n.*
12. advertiser *n.*
13. deal *n.*
14. withstand *v.*
15. spending *n.*
16. layoff *n.*
17. cut *v.*
18. detail *n.*
19. work force *n.*

both up in the quarter.

BT: Any more details about the layoffs and other cuts?

Yang: We want to do it before the holidays, which is why we wanted to let people know that it would affect 10 percent [of Yahoo's work force]. But we also want to make sure that we are cutting to be more effective and not cutting for cutting's sake. We have been growing costs for the last few years while we were investing in new products and platforms, and we have also made a lot of acquisitions and additions. There have been redundancies and geo-consolidation that we had not addressed that we are doing now. I know that sounds generic, but doing this is really important. I look at these cuts as both a short-term and long-term effort. In the short term, we have consolidation and organizational corrections to make. In the long term, we will look at our whole portfolio and are now asking ourselves in each case if we need to be in this business. We're asking ourselves—should we sell it or should we shut it down? That is the kind of comprehensive look we are doing across the company.

BT: And how is your relationship with Carl Icahn going?

Yang: Carl is fine and he has got a lot on his plate as well. But he has been a very useful person to have on the board and, of course, it is a different role for him than before. For the most part, he is very constructive, but he is still Carl and he doesn't hesitate to share what's on his mind.

BT: What is the status of the talks with the Justice Department over your search ad deal with Google?

Yang: I don't have a lot of new things to say. We're still talking, as I have said, and hope to get things resolved. We have not started it, but no one has walked away.

BT: What about your relationship with Microsoft? What did you think of CEO Steve Ballmer's comment last week about doing a search deal?

Yang: I don't have anything new to report either. As we have always said, we are willing to listen to them, to talk to them about anything.

BT: You have been attacked a lot recently for not selling Yahoo to Microsoft, Yahoo's low stock price and your management of the company—why do you think you are the best leader for Yahoo going forward?

Yang: I think if you look at what the company is doing and what we have been going through and the story we have been telling, we have done most, if not all, of what we set out to do, starting last year. My dream is to transform Yahoo as a platform and product company and I think we are on the way to really doing that. And a lot of what we have been doing is starting to translate into value—whether it is our front page, our profiles, our email or our APT ad platform. And, in this uncertain environment, I think I am absolutely the right person. Times like this require a leader who really understands this company and its customers, and I think I do. The world is a different place today than even a month ago and I think I am the best person to guide Yahoo through this volatile time.

雅虎10%的职工[19]的原因，但是我们会确保裁员是有效的，而不是为了裁员而裁员。近些年来，我们一直在增加成本，我们不仅在新的产品和平台上投资，还进行了合并[20]，增加[21]了固定资产。我们还有一些裁员和巩固的工作未完成，现在还在继续做。我知道这听起来有点泛泛而谈，但是做这个确实很重要。我是从短期[22]成果和长期[23]成果来看待裁员。从短期来说，我们要实现整合和组织修正。从长期来说，我们会观察整个组合[24]，在每一种情况下都要问自己，我们是否有必要做这件事。我们不断问自身，是否应该出售或者是关闭[25]？这便是现在我们公司工作的整体状况。

英国电信：您与卡尔•伊坎的关系进展如何？

杨致远：卡尔很好，他有很多事要忙。他在董事会[26]是一个很重要的人，当然，这与他之前的角色截然不同。很大程度上来说，他十分具有建设性[27]，同时，他还是和以前一样，从来都是毫不犹豫地分享[28]他的所想。

英国电信：关于您和谷歌的搜索广告交易问题，与司法部门[29]会谈的情形[30]是怎样的呢？

杨致远：我们没有什么最新的消息可讲。我们仍在会谈，并希望事情可以得到解决，我之前也说过的。我们现在还没开始解决，但是也没有人避开这个问题。

英国电信：您与微软的关系如何呢？您是怎么看待上周首席执行官史蒂夫•鲍尔默对搜索交易的评价的？

杨致远：对这个我也没有最新的消息可讲。正如我们一直说的那样，我们愿意去倾听他们，并和他们交流任何事情。

英国电信：由于未将雅虎卖给微软，雅虎的低价格股票和您的公司管理，您最近受到的打击挺大，您为什么认为您是雅虎的最佳领导者？

杨致远：我想如果你看到我们公司现在所做的，以及我们一直在做的和我们所讲述的，你会知道，如果算不上全部完成的话，我们也已经大部分完成了去年开始的任务。我的梦想就是把雅虎转变[31]成一个平台和产品公司，我想我们现在就在实现它的路上。不管是我们的首页[32]、文件，还是我们的邮件以及高级包装工具广告平台，都在转化为价值[33]。同时，在这个不确定的[34]环境中，我绝对是正确的人选。在这个时候，需要的是一个了解公司和客户的领导，我认为我就是。当今世界与一个月前都是不同的，我想我是领导雅虎走出这段不稳定[35]时期的最佳领导者。

20. acquisition *n.*
21. add *v.*
22. short-term *adj.*
23. long-term *adj.*
24. portfolio *n.*
25. shut down
26. board *n.*
27. constructive *adj.*
28. share *v.*
29. department *n.*
30. status *n.*
31. transform *v.*
32. front page
33. value *n.*
34. uncertain *adj.*
35. volatile *adj.*

1. 斯坦福大学（Stanford University）是美国一所私立大学，被公认为是世界上最杰出的大学之一。它位于加利福尼亚州的斯坦福市，临近旧金山。斯坦福大学拥有的资产属于世界大学中最大的资产之一。它占地35平方公里，是美国面积第二大的大学，也是惟一一所在自然科学（数学、物理、化学、生物、计算机、地理、统计学）方面与麻省理工大学相媲美的名校。

2. come up against的意思是"遭到……的反对"，例如：We expect to come up against a lot of opposition to the plan.（我们预计这个计划会遭到很多人的反对。）

3. 雅虎（Yahoo!）是美国著名的互联网门户网站，20世纪末互联网奇迹的创造者之一。其服务包括搜索引擎、电邮、新闻等，业务遍及24个国家和地区，为全球超过5亿的独立用户提供多元化的网络服务。同时也是一家全球性的因特网通讯、商贸及媒体公司。2012年4月4日美国雅虎公司宣布裁员2000人，约相当于雅虎全球员工数量的14%。

4. 词组show off的意思是"炫耀"，例如：So what if the Chinese government wants to show off how far the country has come in 30 years?（所以，如果中国政府想要炫耀30年来这个国家所取得的成就，又有什么关系呢？）

5. 英语中，一些形容词词尾加后缀"–en"可以变为相应的动词，例如：soften（使缓和）, richen（使富有）, widen（加宽）等，举个例句说明：They are trying to widen the discussion to include environmental issues.（他们正在尽量拓宽讨论范围以纳入环境问题。）

6. 词组juice up的意思是"使活跃，使有生气"，例如：These young men juiced up the conference with their new ideas.（这些年轻人以他们的新思想使讨论会变得生动活泼。）

7. 美国在线（American Online），是美国时代华纳的子公司，著名的因特网服务供应商。2000年，美国在线和时代华纳（Time Warner）宣布计划合并，2001年1月11日该交易被联邦贸易委员会（Federal Trade Commission）证实。合并及以后的运作信息见时代华纳。该企业品牌在世界品牌实验室（World Brand Lab）编制的2006年度《世界品牌500强》排行榜中名列第139位。

8. 2012福布斯全球富豪排行榜第50位，常被冠以诸如"投机家"、"激进投资人"甚至是"企业掠夺者"如此骇人名目的卡尔·伊坎（Carl Icahn）于1936年2月16日出生在纽约皇后区的洛克威（Far Rockaway）。犹太人与生俱来的商业头脑和他作为土生土长的纽约客耳濡目染到的财富诱惑使他具备了一个典型美国追梦人的基本素质。

阿里巴巴创始人：

马云

Founder of Alibaba: Jack Ma

中国企业家马云，浙江绍兴人，阿里巴巴集团主要创始人之一。1995年创办中国第一家互联网商业信息发布网站"中国黄页"。1999年创办阿里巴巴网站，并迅速成为全球最大的B2B电子商务平台，目前已成为亚洲最大的个人拍卖网站。2003年创办独立的第三方电子支付平台，目前在中国市场位居第一。2005年与全球最大的门户网站雅虎战略合作，兼并其在华所有资产，阿里巴巴因此成为中国最大的互联网公司。

马云现任阿里巴巴集团主席和首席执行官，除此之外，马云还担任中国雅虎董事局主席、杭州师范大学阿里巴巴商学院院长、华谊兄弟传媒集团董事等职务。他是《福布斯》杂志创办50多年来成为封面人物的首位大陆企业家，曾获选为未来全球领袖。

9.1 Everyone Should Make Contributions to Protect the Environment

轻松输入十分钟

Reporter: You've incorporated social responsibility into Alibaba, and you've also focused on bringing the Nobel Peace Prize winning microlending institution Grameen Bank into China. You've got a longer term vision than what is typical in the corporate world. Given that, what do you see long-term for China's environment? Where do you think China's environment will be in 10 years or 20 years?

Jack Ma: I think one thing's for sure—China's environment will get better in 10 or 20 years. Business people like myself are beginning to pay attention to social issues including the environment and taking action and really treating this issue very seriously. And we're doing it not for P.R. reasons, but because we know it is important. We know it is serious and that if we don't take action, it will hurt ourselves, our children and our families. I think that, in a way, this growing awareness of the environment as an issue now is good timing. 10 or 20 years ago, China would never have been aware of this kind of problem. Back then, people were focused on how to survive. Now, people have better living conditions and they have big dreams for the future. Now we have the ability to deal with the issue. We have the knowledge. We have the technology to solve our environmental problems. But if we don't take them seriously, we're going to pay a huge, huge price later. The most fun part of business, at least to me, is to contribute to the future. It's not just about making money—it's about making healthy money, enabling people to enjoy their lives. I think the important thing is to wake people up and let them know that our environmental issues need to be addressed. Positive thinking is key: The future is always beautiful.

Reporter: Building on that a bit, how do you see or how could you help or how can other corporate leaders in China get beyond that quarterly-report mentality of profits and into a longer term sustainable future vision?

Jack Ma: As business leaders and entrepreneurs, we always have to ask ourselves: Why did we build this business? As companies grow and become public,

---

incorporate *v.*
融入，吸收

microlending *n.*
小额信贷，小额贷款

vision *n.*
眼力，想象

issue *n.*
问题

awareness *n.*
意识，认识

focused *adj.*
聚焦的，专心的

contribute *v.*
贡献，出力

enable *v.*
使能够，使成为可能

address *v.*
解决，演说

mentality *n.*
心态，智力

sustainable *adj.*
可持续的，可支撑的

entrepreneur *n.*
企业家，承包人

每个人都应该为保护
环境做出贡献

有效学习十分钟

记者：您已将社会责任融入阿里巴巴，并专注于将曾获得过诺贝尔和平奖的小额信贷[1]机构——格莱珉银行引入中国。您已拥有了企业领域特有的长远眼光。鉴于此，您怎么看待中国环境的长期性[2]？您认为十年或二十年后中国环境将会怎样？

马云：我觉得有一点是肯定的——十年或二十年后，中国环境会变得更好。像我一样的商业人士正开始关注包括环境在内的社会问题，并采取行动[3]，真正严肃认真地对待这个问题。我们这样做并非出于公关原因，而是因为我们知道它的重要性。我们知道这很严重，如果不采取行动，就会伤害到自己也会伤害到我们的孩子和我们的家庭。在某种程度上，我认为这种日益增长的环境意识[4]现在出现真是恰到好处。十年或二十年前，中国人绝对意识不到这种问题。那时候，人们只关注如何生存[5]。现在，人们的生活条件[6]好了，对未来也有了远大的理想。现在，我们有能力解决这一问题。我们拥有知识。我们也具备了相应的技术来解决环境问题。但是，如果我们不重视它们，我们以后将付出无比巨大的代价[7]。至少对我来说，从事商业最有趣的部分是为未来作贡献。不只是赚钱——而是在不破坏环境的前提下赚钱，使人们能够享受生活。我认为最重要的是唤醒人们，让他们知道我们的环境问题急需解决。积极思考是关键：未来永远是美丽的。

记者：基于以上那一点，您是如何看待中国其他企业领导人[8]只在意季度盈利报告的？您怎样才能帮助他们或他们怎样做才能超越只在意季度盈利报告的心态，进入一个长期可持续的[9]未来愿景？

马云：作为商业领袖和企业家[10]，我们总是要问自己：为什么我们要成立这个

1. microlending
2. long-term
3. take action
4. awareness *n.*
5. survive *v.*
6. living condition
7. price *n.*
8. corporate leader
9. sustainable *adj.*
10. entrepreneur *n.*

most start to forget about their initial dreams, about why they built the company in the first place, which was to contribute to society and to help customers. Those are their real dreams, and not to produce good quarterly results. Good quarterly results are good, of course, but that's not the purpose of business. That is the by-product and result. For successful business leaders, if their goal is to be rich, they can become very rich. But then what's the point of having all that money? When you have 100 million U.S. dollars, I think that's more than enough for you and your children. Once your net worth exceeds a certain point, that's not your money anymore. It is society's money. It is the money society has given to you, and you should take responsibility to allocate the money in a good way. I started thinking about this issue just two, three years ago. One day I suddenly woke up and wondered, "What's next?"

Reporter: "What's next?"

Jack Ma: Yes. "What's next?" What was the initial dream you had? Go back and think about it. You know, reboot it. You have to reboot your brain, your machine, your computer to run faster, right?

Reporter: Yeah.

Jack Ma: When there is so much software installed, your machine is very slow. Therefore, we all have to reboot and revisit that initial dream we had and why we built our businesses. Was it really to please shareholders? It is best to forget about the quarterly results. It's just one part of the business—it's not the purpose of the business. I believe that customers are number one, employees are number two and shareholders are number three—always in that order.

Reporter: You mentioned that, over the last couple of years, environmental awareness has become a bigger focus in your life. Specifically, you have restricted trading of shark fin products in the platforms that you work in, and you personally have made a public call for rejection of shark fin products.

Jack Ma: Yes.

Reporter: Is that when your interest in the environment and sustainability began, or is it a result of a natural evolution? How did you get involved? Where did you first find I guess we would say in the United States, "find religion" on the environment?

Jack Ma: Well, honestly speaking, before [the shark fin issue] I had never thought about the environment. That was the first environmental issue I dealt with. In the beginning, I did not understand those anti-shark fin guys because I had never given much thought to where shark fin came from and thought it was cultivated.

initial *adj.*
最初的

quarterly *adj.*
按季度的，每季一次的

by-product *n.*
意外收获，副产品

exceed *v.*
超过，胜过

allocate *v.*
分配，拔出

reboot *v.*
重新启动，再发动

install *v.*
安装

shareholder *n.*
股东，股票持有人

restrict *v.*
限制，约束

rejection *n.*
拒绝，抛弃

sustainability *n.*
持续性，永续性

religion *n.*
宗教，宗教信仰

cultivate *v.*
培养，陶冶

公司？随着公司的发展和上市，大多数人会渐渐忘记他们最初的[11]梦想，忘记起初建立公司的原因是贡献社会和惠及顾客。那才是他们真正的梦想，并不是创造出良好的季度业绩。当然，能够产生良好的季度业绩固然不错，但这并不是企业的宗旨；那只是附带结果和意外收获而已。对于成功的企业领导者来说，如果他们的目标是成为富人，他们可以变得非常富有。但那之后，那些钱又有什么意义[12]呢？我认为，当你有1亿美元时，

养活你和你的孩子就已经绰绰有余了。一旦你的净资产超过[13]了某一数值，这些钱就不再是你的了，它是社会的了。这些钱是社会给你的，你应该承担起如何分配[14]好这些钱的责任。两三年前我才刚刚开始思考这个问题。有一天，我突然醒来并想知道，"下一步该何去何从？"

记者："下一步该何去何从呢？"

马云：是的。"下一步该何去何从呢？"您最初的梦想是什么？回想一下。要知道，得重新启动它。为了使运行速度更快，你必须重新启动你的大脑，你的机器，你的电脑，对不对？

记者：对。

马云：当安装了太多的软件时，您的机器就会非常慢。因此，我们都必须重新启动，重新审视这一最初的梦想，我们为什么要成立这个公司。真的是为了取悦股东[15]吗？最好忘记季度业绩。它只是这个公司的一部分——不是其成立的目的。我一直认为顾客应该排在第一位，员工第二位，股东第三位。

记者：您提到，在过去的几年里，环保意识已经成为您生活中一个更大的关注点。具体来说[16]，您在你们公司的平台上限制交易鱼翅[17]，就您个人而言，已经公开呼吁拒绝鱼翅产品了。

马云：是的。

记者：以上举动是当您开始对环境和可持续发展感兴趣时开始的，还是自然发展的结果？您是如何参与的？您是在哪里首次发现通过"发现宗教信仰"来保护环境的？我猜是在美国？

马云：嗯，说实话，在【鱼翅事件】之前，我从没想过环境。这是我第一次处理环境问题。起初，我不理解那些反对吃鱼翅的家伙们，因为我从未考虑过鱼翅是从哪儿来的，并认为它们是培育[18]出来的。

记者：（对于反对吃鱼翅，当时，）您是怎么想的？

11. initial *adj.*
12. point *n.*
13. exceed *v.*
14. allocate *v.*
15. shareholder *n.*
16. specifically *adv.*
17. shark fin
18. cultivate *v.*

Reporter: What did you think about it?

Jack Ma: I didn't know what it was because I'm not fond of food and ate it purely because it tasted good. To me, it was like having noodles. But on the day I discovered where it came from, I made a promise to never eat shark fin. I did not see the point of eating fins of sharks from the ocean. The incident inspired me to think about our business model and how it interacts with the environment. The more I thought about it, the more I wanted to know about what's happening to the environment, climate change and everything. I feel proud that the knowledge was integrated into our work, especially because I didn't force the Alibaba team to remove shark fins from our site. My colleagues and staff asked me about it and we exchanged ideas. The young people in my company sat down and discussed it amongst themselves. They came to their own conclusion and said, "Let's take down this thing." I am proud of the transformation that resulted through education and thoughtful discussion. It's very interesting that so many people, especially those born in '80s and '90s, support this action. I am proud of these young people. They care for the environment more than my generation ever did. If you want to change the future, get the young people on board. If you want to understand young people, you have to think like the young people do and care for the environment.

Reporter: Can you trace your interest in environment and sustainability to that realization, or were there other issues that...

Jack Ma: There are many other things that have inspired me. When I visited the river where I learned to swim as a kid (I almost drowned in there when I was 12 years old), the water was full of garbage. The water used to come up to my chest and now is just barely above my ankle. It has almost completely dried up. I thought to myself, "Oh, my God, what's going on?" Also, my wife keeps telling me: "Be careful of the water that you drink. There is something wrong with it." My father-in-law had recently died of cancer, which has made me re-evaluate a lot of things. I look around and see so many people dying. The more I think about the environment, the more I start to realize and wake up to the issues. Alibaba has helped a lot of small business owners make money through our platforms. But now our challenge is to help more people to make healthy money, "sustainable money", money that is not only good for themselves but also good for the society. That's the transformation we are aiming to make.

Reporter: You've spoken a lot about the idea that small businesses are beautiful in the economic world and small businesses are the future.

Jack Ma: Yes.

---

promise *n.*
允诺，许诺

interact *v.*
互相影响，互相作用

integrate *v.*
整合，使成为整体

colleague *n.*
同事，同僚

amongst *prep.*
在……之中，在……当中

transformation *n.*
转化，改革

generation *n.*
一代，产生

realization *n.*
实现，领悟

garbage *n.*
垃圾，废物

barely *adv.*
仅仅，几乎不

re-evaluate *v.*
重新评估，重新评价

platform *n.*
平台，月台

challenge *n.*
挑战，怀疑

马云：我不知道这是什么，因为我对食物没什么兴趣，吃它纯粹是因为味道不错。对我来说，吃它就像吃面条一样。但从我发现它是从哪里来的那天起，我就发誓再也不吃鱼翅了。以前，我并不知道我们吃的鱼翅是从海洋里的鲨鱼身上取下来的。这一事件激发[19]我去思考我们的商业模式[20]以及它与环境是如何相互作用的。我考虑得越多，就越想知道环境、气候变化[21]和一切都出现了什么状况。让我感到自豪的是，我们的工作是与知识相结合的。特别是因为我没有强迫阿里巴巴团队将鱼翅从我们的网站上移除。我的同事[22]和员工向我询问此事，于是我们交换了意见。我们公司的年轻人都坐下来相互讨论了这件事。他们得出了他们自己的结论："将鱼翅从平台上移除。"我对于这个通过教育和深思熟虑[23]得出来的转变[24]感到很自豪。有意思的是许多人，特别是那些出生在80年代和90年代的人，都支持这一行动。我为这些年轻人感到骄傲。他们对环境的关心超过了我们这一代人。如果你想改变未来，让年轻人也参与进来。如果你想了解年轻人，就必须像年轻人一样思考问题、关爱[25]环境。

记者：您能将您对环境与可持续性的兴趣回溯[26]到现实或其他问题上吗？

马云：有许多其他的事情也启发了我。当我再回到小时候学游泳的那条河时（那时我12岁，差点被淹死[27]），水里满是垃圾[28]。水位曾经高达我的胸部[29]，现在只能勉强没过我的脚踝[30]。河水几乎已经完全干涸了。我心想："哦，我的天哪，这到底是怎么了？"而且，我的妻子总是告诉我："小心你喝的水。水有问题了。"最近，我岳父因患癌症去世了，他的去世让我重新评估了很多东西。我环顾四周，目睹了那么多人的死亡。我越思考环境，就越深刻地开始意识到这个问题。阿里巴巴已经帮助很多小企业主通过我们的平台赚到了钱。但现在，我们面临的挑战是帮助更多的人在不破坏环境的前提下赚钱，"在实现环境可持续发展的前提下赚钱"。那些钱，不仅对自己有好处，对社会也有好处。这才是我们的转变想要达到的目标。

记者：您经常说，在经济领域小企业是很好的企业，而且它们是未来的发展趋势。

马云：是的。

记者：您认为此观点可应用于帮助保护中国的自然和环境吗？那些小型企业中的创

19. inspire *v.*
20. business model
21. climate change
22. colleague *n.*
23. thoughtful *adj.*
24. transformation *n.*
25. care for
26. trace *v.*
27. drown *v.*
28. garbage *n.*
29. chest *n.*
30. ankle *n.*

Reporter: How do you think that applies to helping protect China's nature, China's environment? How can those innovative sources in small businesses or that type of business aid in the protection of China's environment?

Jack Ma: The Nature Conservancy is doing a great job to help preserve huge amounts of beautiful land and is an expert in this area. My thinking is that everybody can do something and each person makes their own small contribution to the environment. People can look at their own community, their own neighborhood, their own lake in front of them and think about what they can do to help. My belief is that small is beautiful and it is about everyone contributing their small part. For me, it is about caring for the river in front of me. It is about caring for the small garden in my neighborhood. This is the movement I want to inspire. I want everybody to take action—do simple and easy things that don't require money but will as a whole make a big difference. And I want to encourage all the grandmothers, grandfathers, those who are retired and living in the community, to challenge those companies who are the source of environmental damage and polluting the water. If you are really committed, you can take action. You don't have to cross mountains in order to address climate change. Being ambitious is good, but every tiny action, every tiny contribution is beautiful. I respect the grandmothers and the young kids who do things in their own neighborhood. This is what I want to encourage in everyone.

Reporter: So that would be a platform that you could create for that individual action and meaningful local action towards improving water, air, natural values, forests?

Jack Ma: Yes. Thirty years ago, you can throw rubbish in Hangzhou's West Lake and nobody would care. But try doing that today and the local people will throw you into the water for littering!

Reporter: Yeah.

Jack Ma: What we want to build up is consciousness and awareness among people. We want people to take these issues seriously so that they think polluting is just as bad as committing a murder. Because, ultimately, it is. Business is important, but it is just as important to take action on these environmental issues as well. I'm not an extremist. We're just taking a stand on what we believe is good for ourselves and our children. And I don't want people to do it merely because they are told it is a responsibility. I hate the word "responsibility". I am taking action because this is something I believe in. It is a way of thinking and a part of my philosophy.

innovative *adj.*
创新的，革新的

preserve *v.*
保护，保存

inspire *v.*
鼓舞，启示

commit *v.*
犯罪，委托

ambitious *adj.*
有雄心的，热望的

individual *adj.*
个人的

littering *n.*
乱丢垃圾

consciousness *n.*
意识

extremist *n.*
极端主义者

新或商业类型的援助³¹如何能够保护中国
环境？

马云：大自然保护³²协会为帮助保护大批美丽国
土做了大量工作，该协会是保护环境方面
的专家。我的想法是：每个人都可以做一
些事情，每个人都能为保护环境做出一
点贡献。人们可以着眼于他们的社区³³，

他们的周边，他们社区前面的湖，想想他们能帮着做些什么。我的信念是：小
即是美，即，每个人都贡献自己的一小部分。对于我来说，是照顾我家前面的
河；是照顾我家附近的小花园。这是我想鼓励的行为。我希望每个人都行动起
来——做简单、容易的事情，不需要钱，但如果所有人都做些事情将会产生很
大的不同。我想鼓励那些退休并住在社区里的所有的祖母、祖父们，向那些破
坏环境和污染水质的公司发起挑战。它们是环境破坏³⁴的来源。如果你是真的
支持环境保护，你就可以采取行动。你不必穿越山脉去解决气候变化问题。雄
心勃勃是好事，但每一个微小的³⁵行动，每一份微小的贡献也是美丽的。我尊
重祖母和儿童在他们自己的社区所做的一些事情。这就是我想要鼓励每个人做
的。

记者：因此，您可能会为改善水、空气、自然价值、森林的个人行为和有意义的³⁶地
方行为创建一个这样的平台吗？

马云：是的。三十年前，你可以将垃圾扔进杭州西湖，没有人会在意。但今天，如果
你想尝试那样做的话，当地的人们会把你当作垃圾扔进水里！

记者：是的。

马云：我们想在人们中间建立起一种意识。我们希望人们能够严肃地对待这个问题，
以至于让他们意识到污染³⁷环境与犯了谋杀罪³⁸一样极其恶劣。因为，在根本上³⁹
也的确如此。商业固然重要，但采取行动解决这些环境问题也一样重要。我不
是极端主义者⁴⁰，我们只是站在了一个我们认为对我们自己和我们的孩子都有
利的立场上来看待这个问题。我不想人们仅仅是因为他们被告知这是一种责任
才去做这件事。我讨厌"责任"这个词。我之所以采取行动是因为这是我所信
仰的东西。它是一种思考方式，也是我的人生观⁴¹的一部分。

31. aid *n.*
32. conservancy *n.*
33. community *n.*
34. environmental damage
35. tiny *adj.*
36. meaningful *adj.*
37. pollute *v.*
38. murder *n.*
39. ultimately *adv.*
40. extremist *n.*
41. philosophy *n.*

1. 渐降法（anticlimax）是与climax（渐进法）相反的一种修辞法，将一系列词语从大到小、从强到弱排列，例如：On his breast he wears his decorations, at his side a sword, on his feet a pair of boots.（他的胸上带着饰品，一侧配有一把剑，脚上穿着靴子。）这句话从上往下描写此人的打扮，用到了渐降法的修辞手法。

2. 英语中，一些形容词后加上后缀-ness可以变为相应的名词，例如：friendliness（友谊），sensitiveness（敏感性），happiness（幸福），business（生意），carelessness（粗心大意）等。

3. 词组contribute to除了有"为……做出贡献"的意思外，还有"向……投稿"的意思，例如：She contributed an article to our magazine.（她向我们的杂志投了一篇稿子。）

4. 移就（transferred epithet）是英语中常见的修辞格，是指把本来应该用来修饰甲事物性质或状态的词用来修饰乙事物。在现代英语中，最常见的是把本来用以修饰人的词组用来修饰事物。例如：The sailors swarmed into a laughing and cheering ring around the two men.（水手们蜂拥而至，汇成欢笑与欢呼的一圈，把那两人围在中间。）这句中用修饰人的laughing和cheering修饰了物ring。

5. quarterly表示"季度的"，annual表示"年度的"，anniversary是"周年纪念日"，要注意英语中这些表示一定时段的词汇。

6. given一词除了是give的过去分词外，还可作介词，表示"考虑到……"的意思，例如：Given the uncertainty over her future, I was left with little other choice.（考虑到她前途未卜，我几乎没有选择的余地。）

7. 词组take down的意思是"拆除"，例如：The Canadian army took down the barricades erected by the Indians.（加拿大军队拆除了印度人设置的路障。）

8. 定语从句中，关系副词why主要用于修饰表示原因的名词（主要是the reason），同时它在定语从句中用作原因状语，why可以用that替换，例如：That's one of the reasons why/that I asked you to come.（这就是我请你来的原因之一。）

9. 英语中表示"仅仅，几乎不"的词有：barely，rarely，merely，only，hardly等，例如：But that would not be a solution if it merely leads to indefinite financing of fundamentally uncompetitive economies.（但如果只是为根本上缺乏竞争力的经济体提供无限量融资，那这就称不上是什么解决办法。）

10. 词组take a stand on的意思是"站在……立场上"，例如：He thought people should take a stand on such an issue.（他认为人们应该对这样一个问题表明立场。）

9.2 / The Unique and Interesting Leadership Style
独特而有趣的领导风格

轻松输入十分钟

有效学习十分钟

Reporter: You've mentioned a couple of times how you work with your team. You have a unique and interesting leadership style with the team you get together to work through these tough issues. How do you do that? What's the mechanism to say: "Hey, guys, you've got to resolve this"?

Jack Ma: I trust my team. They know I will not betray them. We will do anything for the sake of the team, for the sake of the company, for the sake of the customers. Our decisions are based on those priorities: customer, team and shareholders—in that order. I think they—the employees—should feel a sense of ownership in the business.

记者：您已经几次提到[1]您是如何与您的团队工作的。与团队一起工作时，您有一种独特而有趣的领导风格[2]来解决这些棘手的[3]问题。您是如何做到的？采用什么技巧[4]来表达："嘿，伙计们，你们必须解决这个问题"？

马云：我相信我的团队。他们知道我不会出卖[5]他们。只要是对团队好、对公司好、对顾客好的事情，我们都会去做。我们的决定是基于这些优先级的：顾客[6]、团队、股东，以此为序。我认为他们——这些员工——应该感受到了在企业中的所有权。

---

unique *adj.* 独特的，唯一的

mechanism *n.* 技巧

resolve *v.* 解决

betray *v.* 出卖，背叛

priority *n.* 优先级，优先

1. mention *v.*   2. leadership style
3. tough *adj.*   4. mechanism *n.*
5. betray *v.*   6. customer *n.*

Reporter: Well, it's not a very typical management or leadership style. It seems to have worked pretty well for you.

Jack Ma: I like the way things have worked out. I am busy, but 70 percent of my time nowadays is not focused on business. I am busy developing peoples' minds. The more I can inspire my team's minds and the more I share with them, the more they will develop.

Reporter: What has attracted you to The Nature Conservancy? What's the connection for you, and what role do you think the Conservancy can play in assisting entrepreneurs and government people in China to conserve the environment?

Jack Ma: Originally, I had thought TNC was too remote from me. However, on my recent U.S. trip, I started thinking a lot about environmental protection and was lucky to have talked to the right people. My friends were very aggressive in pushing me to work with TNC, to the point where I would feel guilty if I didn't accept the opportunity. I was convinced and said, let's go for it. Now that I am involved with the organization, I feel so proud because TNC is doing some really great work. Now I look back and wonder why I did not get involved sooner. I think TNC should take more on in China, specifically in cultivating Chinese business leaders and other community leaders. I have two key tasks. One, I will be helping TNC raise environmental awareness, so they can engage in conservation in a professional way. Two is promoting that "small is beautiful" concept, encouraging people to make their own individual contributions to saving the environment. TNC can do conservation professionally. They can do bigger. They can do better. They can save more. And nobody had let me know that before. I thought it was just another NGO. There are too many NGOs around. Every day I get hundreds and hundreds, thousands of NGOs talking to me about this and that. You know, I felt really proud yesterday when I told my colleagues that I had just attended a meeting of the trustees committee for TNC/China. My Alibaba colleagues started clapping to show their support and approval. They felt proud of me. I've been sitting on the board of many organizations, but this is the first time they have applauded me for joining a board. This is good. This is very good.

Reporter: Final question: Alibaba is new media. We talked about a platform for the many small things that people can do, and I'm assuming you're sort of thinking about that from a new-media tools, perspective and looking to your team to produce that kind of plain blueprint for people to participate through new media in saving the environment.

---

typical adj. 典型的，特有的

inspire v. 激发，鼓舞

connection n. 连接，关系

entrepreneur n. 企业家，主办者

conserve v. 保护，保存

remote adj. 遥远的，偏僻的

aggressive adj. 极力的，好斗的

guilty adj. 内疚的，有罪的

involve v. 牵涉，包含

cultivate v. 培养，陶冶

conservation n. 保护，保存

promote v. 提高，促进

encourage v. 鼓励，支持

professionally adv. 专业地，内行地

colleague n. 同事，同僚

trustee n. 受托人，托管人

clap v. 鼓掌，拍手

approval n. 赞成，认可

applaud v. 赞同，称赞

platform n. 平台，月台

assume v. 假定，承担

perspective n. 视角，观点

记者：嗯，不是一个非常典型的[7]管理或领导风格。对您来说，似乎非常有效。

马云：我喜欢这样解决事情的方式。我很忙，但现在，我的百分之七十的时间都不是放在企业上的。我正忙于开发人们的思想。越是激发团队的思想，与他们分享得就越多，他们成长得就越快。

记者：有什么东西吸引您去参加大自然保护协会吗？是什么使您与它保持联系？您认为大自然保护协会在协助[8]中国企业家和中国政府人员保护环境方面起着什么作用？

马云：起初[9]，我认为大自然保护协会离我太遥远了。然而，在我最近的美国之旅中，我开始思考很多关于环境保护的问题，而且幸运的是，我的谈话都找对了人。我的朋友们都极力催促我参与大自然保护协会的工作。出于这点，如果我不接受这次机会的话，我会感觉很愧疚[10]。我被说服了并且附和着说："让我们开始行动吧。"参加这个组织我感到很骄傲，因为大自然保护协会正在做一些真正伟大的事情。现在回想起来，我不禁纳闷为什么不早点参加呢？我认为大自然保护协会应该在中国采取更多的行动，特别是在培养中国商界领袖和其他社会活动家方面。我有两个主要任务[11]。第一是：帮助大自然保护协会提高大家的环境意识，以便于他们以更专业的[12]方式参与[13]环境保护。第二是：推进"小即是美"的观念[14]，鼓励人们为保护环境贡献[15]自己的力量。大自然保护协会能够提供专业性的保护。他们可以做得更大、更好、挽救得更多。之前，没有人让我知道这些。我认为大自然保护协会是另一种非政府组织形式。周围有很多非政府性组织，每天都会有数以百计、数以千计的非政府性组织跟我谈论各种问题。要知道，昨天，当我跟同事们说我刚刚参加了一个大自然保护协会中国区的受托人[16]委员会会议时，我感到非常骄傲。阿里巴巴的同事们开始为我鼓掌[17]，以表示他们的支持和赞同[18]。他们都以我为荣。我在很多组织[19]中任职，但这是他们第一次因为我参与了某个组织而鼓掌。这很好，真的非常好。

记者：最后一个问题：阿里巴巴是个新媒体。我们谈到了可供人们做很多小事的平台[20]。我假设[21]您是在从一个新媒体[22]工具的视角[23]考虑，注意团队和产品，提供一个人们可以通过新媒体进行参与[24]拯救[25]环境的普通蓝图[26]。

马云：是这样的。我打算从事许多艰难的工作，包括将那些不关心社会和社区的公司都披露出来。我将利用网络的力量及我的强大平台让全世界都知道那些污染河流的公司。我想人们的意识

7. typical *adj.*
8. assist *v.*
9. originally *adv.*
10. feel guilty
11. key task
12. professional *adj.*
13. engage in
14. concept *n.*
15. contribution *n.*
16. trustee *n.*
17. clap *v.*
18. approval *n.*
19. organization *n.*
20. platform *n.*
21. assume *v.*
22. new-media
23. perspective *n.*
24. participate *v.*
25. save *v.*
26. blueprint *n.*

Jack Ma: Absolutely. I'm going to pursue a lot of tough things, including shining a light on those companies that do not care for their society and community. I'm going to use the power of the Internet and my wonderful platform to let the whole world know about companies that are polluting rivers. I think raising awareness will make hundreds of people start to challenge the companies' unethical behavior and banks will stop their funding. There is so much power in education and raising awareness. We will also offer prizes for the small and medium size companies that are taking action and bettering their community. I want to highlight good actions and encourage people to do good constructively. I am really looking forward to this and think this will become part of my fun activities every year.

Reporter: Well, thank you very much. It's really great to talk to you about this.

Jack Ma: You're welcome. It is my pleasure. I love this topic.

提高后，将会有许许多多的人开始挑战公司的不道德行为[27]，并使银行冻结他们的资金[28]。教育和意识的力量是很强大的。我们将对那些采取行动、改善社区环境的中小企业[29]给予奖励。我想凸显[30]那些好的行为，鼓励人们有建设性地去做好事。对此，我很期待，并认为这将成为我每年有趣活动的一部分。

记者：嗯，非常感谢。很高兴跟您谈论这个话题。

马云：不客气，我很高兴。我喜欢这个话题。

participate v. 参加

shine v. 擦亮，照耀

awareness n. 意识，明白

unethical adj. 不道德的，缺乏职业道德的

highlight v. 突出，强调

constructively adv. 建设性地

27. unethical behavior

28. funding n.

29. small and medium size companies

30. highlight v.

自由输出十分钟

1. 词组for the sake of的意思是"为了……的利益"，例如：For the sake of her daughter's health, she decided to move to a warm place.（为了她女儿的健康，她决定搬到一个气候温暖的地方去。）

2. 大自然保护协会The Nature Conservancy（TNC）是从事生态环境保护的国际民间组织，致力于在全球保护具有重要生态价值的陆地和水域，以维护自然环境、提升人类福祉。由于坚持采取合作而非对抗性的策略，以及用科学的原理和方法来指导保护行动，经过50余年的不懈努力，该协会已跻身美国十大慈善机构行列，位居全球生态环境保护非营利民间组织前茅。

3. right可以做副词，表示"正好，恰好"的意思，例如：Lee was standing right behind her.（李就站在她身后。）

4. 表示"关键的"词汇有：key，pivotal，critical等，例如：A key uncertainty in the experiment lay in the satellite data used, because it spans only a few years.（实验使用的卫星数据中存在一个关键的不确定因素，因为数据只覆盖了最近几年。）

5. 反意法（oxymoron）是英语修辞方法之一，主要是指用两种不相调和的特征形容一个事物，以不协调的搭配使读者领悟句中微妙的含义，例如：No light, but rather darkness visible.（没有光亮，黑暗却清晰可见。）"没有光亮"与"清晰可见"就体现了这种用法。

6. 词组engage in的意思是"从事……"，例如：Faculty who engage in research seem to have more knowledge to pass on to their students.（从事研究工作的教师似乎有更多的知识可以传授给学生。）

7. 英语中一些动词的后面加–ee可构成名词，表示"被……的人"，例如：trustee（受托人），interviewee（被面试的人），trainee（接受训练者），appointee（受任命者），expellee（被驱赶者）等。

8. 定语从句中，若介词放在关系代词前，关系代词指人时用whom，不可用who或者that；指物时用which，不能用that；关系代词是所有格时用whose。例如：The man with whom you talked is my friend.

9. 合成法是英语构词方法之一，英语中有很多合成词，合成词的词义一般为用来合成的各个单词词义的叠加，例如：mindset（心态，精神状态），highlight（最精彩的部分），overall（全部的）等。

10. 词组be supposed to do sth.的意思是"应该做某事"，例如：Markets were supposed to shut down bad ideas in a gradual evolutionary process; what happened in 2008 was more like a mass extinction.（市场本应在一种逐渐演化的过程中摒弃不好的想法；而2008年发生的一切却更像是大规模的灭绝。）

9.3 / Let's Plant the Seeds of Love and Responsibility

轻松输入十分钟

Reporter: Although the government here in China isn't monolithic—there are actually complex relationships among the national and the provincial and the local governments—government as a whole is certainly a major actor here and plays a big role, and business is the other huge sector that's come on in the last 15 and 20 years in China. But one of the sectors that's noticeably missing is the NGO, the charitable, the social civic culture. What role should entrepreneurs and businesses play in helping to create that civil culture?

Jack Ma: We need to give them some time. I think China is making progress. But keep in mind that government people are all human beings, and people should be self-reliant instead of depending too much on government. Second, don't complain about what government should and should not do while you remain passive and are not acting. What we want to do is to raise awareness among as many people as possible on the seriousness of the environmental situation in China, and let them know that everybody can contribute something to make things better. The better we educate people on the issues, the more will happen. With more and more young people joining the government, they will bring an understanding on the importance of the problem and take action. So it is about influencing a whole system. I think we are in the process to building it up right now. We cannot expect change overnight. We need to create the change over time, say five or ten years. That's called a long-term strategy, and is necessary for sustainable action and results.

Reporter: The Sichuan earthquake of 2008 was a catalytic event in this country, something that really changed mindsets and changed people's sense of their ownership of the collective China, beyond the government role. You yourself have been very active in Sichuan. You're still active. What was behind that shift? Was that just the right time and right place sort of thing to spur Chinese philanthropy, to spur consciousness about those things?

Jack Ma: I think this earthquake made some changes in China that have been happening over the past decades transparent to the Chinese people. A lot of Chinese people who have become rich recently have started to think about others and about the environment. I think many hundreds or millions of

monolithic *adj.* 整体的，完全统一的

provincial *adj.* 省的

noticeably *adv.* 明显地，引人注目地

charitable *adj.* 慈善事业的，仁慈的

entrepreneur *n.* 企业家，主办者

self-reliant *adj.* 自力更生的

passive *adj.* 消极的，被动的

seriousness *n.* 严肃，严重性

overnight *adv.* 一夜之间，突然

sustainable *adj.* 可以忍受的，足可支撑的

collective *adj.* 集体的，共同的

spur *v.* 刺激，鞭策

transparent *adj.* 透明的，显然的

让我们播下爱与责任的种子

有效学习十分钟

记者：尽管在中国，政府并不专制——实际上，国家和省级以及地方政府之间有着一种复杂的[1]关系——但政府作为一个整体[2]当然扮演着主要的角色，起主要作用。商业是另一大部门[3]，是在过去的15到20年中发展起来的。但它有一个明显缺失的部门，那就是非政府组织、慈善事业、社会公民文化[4]。在帮助创建公民文化的过程中，企业和企业家们应该扮演什么角色呢？

马云：我们需要给政府一些时间。我认为，中国正在不断取得进步[5]。但需要记住[6]的是，政府人员也都是普通人，人们应该自力更生[7]而非过分依赖政府。其次，当你消极被动[8]、无所作为时不要抱怨政府应该做什么、不应该做什么。我们想要做的是让尽可能多的人对中国环境现状的严重性提高认识，并且让他们知道每个人都能有所作为，让事情变得更好。在这个问题上，人们受到的教育越好，产生的效果就越大。随着越来越多的年轻人参与政府工作，他们也将自己关于环境问题重要性的理解带入政府，并采取行动。因此，这也将影响整个政府系统。我认为我们现在正在构建的过程中。我们不能指望改变在一夜之间[9]发生。我们需要随着时间的推移来创造变化，也许需要五年或十年时间。那就是所谓的长期战略[10]，而且长期战略对可持续性的行动和结果也是十分必要的。

记者：在中国，2008年的四川地震[11]是一起诱发事件[12]，这起事件真的改变了人们的心态[13]，改变了人们对集体所有制的中国所有权的认识，这些事情超出了政府的能力范围。您本人曾在四川十分活跃。现在仍然很活跃。是什么导致了这种转变？只是因为恰当的时间和恰当的地点诸如此类的东西刺激了中国的慈善事业[14]，激发了人们对这些事情的意识吗？

马云：我认为地震给中国带来了一些变化，但这些变化在过去的几十年里也一直在发生，而中国人没有察觉。很多富裕起来的中国人最近已经开始为他人和环境着想了。我认为成百上千万的人已经每天都在做慈善事业，只是地震突然迫使所有人都专注在一件事情上了。中国人并不是从这件事才开始互相关爱的。人们互相关爱的高峰期[15]是在过去的10年或20年里，那时大家都在为彼此做着小事。地震的发生，产生了一个焦点[16]，它将所有人的注意力和焦点都集中在了一起。

1. complex *adj.*
2. as a whole
3. sector *n.*
4. social civic culture
5. make progress
6. keep in mind
7. self-reliant
8. passive *adj.*
9. overnight *n.*
10. long-term strategy
11. earthquake *n.*
12. catalytic event
13. mindset *n.*
14. philanthropy *n.*
15. culmination *n.*
16. focal point

culmination *n.*
顶点，高潮

recover *v.*
恢复，弥补

efficient *adj.*
有效的，有能力的

complain *v.*
抱怨，控诉

seed *n.*
种子，根据

blossom *v.*
开花，发展

fertilizer *n.*
肥料

cultivate *v.*
培养，陶冶

spin *v.*
旋转，纺织

fascinate *v.*
着迷，神魂颠倒

embed *v.*
使深留脑中，使嵌入

biodiversity *n.*
生物多样性

obligation *n.*
责任，义务

rainforest *n.*
热带雨林

people were already doing that every day, but that earthquake suddenly forced everyone to focus on one thing. Chinese people did not start caring from this event. It is more a culmination of the past 10 or 20 years, when everyone was doing small things for each other. When this event occurred, it created a focal point that brought together everyone's attention and focus. It's not like the event suddenly changed China or the Chinese people in their care and love for their neighbors. China is and had already been changing. [The Chinese people have] been recovering the love [for each other] for the past 10, 20 years now. Now is a chance that everybody will start to move, take action. Whether these actions are right or wrong or good enough or efficient enough, we will see. It's improving. So when I complain about these environmental disasters in China, I'm actually being positive towards China. If I can understand and realize what other people can't realize, it's because they have not had a chance to think about it. So let's tell them. Let's communicate our message to them. Now what we want to do is plant seeds of love and responsibility, and 20 years later, they will blossom. If we only complain and do not plant, do not invest in a good fertilizer, do not have land, then it is hopeless. There is love in the heart of every individual. We should "plant" facts, culture, education that cultivate love, and foster appreciation and understanding of others.

Reporter: I love that phrase, "recovering the love". It's a really lovely phrase. I have two questions kind of spinning out of that. First, what you've described sounds a lot like what the Buddhists call "Right Livelihood" or a right focus on participation in society. Is that a social value in China? Is it a personal value? Is it both?

Jack Ma: I'm not strongly religious, but I am fascinated by religion. I love Christianity. I love Buddhism. I love Taoism. I respect all religions and am curious about them. China is largely a Buddhist culture—it's genetic for us. It's been embedded in our culture for hundreds of years. Unfortunately, today, the land has been polluted by so many chemicals that it makes it hard for the Buddhist culture to grow. But the seeds are there.

Reporter: The second thought about that is, as you know, I work for The Nature Conservancy, and it's obviously a global organization. It's mainly based in the United States, and it's focused on biodiversity and nature conservation around the world. The United States has felt an obligation to the rest of the world, I think, where many people feel they have to support NGOs that work not just in our country but internationally. Do you see a China version of that movement in the future? How do you see Chinese working to save the planet not in China? What's the obligation? What's the path for Chinese entrepreneurs who care about Brazilian rainforests or Indonesian rainforests or global water quality or climate change?

Jack Ma: China is a developing nation, and for nature conservation, China is not fully developed in this area yet. The U.S. is pretty developed. I think most of

不像是这件事突然改变了中国，或改变了中国人民对他们街坊邻居的关心和爱护。在四川地震之前，中国就已经在改变了。在过去的10年、20年中【中国人已经】【在彼此之间】复苏了爱。现在正好是一个让大家都行动起来的机会。

至于这些行为是对是错、是否足够好、足够多，让我们拭目以待吧。总之是在改善中。因此，当我抱怨发生在中国的生态灾难[17]时，实际上，我对中国是抱有乐观态度的。如果说我能意识到他人意识不到的，是因为他人没有机会去思考这些。因此，让我们告诉他们。让我们将我们的信息传递给他们。现在，我们要做的就是播下爱和责任的种子。20年后，它们将开花[18]结果。如果我们只是抱怨，不去种植，不施好的肥料[19]，没有土壤的话，那么将毫无希望。每个人心中都有爱。我们应该将培育爱的事实、文化和教育植根于人们心中，以此培养[20]他们的鉴别力[21]和理解力。

17. disaster n.
18. blossom v.
19. fertilizer n.
20. foster v.
21. appreciation n.
22. social value
23. personal value
24. Christianity
25. Buddhism
26. Taoism
27. genetic adj.
28. biodiversity n.
29. nature conservation
30. internationally adv.
31. rainforest n.

记者：我喜欢"复苏爱"这个词语。它真是个令人愉快的短语。对此我有两个问题。首先，您所描述的听起来很像佛家所说的"正命"或者说是一个能使人们参与到社会中的正确的专注点。那是所有中国人的社会观[22]，还是个人的价值观[23]，还是两者皆是？

马云：我不是虔诚的教徒，但我被宗教深深吸引着。我爱基督教[24]、佛教[25]和道教[26]。我尊重所有宗教信仰，并且对其感到好奇。中国是佛教大国——它是世代传承的[27]。佛教植入我国文化已经有数百年的时间了。不幸的是，如今的中国大地已经被太多的化学药剂污染了，佛教文化已经很难在其上面生长了。但它的种子还在。

记者：第二个问题：您是知道的，我在大自然保护协会工作，显然这是个全球性的组织。它主要基于美国，专注于全世界的物种多样性[28]和大自然的保护[29]。

美国人已经感觉到了对世界其他地方的职责。我认为，在美国，许多人都觉得他们必须支持非政府组织，不仅是我们本国的也包括国际性的[30]非政府组织。您能预见未来中国版本的这种行动吗？对于不是在中国的中国人进行保护地球的工作，你是怎么看的？有什么义务吗？中国企业家关心巴西热带雨林[31]或印尼热带雨林或全球水质量或气候变化的途径是什么？

马云：中国是发展中国家。在保护大自然这个领域，中国发展还不充分。美国在这个领域是很发达的。我想很多中国人还没有意识到本国的环境情况有多恶劣。现在，他们仅仅在开始思考怎样做才能解决环境问题。对他们来说，出去旅行了

the Chinese people did not realize how terrible the environmental situation is in their own country. They are only now just beginning to think about what can be done about to address the problems. It is not easy for them to travel and see what is going on outside of their own community. For you, travelling is merely a matter of getting a visa and finding time. For Chinese people, many have never travelled to a neighboring province, let alone visit a different country. Of China's 1.3 billion people, most are still farmers and have not left the countryside. The Chinese people really care about environmental protection in China. That will be their greatest contribution to the world. For me, I have the luxury to think about doing more for Africa. But how many people are like Jack Ma? How many Chinese people have the resources, the opportunity to develop a bigger world view, and have the luxury to see the outside world? Obligation to the world is good, but I think the Chinese people will say they have an obligation to take more action to take care of their own environment. If you don't or can't care for yourself, I don't think you can care for others.

Reporter: That's a great way of putting it. China's contribution to global conservation is working on China.

Jack Ma: China's gas consumption. China's pollution. These can have devastating impact on the world. If the Chinese people solve these issues, they would be making a tremendous contribution to the world.

Reporter: I know from other sources that you're also interested in environmental or organic farming. How are you going to sort of pursue those? Where are you heading with those things?

Jack Ma: I want my team to tell me. I want our young people to tell me and get me involved in it. I don't want to be telling them what to do. If I tell them, it's just going to be another job assignment that they have to complete. I want them to think about it and do research. I want them to come to me and say, "Here's an issue which is destroying the environment and these are the things that we think we should do about it." We should trust the young people. They're smart enough. The good thing is they are waking up to the issues. They have started to think and do research. They are influential because they work for this company and this city. When they go home, they talk to their parents, relatives, classmates and exchange ideas. I think you have to manage philanthropy like the way you manage a business—you always have to be smart. You need to find out what works, what doesn't, what is needed, and what is good. My thinking is very simple. Let's plant the seeds of love everywhere. When spring arrives, we will see green shoots. In five years, they become the trees. I say we start planting.

merely *adv.*
仅仅，不过

visa *n.*
签证

luxury *n.*
奢侈，享受

conservation *n.*
保护，保存

devastating *adj.*
毁灭性的

organic *adj.*
有机的，组织的

assignment *n.*
分配，任务

influential *adj.*
有影响的，有势力的

philanthropy *n.*
慈善，博爱

解自己国家以外的环境问题不是一件简单的事情。对你们来说，旅行仅仅是办签证、有时间而已。对于中国人来说，很多人甚至都没到过邻近的省，更别说出国了。在13亿的中国人中，多数都是农民，没有离开过农村的农民。中国人真的很关心中国的环境保护，这将是中国人民对世界所做出的最大贡献。对我来说，我可以奢侈[32]地去想为非洲多做些什么。但有多少人跟马云一样？又有多少中国人有物力、有机会去培养更大的世界观，并且能够奢侈地去看外面的世界？对世界担负责任是好的，但是我认为中国人会说他们有责任为保护本国的环境做更多的努力。如果你不想或者不能保护本国的环境，我认为你也不能保护其他国家的环境。

记者：这句话说得好。中国人保护本国环境就是中国人对全球性环境保护做出了贡献。

马云：中国的天然气消费量[33]以及中国的污染都会对世界产生灾难性的[34]影响。如果中国人能解决这些问题，他们将对世界做出巨大的[35]贡献。

记者：我从其他渠道了解到您对生态或有机农业[36]也很感兴趣。您打算怎样实现它们？从哪里入手解决这些事情？

马云：我想让我的团队来告诉我。我想让我们的年轻人告诉我，并让我参与进去。我不想告诉他们该做什么。如果由我告诉他们，那就变成了他们必须完成的另一个工作任务[37]了。我希望他们自己思考，去做研究。我希望他们走到我面前跟我说："这儿有一个造成环境破坏的问题，针对这个问题，我想我们应该做这些事情。"我们应该相信年轻人。他们聪明得很。好在他们意识到了这个问题。他们已经开始思考，开始研究了。他们是很有影响力的[38]，因为他们是为这个公司、这座城市工作的。当回到家里时，他们会与父母、亲戚、同学谈论此事并且交换意见。我想你必须像经营企业一样经营慈善事业——必须时刻保持头脑清

醒。你需要找出什么有效，什么无效，需要什么以及什么是有益的。我的想法很简单。让我们处处播下爱的种子。当春天到来时，我们就能看见绿色的嫩芽。五年后，它们就会长成大树。让我们开始种植吧。

32. luxury *n.*
33. consumption *n.*
34. devastating *adj.*
35. tremendous *adj.*
36. organic farming
37. job assignment
38. influential *adj.*

1. 英语中破折号可用在一个解释性的分句或句子前面，例如：How lucky the girls nowadays are! —they can go anywhere, say anything.（今天的女孩子多幸福啊！她们哪儿都能去，什么话都能说。）

2. 英语中，如果同位语与其同位成分关系紧密时不用逗号隔开，例如：He told me that his brother John is a world-famous doctor.（他跟我说，他的兄长约翰是一位世界闻名的医生。）brother和John是同位语，两者关系密切，因此中间不用逗号隔开。

3. NGO是Non-Governmental Organization的缩写，意为"非政府组织，民间组织"，世界上的非政府组织主要有：国际红十字会，博鳌论坛，国际足联，奥委会等。

4. 词组come up with的意思是"想出（一个主意或计划），提出"，例如：To come up with a strong password, some security officials recommend taking a memorable phrase and using the first letter of each word.（要想设置出强大的密码，有些安全专家建议，可以先选择一个好记的短语，然后用这个短语中每个词的首字母作为密码。）

5. 虚拟语气中，有时可将条件从句的连词if省略，但此时应用倒装句型，即把从句中的 were, should, had 等提到句首，例如：Were I you, I would refuse.（如果我是你，我会拒绝。）

6. 比较级的用法中，句型"The+比较级……，the+比较级……"表示"越……，越……"，例如：The busier he is, the happier he feels.（他越忙就越高兴。）

7. 词组spin out的意思是"消磨时间"，例如：Spin out the time by talking.（以谈话来消磨时间。）

8. 英语句子中，如果不定式作表语，且前面主语有do时，后面表语不定式中的to可以省略。例如：What I want to do is stay at home.（我只想待在家里。）这里stay前面的to就省略了。

9. 词组let alone的意思是"更不用说"，例如：When Apple launched the iPad less than a year ago, most people did not know what it was for, let alone how many the company would sell.（不到一年前，当苹果推出ipad的时候，大多数人还不知道它是做什么用的，更别提预测它的销量了。）

10. supposing可作连词用，表示假设，例如：Supposing that there were no war in the world, all the children could be studying in peace in the classrooms.（假如世界上没有了战争，所有的孩子就都能在教室里平静地学习了。）

亚马逊首席执行官：
杰夫·贝索斯
CEO of Amazon: Jeff Bezos

杰夫·贝索斯（Jeff Bezos），1964年1月12日出生于美国新墨西哥州中部大城阿尔布奎克。1986年，获普林斯顿大学电气工程与计算机科学学士学位，并成为美国大学优秀生联谊会会员。1988年，他进入华尔街的Bankers Trust Co.，主要从事计算机系统开发工作，后来该系统管理着2500亿美元的基金。1990年2月，贝索斯成为该公司最年轻的副总裁。

1994年年初开始构想亚马逊，之后他便步步为营，创办了全球最大的网上书店Amazon（亚马逊），并成为经营最成功的电子商务网站之一，引领时代潮流。更可贵的是，随着互联网泡沫的破灭，面对"破产"的批评，贝索斯不畏艰辛，在保持持续增长的情况下，逐步走向盈利，重新树立起电子商务的信心。贝索斯依然是全球电子商务的第一象征。1999年他当选《时代》周刊年度人物。

10.1 Amazon Made Its Decision to Provide the Best Service for Customers

Reporter: Kindle Fire seems to have gone beyond just the "iPad competitors" in this definition.

Jeff Bezos: Yes, Kindle Fire is a deep integration of media products. We believe that the hardware **configuration** is very important in today's electronic products. It is an integral part, but is only part of them.

Reporter: Price is also important to mention. Kindle Fire's price is $ 199.

Jeff Bezos: Amazon has a **unique** marketing strategy that is producing highly cost-effective products. Amazon has always been a **puerile** company, we don't want to **squeeze** too much profits from the consumers, the future as well.

Reporter: What's the number of your Kindle Fires sold in the end? You can't answer my question.

Jeff Bezos: I believe you don't expect me to say.

Reporter: In addition to this, you also release Kindle Fires at a **minimum** price of only $ 79. Why don't you choose to **purchase** a certain number of consumer electronics? You can receive a free Kindle books on the market **strategy**?

Jeff Bezos: This is a very interesting marketing idea. Maybe we will consider this approach in the future. For now, $ 79 is cheap enough for most people.

Reporter: In the past 15 years, what is it for you to keep Amazon **innovative**?

Jeff Bezos: Amazon has a big advantage and that is cultural innovation. Cultural innovation won't **perish**. Many companies don't like this idea, some enterprises will rest on their laurels, follow old roads. But Amazon is not the case, and in the future, we will always work hard.

Reporter: Eric Schmidt has cited Amazon as one of the four **knights** (Google, Apple, Facebook, and Amazon), how do you see?

Jeff Bezos: This list is close to the truth, but we cannot ignore Microsoft, although their innovation has been largely **overshadowed** by the existing business operations, such as Kinect's success. If you look back to 1980, who will be included in the list of four knights ?

Reporter: IBM.

Jeff Bezos: Yes, there will be Intel. But you may also count Commodore or Atari. Every age is the color of some things that can be later **eulogized**. But for companies, you should not indulge in memories of the past, because

---

configuration n.
配置，结构

unique adj.
独特的，惟一的

puerile adj.
未成熟的，幼稚的

squeeze v.
压榨，挤

minimum adj.
最低的，最小的

purchase v.
购买，赢得

strategy n.
战略，策略

innovative adj.
创新的，革新的

perish v.
毁灭，死亡

knight n.
骑士，武士

overshadow v.
黯然失色，使阴暗

eulogize v.
称赞，颂扬

亚马逊致力于为顾客提供最好的服务

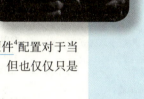

有效学习十分钟

记者：　　　平板电脑[1]好像已经超出"iPad的竞争对手[2]"的定义范畴了。

杰夫·贝索斯：是的，平板电脑是深度集成的媒体[3]产品。我们认为，硬件[4]配置对于当今的电子产品来说是很重要的部分，是构成的主要部分[5]，但也仅仅只是一个部分。

记者：　　　价格也是要提到的一个重要问题，平板电脑的价格是199美元。

杰夫·贝索斯：亚马逊有独特的营销战略，生产高效益成本的产品。它一直是一个薄利多销的公司，不会向顾客榨取[6]太多的利益，将来也不会。

记者：　　　您平板电脑的最终销量是多少？我想您不能回答这个问题。

杰夫·贝索斯：我相信你不会期望我说的。

记者：　　　除了这个以外，您还以79美元的最低[7]价格发行[8]了平板电脑，您为什么不选择购买一定数量的家用电子产品[9]呢，难道您能通过营销战略获得免费的平板电子书吗？

杰夫·贝索斯：这是个有趣的营销想法。我们在将来可能考虑使用这个方法。现在，79美元对于大多数人来说是足够便宜的。

记者：　　　在过去的15年里，是什么让亚马逊持续创新[10]的？

杰夫·贝索斯：亚马逊有一个优势就是文化创新，文化创新是不会消亡[11]的。许多公司不喜欢这种主张，他们依赖头上的光环，不断走老路。但是亚马逊不同，将来我们还会继续努力。

记者：　　　埃里克·施密特把亚马逊列为四大骑士[12]之一（谷歌，苹果，脸谱和亚马逊），您是怎么看待的？

杰夫·贝索斯：这个列表是靠近事实的，但是我们不能忽视微软。尽管他们的创新大多被现存的一些商业操作夺去了光彩[13]，例如游戏机的成功。但是如果你重新回头看1980年那时候，你们把谁列为四大骑士呢？

记者：　　　美国国际商用机器公司。

杰夫·贝索斯：是的，还有英特尔。你还可能把康懋达或者是雅达利算进来。每个时代都带有某些事物的色彩，然后受到赞扬。但是对于公司来说，不能沉浸于过去，因为事物不是永远都有光泽的[14]。对于商业来说，清晰的结构

1. Kindle Fire
2. competitor *n.*
3. media *n.*
4. hardware *n.*
5. integral part
6. squeeze *v.*
7. minimum *adj.*
8. release *v.*
9. consumer electronics
10. innovation *n.*
11. perish *v.*
12. knight *n.*
13. overshadow *v.*
14. glossy *adj.*

things are often not **durable** glossy. What business really needs is a clear structure. Entrepreneurs should provide ideal services for consumers. But many companies have not experienced a downturn in the market environment, so they have not **undergone** the real test.

Reporter: Amazon has gone through difficult stages, the first time when the technology **bubble** bursted, the company's stock price fell sharply, what do you learn from this stage?

Jeff Bezos: Now back in 1999, we find it difficult to keep track of how great the impact was. At that time, a majority of people have lost **passion** for the technology industry. They gave up their career and turned to the IT sector which is considered as a gold sector. When the bubble burst, many people left, they finally realized that they didn't want to do that. Some were **dismissed**, some still stayed there. It was a hard period for our sector. Those people you really like and value also left the Silicon Valley. Not only me but also those people who had gave up IT company **executive** positions. Our **facial** skin began to thicken.

Reporter: Amazon has already started to sell their own books. This is a very bad news for publishers. Do you think Amazon is the latter in this respect? What's the difference?

Jeff Bezos: There are the same—the price, we still think $ 9.99 is the highest book price **acceptable** to consumers.

Reporter: Let's talk about the topic of web services. Amazon's web hosting service has a leading position in the industry, some observers even think that your web hosting service is in the **equivalent** position to Coca-Cola, Pepsi which are in the **beverage** sector in the absence of a **premise**. My question is that why an e-commerce company provides network services for other large companies and institutions, such as NASA, Netflix, *The New York Times*?

Jeff Bezos: 9 years ago, our application engineers and network **infrastructure** engineers would spend a lot of time on internal communications. They realized that if they needed to communicate details, they would let guys of data center do application center's work, and this will provide a set of tools, form a **dependency** structure. Therefore, the company began to build and use this **framework**. Then they realized that any person needs this thing if they want to build a network application. So they decided to start selling.

Reporter: I guess you must have heard many voices of **opposition**, right?

Jeff Bezos: What people focus on is the most questioned "why the Amazon has to enter this industry?" This is a good question, but I have to ask "Why not?" We have enough technology and resources, and have been successful in others, why can't it been sold?

Reporter: Some young start-up companies told me that even if Google provides free hosting services, they will continue to use Amazon's, why?

Jeff Bezos: Our **commitment** is to provide customers with best service even if customers are willing to use worse products. Customers will set the lowest price, technology companies must make some profits but other than

durable *adj.*
耐用的，持久的

undergo *v.*
经历，忍受

bubble *n.*
泡沫，气泡

passion *n.*
热情，激情

dismiss *v.*
解雇，开除

executive *n.*
高管

facial *adj.*
面部的，表面的

acceptable *adj.*
可接受的，合意的

equivalent *adj.*
相等的，等价的

beverage *n.*
饮料

premise *n.*
前提

infrastructure *n.*
基础设施，公共建设

dependency *n.*
从属

framework *n.*
结构，框架

opposition *n.*
反对

commitment *n.*
承诺，保证

是很有必要的。企业家们要为顾客提供他们认同的完美的服务，但是很多公司没有经历过市场的衰退[15]，所以他们没有经受过真正的考验。

记者：　　亚马逊经历了不同的困难阶段，第一次是在技术泡沫[16]爆发的时候，那时公司的股票价格急速下降，您从这个阶段学到了什么呢？

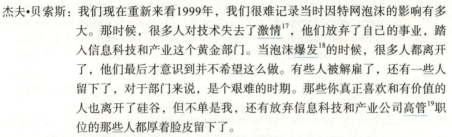

杰夫·贝索斯：我们现在重新来看1999年，我们很难记录当时因特网泡沫的影响有多大。那时候，很多人对技术失去了激情[17]，他们放弃了自己的事业，踏入信息科技和产业这个黄金部门。当泡沫爆发[18]的时候，很多人都离开了，他们最后才意识到并不希望这么做。有些人被解雇了，还有一些人留下了，对于部门来说，是个艰难的时期。那些你真正喜欢和有价值的人也离开了硅谷，但不单是我，还有放弃信息科技和产业公司高管[19]职位的那些人都厚着脸皮留下了。

记者：　　亚马逊开始出售书籍，这对于出版商[20]来说是一个坏消息。您认为亚马逊在这方面是后继者吗，不同点是什么？

杰夫·贝索斯：是一样的，价格是一样的。我们仍然认为9.99美元是顾客可以接受的最高的书本价格。

记者：　　我们来谈谈网页服务[21]这个话题。亚马逊的网页主机服务在行业内占有领先地位，甚至有一些观察者说，在前提缺失的情况下，你们的网页主机服务等同于饮料[22]行业的可口可乐和百事可乐。我的问题是，作为一家电子商务[23]公司，为什么要为美国国家航空航天局、网飞公司、《纽约时报》提供服务？

杰夫·贝索斯：9年前，我们的应用工程师和因特网基础设施[24]工程师在内部[25]交流的时候耗费[26]大量时间，他们就意识到如果要交流细节的话，若能让数据中心的人去做应用中心的活，就能依靠数据中心的人提供很多工具，形成一个独立的结构。于是，公司开始建立并利用这个构架[27]，后来他们意识到建立因特网应用的人都会需要这个，因此决定开始销售。

记者：　　我想您会听到很多反对声音，是吧？

杰夫·贝索斯：人们所关注的焦点是"为什么亚马逊会进入这个行业？"，这是一个好问题，但是我必须要问"为什么不呢？"我们在这方面有足够的技术和资源，并且在他人身上已经成功了，为什么不出售呢？

记者：　　一些刚成立[28]不久的公司说，就算谷歌提供免费的主机服务，他们仍会继续使用亚马逊的，这是为什么？

杰夫·贝索斯：我们的承诺[29]是为顾客提供最好的服务，即使顾客愿意使用更差的产品。顾客会设定最低水平的价格，技术公司通常是盈利的，但是亚马逊要被排除在外，我们是惟一的低盈利[30]技术公司。

记者：　　你们是怎样做到的？

15. downturn *n.*
16. bubble *n.*
17. passion *n.*
18. burst *v.*
19. executive *n.*
20. publisher *n.*
21. web service
22. beverage *n.*
23. e-commerce
24. infrastructure *n.*
25. internal *adj.*
26. consume *v.*
27. framework *n.*
28. start-up
29. commitment *n.*
30. low-profit

Amazon. In fact, we are the only low-profit technology company.

Reporter: How did you do that?

Jeff Bezos: We have a small mistake that is we are very **persistent**. This mistake usually increases our costs, because doing things which needs a lot of spending is unwise. Amazon is focusing on mistakes and shortcomings and finding ways to fundamentally **eliminate** them.

Reporter: **Streaming** video is part of Amazon's prime services. This is a completely different service, why not make a separate charge?

Jeff Bezos: To build a successful company needs two ways: one is trying hard to convince consumers to pay high profit; the other is trying hard to create accesse for customers to allow companies to pay high profit. They are both successful, but I will stand **firmly** with the latter one. To do this is difficult, because you have to reduce errors and be **adequate** and efficient. Our view is we prefer to have a very large customer base and consequent low profits, rather than a smaller user base and higher profits.

Reporter: Currently, Amazon has been integrated into a lot of social **elements**, so how do you think of your company's positioning in the social field?

Jeff Bezos: This is a very open question. If you have a user list of more than 500 friends, what would you do? In this regard, we have an idea and have **conducted** several experiments, but we are not particularly satisfied.

Reporter: 2 years ago, Amazon acquired Zappos. Can we understand that Amazon is **attempting** to learn from their high-quality customer service culture?

Jeff Bezos: No, no. We like their special culture, but we do not have this culture in the Amazon, because we also like our culture. The perfect customer experience of us is that customers needn't to communicate too much with us. As long as customers **contact** us, we will regard that as a mistake. I have said for many years that people should talk with their friends, rather than with businesses. Therefore, we will use customers' information to find the reasons that cause customers to contact with us. For example, what's going wrong? Why do they call us? Why do they spend time talking to us instead of talking to their families? How to solve this problem? While, Zappos is taking a **completely** different strategy. They will take out Yellow Pages to write down your telephone number.

Reporter: You are still **relatively** young, and have been in this position for many years. There are a lot of CEOs the same age with you. They are **half-baked** in technology but still hold the dominated positions.

Jeff Bezos: Don't worry, CEOs are always like that.

Reporter: I think you also miss Steve (Steve Jobs), right?

Jeff Bezos: For any people who are willing to **concentrate** on listening, Steve is a mentor, but unfortunately he left too early.

Reporter: Do you think CEO is the most appropriate position?

Jeff Bezos: I think the answer to this question is open. For me, I am very fond of innovation, and now the Internet has gone far beyond the rate of change in 1995. I can't imagine a better period than the present stage of innovation. So, I wake up every morning excited.

persistent *adj.*
持久稳固的

eliminate *v.*
消除，排除

streaming *n.*
流

firmly *adv.*
坚定地，坚固地

adequate *adj.*
充足的，适当的

element *n.*
因素，元素

conduct *v.*
实施，管理

attempt *v.*
试图，尝试

contact *v.*
联系，接触

completely *adv.*
完全地，彻底地

relatively *adv.*
相对地，相当地

half-baked *adj.*
未完成的，不完整的

concentrate *v.*
集中；浓缩

杰夫·贝索斯：我们有一个错误就是坚持，这通常会增加成本。因为做成本昂贵的东西是不明智的，亚马逊很重视其错误和<u>缺点</u>[31]，并在寻找方法从<u>根本上</u>[32]铲除它们。

记者：视频流是亚马逊的主要服务之一。这是一个完全不同的服务，为什么不单独收费呢？

杰夫·贝索斯：要建立一家成功的公司有两个途径：一个是很艰难地<u>说服</u>[33]消费者为公司支付昂贵的利润，另一个是通过艰难的途径，允许顾客为公司支付较低的利润。他们都是成功的，但是我会坚定地站在后一个立场上。要做到这样是很难的，因为你必须要降低错误，保证充裕和<u>效率</u>[34]。我们的观点是，我们宁愿拥有巨大的顾客群和绵延不断的低收益，也不拥有较小的顾客群和更高的收益。

记者：目前，亚马逊融入了很多社会因素，那么您是怎么看待公司在社会领域的<u>定位</u>[35]的？

杰夫·贝索斯：这是一个很开放的问题。如果你有500多个客户使用列表，你会怎么做呢？对于这个问题，我们有一个想法，并进行了几次<u>实验</u>[36]，但是我们不怎么满意。

记者：两年前，亚马逊收购了捷步，我们可以理解为亚马逊在试图学习他们的<u>高质量</u>[37]消费者服务文化吗？

杰夫·贝索斯：没有，不是的。我们喜欢他们特有的文化，但是并没有把他们纳进亚马逊，因为我们也喜欢亚马逊的文化。我们最完美的<u>客户体验</u>[38]是用户不会和我们交流过多。只要有顾客和我们接触，我们会视其为错误。我已经说了很多年了，人们应该和朋友交流，而不是跟企业交流。我们会利用顾客信息找到顾客接触的原因，例如，什么出错了？为什么打电话给我们？他们为什么花时间和我们交流而不是和他们的家人交流呢？怎么解决这个问题？而捷步则采取完全不同的战略，你若是打电话向他们订购比萨，他们会拿出黄页来记下你的号码。

记者：您相对来说还很年轻，在首席执行官这个职位上已经做了很多年了，还有很多和您年龄一样的首席执行官，他们对技术不熟，却一直占据主导地位。

杰夫·贝索斯：别担心，首席执行官总是有的。

记者：我想您会思念史蒂夫·乔布斯的，是吗？

杰夫·贝索斯：对于愿意<u>专心</u>[39]倾听的人来说，史蒂夫是<u>良师益友</u>[40]，但不幸的是他离得太早了。

记者：您认为，首席执行官是最<u>合适</u>[41]长期任职的吗？

杰夫·贝索斯：我想这个问题的回答是很开放的。对于我，我是很喜欢创新的，现在因特网的变化速率已经远远超过了1995年，我不能想象还有比现在更适合创新的时期了，所以我每天早上醒来都很激动。

31. shortcoming *n.*
32. fundamentally *adv.*
33. convince *v.*
34. efficient *adj.*
35. positioning *v.*
36. experiment *n.*
37. high-quality
38. customer experience
39. concentrate *v.*
40. mentor *n.*
41. appropriate *adj.*

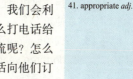

1. 普林斯顿大学（Princeton University），又译普林斯敦大学，位于美国新泽西州的普林斯顿，是美国一所著名的私立研究型大学，八所常春藤盟校之一。学校于1746年在新泽西州伊丽莎白镇创立，是美国殖民时期成立的第四所高等教育学院，当时名为"新泽西学院"，1747年迁至新泽西州，1756年迁至普林斯顿，并于1896年正式改名为"普林斯顿大学"。

2. 亚马逊公司（Amazon.com）是美国最大的一家网络电子商务公司，位于华盛顿州的西雅图，是网络上最早开始经营电子商务的公司之一，亚马逊成立于1995年，一开始只经营网络的书籍销售业务，现在则扩及到范围相当广的其他产品，包括DVD、音乐光碟、电脑、软件、电视游戏、电子产品、衣服、家具等等。

3. 词组keep a close watch on的意思是"密切注意"，例如：Please keep a close watch on the children while they are in the pool.（孩子们在游泳池里的时候，请你一定要好好看着他们。）

4. 平板电脑（Tablet Personal Computer，简称Tablet PC、Flat PC、Tablet、Slates），是一种小型、方便携带的个人电脑，以触摸屏作为基本的输入设备。它拥有的触摸屏（也称为数位板技术）允许用户通过触控笔或数字笔来进行作业而不是传统的键盘或鼠标。用户可以通过内建的手写识别、屏幕上的软键盘、语音识别或者一个真正的键盘来操作使用。

5. 词组set out可以表示"开始努力"的意思，例如：He has achieved what he set out to do three years ago.（他已经完成了3年前开始努力做的事情。）

6. 在倒装结构中，部分倒装有承上启下的作用，表示同意和赞同，例如：A: I couldn't do anything for her.（我帮不了她。）B: Nor you could, but you might have got somebody to help her.（你是不能帮她，但你本可以找人帮她的）。Nor you could就是部分倒装表示同意A说的话。

7. 词组might as well的意思是"不妨，倒不如"，例如：We might as well make hay while the sun shines. Let us finish the task before the boss comes back from his business trip.（我们不妨利用大好时机。让我们在老板出差回来前把任务完成。）

8. 介词whether可以引导宾语从句，例如：We are talking about whether we admit students into our club.（我们正在讨论是否让学生加入我们的俱乐部。）

9. 词组keep in mind的意思是"记住"，例如：The Ford Moter Company had close to half a million employees around the world and I had to keep in mind that I was only one of them.（福特汽车公司在全世界的雇员将近50万人，我必须记住我只是其中的一员。）

甲骨文公司首席执行官：
拉里·埃里森
CEO of Oracle: Larry Ellison

　　拉里·埃里森(Larry Ellision)，美国犹太人，俄罗斯移民，1944年出生于曼哈顿。他是世界上最大数据库软件公司Oracle（甲骨文）的老板，产品遍布全世界。埃里森在32岁以前还一事无成，读了三所大学，没得到一个学位文凭，换了十几家公司。1977年6月，埃里森与另外两个合伙人出资成立了软件开发研究公司，开始创业时他只有1200美元，却使得Oracle公司连续12年销售额每年翻一番，成为世界上第二大软件公司，他自己也成为硅谷首富。

　　埃里森被《财富》杂志列为世界上第五富的人，2004年《福布斯》杂志全球富豪排行榜显示，他的个人净资产为187亿美元，排名第12位。他拥有的Oracle公司是世界上最大的数据库软件公司，而且Oracle公司的客户大多是赫赫有名、名列财富500强的大型公司。

We Are Definitely Not Going to Exit the Hardware Business

轻松输入十分钟

Reporter: Why does Oracle, a company that prides itself on high margins, want to get into the low-margin hardware business? Are you going to exit the hardware business?

Ellison: No, we are definitely not going to exit the hardware business. While most hardware businesses are low-margin, companies like Apple and Cisco enjoy very high-margins because they do a good job of designing their hardware and software to work together. If a company designs both hardware and software, it can build much better systems than if they only design the software. That's why Apple's iPhone is so much better than Microsoft phones.

Reporter: OK, Apple and Cisco have proven that they can do it, but what experience does Oracle have in designing hardware and software to work together?

Ellison: Oracle started designing hardware and software to work together a few years ago when we began our Exadata database machine development project. Some of our competitors, Teradata and Netezza for example, were delivering preconfigured hardware/software systems, while we were just delivering software. The combination of hardware and software has significant performance advantages for data warehousing applications. We had to respond with our own hardware/software combination, the Exadata database machine. Oracle's Exadata database machine runs data warehousing applications much faster—at least ten-times faster than Oracle software running on conventional hardware. All the hardware and software pieces, database to disk, are included. You just plug it in and go—no systems integration required.

Reporter: Alright, Oracle's done integrated hardware and software design with the Exadata database machine. But Exadata uses standard Intel chips. Are you going to discontinue the SPARC chip?

Ellison: No. Once we own Sun we're going to increase the investment in SPARC.

definitely *adv.*
肯定地，明确地

hardware *n.*
硬件，五金器具

database *n.*
数据库，资料库

preconfigured *adj.*
预先购置的

significant *adj.*
重大的，有效的

warehousing *n.*
储仓，周转性短期贷款

conventional *adj.*
常见的，符合习俗的

plug *v.*
插入，塞住

integration *n.*
综合，集成

alright *adv.*
好吧

chip *n.*
芯片，筹码

我们绝对不会退出硬件业务

有效学习十分钟

记者： 甲骨文公司，一家以其高利润率[1]著称的公司，为什么想进入低利润的硬件行业[2]？您打算退出硬件业务吗？

埃里森：不，我们肯定不会退出[3]硬件业务。虽然大多数硬件企业是低利润的公司，但像苹果电脑和思科这样的公司都有非常高的利润，因为他们以良好的设计让硬件和软件协调运作。如果一家公司同时设计硬件和软件，它会比只设计软件的公司建立更好的系统。这就是为什么苹果的iPhone如此明显地优于微软手机的原因。

记者： 嗯，苹果和思科公司已经证明他们能做到这一点，但什么能让甲骨文硬件和软件配合运作？

埃里森：几年前，在我们开始Exadata数据库装置[4]开发项目[5]时，甲骨文就开始设计让硬件和软件一起工作。我们的一些竞争对手[6]，比如Teradata和Netezza公司，提供预配置的硬件或软件系统，而我们只是提供软件。在数据仓库应用[7]中，集成的硬件和软件有着显著的性能优势。作为回应，我们已推出自己的硬件/软件组合，即Exadata数据库装置。甲骨文Exadata数据库装置将更快地运行数据仓库应用程序，至少比甲骨文软件在常规硬件[8]中快10倍。所有的硬件和软件、数据库、光盘都包括在内。只需将其插入——无须系统集成[9]。

记者： 好吧，甲骨文做集成的硬件和软件设计与Exadata数据库装置。但是Exadata使用的是标准的英特尔芯片[10]。您要放弃SPARC芯片吗？

埃里森：不。一旦我们拥有了Sun,我们就会增加SPARC的投资[11]。我们认为自己的芯片设计是非常非常重要的。即便是苹果现在也在设计自己的芯片。现在，

1. high margin
2. hardware business
3. exit *v.*
4. database machine
5. development project
6. competitor *n.*
7. data warehousing
   application
8. conventional hardware
9. system integration
10. chip *n.*
11. investment *n.*

We think designing our own chips is very, very important. Even Apple is designing its own chips these days. Right now, SPARC chips do some things better than Intel chips and vice-versa. For example, SPARC is much more energy efficient than Intel while delivering the same performance on a per socket basis. This is not just a green issue, it's an economic issue. Today, database centers are paying as much for electricity to run their computers as they pay to buy their computers. SPARC machines are much less expensive to run than Intel machines.

Reporter: So is that your plan, to use SPARC to compete by lowering a data center's electricity bills?

Ellison: No, our primary reason for designing our own chips is to build computers with the very best performance, reliability and security available in the market. Some system features work much better if they are implemented in silicon rather than software. Once we own Sun, we'll be able to plan and synchronize new features from silicon to software, just like IBM and the other big system suppliers. We want to work with Fujitsu to design advanced features into the SPARC microprocessor aimed at improving Oracle database performance. In my opinion, this will enable SPARC Solaris open-system mainframes and servers to challenge IBM's dominance in the data center. Sun was very successful for a very long time selling computer systems based on the SPARC chip and the Solaris operating system. Now, with the added power of integrated Oracle software, we think they can be successful again.

Reporter: Your management team has no experience with delivering hardware. There is a lot of risk in going into an unfamiliar business.

Ellison: Obviously, we want to hold on to Sun's experienced team of first-rate hardware engineers. For years, Sun has led the industry in building and delivering innovative systems. For example, Sun was the first company to deliver systems built on a multicore processor—what Sun called the Niagara chip—and the industry followed. Oracle has a good track record of retaining the engineering talent from acquired companies; Sun will be no different. In addition, over the last couple of years Oracle gained a lot of experience developing and delivering our first integrated hardware and software system, the Exadata database machine. We have lots of hardware experience inside of Oracle. Hundreds of Oracle's engineers came from systems companies like IBM and HP. Even I started my Silicon Valley career working for a hardware company that worked with Fujitsu to design and build the first IBM compatible mainframe.

Reporter: OK, so you have engineers who are experienced at designing hardware as

---

performance *n.*
性能，表演

socket *n.*
插座，窝

reliability *n.*
可靠性

implement *v.*
实施，执行

synchronize *v.*
使同步，同时发生

microprocessor *n.*
微处理器

mainframe *n.*
主机，大型机

innovative *adj.*
创新的，革新的

multicore *adj.*
多芯的

retain *v.*
保持，留住

compatible *adj.*
兼容的，能共处的

SPARC芯片在某些方面优于英特尔芯片，反之亦然[12]。举例来说，SPARC比英特尔在每插槽提供相同的性能时有更高的能源效率[13]。这不仅是一个环保的问题，也是一个经济问题。今天，数据库中心[14]支付高额电力费用来运行自己的计算机，就像他们付费购买计算机一样。运行SPARC的机器比英特尔更便宜。

记者：   所以，您的计划是使用SPARC的竞争力来降低数据中心的电费？

埃里森： 不，我们自己设计芯片的首要原因是实现市场上的电脑最佳性能、可靠性[15]和安全性[16]。有些功能在硅[17]这个级别上执行比在软件上执行要好得多。一旦我们拥有了Sun，我们就可以进行从硅到软件的新功能的同步规划，就像IBM和其他大的系统供应商一样。我们希望与富士通合作，以先进的设计融入SPARC微处理器[18]，旨在改善甲骨文数据库的性能。在我看来，这将使SPARC的Solaris开放系统主机[19]和服务器[20]挑战IBM在数据中心的优势。Sun曾在很长一段时间内非常成功地销售基于SPARC芯片和Solaris的操作系统。现在，随着功率集成甲骨文软件的加入，我们认为它们会再次成功。

记者：   您的管理团队[21]没有任何硬件经验。进入不熟悉的业务会有很多风险的。

埃里森： 显然，我们要保留Sun公司经验丰富的一流硬件工程师团队。多年来，Sun公司在建设和提供创新系统方面引领业界。例如，

Sun公司是第一家提供多核处理器[22]系统的公司——Sun公司的Niagara芯片，后来这个业界都开始做。甲骨文公司有从收购的公司中留住工程技术人才[23]的良好记录；Sun公司也将会一样。此外，在过去的几年里，甲骨文得到了丰富的经验，开发并提供我们的第一个综合硬件和软件系统，Exadata数据库装置。甲骨文在公司内部也有硬件生产经验。甲骨文有数百名工程师，他们来自如IBM和惠普这样的系统公司。就连我自己刚开始工作的时候也是在硅谷的一家硬件公司，这家公司与富士通合作设计和建造了第一台IBM的兼容大型计算机[24]。

12. vice-versa
13. energy efficient
14. database center
15. reliability *n.*
16. security *n.*
17. silicon *n.*
18. microprocessor *n.*
19. open-system mainframe
20. server *n.*
21. management team
22. multicore processor
23. engineering talent
24. compatible mainframe

well as software, but Oracle outsourced the manufacturing of the Exadata machine to HP. You have no experience in manufacturing.

Ellison: Just because we're buying Sun does not mean Oracle is becoming a manufacturer. Sun outsources almost all of its manufacturing to companies like Flextronics and Fujitsu. With one tiny exception, Sun does no manufacturing; neither will we.

Reporter: There has been a lot of speculation in the press that Oracle is going to sell some or all of Sun's hardware businesses. From your previous answers it certainly seems like you are keeping the SPARC Solaris systems business. Are you keeping the disk storage and tape backup businesses?

Ellison: Yes, definitely. We believe the best user experience is when all the pieces in the system are engineered to work together. Disk storage and tape backup are critical components in high performance, high-reliability, high-security database systems. So, we plan to design and deliver those pieces too. Clearly many Sun customers choose disk and tape systems from other vendors. That's what open systems are all about: providing customers with a choice. But Oracle expects to continue competing in both the disk and tape storage businesses after we buy Sun.

Reporter: Is Exadata moving to Sun SPARC Solaris?

Ellison: Exadata is built by HP using Intel microprocessors. We have no plans for a SPARC Solaris version of Exadata. We have an excellent relationship with HP that we expect to continue. The Exadata database machine delivers record setting database performance at a lower cost than conventional hardware. Customers love the machine. It is the most successful product introduction in Oracle's 30 year history. The Sun acquisition doesn't reduce our commitment to Exadata at all.

Reporter: Looking back on your childhood, can you see the Larry Ellison of today taking root when you were young?

Ellison: I don't think my personality has changed much since I was five years old. The most important aspect of my personality, as far as determining my success goes, has been my questioning conventional wisdom, doubting the experts, and questioning authority. While that can be very painful in relationships with your parents and teachers, it's enormously useful in life.

outsource *v.*
外包，外部买办

speculation *n.*
投机，推测

tape backup
磁带备份

vendor *n.*
供应商

storage *n.*
存储

acquisition *n.*
收购

enormously *adv.*
巨大地，庞大地

记者：　好，您已经有了有经验的硬件以及软件设计工程师，但甲骨文将Exadata机的制造外包给了惠普。你们没有任何制造[25]经验。

埃里森：收购Sun并不意味着甲骨文正在成为制造商。Sun几乎外包其所有的制造业，比如外包给Flextronics公司和富士通。但有一个小小的例外，Sun公司没有任何制造的历史，我们也不会有。

记者：　很多媒体猜测，甲骨文公司将出售部分或全部的Sun公司的硬件业务。您先前的答案是肯定的，好像您是要保留SPARC Solaris系统业务。您是否会保留磁盘存储[26]和磁带备份[27]的业务？

埃里森：是的，绝对会。我们认为最好的用户体验是当所有的要素在系统里被设计来共同工作的时候。磁盘存储和磁带备份是数据库系统高性能[28]、高可靠性[29]、高安全性[30]的关键组件[31]。所以，我们计划设计和提供这些东西。显然，许多Sun的客户选择其他厂商的磁盘和磁带系统。这就是开放系统：为客户提供一种选择。但是，甲骨文公司收购Sun后，预计将继续同时竞争磁盘和磁带存储业务。

记者：　Exadata是否会被移到Sun公司的SPARC Solaris里呢？

埃里森：Exadata是由惠普在英特尔微处理器上构建的。我们没有SPARC Solaris版本的Exadata计划。我们和惠普有着良好的关系，并将继续下去。比起传统的硬件装置，Exadata数据库装置以更低的成本提供了创纪录的数据库性能。这是客户喜欢的机器，也是甲骨文公司30年历史中推出的最成功的产品。收购Sun不会减少我们对Exadata所有的承诺。

记者：　回顾您的童年，能在小拉里·埃里森身上看到现在的影子吗？

埃里森：5岁以后，我的性格基本没有变过。其中，对我成功最重要的方面是质疑传统智慧[32]、专家言论和权威[33]。尽管这在处理与老师和父母的关系时会带来很多令人痛苦的麻烦，对生活却有巨大的帮助。

25. manufacturing *n.*
26. disk storage
27. tape backup
28. high performance
29. high-reliability
30. high-security
31. critical component
32. conventional wisdom
33. authority *n.*

135

10 min 自由输出十分钟

1. 同位语从句属于名词性从句，大多由从属连词that引导，常常跟在fact, idea, opinion, news, hope, belief等名词后面。同位语从句一般用来解释或说明这些名词的具体含义或内容，在逻辑上表现为同位关系。例如：They are familiar with the opinion that all matter consists of atoms.（他们很熟悉这一观点，所有的物质都是由原子构成的。）

2. prove一词是"证明"的意思，但它不能用于被动语态中，例如：In fact, he has proven to be wrong.（事实证明，他是错的。）而不能说成是In fact, he has been proved to be wrong.

3. Oracle是殷墟出土的甲骨文（oracle bone inscriptions）的英文翻译的第一个单词，在英语里是"神谕"的意思。Oracle是世界领先的信息管理软件开发商，因其复杂的关系数据库产品而闻名。Oracle数据库产品被《财富》排行榜上的前1000家公司所采用，许多大型网站也选用了Oracle系统。

4. 公共场所的一些表示禁止性的标识语中，通常会用到no，例如：No Smoking.（禁止吸烟。）；No Parking.（禁止泊车。）等。这体现了标识语的简洁性。

5. "vice versa"是"反之亦然"的意思，例如：A husband may claim deduction for payments made by his wife, and vice versa.（丈夫可申诉扣除其妻子所缴付的款项，反之亦然。）

6. 表示"除了……"的词汇或词组有：in addition to，except，besides，either...or...等。

7. 词组take root意为"扎根"，例如："I wanted these works to take root in the soil and culture here," he said.（他说："我想要这些作品根植在这里的土地和文化中。"）

8. 表示"确定，肯定"的副词有：definitely，absolutely，certainly等。

9. 英语中有一些名词可以作为动词使用，例如：question，school等，分别意为"提问"，"受教育"。

11.2 Most Achievers Are Driven Not By the Pursuit of Success, But By the Fear of Failure

大多数成功者的动力不是对成功的追求，而是对失败的恐惧

轻松输入十分钟

有效学习十分钟

Reporter: How did you become involved with relational database programming?

Ellison: Relational database technology was invented by a guy by the name of Ted Codd at IBM. It's based on relational algebra and relational calculus. It is a very mathematically rigorous form of data management that we can prove mathematically to be functionally complete. This work was done in the early seventies by an IBM fellow by the name of Ted Codd. He published his papers, and really, based on those publications, Oracle decided to see if we (we were four guys) couldn't beat IBM to market with this technology, based on the published IBM research papers.

记者： 您是如何开始与关系数据库[1]设计工作扯上关系的？

埃里森： 关系数据库是由IBM的泰德·阔德发明的。它建立在关系代数[2]和关系微积分[3]的基础之上，是一个非常缜密的数据管理[4]程序，我们可以把数学上的东西最终以功能的形式[5]实现。这项工作是IBM的泰德·阔德在上世纪70年代完成的。他发表了自己的论文。而正是因为这些论文的出版，甲骨文决定看看我们（4个人）是否能根据IBM发表的研究论文，在这项技术上

relational *adj.* 有关系的，亲属的

algebra *n.* 代数学

calculus *n.* 微积分学

rigorous *adj.* 严密的，严格的

mathematically *adv.* 数学上地，算术地

1. relational database   2. relational algebra
3. relational calculus   4. data management
5. functionally *adv.*

137

And in fact we did.

Reporter: What is the biggest obstacle you've ever had to face in your professional life? Was there a time that you thought you actually might fail?

Ellison: There were lots of times, especially in the early days, that were very, very difficult. I think the most difficult experience I had was in 1990 when Oracle had its only loss quarter in history. We've been in business for 20 years, and after 20 years we lost money one quarter. We had a very difficult time. We had virtually doubled our sales every year for ten years. Nine out of ten years, ten out of eleven years. It was really quite an amazing run. We were the fastest growing company in history, and still are the fasting growing company in history over a long period of time. Suddenly we hit a wall. We reached a billion dollars in revenue, and we were having senior management problems all over the place. The people who were running the company, the billion dollar company, were the same people that had run the company when we were a 15 million dollar company, one twentieth the size. I had an incredible sense of loyalty to those people who had worked with me to build Oracle. It was a very painful realization in 1990 that I was going to have to change the management team. The company had outgrown the management. People who are good at running a 15 million dollar company don't use the same skills. They're just different, not one is better or worse, just an entirely different skill set in running a 15 million dollar company than a billion dollar company. Both skill sets are rare and precious. But we needed a different group of managers, and virtually the entire management team had to be replaced. That means I had to ask people who I had worked with for a decade to leave. I had to fire people. That was the most difficult thing I had to do in business, asking a bunch of people to leave Oracle.

Reporter: What kept you going through that time?

Ellison: That I had no choice. I had to ask them to leave Oracle, or everyone had to leave Oracle, because there wouldn't be any Oracle left. In that sense, it was a simple choice. Thousands of people worked for Oracle. They deserved the best leadership you could find. My primary responsibility was to the company and to all of the staff, all of our shareholders, and all of our customers. Therefore, I had to choose. And if I couldn't make that decision, then I had to go.

Reporter: Have you ever been deeply afraid?

Ellison: Deeply afraid? Yes, only once. The most deeply afraid I can ever remember being was once my mother came —I might have been six—and I went to school, and my mother came home very late from work. It was six o'clock,

obstacle n.
障碍，干扰

virtually adv.
事实上，几乎

revenue n.
收入，税收

outgrow v.
长大（或发展）得
使……不再适用，
出生

precious adj.
珍贵的，宝贵的

deserve v.
值得，应得

shareholder n.
股东，股票持有人

打败IBM。事实证明，我们做到了。

记者： 您职业生涯中曾遇到过的最大障碍[6]是什么？你有觉得自己会失败的时候吗？

埃里森： 有很多这样的时候，尤其是刚开始的时候，我们创业很艰难。我认为最困难的时候是1990年甲骨文经历历史上惟一一个亏损季度[7]的时候。我们的生意经营了20年，20年后我们有一个季度亏损了。那是一段艰难的时期。10年间我们每年的营业收入一直是翻倍的。其中10年中有9年，11年中有10年。这样的运营成果真的是令人吃惊。我们是历史上增长速度最快的企业，也是很长一段时间内增长最快的企业。突然之间，我们遇到了障碍。我们的收益达到了10亿，而且我们遇到了各方面的高级管理[8]问题。经营这家10亿美元公司的依然是当初经营那家1500万美元公司的那些人，仅是现在规模的1/20。对于与我一起创立甲骨文的那些人，我有一种令人难以置信的忠诚感[9]。1990年残酷的现实令人悲痛，我必须要调整管理团队[10]。目前的团队已无法很好的管理公司了。擅长经营1500万美金的公司的人不用相同的技巧。只是不同而已，没有哪个更好或哪个更差的说法，只是这两家公司需要不同的管理技巧而已。两种技巧都弥足珍贵。但我们需要一套不一样的管理技巧，事实上，我们需要替换整个管理团队。这就意味着我要让那些跟我一起工作了10年的人离开公司。我必须辞掉他们。这是让我最难做的事情，我要让他们离开甲骨文。

记者： 是什么让您坚持了下来？

埃里森： 我别无选择。我必须让他们离开甲骨文，不然的话所有人都得离开甲骨文，因为那样的话甲骨文也就倒闭了。这样来看，这是一个简单的选择。上千个人为甲骨文工作，他们有权享有最好的领导。我最重要的责任就是对公司和全体员工负责、对所有股东[11]负责和对所有客户[12]负责。因此，我必须要做出选择。如果我不能，我就要离职。

记者： 您有过害怕至极的时候吗？

埃里森： 害怕至极？有，仅有过一次。我最害怕的是一次我妈妈回来的时候——那时我大概6岁，我去上学，我妈妈很晚才下班回家。那时是6点钟，没有人在家。我很担心妈妈会不回来了，很害怕。那是我能够记起来的惟一的一次

6. obstacle *n.*

7. loss quarter

8. senior management

9. sense of loyalty

10. management team

11. shareholder *n.*

12. customer *n.*

so no one was home. I was very worried that my mother wouldn't come home, and I was deeply afraid. That's the only time I can remember being deeply afraid. I was also making deals with God, if he would return her to me.

Reporter: With all of the risk that you take in your professional and your personal life, how do you deal with the fear factor?

Ellison: There's a mild degree of fear; a sociobiologist would tell you that fear is the prevalent human emotion. I certainly feel a little stress, if I just bought a jet fighter and I'm flying it for the very first time, and doing aerobatics very low to the ground. I wouldn't call it fear, but it's a little bit of a rush. That gets the adrenaline going, and I thrive on it. I don't really call that fear. That's a somewhat pleasant experience for me. Extreme fear is awful, but out-on-the-edge a little bit, where you have a mild sensation of apprehension and concern, is something I actually enjoy.

Reporter: You had so many questions about your parents' values, do you think that independence you had as a child had something to do with developing your self-confidence?

Ellison: No doubt. We're constantly testing ourselves. We're trying to understand our own level of competency; our ability to control our own world; our ability to put ourselves at risk, and then save our own lives. There's always an element of risk. You're risking your ego when you play in a chess match; you're risking your ego, and sometimes your life, when you're doing certain kinds of flying. But I really don't do things that endanger my life when I fly. We were in a very nasty boat race, from Sidney to Hobart, where we were in a storm for 14 hours. But I really never felt like I was going to die. Sometimes I felt like I wanted to die, because literally everyone on board got pretty sick. They're all professional sailors. It was a horrible storm; we had a lot professional sailors who were puking. But I never really felt the same kind of deep fear that I felt as a child.

Reporter: What about fear of failure?

Ellison: Oh, absolutely. I think most great achievers are driven, not so much by the pursuit of success, but by the fear of failure. Unless failure gets very close, that fear doesn't reach profound levels, but it drives us. It drives me to work very hard. It drives me to make sure that my life is very orderly, that I'm in control of my company, or in control of the airplane or boat or what-have-you, so that I'm not at risk of failure. Whenever I feel even remotely close to being at risk of failure, I can't stop working.

Reporter: Your showmanship and your public image are attributes that have received a lot of comment, both negative and positive. How do you deal with

sociobiologist n.
社会生物学家

prevalent adj.
普遍的，流行的

aerobatics n.
特技飞行，航空表演

adrenaline n.
肾上腺素

apprehension n.
恐惧

competency n.
能力，资格

nasty adj.
险恶的，肮脏的

horrible adj.
可怕的，极讨厌的

puke v.
呕吐

profound adj.
深厚的，意义深远的

remotely adv.
遥远地，偏僻地

令我恐惧的事情。我还祈祷上帝[13]送她回到我身边。

记者：　当您生活中或工作中遇到风险时，您是如何处理恐惧因素[14]的？

埃里森：有一种很轻微的恐惧，一位社会生物学家[15]会告诉你恐惧是人类普遍的情感。如果我刚买了一架喷气式飞机[16]并且第一次驾驶，做离地很近的飞行活动，我当然会感觉到一些压力。我认为这不是恐惧，倒是有一点匆忙。这会刺激肾上腺素[17]分泌，我喜欢。我不认为这是真正意义上的恐惧感。在某种程度上，这对我来说是愉快的经历。极度恐惧太可怕了，但是我还是很喜欢有一点恐惧[18]和焦虑的感觉的。

记者：　您对于您你母的价值观[19]有很多疑问。您认为童年的独立对您成长过程中自信心的建立有帮助吗？

埃里森：毫无疑问。我们在不断地检验自己。我们努力了解自己的能力[20]，掌控自己的世界的能力，挑战并战胜风险的能力。随时都有风险因素存在。你下象棋的时候是在挑战自我[21]，你飞行的时候也是在挑战自我，有时甚至是在挑战生命。但我飞行的时候从不做危害自己生命的事情。我们曾经历一场令人生厌的[22]赛船，从悉尼到霍巴特，我们要经历14个小时的暴风雨。但我真的从未认为我们要死了。有时我觉得我好像要死了，因为确实甲板上的每个人都非常虚弱。他们都是专业的水手[23]。那场暴风雨很可怕；很多专业水手都吐了。但是我从没有感觉到像童年时那样深的恐惧感。

记者：　对失败的恐惧呢？

埃里森：哦，绝对。我认为最成功的人，他们成功的动力不是对成功的追求[24]，而是对失败的恐惧。失败离得很近的时候才会产生强烈的恐惧感，但是它一直在驱动着我们。它让我很努力地工作。让我确定我的生活很有规律[25]，让我很好地掌管着自己的公司，掌管着自己的飞机或者轮船，或者其他属于我的东西。因此，我并没有失败的风险。无论何时，只要轮我远远地感觉到了失败的危险，我就不停地工作。

记者：　您的表现力和公众形象受到了很多不同的评论，有正面的[26]也有负面的[27]。您怎样对待这些批评？包括工作和个人生活。

埃里森：这个世界上有很多人总是想要标准答案[28]。他们想让每个人都有一样的发型，每个人都以同样的方式做生意，每个人都穿成一样，每个人都去同一座教堂。如果你不这么做，他们就

13. make deal with God
14. fear factor
15. sociobiologist
16. jet fighter
17. adrenaline *n.*
18. apprehension *n.*
19. value *n.*
20. competency *n.*
21. ego *n.*
22. nasty *adj.*
23. sailor *n.*
24. pursuit *v.*
25. orderly *adj.*
26. positive *adj.*
27. negative *adj.*
28. standard answer

critics, both professionally and personally?

Ellison: There are an enormous number of people in the world who really want standard answers. They want everyone to wear their hair the same way, everyone to conduct business the same way, everyone to dress the same way, everyone to go to the same church. And if you wander out of these norms, people are highly critical, because this is threatening to them. They're living their life one way, and they believe that's the proper way to live their life. If you live your life a different way, and you answer questions differently, that makes them feel very uncomfortable. They say, "Well, this person's different from what I am." Then they seem to go a little further, and they say, "This person's different and wrong, and I'm different and right." So people have been very, very critical, and will be critical of you if you do things a little bit differently. It takes a certain amount of strength not to succumb to fashion.

Reporter: How do you persevere through it?

Ellison: I try to think things through. I try to always ask two questions about my personal policies in life. Are they fair, are they morally correct? And do they work? I try to reason things back to first principles. I try to think about things, and come to conclusions and make my own decisions. If anyone has a logical criticism and can explain to me why what I'm doing is wrong, and they can convince me, I'll change. If they have good reasons, I'll just alter my behavior. I love it when people point out when I'm wrong, and explain to me why I 'm wrong. That' s great. I don't want to be wrong. I would love to be right. If I am wrong, I love it when people stop me. But sometimes people just throw labels at you and throw criticisms around that are not rational, and they call your names. You can't change behavior that you think is right, just because someone is calling your names, and it's not the conventional way of behavior.

Reporter: Does it make you feel defensive, or do you just let it go?

Ellison: It depends on what they say. Most of the time I let it go. Sometimes people say things that are so hurtful and so offensive—or say things that are just patently untrue—that I feel like I have to defend myself. If someone says something that is factually an error, then I'll defend myself. If it's just calling me a random name, then I forget it.

Reporter: How important do you think academic success is to one's career?

Ellison: Generally, for most people it's important. I think academic success is an advantage, but it by no means assures success in business. If you're an outstanding student you'll probably be reasonably successful in business, but you might not be among the most successful in business, or even in science.

enormous *adj.*
巨大的，庞大的

norm *n.*
规范，基准

uncomfortable *adj.*
不舒服的，不安的

succumb *v.*
屈服，被压垮

morally *adv.*
有道德地，确定地

conclusion *n.*
结论，总结

rational *adj.*
合理的，理性的

defensive *adj.*
防卫的，防御用的

offensive *adj.*
无礼的，冒犯的

factually *adv.*
确实地

random *adj.*
任意的，胡乱的

academic *adj.*
学术的，理论的

assure *v.*
确保，保证

会批评你，因为这威胁到了他们。他们用一种方式生活，他们深信那就是最适合他们的生活方式。如果你过着一种不同的生活，然后你从不同的角度回答了问题，会让他们觉得不舒服。他们说，"这个人和我不一样。"然后他们会更进一步地说，"这个人是不一样的，是错的；而我是不一样的，是对的。"所以，如果你有什么不一样的行为，人们就会批评你是错的。不屈服于[29]世俗需要很大的力量。

记者：　您是如何坚持[30]的？

埃里森：我试着把问题想明白。我经常问自己两个关于人生个人政策的问题。这样公平吗？道德上对吗？有效吗？我试着回到第一原则上想问题。我尝试着通过思考得出结论并做出自己的决定。如果有任何人的批评是有逻辑的[31]并且可以解释我正在做的为什么是错的，那他们就能说服[32]我，那么我会做出改变。如果他们有好的理由，我就会改变自己的行为。我喜欢人们指出我的错误并向我解释我为什么错了。这很好。我不想做错。我喜欢做正确的事。我喜欢大家在我做错的时候及时阻止我。但是有时候，人们只是向你投来批评和不理性的指责、谩骂。你不可能仅仅因为有人在骂你，或者因为这并不是约定俗成的[33]做事方式就改变自己认为是正确的行为。

记者：　您会为自己辩护[34]吗？还是只是对这些置之不理？

埃里森：这要看他们说什么了。大多数时候我都会不予理睬。有时人们说的话很伤人，有攻击性或者公然地说假话，我感觉这时我得为自己辩护。如果某人说的话事实上是错误的，我会辩护。如果只是随便说说我的坏话的话就算了。

记者：　您觉得对一个人的职业生涯来说，学术上的[35]成功有多重要？

埃里森：对于大多数人来说，学术成功是重要的。我认为学术成功是一种优势，但这并不能保证在生意上的成功。如果你是一名出色的学生，按道理来讲，你可能是一位好的商人，但你可能不是最成功的商人之一，或者甚至在科学领域也不是。

29. succumb to
30. persevere v.
31. logical adj.
32. convince v.
33. conventional adj.
34. defensive adj.
35. academic adj.

自由输出十分钟

1. 虚拟语气用来表示说话人的主观愿望或假想，而不表示客观存在的事实，所说的是一个条件，不一定是事实，或与事实相反。表示与现在事实相反的应该是"主语+should/would/could/might + do"，例如：If I knew his telephone number, I would tell you.（如果我知道他的电话号码，我就会告诉你。）而事实上是他并不知道。

2. 只能修饰不可数名词的表示数量的词组有：much，a deal of，a bit of，an amount of，amounts of等。

3. 词组be in business意为"经商，做生意"，例如：No one I talk to can remember a tougher time to be in business.（与我交谈的人都认为，眼下是经商最困难的时期。）

4. 注意"几分之几"的写法，例如："十分之三"应写为three out of ten。

5. 词组trace back to意为"追溯到……"的意思，例如：His family can trace its history back to the Qing Dynasty.（他的家族史可追溯到清朝。）

6. 前缀socio–表示"社会的，社会方面的"，可与其他单词组成合成词，例如：sociolinguistics（社会语言学）；socioeconomic（社会经济学的）等。

7. 词组at risk意为"担风险"的意思，例如：It isn't clear how much of that debt is at risk of going bad.（这些债务中有多少可能会变为坏账还不得而知。）

8. 表示"必须"意思的情态动词must与have to的区别是：have to表示"不得不……"，有一种别无选择的意味，而must则没有这一层意思。

9. 词组by no means意为"决不……"，例如：However, these notations were by no means a standard.（然而，这些记号绝不是一种标准。）

12

易趣创始人之一：
皮埃尔·奥米迪亚
Co-founder of EBay:
Pierre Omidyar

皮埃尔·奥米迪亚，1967年出生于巴黎，父母都是留学法国的伊朗人。1988年，奥米迪亚从塔夫特大学计算机系毕业，先后进入硅谷最有名的几家公司工作。他建立了自己的几家网站，其中的eSHOP被微软公司收购。

1995年，奥米迪亚萌发出了网上拍卖的念头，28岁的他写下了eBay的源代码，而后以自己工作的咨询公司Echo Bay为这一网络拍卖系统命名，但未能申请下echobay域名，于是改名为eBay。他是全球电子商务领头羊eBay公司的创始人，用网络拍卖引发了电子商务的变革。eBay让奥米迪亚成了亿万富翁，但是比这更加重要的是，它使得无数创业者通过在eBay的网上销售成就了自己的事业。目前，奥米迪亚在为推动社会变革的组织和企业积极投资。

12.1 Omidyar Was Interested In Gadgets

轻松输入十分钟

Reporter: Where did you grow up, and what you were like as a kid?

Omidyar: I was born in Paris, France. I lived there until I was six years old actually, and I went to bilingual school as I was growing up during that period so I learned English. And at age six moved to the United States, moved to the east coast of the US, Washington, D.C. area, and grew up in the D.C. area actually through high school. I had a brief stint actually in Hawaii in junior high school, eighth and ninth grades. Then back to the Washington, D.C. area, college in Boston and then after college moved to California. The longest I was in one place was in college, four years. Before that it was the last three years of high school. Before that we were moving every two to three years. I wasn't part of a military family, which is usually the cause of that. It just kind of happened.

Reporter: How did that affect you? All that moving around when you were growing up?

Omidyar: I didn't really realize until we moved after ninth grade—which was my last year in Hawaii—that I had missed people. In eighth and ninth grade, I had finally started to make some close friends in school, and leaving after ninth grade was kind of tough. It was tough for me personally. Before that it was just what I knew. It was the way I was raised and it was fine. There weren't a lot of kids around, and when I was younger I ended up hanging out with adults a lot more, because I had to. In retrospect, I may have been cheated a little bit on the childhood side. I kind of grew up very quickly and became a little more mature more quickly than I see some of my relatives these days.

Reporter: How would you describe yourself as a kid?

Omidyar: I was actually interested in gadgets, little electronic gadgets. Whether it was calculators—actually I remember early on going out shopping for a calculator—and this was when calculators were like $100, you know, I mean—and with my dad, I think. And so I was always fascinated by these little gadgets and I always managed to break them for one reason or another, of course, as kids do, and then I would take them apart and try to fix them, which I was never able to.

Reporter: Do you recall early influences in your life? Who was important to you?

Omidyar: I think it's both my mom and my dad. They were separated when I was two, I think, but my dad was always part of my life. I lived with my mom,

bilingual *adj.*
双语的

military *adj.*
军人的，军事的

tough *adj.*
难过的，艰难的

personally *adv.*
就自己而言，亲自地

retrospect *n.*
回顾，追溯

mature *adj.*
成熟的，充分考虑的

gadget *n.*
小玩意，小器械

calculator *n.*
计算器，计算者

fascinate *v.*
着迷，入迷

recall *v.*
回想起，记起

奥米迪亚对小器械很感兴趣

有效学习十分钟

记者：　您在哪儿长大的？您小的时候是什么样子的？

奥米迪亚：我出生在法国巴黎。我6岁之前一直住在那里，到了上学的年纪我上了双语学校[1]，所以我也会说英语。6岁的时候我搬到了美国的东海岸，华盛顿特区。在那里一直生活到高中阶段。我有很短的一段时间是在夏威夷，是在初中八九年级的时候。然后又回到了华盛顿特区，在波士顿上大学，毕业之后又去了加利福尼亚。我在一个地方待得最长的时间是上大学的时候，待了4年。那之前是高中的3年。那之前我们每两三年就换一个地方。我不是军队家庭[2]，军队家庭才经常搬迁。只是我们也是那样而已。

记者：　这对您有什么影响？在您成长的过程中一直在搬家[3]？

奥米迪亚：在我9年级搬家那次之前，我并没有意识到这个问题——那是我在夏威夷的最后一年，我想念[4]一些人。八年级和九年级的时候，我开始在学校里结交了一些非常好的朋友，上完九年级离开的时候很难过。对我个人而言是很难过的[5]。在那之前我已经习惯了经常搬家的生活，我就是这样被带大[6]的，并且茁壮成长。我周围并没有很多小朋友，在我很小的时候我就跟大人打交道[7]了，因为我别无选择。回顾一下[8]，我觉得自己的童年可能或多或少地被欺骗了。我似乎很快就长大了，而且比我现在看到的一些孩子还要更快地走向成熟[9]。

记者：　您怎样来描述自己小时候的样子？

奥米迪亚：实际上，我对小器械很感兴趣，小的电子器械[10]。不管是不是计算器[11]——事实上，我还记得小时候去买过计算器，那个时候计算器差不多要卖100美元，我记得是跟我爸爸一起去的。所以，我总是被这些小器械吸引，而且我经常会出于各种各样的原因把它们拆掉。当然，就像其他小孩子一样。我会把它们拆开[12]，然后试图修好它们，但是我从来都没有成功过。

记者：　回想[13]一下，什么对您的生活有影响[14]？谁是对您来说最重要的人？

奥米迪亚：我想应该是我的父母。在我两岁的时候，他们就离婚[15]了。但是我觉得，爸爸永远是我生活的一部分。我跟妈妈一起住，但是爸爸经常在身边。我记

1. bilingual school
2. military family
3. move around
4. miss v.
5. tough adj.
6. be raised
7. hang out with
8. in retrospect
9. maturity n.
10. electronic gadget
11. calculator n.
12. take apart
13. recall v.
14. influence n.
15. be separated

147

but my dad was always around. I remember when I was younger spending weekends with my dad, who is a surgeon and medical doctor, doing rounds with him. We would spend maybe 45 minutes in the car going from one hospital to the next and we'd have some great conversations. That's one of my fond childhood memories.

Reporter: What did you talk about?

Omidyar: My dad still does have a fascinating kind of grasp of all things, and we'd talk about history and art. When I say conversation, that's not quite accurate. It was mostly one way. Now that I'm older—I'm 33 now—I think if I was in his shoes I'd think, "This kid isn't hearing anything I'm saying," from my reaction. It's funny now that I look back on it, it was a precious time for me.

Reporter: Were you a good student?

Omidyar: I was one of these guys that didn't really study, so I don't think I was a good student. I am very proud to say that I graduated from Tufts University with better than a 3.0 average. It was actually 3.01. During my entire four years there at Tufts my GPA improved every single semester, which gives you an idea of where I started. No, I was not a good student.

Reporter: Were there any subjects you were particularly interested in? Any books that influenced or were important to you?

Omidyar: I've been asked before, "Who are your heroes?" and these types of questions. I always find it hard to identify a single person or a single book or this sort of thing. I've always been forward looking. I was raised with the notion that you can do pretty much anything you want. You're able to accomplish anything you set out to accomplish. I was given a sense of confidence and I never really felt the need to—or I've never had the benefit, I should probably say—of being inspired by outside heroes.

Reporter: But early on you were interested in gadgets, including computers. How did this manifest itself?

Omidyar: I've always been into the gadgets and I guess when I first saw a computer—I'm trying to think if it was third—it might have been third grade. It was pretty early on actually and it was an early TRS-80, you know, Radio Shack. Kind of the original Radio Shack TRS-80 computer, 4K of memory. I think this one had the 4K or the 8K expansion module, which was like as big as a desk, you know, and learned how to program Basic on it. And I used to actually cut gym and sneak into the computer room—which wasn't really a room, it was a closet where they kept the computer between classes— and played on the computer.

Reporter: Did you pass gym?

Omidyar: Good question. I don't know if I failed gym or not. I don't think I failed.

Reporter: It sounds like even then you were kind of entrepreneurial.

Omidyar: I always kind of just went ahead and tried things and one of the things I learned later—you know, more kind of professionally—is that a lot of people don't just go ahead and try things. They'll have an idea and they'll say— they'll convince themselves or other people will convince them that it can't be done. You know, one or the other. Actually I think that the first is even more

---

surgeon *n.*
外科医生

conversation *n.*
交谈，会话

grasp *n.*
掌握，抓住

accurate *adj.*
精确的

semester *n.*
学期，半年

identify *v.*
鉴定，确定

accomplish *v.*
完成，实现

inspire *v.*
启发，激发

manifest *v.*
显示，表明

module *n.*
模块，组件

sneak *v.*
溜，偷偷做

closet *n.*
壁橱，密室

entrepreneurial *adj.*
企业家的，创业者的

professionally *adv.*
专业地，内行地

得我小的时候跟爸爸一起过周末，他是一位外科医生[16]，也是一名医学博士[17]，我一直跟着他。我们经常开车45分钟从一所医院到另一所，我们有过很多很美好的对话[18]。这是我很喜欢的童年回忆[19]之一。

记者：　你们都谈些什么？

奥米迪亚：我爸爸对事物有很好的掌控[20]能力，我们经常谈关于历史和艺术的话题。说是"谈话"，其实不是特别准确。因为基本就只是单方面地说。现在我长大了——33岁了，我想我理解他了，他对我的反应就是"这孩子根本没听我说话。"现在回顾[21]的时候觉得很有意思，这对我来说是一段珍贵的[22]回忆。

记者：　您是一名好学生吗？

奥米迪亚：我是那种基本不学习的学生，所以我并不认为自己是一名好学生。我很骄傲自己从托弗斯大学毕业，而自己的成绩要高于平均分3.0，确切地说是3.01。在我四年大学生活中，我的平均分数[23]每个学期[24]都有提高，这样你就可以看出我的起点了。不，我不是好学生。

记者：　您对哪个科目特别感兴趣[25]呢？有没有什么书给您带来很大的影响或者对您来说很重要？

奥米迪亚：以前有人问过我："谁是你心目中的英雄？"以及很多类似的问题。我总是觉得很难找出一个人或者一本书或者这类的东西。我一直在寻找。从小到大我都被灌输这样的理念[26]，你可以做很多你想做的事情。你可以完成你给自己设定的任何任务。我的自信心[27]被培养起来，我从没觉得自己需要一个外界的英雄来激励[28]自己——或者我应该说，我从来没有这样的经历。

记者：　但是之前您对小电器感兴趣，包括电脑。您对这怎么解释？

奥米迪亚：我一直研究小器械，我回想我第一次看到计算机的时候——我想是不是在三年级，可能是在我三年级。那是很早的时候，是早期的TRS-80，你知道吧，Radio Shack。就是类似于原始的Radio ShackTRS-80计算机。它的内存[29]是4K，它有一个4K到8K的扩展模式[30]，像一个桌子一样大，我用它学习如何编程[31]。我在体育课的时候逃课偷偷溜进电脑房——实际上并不是一个房间，就是两个班之间像一个小壁橱[32]一样的地方，用来放电脑——我在那里玩电脑。

记者：　那您体育[33]考试通过了吗？

奥米迪亚：好问题。我也不知道我的体育成绩是否及格了。我想应该及格了。

记者：　听起来，那个时候您就很有企业家的[34]气质了。

奥米迪亚：我经常会提前做一些事情，提前尝试我之

16. surgeon *n.*
17. medical doctor
18. great conversation
19. childhood memory
20. grasp
21. look back on
22. precious *adj.*
23. GPA (Grade Point Average)
24. semester *n.*
25. be interested in
26. notion *n.*
27. a sense of confidence
28. inspire *v.*
29. memory *n.*
30. expansion module
31. program *v.*
32. closet *n.*
33. gym *n.*
34. entrepreneurial *adj.*

dangerous and more serious. It's convincing yourself that it can't be done. And I never learned that for some reason, so I just kind of had this naive approach to—well, gee, you know, why not? I'll just go ahead and do it.

Reporter: We've read that early in high school that you wrote a program to print catalogue cards at six bucks an hour. Was that your start?

Omidyar: That was my professional debut. Six bucks an hour. And it's funny too, thinking about it, because it was using computer technology to print out library cards for the card catalogue. And so all it was, was a program to just format. You know, somebody would type in the information and it would format it the way the librarian wanted, so they could put the cards into the card catalogue. So this is incredibly basic computer technology. This is no database there. No search engine, nothing like that. But yeah, six dollars an hour. And also, at that time I also worked on the software to help schedule classes, which was key. This was in high school at tenth or 11th grade, I think, when I was working on that, and I resisted the temptation to put in some code there to make sure I never had classes on Friday, because I wouldn't have been able to get away with it, but I thought about it.

Reporter: Was there ever any doubt in your mind that computer science was what you wanted to do?

Omidyar: I always wanted to be involved with computers. My original kind of career choice, what I thought I was going to do was more computer engineering, which was, I thought—you know, figure out the hardware and the software and combine the two to learn about computers. When I got to college at Tufts I was accepted into the engineering school to do an electrical engineering and computer engineering program. I learned quickly there in my first semester—actually my second—well, I learned very quickly that the engineering program was a little bit too rigorous for me, and I took a class. I took a chemistry class, and I think that was the second semester of freshman year, because it was required for the engineering program, taking chemistry. I had no interest in chemistry. And I had worked—I worked so hard for that class trying to understand what was going on and study for the test and everything, and did so poorly. I remember for the mid-term I had studied harder than I had for anything else and got 25 out of 100 on the test. And it was at that point I said, "You know what, this is kind of ridiculous." So I transferred out of the engineering college and went to liberal arts and just did the pure computer science.

Reporter: What else do you recall from college in terms of influences and life changing experiences or ideas?

Omidyar: When I was in college I taught myself how to program the Macintosh. A big foundation actually for that was a class. It was actually—so it wasn't completely self-taught—it was a C programming class called "Data Structures". It was the big kind of the "weed-out" class for the computer science program. I learned how to program C. A great, great professor. Probably one of the best I've ever had, and a couple of things stem from that story.

---

naive *adj.*
天真的，幼稚的

debut *n.*
初次登台，开张

buck *n.*
（美）钱，元

format *v.*
格式化，设计版式

database *n.*
数据库，资料库

temptation *n.*
引诱，诱惑物

rigorous *adj.*
严格的，严密的

freshman *n.*
新手，生手

ridiculous *adj.*
荒谬的，可笑的

foundation *n.*
根据，基础

completely *adv.*
完全地，彻底地

后会学到的东西——你知道，有点更专业性，很多人并不会提前去做一些尝试。他们会有一个想法，会说——他们会被自己或者他人说服，认为这是不可能实现的。你知道，不是这个就是那个。事实上，我认为前者更危险、更严重。就是你说服自己你的想法是行不通的。由于某些原因，我并没有这样的概念，所以，我就是用这样有点幼稚的方法——嗯，你知道，为什么不呢。我会尝试去做一下。

记者：　您早期在高中的时候写过印刷目录卡片的程序，每个小时6美元。那是您事业的开始吗？

奥米迪亚：那是我的专业技能的处女作[35]。每个小时6美元。想起来也很有趣。因为那是用电脑技术去给卡片目录印刷图书卡片，就是排版程序而已。你知道，有些人输入一些数据，就会像图书管理人员希望的那样排版，这样他们就可以把这些卡片放入卡片目录了。所以这是令人难以置信的基础电脑技术。没有数据库，没有搜索引擎[36]，没有任何类似的东西。但是，是的，每个小时6美元。同时，那时我还用软件帮忙做课程表，这很关键。那时我是高中10年级或是11年级，正在编课程表。我经受住了诱惑，没有通过一些编码的操作来保证自己星期五的时候不用上课，我不能那样做，但我那样想过。

记者：　您对自己想要从事计算机科学这个行业有过任何怀疑吗？

奥米迪亚：我一直想跟计算机打交道。从我最初的职业规划[37]来看，我认为我更有可能成为一名电脑工程师，我认为，你知道，把软件和硬件结合在一起，弄明白计算机。在托弗斯大学上学的时候我曾被选去工程学院，做一个电机工程和一个计算机工程程序。第一个学期我学得很快——事实上是我的第二个学期，嗯，我很快明白了工程程序对我来说有一点过于缜密了，我参加了一个课程。我参加了一个化学课，我认为那是对于新生来说的第二个学期，因为工程程序要求掌握化学课的内容。我对化学一点都不感兴趣。那门课我很用功，努力理解到底是怎么一回事，努力学习通过考试，但是结果学得并不怎么样。我记得期中考试的时候，我从来没有那么认真过，只得了25分，100分满分。所以那时我说："你知道的，这也太可笑了。"所以我就离开了工程学院，开始学习自由艺术，只做计算机科学。

记者：　您大学时代的回忆中，还有什么影响或者改变了您人生的经历或者想法？

奥米迪亚：我在大学的时候自学了如何为苹果机编程，很多的基础部分实际上是一门课程。事实上那是一门C语言编程课，叫做"数据结构"——所以不能算是完全自学的。它是计算机科学程序的一门"剔除"类课。我学会了如何编写C语言。老师是一位超级厉害的教授，或许是我遇见过的最好的教授，给我留下了很多回忆。

35. debut *n.*
36. search engine
37. career choice

1. 英语中，破折号可用在一个解释性的插入语前面和后面，相当于一个括号。例如：Then the proposals—both Tom's and mine—were adopted.（后来两个建议——汤姆的和我的——都被采纳了。）

2. 词组"take apart"意为"拆卸"。例如：The child wants to take apart a watch to see what makes it work.（那个小孩想拆开手表看看，是什么使它走个不停。）

3. 词组In retrospect意为"回顾往事"，可做副词使用，例如：In retrospect, it's easy to see why we were wrong.（回顾一下，就可以很容易看到为什么我们错了。）

4. 前缀re-表示"又，再一次"的意思，所以加在单词前面可表示动作或行为的重复，例如：recall（召回），restart（重新开始），reborn（重生）等。

5. 条件状语从句是指由连接词if或unless引导的状语从句，表示"假如"的意思。例如：If you ask him, he will help you.（如果你请他帮忙，他会帮你的。）

6. it置于句子开头的时候通常作形式主语，例如：It is obvious that I am glad to answer your question. 其真正的主语是"I am glad to answer your question"。但为了避免句子显得头重脚轻，所以用it来代替主语置于句首。

7. 委婉语（euphemism）也是英语中的修辞手法，是指用委婉、文雅的方法表达粗恶、避讳的话，例如：His relation with his wife has not been fortunate.（他与妻子关系不融洽。）这里用"不幸运"来表示关系不好。

8. be convinced of意为"确信，深知"的意思，例如：It is a wonder that he shouldn't be convinced of his mistakes.（说来也怪，他竟然认识不到自己的错误。）

9. 英语口语中，经常会用到gonna一词，它等同于going to，例如：I'm gonna go.=I'm going to go.（我要走了。）

13

维基百科创始人之一：
吉米·威尔士
Co-founder of Wikipedia: Jimmy Wales

吉米·威尔士，1966年8月7日出生于美国阿拉巴马州的一个偏僻小镇汉斯维尔（Huntsville）。1989年，他从欧本大学的金融系毕业，后来他又取得了印第安纳大学的经济学博士学位，研究方向是期权定价。1994年，威尔士离开学术界决定从商，并前往芝加哥发展。在芝加哥的几年时间里，他从事利率和外汇的投机。4年后，他移居圣地亚哥并开了一家网络公司。2001年，威尔士应用wiki技术开拓了维基百科全书。

吉米·威尔士是维基百科（Wikipedia）的创始人之一。现为维基媒体基金会理事会荣誉主席，同时拥有一家名为维基亚（Wikia）的营利公司。2006年5月，威尔士被《时代周刊》选为100个最具影响力人物之一。

13.1 Wikipedia Is A Social Innovation, Not A Technical Innovation

轻松输入十分钟

foresee v.
预测，预知

editable adj.
可编辑的

innovation n.
创新，革新

database n.
数据库，资料库

collaborative adj.
合作的，协作的

fluid adj.
灵活的

slightly adv.
稍微地

antichrist n.
反对基督者，基督的敌人

shortcoming n.
缺点，短处

tease v.
玩笑，戏弄

thrust n.
推力

misplace v.
错放，错位

overview n.
概述，综述

philosophy n.
哲学，人生观

automatic adj.
自动的，无意识的

deduction n.
减少，扣除

Reporter: How do you think Wikipedia will evolve as technology evolves? Can you foresee, by say 2020, a way for Wikipedians to create editable, interactive videos about a topic?

Wales: I think we'll see a lot of advances in video. One of the things I like to point out is that Wikipedia is a social innovation, not a technical innovation. All the tools necessary to create Wikipedia existed in 1995 when Ward Cunningham invented the wiki editing concept. Web server, web browser, database, wiki.

Reporter: What technologies already exist today for collaborative video editing?

Wales: Well, having said that, I will also say that words are far more fluid than video, and always will be. If I don't quite like what you have written, I can adjust it slightly until we are both satisfied. But once a video has been shot, there is a very limited set of things that can be done about it.

Reporter: British-American author Andrew Keen, the self-described antichrist of Silicon Valley, gets a kick out of regularly blasting Wikipedia. He pointed out that the Harry Potter article is longer than the Hamlet article, and because Hamlet is more historically significant, this some how represents a shortcoming in Wikipedia. Do you find his logic lacking?

Wales: I don't think the words "Andrew Keen" and "logic" generally belong in the same sentence. No, I'm just teasing! The overall thrust of his argument is not compelling to me. Regarding the question of the length of Wikipedia entries, I don't find the argument compelling at all. Some criticisms about Wikipedia entries of various lengths is actually misplaced simply due to how we slice-and-dice the world. It is likely that our entry on "China" is shorter than our entry on "Harry Potter" too. But that's more because we have a short overview article on "China" and then break out specific topics into separate articles. What happens normally is that when one entry gets too long, people will naturally want to break it up.

Reporter: When I was a student at Ohio State, I had Wikipedia co-founder Larry Sanger as a philosophy professor. Sanger had a policy that if you used Wikipedia as a source on a paper, you would receive an automatic five point deduction. Do you think Wikipedia is reliable enough at this stage to pass as

维基百科是社会革新
而不是技术革新

有效学习十分钟

记者： 随着技术的不断发展，您认为维基百科[1]将会怎样发展？您预测到2020年，维基百科会针对某些词条[2]增加可编辑的[3]互动[4]视频吗？

威尔士： 我认为我们会看到视频方面的很多进步。有一点我需要指出，维基百科其实不是技术革新[5]，而是社会革新。它需要的所有技术工具——网络服务器[7]、网络浏览器[8]、数据库[9]和维基百科——在1995年沃德•坎宁安发明维基百科编辑概念[6]时就都存在了。

记者： 协同[10]视频编辑现有哪些技术？

威尔士： 嗯，说到这一点，我认为，文字的灵活性[11]比视频好得多，以后也是这样。如果我对你提供的文字材料并不认同，就可以稍作更改[12]，直到大家达成共识为止。视频材料一旦拍摄[13]完成，剩下能做的事就很有限了。

记者： 美国硅谷有一位自称为[14]伪基督徒[15]的美籍英国作家安德鲁•基恩，定期地猛烈抨击[16]维基百科。他的论据之一就是，"哈利•波特"条目[17]的长度居然超过"哈姆雷特"，因为哈姆雷特更具历史意义，这就显出[18]了维基百科的不足。您觉得他的分析缺乏逻辑[19]吗？

威尔士： 我觉得"安德鲁•基恩"和"逻辑"根本不应该出现在同一个句子里。不，我只是在开玩笑。我不觉得他的批评令人信服。说到维基百科词条的长度，它根本不能说明什么。实际上一些关于维基百科词条长度并不合适的批评依据的仅仅是我们的世界观。"中国"条目的长度可能都超不过"哈利•波特"，但这是因为"中国"条目只是一个概览[20]，更多的内容都在各个子条目中。当一个条目太长时，人们通常[21]会很自然地想要将它分开。

记者： 我在俄亥俄州上学的时候，哲学教授拉里•桑格是维基百科的合伙创始人[22]，规定论文中不得引用[23]维基百科的内容，违者一律扣除5分。您是否同意，维基百科是否足够可靠，可以在学术性[24]文章中引用？

威尔士： 如果我是大学老师的话，我也会采取同样的做法。我同样也会对从大英百科全书[25]中引用扣除5分。在研究领域不管百科全书[26]写得多么好，它都不是用来引用的。一部高质量的百科全书只是一个起点[27]，告诉你一些宽泛的[28]背

1. Wikipedia
2. topic n.
3. editable adj.
4. interactive adj.
5. innovation n.
6. concept n.
7. server n.
8. browser n.
9. database n.
10. collaborative adj.
11. fluid adj.
12. adjust v.
13. shoot v.
14. self-described
15. antichrist n.
16. blast v.
17. article n.
18. represent v.
19. logic adj.
20. short overview n.
21. normally adv.
22. co-founder
23. source v.
24. academic adj.
25. Britannica n.
26. encyclopedia n.
27. starting point
28. broad adj.

a source on an academic paper?

Wales: I would do the same thing if I were teaching a course at a university. I would also deduct 5 points for citing Britannica. This is simply not the proper role for an encyclopedia, no matter how good, in the research process. A high quality encyclopedia is a starting point, giving us broad background knowledge and helping us to firmly and correctly fill in gaps, not an original source. The right thing to do is to quickly read the Wikipedia entry to get your bearings, and then go to read the original sources.

Reporter: In 2007, Wikipedia decided to add no-follow tags to all of its external links. This drew the ire of some and sparked the creation of anti-Wikipedia wordpress plugins that automatically turn all the Wikipedia links on a person's blog to no-follow. Has the community's decision to place no-follow tags around external links kept out spam, and do you think Wikipedia would ever decide to flip the switch back?

Wales: I was opposed to the change, and only reluctantly agreed to it after Matt Cutts of Google recommended it. I am still not sure it is the right answer. After all, Wikipedia prides itself on public service, and our external links are generally quite carefully vetted. On the other hand, it is also true that when we were not using 'nofollow' we had a bigger problem with skeevy "SEO" experts doing everything they could to get Wikipedia links. Even today, of course, a link in Wikipedia can drive a significant amount of traffic so we have to deal with inappropriate self-promotion. But my vague sense is that the troubles have declined.

Reporter: Apparently you sat at a long dinner table with Mahalo CEO Jason Calacanis at Wikimania in 2006, and during this dinner, Calacanis "begged you" (his words) to sell ads on Wikipedia. He claimed that if you put a leaderboard up, Wikipedia would generate over $100 million a year. He later offered a more modest revenue proposal, one that involved putting a search box on the Wikipedia. He estimated this would make $6 million a year, which is ironic considering $6 million is what you raised last year via charitable donations. Can you ever envision a scenario in which the Wikipedia community would agree to put ads on the site, especially in light of the fact that it met its $6 million donation goal last year?

Wales: Actually, I sat next to Jason, but I didn't know who he was. Afterwards, when he published his post about the dinner, I didn't really remember him. I regret saying so publicly, because this seems to have hurt Jason's feelings. I was exhausted that evening, and the fault was entirely mine. The thing is, lots and lots of people propose that Wikipedia should accept ads. And it is not an unreasonable position. I am opposed to it, but I am actually a moderate about it. I think there are a set of circumstances in which the Wikipedia community

cite v.
引用，想起

encyclopedia n.
百科全书

bearing n.
方位

tag n.
标签，名称

spark v.
鼓舞，发动

plugin n.
插件，相关插件

spam n.
垃圾邮件

flip v.
轻击，掷

reluctantly adv.
不情愿地，嫌恶地

recommend v.
推荐，介绍

skeevy adj.
质量差的，令人厌恶的

inappropriate adj.
不适当的，不相称的

self-promotion n.
自我促进，自我推销

leaderboard n.
通栏广告

generate v.
产生，发生

modest adj.
谦虚的

charitable adj.
慈善事业的

scenario n.
方案，剧本

donation n.
捐款，捐赠物

exhausted adj.
疲惫的，耗尽的

circumstance n.
情况，环境

景知识，帮助你正确地认识问题，并不能取代原始材料。正确的做法是，读完百科全书中的介绍后，确定方向，再去读原始[29]材料。

记者：2007年，维基百科决定为所有外部链接[30]添加"不准跟踪链接"属性。一石激起千层浪，很多反维基百科者编写了博客插件[31]，可以自动将个人博客里的维基百科链接更改为不准跟踪链接。为外部链接添加不准跟踪链接，这种做法对防止垃圾信息的发送是否有效？您觉得未来会恢复回去[32]吗？

威尔士：我是反对这种改变的。最后，只是因为谷歌的工程师马特•卡茨不断劝说，才勉强同意。直到今天，我都不确定这种做法是否正确，毕竟维基百科的使命是服务公众，而且我们的外部链接都是经过精心审查的。但是，另一方面，以前我们不用"不准跟踪链接"的时候，总是有一些所谓的"SEO"专家，想尽办法来得到维基百科链接。即使是现在，当然，维基百科中的链接会带来很大的流量，因此我们就要解决那些不合适的自我宣传。我大致可以感觉到，这为我们减少了一些麻烦。

记者：2006年，您与Mahalo（一款人力搜索引擎）的总裁贾森•卡拉卡尼斯一起共进晚餐，其间卡拉卡尼斯"乞求"（原话）您给他们一个在维基百科上做广告的机会。他承诺如果您允许安装广告，维基百科每年将有超过10亿元的进账。之后他还给出了更高的价格，希望可以在维基百科中添加搜索框[33]。他估计这大概每年会有600万美元的收入，而讽刺[34]的是，去年你们通过慈善捐赠募集600万美元的经费很辛苦。有没有想过在维基百科上放置广告，尤其是从去年的情况来看，很可能会给你们带来600万美元的收益？

威尔士：事实上，我坐在贾森旁边却不知道他是谁。之后他发表了关于那顿晚餐的一篇帖子，我还是没有想起来他是谁。我很抱歉这样公开地说了这件事，因为这有点伤害贾森的感受。那天晚上我很累，是我做得不对。确实有许许多多的人提议维基百科应该接受广告。这种提议是合情合理的，但是我还是持反对态度，尽管实际上我对此持中立态度。可能在某些情况下，我们会接受广告，但是目前不太可能出现，我希望将来也不要出现。但是时间会揭示一切。我的观点是，我们——不仅仅是我，整个董事会[35]和目前的社区，而应该是每个把自己看作是网络世界和真实世界中的一分子的人——我们应该将维基百科视作世界的基础设施之一，而不是互联网上的一个竞争性组织。维基百科并不仅仅是一个网站，而是一种更深刻的东西，文化方面的潜在的价值观。我们考虑问题，不是只考虑下个季度、下一年、或者未来5年，我们

29. original *adj.*
30. external link
31. plugin *n.*
32. switch back
33. search box
34. ironic *adj.*
35. board *n.*

157

would accept ads, but we are nowhere near it and I personally hope we never get there. But, time will tell. My view is that we should all—not just me, not just the board, not just the current community—but everyone who thinks of themselves as a citizen of the Internet, a citizen of the world—we should all think about Wikipedia as part of the infrastructure of the world, not a competitor in the Internet space, not just a website, but something deeper, cultural, and potentially of value to everyone. As such, we should think about the long run—not the next quarter, not the next year, not the next 5 years. What about 50 years? What about 100 years? What's best for the world in the long run? We desperately need to make sure that everyone on the planet has access to high quality information. We are on a small and crowded planet that will get more crowded in this century. We need to live together in peace and productivity. We need to take individual rights seriously. We need to have political decisions that are rational and fact-based. We need to have culture and joy and art and love. These are heavy responsibilities for us all. And slapping a "leaderboard" on Wikipedia to bring in short-term revenue might not be the best plan. (Or it might. But we need to think like adults about it.)

Reporter: Will it be harder or easier for you to reach a $6 million donation goal in 2009?

Wales: Since traffic is growing (according to Comscore) by 4% per month still, I think it will be easier to reach $6 million since we will be 66% larger in terms of reach by next fundraiser as compared to the last fundraiser. On the other hand, I suppose everyone is watching with nervousness about the financial crisis!

Reporter: You've set a tone that Wikipedia has a much deeper responsibility to the world than to act, simply, as an encyclopedia. In what ways do you think Wikipedia will permanently change the fabric of humanity?

Wales: Well, if we do our job right, we will be a positive change for the world. Wikipedia will be a little bit dry, a little bit uncontroversial, but a place where people of all stripes turn for clear explanations and information that allows them to have more difficult debates in a rational and evidence-based manner.

Reporter: Did you catch this *CollegeHumor.com* satire of Wikipedia? Did you find it amusing?

Wales: Hilarious!

Reporter: I'd like to see a roundtable discussion involving you, and Rew Keen, Jason Calacanis, Noam Chomsky and Ron Paul. 55 minutes into the discussion, a thunderous gong would go off and a mystery guest would emerge and immediately inject himself into the conversation. As odd as this sounds, I am 100% serious about one day setting this up. There's no doubt a video of the event would serve as tremendous linkbait—quite an interesting collection of people. Would you participate in this roundtable discussion if your airfare was paid for?

Wales: Yes, gladly. What an interesting set of characters.

infrastructure *n.*
基础设施，公共建设

desperately *adv.*
极度地，绝望地

slap *v.*
(无理地或者盲目地) 强加

fundraiser *n.*
资金筹集活动，资金筹集人

uncontroversial *adj.*
不会引起争论的，非争论性的

hilarious *adj.*
有趣的，滑稽的

roundtable *adj.*
圆桌的，圆台的

考虑的是长期发展。维基百科应该怎样做，才能在未来50年甚至100年中对整个世界最有利。我们竭尽全力[36]，确保这个星球上的每个人都能够得到高质量的信息。地球已经很小很拥挤了，未来的这个世纪还会更拥挤，人类需要和平合作地生活在一起。我们需要严肃地对待个人的权利，需要理性[37]和客观的[38]政治决策，需要文化、乐趣、艺术和情感。这些都是非常重大的责任。如果我们为了短期的[39]收入，在维基百科上放置广告，这并不一定有利于达到我们的目标。（它也可能会有帮助，但是我们一定要像成人一样思考。）

记者：2009年募集600万美元经费的任务，实现起来会更难还是更容易？

威尔士：根据康姆斯克的数据，我们的访问量[40]每个月大概增长4%，所以我想应该更容易一些吧。因为下一次开始募集的时候，从访问量上来看，我们的规模比上一次大了66%。另一方面，我认为每个人都在为金融危机而担忧！

记者：您为维基百科设定了宏伟的目标，远远超过了百科全书本来的角色。您觉得维基百科会通过什么方式永久地改变人性呢？

威尔士：是这样的，如果我们做好这个项目，我们就会为世界带来一些积极的变化。维基百科可能有一点枯燥[41]并且不会引起争端，但是人们会从维基百科上得到清晰的解释和足够的信息，这使得他们可以更理性和客观地探讨更难的问题。

记者：您看过大学幽默网站关于维基百科的讽刺漫画了吗？您觉得好笑吗？

威尔士：非常有趣！

记者：我希望您和安德鲁·基恩、贾森·卡拉卡尼斯、诺姆·乔姆斯基以及罗恩·保罗可以进行一次圆桌[42]讨论。讨论进行55分钟，响亮的铜锣声响起，这时神秘嘉宾登场并立即融入对话当中。这听起来很奇怪，但是我100%肯定有一天我一定会把这件事办成。毫无疑问，这次会议的视频会吸引很多人

来点击——这是非常有趣的一伙人。如果我们支付您的机票[43]的话，您愿意加入到这次圆桌讨论中来吗？

威尔士：好的，很高兴有机会参加。这会是个有趣的会议。

36. desperately *adv.*
37. rational *adj.*
38. fact-based
39. short-term
40. traffic *n.*
41. dry *adj.*
42. roundtable *n.*
43. airfare *n.*

每天30分钟，轻松听懂读懂名家访谈

自由输出十分钟

1. 维基百科（英语：Wikipedia，是维基媒体基金会的商标）是一个自由、免费、内容开放的百科全书协作计划，参与者来自世界各地。这个站点使用Wiki，这意味着任何人都可以编辑维基百科中的任何文章及条目。维基百科是一个基于wiki技术的多语言百科全书协作计划，也是一部用不同语言写成的网络百科全书。

2. 可以用来修饰比较级的副词有：far，quite，much，even，a little，a bit等。例如：Tom looks even younger than before.（汤姆看起来甚至比以前更年轻.）

3. limited表示"限制的"，同时也表示"有限公司"的意思，例如：Jack Ma, the CEO of Alibaba Group Holding Ltd.(limited) is something of an exception, with some Jobs—like characteristics.（阿里巴巴集团有限公司首席执行官马云在某种程度上是个例外，他有一些与乔布斯相类似的性格特点。）

4. 英语中有名词修饰名词的情况，例如：women teacher（女老师），mother language（母语），dog shop（卖狗狗的商店）等。

5. Hamlet（《哈姆雷特》）是莎士比亚著名的四大悲剧之一，另外三部包括《奥赛罗》、《李尔王》、《麦克白》。

6. 词组slice-and-dice意为"分开"，例如：The pundits like to slice-and-dice our country into Red States and Blue States.（权威们喜欢把我们的国家煞有介事地分成红色州和蓝色州。）

7. 表示开玩笑的表达法有teasing，kidding等。例如：John was only kidding you when he said he's a gay.（约翰跟你说他是同性恋时只是在开你玩笑。）；I am just teasing.（我只是在开玩笑。）

8. 词组in the charge of的意思是"由……负责"，例如：The preparation committee, in the charge of Prof. Smith, will see to everything concerning the meeting.（由史密斯教授负责的筹备委员会将负责有关会务工作。）

9. tell一词除了常见的"告诉"之意外，还可表示"辨别"，例如：A new study has shown that the ability to tell the differences between right and wrong is a skill which even babies can possess.（一项新研究显示，即使是婴儿也能够明辨是非。）

微软公司首席执行官：
史蒂夫·鲍尔默
CEO of Microsoft: Steve Ballmer

　　史蒂夫·鲍尔默是全球领先的个人及商务软件开发商——微软公司的首席执行官。他毕业于哈佛大学，获得了数学和经济学学士学位，并在斯坦福商学院获得了工商行政管理硕士学位。史蒂夫·鲍尔默最引人注目的特点就是"易于激动"。激动的时候，鲍尔默习惯于把任何东西都强调三遍，他是天生的销售明星和演说家，一站上演讲台就会有难以抑制的澎湃活力。

　　鲍尔默于1980年加盟微软，他是比尔·盖茨聘用的第一位商务经理。从此，他的热情及领导艺术成为他任职期间的特点。在过去二十年里，鲍尔默先生先后担任了微软公司的多项重要职位，负责公司运营、操作系统的开发、销售和支持。2000年1月，他接任公司CEO一职。

14.1 Our Business Is Very Promising

轻松输入十分钟

Reporter: You're back in Silicon Valley—what bring you here?

Ballmer: We do an annual event where we bring together venture capitalists, and try to make sure they understand where we're going, and we understand where they're going, 'cause there're going to be opportunities for us to partner with their portfolio companies, try to get their portfolio companies to build on and alongside of things that we do. There'll be chances for acquisition, and we do that once a year and we happen to be doing that today. I'm down in the valley probably 7 times a year, and this is sort of more of a valley day because we're with the VC community.

Reporter: The last time you were in the valley, is that when you did the Yahoo deal?

Ballmer: Last time I was down here probably was the announcement of the Yahoo deal. I've had kind of a quiet two months of travel since I was down here at the end of July for that.

Reporter: I have a couple questions about that but we can hit those later. You guys have a lot of new product initiatives, I think some are big ideas, big new businesses, possibly some are what you call an enabler, something like that. You've got big buckets—Bing is out, Windows 7 is coming out, Azure, I think you guys have said by the end of the year, Mesh is there, Project Natal, and others. How do you feel about big buckets and all of these products—your babies?

Ballmer: Well, it's great to have a year where you have a lot of stuff that you can kind of be excited about, if you lead a company like ours we have a lot of very exciting products for the consumer and frankly for the enterprise customer, although that tends to get a little less press attention I would say, but it's a fun year. It also is a good year to say then that it's a good year to go to build business and it's a good year to lay the seeds for the next generation of businesses that can be good, and whether it's what we're trying to do with Bing, or do with Natal, the next 12 months is shaping up to be very promising.

Reporter: One of the big things you talk about is something you call "three screens

---

annual *adj.*
每年的，一年的

portfolio *n.*
投资组合，公文包

acquisition *n.*
收购，获得物

valley *n.*
硅谷

announcement *n.*
宣告，通告

initiative *n.*
主动权，首创精神

bucket *n.*
项目，水桶

stuff *n.*
材料，物品

enterprise *n.*
企业，事业

generation *n.*
产生，一代

我们的业务是非常有发展前景的

有效学习十分钟

记者：　如今您又回到硅谷了——能告诉我们其中的原因吗？

鲍尔默：我们每年都会组织风险资本家[1]在此举办一场年会[2]，试图确保他们了解我们的发展动向，我们也了解他们的投资方向。我们之所以这么做主要是因为我们与他们的投资公司之间存在很多合作的机会，试图让他们的投资公司能够参与到我们做的事情里来。其中可能会有收购行为，我们每年召开一次这样的大会，今天刚好是这个日子。我大概每年来硅谷七次，今天的特殊之处在于我们与风险投资社区合作。

记者：　上一次您在硅谷的时候是不是正在处理雅虎合并案[3]？

鲍尔默：上次我来硅谷好像是为了宣布雅虎合并案。自从七月底来到硅谷，我在这里度过了很安静的两个月。

记者：　关于这个方面我有一些问题，但我们稍后再接着讨论。我知道微软有很多新产品开发首创精神，其中一些是了不起的想法，大单新业务，可能有一些会像您说的起到类似于促进者[4]的作用。微软已经研发了大项目——必应搜索引擎[5]和Windows7已经研发出来，Azure也预计在年底推向市场。无线蜂窝网格网络（Mesh）已经建好，还有Natal项目和其他内容。您对于这些大项目以及所有这些产品感觉如何——像您的孩子一样吗？

鲍尔默：嗯，如果你领导像微软这样的公司，在一年内拥有这么多令人兴奋的产品提供给客户，更确切地说，是企业客户[6]，尽管媒体关注略少些，但是我们还是要说今年是愉快的一年。今年也是建立新业务、为下一代业务播撒种子的好时机，无论我们是否要继续发展"必应"或是Natal，接下来的一年里，我们的业务是非常有发展前景[7]的。

记者：　微软今年的一件大事情就是您口中的"三个屏幕一片云"。我们很想请您深入介绍一下这个项目，不仅从一个企业的角度而且从一个用户的角度来看意

1. venture capitalist
2. annual event
3. the deal *n.*
4. enabler *n.*
5. Bing
6. enterprise customer
7. promising *adj.*

standpoint *n.*
立场，观点

alliteration *n.*
头韵，押头韵

fundamental *adj.*
根本的，基本的

paradigm *n.*
范例，词形变化

mainframe *n.*
主机，大型机

platform *n.*
平台，月台

security *n.*
安全，防备

revitalize *v.*
复兴，使复活

graphical *adj.*
图解的，绘画的

application *n.*
应用程序，申请

competition *n.*
竞争，比赛

integrate *v.*
整合，使完整

infrastructure *n.*
基础结构，基础
建设

proprietary *n.*
所有权，财产

synergy *n.*
共同作用，合力

perspective *n.*
观点，洞察力

and the cloud". I'd love if you could dive a little bit into what that means from a business standpoint but also from a user standpoint and what they're going to get out of this when it finally comes together.

Ballmer: Yeah, the reason I like the little phrase "three screens and the cloud" isn't just that it's true and it's what we started talking about it at CES but I kind of like the alliteration of "Three Men and a Baby". Every time I say it I think, "three screens and the cloud," "Three Men and a Baby" if you remember the movie, but I think what it really refers to is a fundamental shift in the computing paradigm. We used to talk about mainframe computer, mini computer, PC computing, client server computing, graphical computing, the Internet; I think this notion of "three screens and a cloud", multiple devices that are all important, the cloud not just as a point of delivery of individual applications, but really as a new platform, a scale-out, very manageable platform that has services that span security contacts, I think it's a big deal. You lay natural user interface technologies on there, and platforms on there, and then you start revitalizing the UI platform. What you're seeing on phones and TVs, people want more than what's called the classical graphical user interface: touch, voice, camera, gestures —all of that stuff whether it's Natal or the touch stuff, in iPhone or Windows 7 or whatever it is. It is the next big generational shift in the computing platform. And people are going to want applications, I'll call them that, or services, depending on whether you like old-fashioned words or new words, but they're going to want things that serve them across those environments. So when I'm away and just have my phone with me I still may want to check in on the action—my favorite box competition, or I may want to play games with somebody who's in a different environment. We're sitting watching television, and we want to share with somebody who's not physically present—we want that to work to somebody who might be a family member, who's on their PC in a hotel room traveling tonight. So you got to think about it as one integrated computing infrastructure. Now, whether it will all come from one company, and what are the standards, and what are the points of proprietary differentiation, all of that's going to get kind of played off. Now in our own case, you know we're going to try to share technologies, so that we get kind of synergy from a developer's perspective. Windows on the phone, you know, Windows PCs controlling TVs, the Windows PC of course itself, Windows Azure in the cloud, so we have a lot of work that's trying to share technology, but obviously you don't want exactly the same experience on a little screen and a very big screen and a mid-size screen.

Reporter: OK, you talked about Azure in the cloud, but does it work if somebody's

味着什么。当这个项目建成时，企业与用户能够从中获得什么？

鲍尔默： 是的，我喜欢"三个屏幕一片云"，不仅仅是因为它的真实性和我们在消费电子展[8]时就开始对其进行讨论，而是因为我有点喜欢"三个奶爸一个娃"的头韵[9]。每次我提到"三个屏幕一片云"就会联想到"三个奶爸一个娃"，不知道你是否还记得这部电影。我想"三个屏幕一片云"真正的所指就是计算机范式的根本转变[10]。我们过去常常谈到大型电脑、迷你电脑、个人电脑、客户服务器[11]、图形处理技术[12]、互联网；我认为"三个屏幕一片云"的想法，多重设备都是很重要的，云不仅仅指每个应用程序[13]的传输点，而且它是一个新平台，一个全面易管理的平台，在这个平台上程序能够保持安全连接[14]，我认为这是一个很大的项目。你可以添加电脑自带的用户界面[15]技术和各种平台，然后重启UI平台。从手机和电视上可以看出，人们已经不满足于经典图形用户界面：触摸屏[16]、声控[17]、摄像、手势等等，不管是Natal还是触摸式的，是不是应用于iPhone或者Windows7或者其他任何东西里。这是计算机平台的又一次大转型。人们将会对应用程序有新的需求，或者也可以说对服务有新要求，就看你是喜欢用新词汇还是老词汇了，但是他们需要在这些环境下为他们提供服务的东西。所以当我不在电脑前只有手机在身上的时候，我仍然想要知道电视节目的情况——我最喜欢的拳击比赛，或者我想与处在异地的人一起玩游戏。当我们坐在电视机前，想要与不在电视机前的人共享节目时——这个人可能是我们的家人，也可能是坐在宾馆的电脑前正在度假的某人。所以你需要将其视为一个整合的计算机设备。如今无论是来自一个公司还是采用不同标准[18]，不同版权商[19]的产品，都会暴露[20]些缺点。现在我们正在打算分享[21]技术，这样我们从开发商[22]的角度进行协作。比如，手机上的Windows操作系统[23]，Windows计算机控制的电视设备，Windows个人电脑本身，云中的Windows Azure，我们做很多用来分享的科技，但是显然你希望可以在小屏幕、大屏幕和中等[24]屏幕上有不同的体验[25]。

记者： 好，您刚提到云中的Azure，但是如果有人使用亚马逊网页服务器[26]或者类似的服务器，Azure也能运行吗？尽管我们大多数都是从开发商的角度来谈的，但是您真的打算与其他开发商尽可能多地进行交互操作[27]吗？

8. CES (Consumer Electronics Show)
9. alliteration n.
10. shift n.
11. client server
12. graphical computing
13. application n.
14. contact v.
15. user interface
16. touch n.
17. voice n.
18. standard n.
19. proprietary n.
20. play off
21. share v.
22. developer n.
23. Windows
24. mid-size
25. experience n.
26. web service
27. interoperate n.

using Amazon web services or something like that? Although we're talking more about the developer side now, but are you planning to interoperate as much as possible?

Ballmer: As much as possible implies that infinite complexity's a good thing. Of course, it's unreasonable to say that you're going to completely support only your own three screens and only your own cloud. We have to make our screens and our cloud first and best, but clearly there are going to be people for example who don't want to be in the cloud, that want to be on Premise, that for whatever crazy reasons don't want to be on Windows, might want to be on Linux, for gosh sakes.

Reporter: Yeah, crazy.

Ballmer: For me, I'm allowed to say that. And we need to interoperate, but we do need to be first and best in support and in integration of our own platforms.

Reporter: OK, fair enough. Search. Congratulations, Bing is now one of the major services, they're saying Bing has now achieved 10% of the market share, up actually quite a big percent over 8, 8 and a half—that's a big percentage jump, and it seems to be pretty quick, and it seems to be steady and sticking. So congratulations on that.

Ballmer: Thank you.

Reporter: But, I think everyone agrees, Bing is a good step forward. I think people who thought they would test them out, a lot of them are sticking, but looking forward 5 years from now, search innovation over the last say, 10 years has been somewhat interesting but will the next 10 years of search innovation be more interesting than the last 10 years?

Ballmer: Let me say something dramatic—I think the first five years there was innovation in business model, there was innovation in approach, give credit to competition, the last 5 years there's been some, quote, innovation, which is really things like digitizing, maps and books, or whatever the case may be, adding the larger content base to the corpus of information. But in some senses the UI, the approach, the algorithms have changed less in the last five years, so I think if you look out the next 10 years we're going to see more innovation in search. And, of course, that'll be best served by good competition in the market and, you know, at this stage, hopefully with the government approval of our deal with Yahoo, the good competition better come from us. Otherwise I don't think we'll see some of that innovation. But whether it's natural language, visualization, change in the UI, change in the business model... Business model on search is making life tough for other content providers, makes life tough for some of the merchants...

interoperate *n.*
互用，交互操作

unreasonable *adj.*
不合理的，过度的

for gosh sakes
[口语][用于加强语气]天哪，哎呀

stick *v.*
牢固，粘住

innovation *n.*
创新，革新

dramatic *adj.*
激动人心的，戏剧性的

digitize *v.*
数字化，计数化

corpus *n.*
语料库，文集

algorithm *n.*
算法，公式

visualization *n.*
可视化，形象化

鲍尔默： "尽可能多地"暗示[28]了无限的复杂性是件好事情。当然，如果你说只支持自己公司研发的"三个屏幕一片云"的计算环境，那是不合理的。我们必须首先使自己公司的屏幕和云产品达到最优，但是也会有些人，比如说不想用云计算环境[29]，

而喜欢Premise，处于一些近似病狂的理由不想用Windows操作系统，想要Linux操作系统。

记者： 是的，很疯狂。

鲍尔默： 对于我来说，我可以这样说，我们需要合作，但是我们更需要在支持和整合自己的平台上做到最好。

记者： 好，很公平。要说搜索引擎[30]方面，恭喜，必应如今已经是市场上主要服务之一。有人说必应现在已经占到市场份额[31]的10%，提高了8个多百分点，8个半——这是很大的飞跃[32]。这种增长速度是非常迅速的，而且发展平稳[33]、牢固。所以，我要说，恭喜恭喜。

鲍尔默： 谢谢。

记者： 但是，我想没有人会反对，必应系统进步很大。我认为很多人曾想对他们进行充分考察[34]，其中有很多在坚持，但是我们向前看5年，过去10年中的搜索创新是有点意思的，但是在下一个10年中会更有意思吗？

鲍尔默： 让我说一些激动人心的事情——我认为前5年商业模式有所创新[35]，方法有所创新这要归功于竞争。最近5年有一个引用上的创新，就像数字化、地图、书籍等增加更多内容到语料库[36]信息中。但是从某种角度上说，UI平台、方式和算法在近5年的变化已经少了很多，我想在未来的10年中，我们会看到搜索方面会有更多的创新。当然，由于市场竞争的加剧，计算机服务会更加健全。你知道的，希望政府同意微软与雅虎的合作案，那么我们在搜索引擎方面就会更有竞争力。否则，我认为也许我们在这方面的创新将会比较少。但是无论是自然语言、可视化、UI平台的变化还是商业模式的变化……搜索引擎的商业模式正在给其他信息提供商和商家带来困难……

28. imply *v.*
29. be in the cloud *n.*
30. search
31. market share
32. jump *v.*
33. steady *adj.*
34. test out
35. innovation *n.*
36. corpus *n.*

1. 硅谷 (Silicon Valley) 地处美国加州北部旧金山湾以南，早期以硅芯片的设计与制造著称，因而得名。后来其他高技术产业也蓬勃发展，硅谷的名称现泛指所有高科技产业。自80年代后，世界各国和地区为促进高科技发展，都试图建立起自己的硅谷，如美国波士顿的"第二硅谷"、"日本硅谷"、"韩国硅谷"等。中国也不例外，有北京中关村硅谷、上海浦东硅谷（位于浦东张江）和广东深圳硅谷，浙江杭州也有一个"天堂硅谷"。

2. fun一词既可做名词也可做形容词，做名词时不可数，例如：Those girls at the telephone office have very sharp tongues and they like to make fun of others.（电话所的女电话员们个个尖嘴嚼舌，总和他人开玩笑。）

3. 微软公司于2009年5月29日正式宣布推出全新中文搜索品牌"必应"，打造全新的快乐搜索体验。此次"必应"中文搜索品牌的发布将于微软全球搜索品牌Bing同步，是微软全球搜索服务品牌战略发布的一个重要组成部分。

4. 词组shape up to的意思是"面对（困难等）"，例如：I think you have the courage to shape up to your mistakes.（我相信你有勇气面对你的错误。）

5. 排比（parallelism）是把两个或两个以上的结构大体相同或相似、意思相关、语气一致的短语、句子排列成串，形成一个整体的修辞方法。例如：No one can be perfectly free till all are free; no one can be perfectly moral till all are moral; no one can be perfectly happy till all are happy. 这句话就是一个明显的排比。

6. a big deal的意思是"重要的事或人"，例如：So, for us, to have any patch of woods to play in was a big deal.（所以对于我们来说，拥有一片可以在其间玩耍的树林是一件天大的事。）

7. gosh是英语口语中的一个感叹词，相当于汉语中的"天啊"，例如："Gosh," I said, "it must be a more common name in Canada than I realised."（"天啊！"我说，"这个名字在加拿大肯定比我原来想象的更常见。"）

8. 表示转折的副词有：however，nevertheless，but，yet，while等。例如：The news may be unexpected; nevertheless, it is true.（这消息可能是出乎意料的，然而是真实的。）；She didn't realize her mistake yet.（她还没有意识到她的错误。）

9. 在英语口语中，wanna是want to的口语形式，例如：I don't wanna pick up such a job.=I don't want to pick up such a job.（我不想做这份工作。）

15

摩托罗拉联合首席执行官：
桑杰·贾
CEO of MOTOROLA: Sanjay Jha

　　桑杰·贾于1967年出生在印度一个贫苦家庭，曾获得苏格兰斯特斯克莱德大学电子与电机工程学博士学位。1994年他加盟高通公司，主抓芯片业务。此外，他还负责高通的研发、销售、软件业务，并积极促成了高通与谷歌的合作。1998年，桑杰·贾荣升为QCT的工程设计高级副总裁。

　　2002年，桑杰·贾负责组建美国高通公司技术与风险投资部门，并担任高级副总裁兼总经理，主要管理高通公司技术投资组合及新技术事业部。2003年，桑杰·贾成为美国高通公司执行副总裁兼美国高通CDMA技术集团(QCT)总裁。2006年12月，他被任命为首席运营官。桑杰·贾于2008年加盟摩托罗拉，现任美国摩托罗拉公司CEO一职。

15.1 Motorola Represents Wild, Cool, and Quality

轻松输入十分钟

Reporter: What a quarter for Motorola. Now I know everything is so convoluted after the close, people think that Intel (INTC) didn't deliver, or there's some problem with Yahoo! (YHOO). And it is beginning to impact a company that it shouldn't, which is Motorola, and that's why I want to speak to Sanjay Jha right now. He is the CEO, has put this company on a monster, monster return, a fantastic comeback. How big is the ultimate (ph) cell phone opportunity? There are 6 billion people, only 750 million cell phones, what is ahead of us?

Jha: Oh, that is good, Jake. Thanks very much for the nice compliment, first of all.

Reporter: Absolutely.

Jha: We did have a great quarter, by the way, and I hope that comes through. We really.

Reporter: Well, I know there was a problem in the way it was reported on the network. You guided up significantly in the third quarter, this was—and I want that corrected right now, right?

Jha: Yes, we had a great Q2, first of all, 52 percent up in earnings, 70 percent in sales, took market share and exceeded all of the First Call numbers. And Q3 we actually guided up based on First Call too. So we are feeling very confident about our business and all of the numbers in the right direction, generated over a billion dollars in operating cash flow. So a great, solid quarter. And we're looking good for Q3 too.

Reporter: OK, can you give me a sense, because I've got a very big audience that's not just limited to the hedge fund guys. You seem, in all the interviews I've read, incredibly excited about music. Can you tell us about Motorola and music and what you've got planned?

Jha: Well, I'm excited about all the applications and capabilities of the device we formerly called the cell phone. It is just being—incredibly new capabilities every day, whether it is video, whether it is music, and some of the other commercial applications. Music is going to be big, it is big right now outside the United States. We are doing incredibly well in Brazil and places in Europe with some of our music capabilities. We will be showing some products next week at our analyst meeting. As you know, during this quarter we will also be delivering on

---

convoluted *adj.*
复杂的，费解的

impact *v.*
影响，冲突

monster *n.*
巨人，怪物

comeback *n.*
回归，复原

compliment *n.*
称赞，恭维

significantly *adv.*
意味深长地，值得注目地

exceed *v.*
超过，胜过

solid *adj.*
可靠的，固体的

hedge fund
对冲基金

capability *n.*
性能，才能

formerly *adv.*
以前，原来

application *n.*
应用，申请

analyst *n.*
分析者，分解者

摩托罗拉代表了狂野、冷静和质量

MEET THE FIRST PHONE WITH SOCIAL SKILLS

有效学习十分钟

记者：这对摩托罗拉来说是个多么重要的季度啊。现在我知道了在结束之后所有的事情都很繁杂，人们认为英特尔公司并没有解脱[1]，雅虎公司仍然存在一些问题。这正逐渐影响到本不该受影响的摩托罗拉公司。这就是为什么我现在和桑杰·贾进行访谈，他是公司的首席执行官，他让这家公司成为巨人[2]，现在巨人完美回归了。手机最终会有多大的机遇呢？全球有60亿人口，但只有7.5亿部手机，我们面临的是什么？

贾：哦，好的，杰克，首先非常感谢你对我的夸赞[3]。

记者：那是当然。

贾：我们确实拥有一个很好的季度，顺便说一下，我希望我们能够大获全胜[4]，我们的确可以。

记者：嗯，网络上报道公司现在遇到了一个问题。在第三季度您成功地领导了公司，我想问题已经得到了改正，是吗？

贾：是的，我们第二季度的业绩很好。首先，收入增加了52%，销售额[5]增加了70%，我们获得了市场份额，并且在所有数值上都超过First Call。在第三季度我们实际上与First Call相比也处于领先地位，所以我们对我们的业务非常有信心，并且所有的数字表明我们的发展方向是正确的。营业现金流[6]已经超过10亿美元。这是发展态势好且稳固[7]的一个季度，我们也看好第三季度的情况。

记者：好，您能给我个具体概念吗？因为该节目不仅只针对那些做对冲基金[8]的专家，还有很多大众。从我读过的所有采访中，您好像对音乐非常地狂热。能告诉我您对于摩托罗拉和音乐有没有什么计划？

贾：我对所有被我们称之为手机的应用程序和设备都感到非常兴奋。令人难以置信的[9]是，几乎每天都有新功能出现，不管是视频、音乐还是其他一些商业应用程序。音乐将会是很重要的一部分，它现在在美国以外的地区非常受重视。在巴西以及欧洲地区，我们的音乐功能都取得了极大的成功。我们下周将在分析会上展出一些产品。就像你所知道的，在这个季度，我们同样将宣布对苹果iTunes的承诺。所以我们不仅对音乐能带来的效应十分乐观，同样对掌上[10]设备

1. deliver *n.*
2. monster *n.*
3. compliment *n.*
4. come through
5. earnings *n.*
6. operating cash flow
7. solid *adj.*
8. hedge fund
9. incredibly *adv.*
10. handheld *adj.*

our commit on Apple (AAPL) on iTunes. So we're pretty bullish on what music can bring, but also bullish on the overall market for handheld devices.

Reporter: OK. Could you give us a sense, everybody loves the Razor. I mean, I go into Verizon (VZ). The first thing Verizon says is, hey, I know we don't have the Razor, but, you know, Razor—we've got something really good. Give us a sense of the demand for Razor and whether you can meet it.

Jha: We are meeting it. We announced at our release or our earnings call that we had shipped over 5 million now, Razors, and we will be shipping a lot more. And we will have one for Verizon too before the end of this year. I'm really excited about Razor and Razor derivative products. We'll again be showing some products next week that are coming up for Razor. So there will be lots of thin, thin, thin, and we've got a lot of great products around the slim design.

Reporter: Are you able—and this is a tough question, but can you keep your brand in front of the customer when the carriers—look, the carriers all want to do private label, they want to claim that the phone that I have —you know, that my phone is a Verizon phone, but it is a Motorola phone.

Jha: Well, I don't think that is the case in all areas. We have worked just incredibly well on Razor. And I think they have benefited, we have benefited. I think that Batwing, the M is becoming more well-known around the world. We are working with people like T-Mobile and even Verizon now with the 815 we just introduced is running commercials across the TV and through the press. So I think we—if we build well products, which is what we are doing, working with our carriers on private-branded type products for some of the applications and services, we are both going to win the marketplace. People want Motorola now, it represents wild, it represents cool, and it represents quality.

Reporter: Absolutely. Hey, listen, there are rumors, and you can't, but I would love you to do it on my show, that you have a Blackberry killer coming out. Can you speak to it?

Jha: If I told you, I'd have to hurt you, Jim.

Reporter: Oh, come on, man! I need this!

Jha: What is it worth to you?

Reporter: Ah, no, can't break any rules.

Jha: We've got a lot of good surprises, and maybe next week we'll show you some of them.

Reporter: I hope so. Now I know your stock is up from 15. I'm sure there is going to be profit-taking. But this was a great quarter, great working—thanks for coming on my show, man.

Jha: My pleasure.

Reporter: I have always banked with you, you have always delivered.

Jha: All right. Thanks a lot.

handheld adj.
掌上型的，手持型的

release n.
发布会

derivative adj.
派生的，引出的

tough adj.
困难的，艰苦的

private adj.
私人的，私有的

incredibly adv.
难以置信地，非常地

benefit v.
受益，得益

commercial n.
商业广告

rumor n.
谣言，传闻

profit-taking n.
见利抛售

bank v.
存入银行，倾斜转弯

的市场充满信心。

记者：那么，您能给大家一个概念吗？每个人都喜欢Razor。我的意思是当我进入到威瑞森，他们说的第一件事是：嘿，我知道我们没有Razor，但我们有一些很好的东西。告诉我们，消费者对Razor有哪些需求以及贵公司是否都能满足。

贾：我们正在满足这些要求。我们在发布会或者销售电话中说到我们现在已经推出500万台Razor了，并且我们将会推出更多。我们在今年年底的时候同样会向威瑞森推出。我对Razor及其衍生品[11]感到非常激动，我们下周将展出一些产品，它们都是专门为Razor设计的。我们的产品会变得非常轻和薄，并且我们有很多款成功的产品也都是轻薄[12]设计。

记者：这是个棘手的[13]问题，就是您能保证您的品牌始终被消费者关注吗？所有的运营商[14]都希望有私人商标，他们想说明自己的手机是一台威瑞森手机，但它其实是一台摩托罗拉手机。

贾：我不认为这是个普遍情况。我们在Razor上已经做得很好了，我认为我们双方都得到了利润。我想Batwing的M在世界上已经越来越有名了。我们正在和T-Mobile，甚至威瑞森之类的人合作推出815，我们正为其在电视和出版物[15]上做各种商业广告。所以我认为就像我们现在所做的那样，如果我们制造很好的产品，在某些私人品牌产品的应用程序及服务器[16]上与承运商一起合作，那么我们双方都将赢得市场。现在人们都需要摩托罗拉，它代表了狂野[17]、冷静[18]和质量。

记者：那是一定的。现在有一些传言[19]，我希望您能在我的节目[20]里说明，您将会推出一款击败黑莓的产品，您能谈谈它吗？

贾：如果告诉你的话，我就不得不伤害你了，吉姆。

记者：哦，说吧，哥们儿！我需要这个！

贾：它对你来说算什么？

记者：哦，不，不能破坏任何规则。

贾：我们有很多惊喜[21]，可能下周我将为你展示一些。

记者：希望如此。我知道您的股票从15开始上升，我相信未来一定会很赚钱。这是一个非常优秀的季度，干得好。谢谢您来参加我们的节目，兄弟。

贾：荣幸之至。

记者：我总喜欢把钱存在您这儿，您也总是不负众望[22]。

11. derivative product
12. slim *adj.*
13. tough *adj.*
14. carrier *n.*
15. press *n.*
16. service *n.*
17. wild *adj.*
18. cool *adj.*
19. rumor *n.*
20. show *n.*
21. surprise *n.*
22. deliver

Reporter: Motorola is one of the key companies here at the Consumer Electronics Show. You mentioned those deals with Google and Yahoo. The company is riding the wave of the success of its Razor cell phones. But this just goes to show you that the Motorola's dramatic turnaround shows the power and drama that is consumer electronics.

Jha: It's all we've been talking about for a couple of years. So it's finally coming to reality. We're—the convergence of communications, contents and clients. and the Internet goes there. It's more than broadband Internet.

Reporter: The toys that you're unveiling here, what's getting you excited? What is the latest and greatest for Motorola?

Jha: Well, we've been doing great iconic products now for a year or two. It's wickedly cool iconic products like Razor and Razor derivatives. And I have a whole bunch of them. What's now, we're moving to the next generation of experiences. So we announced a big deal with Kodak last night. How do we take pictures out of these phones and print them? We announced something with Yahoo, something with Google. How do we get more experiences that are really wickedly compelling? And I think that's what you're seeing here today with a lot of the content players.

Reporter: So show us some of these.

Jha: Oh, well, this is something called iRadio. And this is effectively—allows you to 500 channels of your own defined radio. You become your own disc jockey. You become your own radio station. And we did a deal with some of the major music companies to bring that kind of capability to this market. I got a lot of things on me. I feel like a—this is our new product. This takes the QWERTY device to the next level. Not only is it full Microsoft mobile but it plays video, music, camera in a very, very small pack damage as you can see here today.

Reporter: The Treo killer?

Jha: It's even more than that because it's a personal device. It allows you to do things with videos and your favorite personal content on these devices. Something we introduced last night, which is revolutionary, the next generation of Bluetooth. This is the smallest Bluetooth device. Not only does it go into your ear very easily, but it has noise suppression capabilities. So it actually—the microphone actually plays off your jawbone in your inner ear and really brings—you know, if you're driving on the road, for example, or you're in noisy environment, the noise suppression is very, very good. So we're perfecting this. And we also have, you know.

Reporter: The Oakley glasses.

Jha: Well, the Oakley glasses for the next generation because this is now full MP3 stereo. Basically, you know, instead of walking around with those things hanging out of your ears, cut those cords, put your phone on, play music like this on into your ears.

---

ride v.
控制，骑

dramatic adj.
戏剧的，引人注目的

convergence n.
集合，会聚

unveil v.
使公之于众，揭幕

iconic adj.
形象的，图标的

wickedly（美国俚语）adj. 精彩的，了不起的

derivative n.
衍生物，派生物

disc jockey
广播电台

damage n.
损害，损毁

content n.
内容，目录

revolutionary adj.
革命的，旋转的

suppression n.
控制，镇压

jawbone n.
美国一家蓝牙耳机公司的名称

stereo n.
立体声，立体声系统

贾： 是的，非常感谢。

记者：摩托罗拉公司是电子消费产品展览[23]中的一家重要公司。您提到了与谷歌和雅虎的交易，公司推出的Razor手机已经取得了成功，但这只是表明了摩托罗拉奇迹般的[24]转向显示了电子消费产品的力量和奇迹。

贾： 这是我们近几年来一直在讨论的问题。最后这变为了现实。我们是通讯、内容以及客户的融合，并且网络也在往这个方向发展。这比宽带[25]网络有更加重要的意义。

记者：您今天所展示的这些产品，是什么让您如此兴奋？摩托罗拉最好、最新的产品又是什么？

贾： 嗯，我们的形象[26]产品已经做了一两年了。像Razor和其衍生品一类就是绝妙的形象产品。并且公司生产了一系列这些产品。现在我们正向下一代体验迈进。我们昨晚宣布了与柯达公司的合作。怎样才能从手机中把图片提取并打印[27]出来呢？我们与雅虎和谷歌一起推出了一些程序。怎样才能得到更多引人入胜的使用体验呢？我想这就是你和一些体验者今天所看到的。

记者：那么给我们展示一些吧。

贾： 哦，好的，这款产品叫做iRadio，它很高效，可以让你拥有500个自定义的[28]广播频道。你自己就能成为电台DJ。你成为了自己的广播电台。并且我们通过与一些主要的音乐公司合作将这种功能带向市场。因此我有很多事情要做。这是我们的新产品，它将全键盘[29]设计带到一个新的水平。这将不仅仅是一款微软手机，它还可以播放视频和音乐，并具有照相功能。正如你今天看到的摄像头，损坏率非常低。

记者：它会成为Treo的克星[30]吗？

贾： 比那还要出色，因为它是个人装置。你可以在这些设备上看视频和自己喜欢的私人内容。昨天晚上我们推出的产品是具有革新性的[31]，是下一代的蓝牙[32]产品。也是最小的蓝牙设备。它不仅可以轻松将信息传入你的耳朵，还有消除杂音[33]的功能。实际上扩音器[34]将声音传输到你的耳朵里，比如当你开车时，或者当你在一个嘈杂的环境中，这个噪音消除功能非常非常好。我们也在完善这个功能，我们还有别的产品，你知道的。

记者：奥克利眼镜。

贾： 是的，下一代的奥克利眼镜有MP3立体声[35]功能。基本来说，不用把这些东西挂在耳朵外面，拉开绳子，直接打开手机，就像这样让音乐进入你的耳朵。

23. Consumer Electronics Show
24. dramatic *adj.*
25. broadband *n.*
26. iconic *adj.*
27. print *v.*
28. of your own defined
29. QWERTY(键盘第一行的前六个字母)
30. killer *n.*
31. revolutionary *adj.*
32. Bluetooth
33. noise suppression
34. microphone *n.*
35. stereo *n.*

1. 雅虎（Yahoo!）是美国著名的互联网门户网站，20世纪末互联网奇迹的创造者之一。其服务包括搜索引擎、电邮、新闻等，业务遍及24个国家和地区，为全球超过5亿的独立用户提供多元化的网络服务。同时也是一家全球性的因特网通讯、商贸及媒体公司。

2. 虚拟条件句中，结果主句和条件从句的谓语动作若不是同时发生时，虚拟语气的形式应作相应的调整，这种条件句叫错综条件句。例如：If they had informed us, we would not come here now.（如果他们通知过我们的话，我们现在就不会来这里了。）这句话中从句的动作与过去的事实相反，而主句的动作与现在或现在正在发生的事实不符。

3. 词组come through的意思是"经历"，例如：How did you manage to come through the Second World War without even a scratch?（你怎么经历了第二次世界大战还会安然无恙呢？）表示经历意义的词还有：experience，undergo，go through等。

4. whether和if都可以和or not连用，但whether之后可以直接跟or not，而if则不能。例如：我们可以说 "I don't care whether or not your car breaks down." 但不能说 "I don't care if or not your car breaks down."。

5. 词组out of question的意思是"毫无疑问"，例如：Freedom of navigation in the South China Sea is out of question.（南海的航行自由没有任何问题。）注意其与out of the question的区别，out of the question指的是"不可能，不知底细，根本谈不上"，例如：I cannot say she has never given me happiness, but peace of mind with her is out of the question.（我不能说她从来就没给我带来过幸福，但是与她相处是不可能有内心的宁静的。）

6. 英语中，分号有时又称为小句号。它表示一个停顿，其停顿时间在逗号与冒号的停顿时间之间。当两个主句之间没有任何连接词（如and, but, or, nor, for）连接，这时最好采用分号使之分离。例如：You don't write because you want to say something; you write because you've got something to say.

7. 英语词汇的一词多义是很普遍的现象，一些常用词语用在不同的句子里可能会失去基本含义，而表示另外一些意思。我们平时要在大量的阅读中根据不同的上下文去揣摸才能准确地理解，避免闹出笑话。下面举一些示例供参考：①dead，death，die不是"死"的意思。例如：He is a dead shot.（他是个神枪手。）He cut me dead at the meeting.（在开会时他假装不认识我。）His feet feel dead.（他的脚冻僵了。）②hand不仅仅是"手"的意思。例如：He had no hand in the matter.（他跟那事毫无关系。）The terminal examination is at hand.（期末考试快到了。）③see一词可以表示"考虑"的意思。例如：Jack saw any man who spoke to his wife as a potential threat.（杰克认为任何一个与他妻子说话的男人都是一个潜在的威胁。）

8. 词组give a sense of意为"给人以……感"。例如：But these pursuits give a sense of fulfillment, of being the best one can be, particularly in the long run.（但这种追求从长远意义上来讲，会给人以成就感，更好地实现自己的价值，做最好的自己。）

9. first of all与first、firstly一样，都是表示"首先"的意思，可以在句中做状语。例如：First of all, we should chase these fears from his mind.（首先，我们应当消除他心中的恐惧。）

16

摩根集团首席执行官：
杰米·戴蒙
CEO of Morgan Corp.:
Jamie Dimon

　　杰米·戴蒙，1956年3月出生在纽约。1982年获得哈佛大学MBA后进入当时的美国运通公司，给时任美国运通总裁的桑迪·威尔当助手。1999年出任美国第一银行（Bank One）CEO一职。2004年，第一银行与J.P.摩根大通合并，戴蒙出任摩根大通的首席运营官（COO）一职。从2006年起，杰米·戴蒙正式成为摩根大通新一任CEO。摩根大通在戴蒙的带领下不仅在每个季度均保持盈利近20亿美元的水平，而且其投资银行等业务还在五大投行纷纷倒台的情况下逆市走高，更让摩根大通在风暴中屹立不倒。

　　杰米·戴蒙是世界上最令人敬畏的银行家。他是全球500强最年轻的总裁，《财富》杂志评选的25位最具影响力的商界领袖之一，《名利场》杂志"信息时代百名权势人物"排行榜TOP10之一，深得奥巴马的信赖。

16.1 / We Must Restore Confidence

轻松输入十分钟

Reporter: I'm here with Jamie Dimon. Thank you for stepping out of the hearing and talking to us. Tell me what your reaction is. How did it go in there?

Dimon: I think it's completely appropriate that the government looked into a situation like this. It's unprecedented and has future implications of policies. I think the senators asked smart questions and they are thinking about the right issues.

Reporter: Can you give us a sense of how it went down at that weekend, how you came up with the valuation of $2 and then $10, how it was that you actually came up with this price.

Dimon: It's really hard to do that because I think it's unprecedented in the 48-hour period that two companies and the government get together and pull up a transaction like that. A lot of the price had much more looking at the downside, how much risk could JPMorgan bear. Not the upside. We want to make sure that JPMorgan was never put in a position where its financial position was jeopardized in any way, shape or form.

Reporter: And you're talking about a risk of 300 billion of assets.

Dimon: That's correct. And we took an unprecedented guarantee of customers & liabilities and I think the Bear Stearns employees, we want to win their hearts and minds. We think they have some great people. They've been there for a long time. They are proud and should be proud. So we want to welcome a lot of them to our company too.

Reporter: A lot of people are talking about the relationship between you and Tim Geithner, how you and the fed got involved. Were there any other bidders at the table? Yours was the only bank that had the capacity to do this.

Dimon: I know other people that there were there and in the proxy they will have to disclose some of that, but I think—and I'm going to speak about Tim Geithner and secretary treasury Paulson and chairman of the receive Bernanke. I think we're lucky to have public officials that dedicated, hard, creative and can go to work around the clock like they did.

---

appropriate *adj.*
适当的，恰当的

unprecedented *adj.*
史无前例的，空前的

senator *n.*
参议员，评议员

valuation *n.*
评价，估价

transaction *n.*
交易，事务

downside *n.*
底侧，下降趋势

jeopardize *v.*
危害，使陷危地

liability *n.*
负债，责任

bidder *n.*
投标人，出价人

proxy *n.*
代用品，委托书

disclose *v.*
公开，揭露

dedicate *v.*
致力，献身

我们必须重拾信心

有效学习十分钟

记者：我现在与杰米•戴蒙先生在一起，很感谢您能够暂别[1]听证会[2]来参加我们的谈话节目。请跟我们说一下您的感想，事情是如何发展到这个地步的呢？

戴蒙：我认为，政府调查这个情况的举动是非常恰当的，这是史无前例的，并且对未来政策的制定也是有积极影响的。我认为参议员们提出的都是很明智的[3]问题，他们所考虑的事情也都是值得考虑的。

记者：您能跟我们说一下周末事情是怎样发展的吗？您是怎样首先估价[4]2美元，然后又变成了10美元的呢？您到底是如何得出这个价格的呢？

戴蒙：那是很难做的，因为我们无法预测在接下来的48小时内，政府会与两家公司一起合作并且进行一场交易[5]。无论摩根集团能够承受[6]多大的风险，很多价格看起来都是呈现下降趋势，而不是上升趋势。我们想要确保摩根集团在金融界的地位无论是形式[8]还是构成[9]方面都不会受到任何程度上的损害[7]。

记者：您提到3000亿美元资产[10]的风险。

戴蒙：是的。我们用史无前例数量的顾客和债务[11]来做担保，我们想要赢得贝尔斯登公司员工的心，使他们信任我们。我想贝尔斯登公司有很多很伟大的人，他们在自己的岗位上已经做了很久。他们感到很骄傲，也应该感到骄傲。所以我们也非常欢迎他们能够来到我们的公司。

记者：很多人都谈论您和提姆•盖特纳之间的关系，谈论您和美联储是怎样涉及[12]于此的。那里还有其他的投标人[13]吗？还是摩根集团是有能力那样做的惟一一个集团。

戴蒙：我还认识其他一些相关人员，在代理权[14]问题上他们必须要向人们表明一些什么，但是我想，我现在要谈论一下提姆•盖特纳，财政大臣保尔森以及伯南克。我想，我们能够有像他们那样乐于奉献、努力工作、有创造力并且能够昼夜不停[15]工作的人，我们真的很幸运。

记者：当股东们开始进行投票选举，最终结果还没有出来的时候，您期望会发生些什么呢？

戴蒙：额外的[16]保证以及更高的价格，实际上我们将拥有其39.5%的股份，这是我们意

1.step out of

2.hearing n.

3.smart adj.

4.valuation n.

5.transaction n.

6.bear v.

7.jeopardize v.

8.shape n.

9.form v.

10.asset n.

11.liability n.

12.involve v.

13.bidder

14.proxy n.

15.around the clock

16.additional adj.

Reporter: What are you expecting as far as the shareholder vote when that happens, as far as the Bear Morgan conclusion.

Dimon: The additional guaranties, the higher price, the fact that we are going to own 39.5% is a foregone conclusion.

Reporter: The environment was a big part of that in there. Where would you say we are in terms of the ending?

Dimon: I never forecast the future because no one really knows. I try to make sure as a company we're prepared for additional bad times or hopefully good times. But I just don't know.

Reporter: Can you give me a sense of what you'll be keeping as far as the Bear Stearns portfolio?

Dimon: We're treating it like a real merger. We're trying to bring in all their prime correspondents, brokers, equity, bear energy and really try to get the best of both companies.

Reporter: You only had 48 hours to do the due diligence, correct?

Dimon: That's correct.

Reporter: That had to be a huge risk.

Dimon: It's the last time I will ever do something like that. You have to know that there were 200 people in JPMorgan and probably an equal amount of people from Bear Stearns working around the clock, didn't go to sleep for a two or three-day period and are just watching that teamwork of those folks really is something special. You should know, we really went out of our way to try to get every last person a job because there will be job loss in this but we want to make sure those great people find other financial companies in New York and maybe CNBC.

Reporter: OK. Tell me what it was like to be in the middle of the storm. The storm that you've been in for a year, knowing the pressure, knowing the pain that so many people were beginning to suffer, knowing the uncertainty that existed in the country as we watched this go from catastrophe to catastrophe to catastrophe, watching a government trying to do something, but not knowing exactly what to do.

Dimon: You're right. There's not an owner's manual of how to deal through this kind of an event or this kind of a market.

Reporter: Because it's once in a lifetime.

Dimon: It is unprecedented.

Reporter: Because of the housing crisis and the collapse of the bubble and all of that.

Dimon: Exactly. And so—and so a lot of the right things have been done, but not everything that has been done has worked.

Reporter: Which brings me to this question. The issue in many cases is when will we

---

shareholder *n.*
股东，股票持有人

foregone *adj.*
先前的，过去的

forecast *v.*
预测，预报

portfolio *n.*
投资

merger *n.*
并购，合并

teamwork *n.*
团队合作，协力

folk *n.*
人们，民族

financial *adj.*
金融的，财政的

suffer *v.*
遭受，忍受

manual *adj.*
手工的，体力的

collapse *v.*
瓦解，倒塌

bubble *n.*
泡沫，气泡

料之中的结果。

记者：环境也是其中很大的一部分。您在什么时候会说
我们已经得到我们想要的结果了呢？

戴蒙：我从来不对未来做预言，因为没有人会真正地知
道未来会发生什么事情。我试图确保，作为一家
公司，我们已经为不景气或者是我们所希望的繁
荣都做好了准备，但是我不知道未来会发生什
么。

记者：您能告诉我们，您将会保持对贝尔斯登的投资不
变吗？

戴蒙：我们将把它视为一次真正的合并，我们会试着接纳[17]他们原有的所有主要的通讯
员、代理商、普通股[18]以及能源等，来充分利用两个公司的优势。

记者：您只有48个小时去进行尽职审查[19]，是吗？

戴蒙：是的。

记者：风险肯定很大。

戴蒙：这将是我最后一次做这样的事情。你必须要知道，在摩根集团有200个人，贝尔
斯登里也许也有这么多人，大家都是在彻夜不眠地工作着，两三天的时间不睡
觉，就是为了看那些人的共同努力是会起到一定作用的。你应该知道，我们真
的不厌其烦地为每个人都安排好工作，因为如果我们不那样做的话，失业率就
会上升，我们会尽力确保那些优秀的人们都能够在纽约的金融公司或者是美国
财经频道[20]有一份工作。

记者：好的。那么请跟我们说一下现在处于金融风暴之中的感受。金融危机已经有一
年的时间了，了解到其中的一些压力，了解到人们所承受的痛苦，了解到我们
国家中的一些不确定性[21]，到处都是灾难，看到政府想要为此做些什么但是却又
不知道该做些什么的场景，您对此都有些什么看法呢？

戴蒙：是的，没有人能够通过自己的力量解决这次的困难，或者是救助这样一个遭受
打击的市场。

记者：因为这是千年不遇的。

戴蒙：史无前例的。

记者：那是由房产危机和经济泡沫[22]的破灭而导致的。

戴蒙：是的，所以人们采取了很多恰当的措施，但并不是每项措施都有效地发挥了其
自身的作用。

记者：这使我想到了一个问题，那就是我们所采取的补救措施什么时候能够发挥作用[23]，
那样的话银行除了借钱给人们，还能够发挥很多其他的作用。

戴蒙：我想银行已经开始发挥作用了，现在正在发挥其他作用。说银行没有向外贷款

17. bring in
18. equity *n.*
19. due diligence
20. CNBC (Consumer News and Business Channel)
21. uncertainty *n.*
22. bubble *n.*
23. take effect

have all this rescue effort taking effect so that banks will begin to do more of the function they do, which is lend money?

Dimon: It's starting to happen. I think it is happening. It's not fair to say that lending isn't happening. It's just fair to say it isn't happening in the same quantity in which it has happened.

Reporter: By a wide margin.

Dimon: Again, different things in different areas.

Reporter: But that's a trust and confidence that you have got to acknowledge was there. Banks were not willing to loan to each other, because they didn't know the financial circumstance of the other bank.

Dimon: It's an issue for Wall Street. It's an issue for Main Street. It's an issue for the central bankers. It's an issue for the Treasury. Our combined issue, step number one, you have got to restore confidence, because confidence is a necessary condition for anything else.

Reporter: There are many people who believe that people who lead financial institutions who got us in this economic catastrophe in part because of these toxic securities owe an apology to the American people and those people who've suffered so much because of it and those who risked their jobs and lots of other things. Isn't that appropriate, to ask explanation and apology for what has happened and what this country is going through, on the part of the leaders of the financial community, who helped and OKed and made the decisions that got us where we are now?

Dimon: And I can completely understand how people on Main Street, people who are not close to this industry, would be furious at what has happened, and furious at kind of where we've gotten to. In lots of different ways that is affecting them. And their housing prices are down; their nest eggs are down. I mean, there's a lot that's going on, which is something that would make me extremely furious.

Reporter: And they are furious in many ways, as you know.

Dimon: Exactly.

rescue v.
援救，营救

quantity n.
数量，大量

acknowledge v.
承认，答谢

combined adj.
组合的，结合的

restore v.
恢复，修复

catastrophe n.
大灾难，大祸

explanation n.
解释，说明

completely adv.
完全地，彻底地

furious adj.
狂怒的，激烈的

extremely adv.
非常，极其

是不公平的，我们应该说只不过没有以前那么多罢了。

记者：还有广泛的回旋余地[24]。

戴蒙：不同的事物在不同的领域会不同而已。

记者：但是你必须要承认，现在，信任和信心还是存在的。银行过去不愿意借钱给彼此，是因为他们不了解其他银行的金融情况。

戴蒙：这是华尔街遇到的问题，这是主体街遇到的问题，这对于中央的银行家来说是个问题，这对于财政部来说也是个问题。我们的一个共同问题就是，我们必须要重拾[25]信心，因为信心是保证一切事物的必要条件[26]。

记者：很多人认为，那些领导金融机构的人在某种程度上就是使得我们进入这次经济危机的人，他们应该为那些不良的[27]有价证券[28]向美国人民道歉，向那些因此承受很多苦难的人道歉，那些人可能因为这次经济危机失去了工作，失去了很多东西。为了那些已经发生的事情，为了我们国家现在正在经历[29]的事情。向那些金融机构的领导人要求一个解释[30]和道歉，是恰当的[31]做法吗？是他们帮助并通过的决策把我们带入今天的处境。

戴蒙：我完全能够理解为什么主体街[32]上的人们，那些不了解我们产业[33]的人们，会对发生的这一切以及我们要做的事感到如此愤怒[34]。我知道，经济危机从很多方面都影响着他们。他们的房产价格下降，他们的养老储蓄[35]减少。我的意思是，现在确实是有很多正在发生的事情也使我感觉很愤怒。

记者：他们以很多方式来发泄他们的愤怒之情。

戴蒙：是这样的。

24. wide margin
25. restore *v.*
26. necessary condition
27. toxic *adj.*
28. security *n.*
29. go through
30. explanation *n.*
31. appropriate *adj.*
32. Main Street
33. industry *n.*
34. furious *adj.*
35. nest egg

自由输出十分钟

1. 摩根大通集团（JPMorgan Chase& Co.），业界俗称细摩或小摩，总部位于纽约，总资产20360亿美元，总存款10093亿美元，占美国存款总额的10.51%，分行5410家，为美国第二大金融服务机构。摩根大通于2000年由大通曼哈顿银行及J.P.摩根公司合并而成，并分别收购芝加哥第一银行和贝尔斯登银行和华盛顿互惠银行。2012年4月4日，该公司涉嫌违法事件被指控，同意支付约2000万美元的罚款。2012年5月摩根大通宣布一项交易组合亏损20亿美元，引发了金融市场的轩然大波，在随后的15日里美国联邦调查局(FBI)介入摩根大通巨亏丑闻的清查。

2. CEO是chief executive officer的缩写，意为"首席执行官"；COO是chief operating officer的缩写，意为"首席运营官"；MBA是Master of Business Administration的缩写，意为"工商管理硕士"。

3. 词组look into意为"调查"，例如：I would be very grateful if you could look into the matter as soon as possible. And I am looking forward to an early reply.（如果贵方能尽快调查此事，我将万分感激。望早日做出答复。），表示此含义的词还有survey，investigate等。

4. *Vanity Fair*(《名利场》)是美国著名生活杂志，是主要宣扬当代文化的刊物，内容包括政治、名人、图书、幽默、新闻、艺术和摄影。如今，Vanity Fair(《名利场》)已经成为公认的美国最重要的杂志之一。它是造星工厂，是华府政客的读本，也是追名逐利的芸芸众生看世界的一个窗口。

5. 在It is necessary/important/strange/natural；It is requested/suggested/desired/proposed；it is a pity等结构后的主语从句中要用虚拟语气，即用should+动词原形或只用动词原形。例如: It is requested that Professor Li（should）give us a speech.（我们要求李教授为我们做演讲。）

6. due diligence的意思是"尽职调查"，是经济学中的专业术语，例如：Mr. Bolton is now using an independent company to help him do due diligence on potential and existing investments.（目前，波顿先生已聘用一家独立公司帮助自己对潜在的及现有的投资项目作尽职调查。）

7. 排比（parallelism）是英语中常见的修辞手法，运用这种结构写出的文章结构匀称，说理有力，叙事生动，抒情深刻。例如：Without the health, you can't enjoy the happy life; without the health, your dream can't be true; without the health, wealth is useless for you.

8. 表示"灾难"的名词有: suffering，calamity，disaster，catastrophe等。其中，catastrophe表示程度较大的灾难，例如：We are on the edge of a potential catastrophe for the euro and that's not going to be good when it happens.（欧元濒临崩溃的边缘，如果这真的发生了，结果会很糟糕。）

9. happen一词可表示"恰巧，令人惊奇的是"，例如：As it happens, I have a spare set of keys in my office.（碰巧我在办公室有一套备用钥匙。）

百思买首席执行官：
布莱恩·邓恩
CEO of Best Buy: Brian Dunn

布莱恩·邓恩，是全球最大消费电子产品零售商百思买集团的CEO。2009年6月25日，在百思买美国总部举行的年度股东大会上，49岁的布莱恩·邓恩正式被任命为百思买集团（纽约证交所代码：BBY）首席执行官。同时被任命加入百思买董事会，并参选了2010年股东例会。此前邓恩担任集团主席兼首席运营官（COO）一职。

邓恩于2012年3月29日宣布了对百思买的大规模重组和裁员计划。在其推动下，百思买公司关闭50家大卖场，开设100家小型手机连锁店以及裁员400人。通过这一系列措施，公司希望在2015年前削减8亿美元的预算。同年4月10日，百思买董事会宣布，为公司效力28年之久的布莱恩·邓恩已辞去首席执行官和董事职务。

17.1 Staying In Touch With Employees All the Time

轻松输入十分钟

Reporter: Tell me about some of the leadership lessons you've learned.

Dunn: I didn't realize it at the time, but the first deep leadership lesson I learned was when I was 14 years old and working in a grocery store. The manager at the time, a gentleman named Ken, came up to me and said, "What do you think about this process we're using here in the front end to tell people to pick up their groceries?" A seemingly simple challenge, and I gave him some sort of innocuous, nonspecific answer—sort of, "Everything's fine." And he pulled me aside and he said, "Now listen, I asked you about this 'cause I really care what you think. You're doing this every single day and I want to know what you think about it." I know it seems simple, but just that notion of learning from people who are actually doing the work, and the encouragement he gave me to tell him exactly what I thought really stayed with me, and it was a recurring thing throughout the time I worked for him.

Reporter: What else?

Dunn: Be really careful about what you believe about yourself. You're never as good as they say or as bad as they say. When I was made CEO on June 24, I didn't wake up that morning smarter; I didn't wake up with a massive IQ expansion; I did wake up with a new responsibility. Another piece that I think is really, really important is you have to be curious. I describe it as "active learning". And one of the things I do is setting out across our enterprise and look for ideas, people doing things in ways that are different, doing things that are important for our future. And it's not just inside our enterprise; it's outside the enterprise, as well. One of the things that became pretty clear to me, in my last role as president and chief operating officer at Best Buy, is that people don't line up outside my door to tell me how they've screwed something up. You know, you sort of get the "Yep, everything's going terrific and it's A—OK". So it's really important to me to get out where the customer experiences the brand, and that means I surf our web pages. It means I call our call center. It means I visit our stores and talk to our associates about what's working, what's not.

Reporter: How would you say your leadership style has evolved over time?

Glossary

grocery n.
食品杂货店

seemingly adv.
看来似乎，表面上看来

innocuous adj.
无害的，无伤大雅的

notion n.
概念，见解

encouragement n.
鼓励

recurring adj.
再发的，循环的

massive adj.
巨大的，大量的

enterprise n.
企业，事业

screw v.
旋，拧

terrific adj.
极好的

surf v.
浏览，冲浪

associate n.
同事，伙伴

时刻与员工保持联系

有效学习十分钟

记者：请跟我们说一下，您所学到的有关领导方面的知识。

邓恩：在那时我并没有意识到，但是我第一次学习到深入的[1]有关领导方面的东西，是14岁在一家杂货店[2]工作的时候。杂货店的经理是一位叫肯的绅士，他有一天走过来跟我说："你对于我们现在帮助顾客挑选[3]商品的做法有什么看法呢？"那看起来是一个很简单的任务，然后我给出了他一些不会招致反对的、不特定的[4]答案，就像是"我们所做的一切都很好"这样的说法。然后他把我拉到一边[5]，跟我说："听着，我问你这个问题是因为我真的关心你对此的想法，你每天都在做这个工作，所以我想知道你的意见是怎样的。"我知道这看似很简单，但是要向真正做那份工作的人们了解情况，而且他鼓励我对他说出我内心真实的想法，这些都深深地烙在了我的心中。而且在我为他工作的时候，这种情况也时有发生。

记者：还有别的吗？

邓恩：不要想当然地认为自己很了解自己。一个人永远不会像别人说的那么好，也不会像别人说的那么坏。我6月24日被任命为首席执行官的时候，那天我并没有比以往更聪明一些或是拥有更高的智商，我多的只是一份新的责任。我想到的另外一点非常重要的就是，一个人要乐于求知[6]，我称之为"主动学习"。我所做的事情之一就是，在公司范围内寻求新的发展想法，因为人们的工作方式都是不一样的，但是大家做的都是有益于公司未来的事情。这不仅仅是在公司内部，对于公司外部来说也是这样的。当我在百思买担任主席和首席运营官一职的时候，我清楚了一件事情，那就是人们不再在我的办公室门前排着队[7]来告诉我说，他们是怎样把事情搞糟[8]了。你知道，这就会让人觉得"我们的公司运营得很好，每一件事都很好。"所以对我来说，能够了解[9]到顾客对于我们产品的看法是很重要的，这就意味着我得查看网页[10]，给我们的电话中心[11]打电话，还有去商店与我们的同事一起讨论什么事情我们做得很好，而什么不好。

记者：随着时间的流逝，您的领导风格[12]发生了怎样的变化呢？

邓恩：关于这个问题，我给你讲一个我个人的故事。我妻子得乳腺癌[13]，已经7年了。7年前我们对于这个感到非常害怕。那时候你会明白，世界上最重要的事情就是

1. deep *adj.*
2. grocery *n.*
3. pick up
4. nonspecific *adj.*
5. pull aside
6. curious
7. line up *adj.*
8. screw up
9. get out
10. web page
11. call center
12. style *n.*
13. breast cancer

Dunn: I'll give you a very personal story about this. My wife just had her seven-year anniversary, all clear, from breast cancer. We had a big scare seven years ago. And at that moment, you get this gift of utter clarity—that the most important thing in the whole world was making sure my wife and my three children got through this.

Reporter: How did it affect your career?

Dunn: It changed me as a leader. I got really focused on: What are the big rocks that we need to move? I still can fall into some of the petty traps, but I worked really hard to say, is this really important or is this just like a little ego thing for me?

Reporter: Tell me about the best boss you've worked for.

Dunn: Let me tell you a quick story that I think will illustrate it the best. My first day at Best Buy in 1985, I got handed a sales book and I got sent out on the floor, and essentially that was the training. And the store manager came up to me a couple days later and said, "How do you like it here?" And I said: "You know what? I hate it. There's no training. I've got people grabbing at me." And then he looked at me and he started talking to me about the Minnesota Twins—this was in Minnesota. Started talking to me about the Vikings, talking to me about my fiancée, and then talked to me about fishing. He started to get to know me and then he said: "You know, I come in early on Saturdays. If you want to spend some time, I'll teach you a little bit about how to sell." He did that for three successive Saturdays, and by the end of the three weeks, I was really pretty good and I liked it. He taught me how to sell, and you can feed yourself for a lifetime when you know how to sell. And what he really did was starting to open doors for me, and start to find things out in me that I didn't understand about myself.

Reporter: How do you use technology to keep in touch with employees and customers?

Dunn: I leverage video to reach our folks. We have a quarterly enterprise-wide town hall that we started last year that is really an interesting couple of hours. We have folks from China, London, Mexico—all our operations around the world—and I typically start that off with, "Here's a 15-minute update on where we are" and then we get questions from around the world. The other thing I will do is to go on Twitter and listen to what people are saying about us. I think those opinions are important for us. I also have a program that searches the Internet anytime somebody mentions Best Buy out there. Sometimes it's really a great thing, sometimes it's obscenity-laden, but I have a huge appetite for it. If I see customers have problems with things, I will contact the appropriate person in our company and have them contact that customer. Sometimes I contact the customer.

Reporter: Hearing from you probably scares the heck out of them.

Dunn: It does freak them out a little bit. But I do think that the social media

---

evolve v.
发展，进化

breast n.
胸部，胸怀

utter adj.
十足的；绝对的

trap n.
陷阱，圈套

ego n.
自我，自负

illustrate v.
阐明，举例说明

essentially adv.
本质上，本来

fiancée n.
未婚妻

successive adj.
连续的，继承的

feed v.
供给，喂养

enterprise-wide adj.
整个企业的，企业范围的

update n.
最新知识；最新资料

appetite n.
欲望，嗜好

contact v.
联系，接触

freak out v.
（使）吓得要死

让我的妻子和3个孩子能够渡过[14]这个困难的时期。

记者：那对于您的事业有怎样的影响呢？

邓恩：那使我作为一位领导改变了很多。我关注[15]的是：在前进的道路上我们需要克服的困难都有哪些？在发展的过程中，我们仍有可能掉进[16]一些陷阱[17]中，但是我工作非常努力，因为我想要确定哪些事情对我们是真正重要的。

记者：请跟我们说一下您工作过程中遇到的最好的老板。

邓恩：让我给你讲一个能够很好地阐述[18]这个问题的故事。我第一天到百思买上班是在1985年，那天我拿到了一本销货簿[19]，我被派送到楼上，而这实际上就是我们的培训。几天之后，部门经理来问我说："在这里工作感觉怎么样呢？"我说："你知道吗，我不喜欢这里的工作，连个培训都没有。人们抓着我不放[20]。"他看了看我然后开始跟我讲有关明尼苏达双城的事情，那是在明尼苏达谈论维京部族，谈论我的未婚妻[21]，谈论钓鱼等等。他对我有了一定的了解之后又跟我说："我周六早上都会很早来公司，如果你想学的话，我可以教你一些销售的知识。"然后他连续[22]教了我三周，三周之后，我可以做得很好了，并且我喜欢上了那份工作。那位经理教我如何销售，一个人如果学会了销售的话，那就足以养活[23]他一辈子[24]了。而他所做的就是为我开启[25]了事业的大门，并且在我身上发掘[26]了很多我自己并不知道的优点和闪光点。

记者：您如何运用科技来与您公司的员工和顾客们保持联系[27]呢？

邓恩：我利用视频[28]与我们的员工保持联系。从去年开始，我们每一个季度[29]都会与我们的员工进行交谈，那几个小时很有意思。我们的员工来自中国、伦敦、墨西哥等世界上很多不同的地区，我通常[30]会在最开始的时候说，"我们现在有15分钟的时间来讨论我们公司的进程[31]"，然后我们就可以从全世界范围内得到一些问题的反馈。我会做的另外一件事情就是去Twitter了解人们对于我们的看法。我认为那些看法对我们很重要。我们还有一个程序，能够在任何时间在因特网上追踪[32]到人们提及[33]"百思买"，有时候大家说的是好的事情，有时候是一些充满猥亵的[34]事情，但是我总是很关注这个。如果我发现顾客对于我们的产品有什么问题的话，我会与相关部门的人员联系，让他们与那位顾客进行沟通，有的时候我会直接联系顾客。

记者：人们直接收到您的来信可能会使他们受到惊吓[35]。

邓恩：的确会有一点，但是我认为，社会媒体就是为我们创造一些有趣的平台，使人们能够彼此进行联系并更好地了解事物，我觉得这很好。

记者：作为一位领导和经理，您为自己设定[36]的目标是什么呢？

14. get through
15. focus on
16. fall into
17. trap
18. illustrate v.
19. sales book
20. grab at
21. fiancée n.
22. successive adj.
23. feed v.
24. lifetime n.
25. open v.
26. find out
27. keep in touch with
28. video n.
29. quarterly adj.
30. typically adv.
31. where we are n.
32. search v.
33. mention v.
34. obscenity-laden
35. scare the heck out of
36. set v.

we have out there create interesting platforms for people to make those connections and to know things better. I think it's just fascinating.

Reporter: What goals have you set for yourself as a leader and manager?

Dunn: I've set a couple. One, I have spent my career working in the United States, and I am going to be spending a lot of time visiting our operations in China and Europe and around the globe to get very connected to those businesses. Personally, I want to make sure I keep learning. I think the CEO's job is designed to insulate people from things that really happen. I want to make sure that I'm sort of out there in the white noise and the messiness of it all. If you don't, you run the risk of becoming insulated and ineffective.

Reporter: You said the job is set up to insulate the CEO. What do you mean?

Dunn: Most people don't run in and tell you, "Hey, we've got a problem here," or "I think I messed this thing up." It's human nature; everybody wants to look good. I think that the truth of the matter is that if you're really going to look at it with clear eyes, there are things we do really well. There are things we're OK at. There are things that we're not great at. I think I've got a classic bell curve. I think 20 percent of my stores are great, 60 percent are good, and I've got 20 percent where I've got some serious work to do. I know that quite clearly.

Reporter: Let's talk about hiring. Walk me through what you're looking for in the interview process, your key questions.

Dunn: By the time these individuals get to me, we've had a thorough sort of scan of their technical capabilities and all that. So my discussion with them is very little about technical capability and competence and very much about cultural fit. And the thing I really focus on is: "What are you passionate about? What do you really care about and what do you do with that?" And I don't care if it's coaching a basketball team or something else. I want to understand how they think about their passion.

Reporter: What are you listening for?

Dunn: I want to know what you've done with it and how you feel and what you think about and what's the impact you've had with people.

Reporter: Talk about how you run meetings.

Dunn: I lose interest quickly with the endless pontification. Because that drives me crazy. For the most part, I view meetings as a necessary evil, although I do enjoy our staff meetings when we get together and talk about where the business is and where we're going. I like all those elements. But the endless meeting can really get a little bit tedious for me, so I tend to want to get to the point directly.

Reporter: What big-picture advice do you give your kids about work?

Dunn: Listen carefully, and when you're asked what you think, tell people what you think. And even if you end up on the short end of an interaction, I think you're better off in the long run for finding that voice and putting it forward.

fascinate v.
使着迷，使神魂颠倒

operation n.
操作，经营

insulate v.
隔离，使孤立

messiness n.
混乱，乱糟糟

mess v.
弄乱，毁坏

thorough adj.
彻底的，十分的

scan v.
了解，浏览

passionate adj.
热情的，易怒的

coach v.
指导，训练

endless adj.
无尽的，连续的

tedious adj.
冗长乏味的，沉闷的

邓恩：我给自己设立了几个目标。第一，现在我大部分的工作时间都是在美国的企业，但是接下来我准备利用一些时间去我们在中国、欧洲以及全球范围内的企业，去真正地了解我们的产业。就我个人而言，我想要继续不断地学习。我认为，首席执行官的职位就是将人们与真实发生的事情隔离。我想要走出它的限制，如果不那样做的话，你就有可能冒着被隔离[37]、工作没有成效的危险。

记者：您说，这个职位是用来隔离首席执行官的，您的意思是什么呢？

邓恩：当你成为首席执行官之后，很多人可能并不会来跟你说"我们这里出现了一个问题。"或者是"我把事情搞砸了。"这是人性[38]，每个人都希望自己看起来很好。我想，事实的真相就是，当你真正地去看事情发展状况的时候，你会看到有些事情我们做得很好，有些事情我们做得还可以但并不是非常好，有些事情我们做得不好。我觉得我们得到了一个经典的贝尔曲线[39]。我认为我们的商店中，20%做得是非常好的，60%做得是比较好的，而另外的20%我们还需要继续不断地做工作、进行改造。我很清楚这一点。

记者：让我们来说一下有关招聘的事情。请跟我们说一下，在面试过程中您注重的是什么，您提出的主要问题都有哪些呢？

邓恩：当人们来参加我们面试的时候，我们已经彻底地对他们的技能水平和其他一些方面有所了解。所以在面试过程中我们很少会提及他们的技能、能力等方面，而主要是关注他们的文化修养。我特别关注的就是，"你对什么事情充满激情[40]？你真正感兴趣的是什么以及你会怎样发展自己的兴趣？"。我不管那是否是训练一个篮球队还是什么，我只是想要了解他们对于自己的热情是如何看待的。

记者：那么您想听到的内容是什么呢？

邓恩：我想要知道你是如何发挥自己的热情的，你对此的感觉怎样，是如何看待它的，以及你对人们带来的影响有哪些。

记者：请跟我们谈一下您是如何主持[41]会议的。

邓恩：对于无休止地大发议论[42]，我很快就会失去兴趣，那使我感觉很崩溃。就大部分而言，我将会议视为一件不可避免的恶事，尽管我很喜欢参加我们的员工会议，因为在员工会议上我们可以聚集在一起，谈论我们所取得的成绩以及公司的未来发展，我喜欢这些。但是无休止的会议会让我觉得很乏味，所以我总是想要尽快切入正题。

记者：您对您的孩子在工作方面的宏观建议[43]是怎样的？

邓恩：要学会认真聆听，当你被问及自己的意见时，告诉人们你真实的想法。即使在交谈过程中你可能处于劣势，但是从长远利益来看，你提出那样的意见很有可能会是一件好事。

37. insulate v.
38. human nature
39. bell curve
40. passionate n.
41. run v.
42. pontification n.
43. big-picture advice

1. 百思买（BEST BUY）是全球最大的家用电器和电子产品的零售、分销及服务集团。BEST BUY企业集团包括 BEST BUY零售、音乐之苑集团、未来商场公司、Magnolia Hi-Fi 以及热线娱乐公司、Future Shop、五星电器。BEST BUY在北美同行业中处于领先地位，着眼于企业展望、使命和价值观。BEST BUY名列全美《财富》200 强第 66 位，全球500强企业第142位。

2. 同位语从句是名词性从句中的一种，其作用相当于名词，对前面的名词（短语）加以补充说明。that可以引导同位语从句，例如：The idea that you can do this work well without thinking is quite wrong.（你认为不动脑筋就能做好这件工作的想法是完全错误的。）

3. 词组pick up可表示"获取"的意思，例如：If it was the Big Bang we were going to pick up, it would sound like this.（如果我们所要获取的声音是宇宙大爆炸发出的，它听起来会像这样。）

4. 前缀non-表示否定的意思，例如：nonpartisan（无党派之见的），nonpayment（未支付），nonnegotiable（不可谈判解决的），nonnative（非本地的）等，表示否定的前缀还有in-、im-、dis-、il-等。

5. IQ是"intelligence quotient（智力商数，简称智商）"的缩写；EQ是"emotional quotient（情感商数，简称情商）"的缩写。

6. 词组screw sb. up的意思是"使神经不正常"，例如：Her father's death really screwed her up.（父亲死后，她真是万念俱灰。）

7. 在英语中，现在分词可以作为名词充当主语，例如：Helping you is helping myself.（帮你就是帮我自己。）

8. 受文化及生活方式等方面的影响，英语中的一些颜色词与汉语的颜色词具有不一样的意义，例如：to be in the blues 闷闷不乐（蓝色在汉语中无此象征意义）；a very white man 非常忠实可靠的人（而中国京剧脸谱中"白脸"代表奸诈）等。

9. big-picture是一个由big和picture两个单词组成的合成词，意为"全局的"，例如：Big-picture economic forces still have the power to move the markets.（整体经济力量仍有推动市场的作用。）

18

星巴克行政总裁:
霍华德·舒尔茨
Chief Executive of Starbucks: Howard Schultz

　　霍华德·舒尔茨,星巴克的董事长、首席战略总监。 1952年出生在纽约的布鲁克林区。舒尔茨毕业于美国北密歇根大学。1975年进入施乐公司工作,1982年成为星巴克的市场部和零售部经理。四年后,他离开星巴克开设了自己的第一家咖啡店。而后在1987 年,舒尔茨召集一批投资者买下星巴克公司。1992年,星巴克在美国上市;星巴克咖啡于1999年进入中国,积极致力于将中国做成在美国之外最大的国际市场。2006 年,舒尔茨跻身《福布斯》400 富豪榜,身价在10亿美元以上。

　　目前,星巴克的发展势头让人眼红。它的年财政收入持续增长20%以上。"同一店铺"的销售量在去年十一二月份暴增了11%,为十多年来所罕见。另外,星巴克股票比去年上涨56%,与1992年首次发股上市的市值相比增长了30.28%,达到历史新高。

18.1 Starbucks Pays More Attention To Customers' Experience

轻松输入十分钟

Reporter: Our guest tonight is Howard Schultz, the chairman of Starbucks Coffee Company. He has turned his passion for coffee into a multi billion dollar global business with stores in over 10,000 locations worldwide including Turkey.

Schultz: Yes.

Reporter: Thank you for being with us, Schultz.

Schultz: That's my pleasure, thank you.

Reporter: I think our viewers would be very interested to know about your early days, how Starbucks entered into your life and perhaps more appropriately how you entered into the life of Starbucks in the early 80's. Could you elaborate a little bit about that?

Schultz: Sure. Well, the story is that I actually joined Starbucks as an employee. In the fall of 1982. And when I joined the company we had three stores, getting ready to open up our 4th. What attracted me to the company at that point was the entrepreneurial opportunity and I was really drawn to the quality of the coffee and the fact that Starbucks at the time was educating the entire community, the city of Seattle on what good coffee really is. I honestly never dreamed at the time that I would one day own the company and be in a position where we would have as you said 10,000 stores around the world, which has just been an incredible journey for all of us.

Reporter: Actually now you are present in Turkey as well and I know in the course of approximately three years you have over 20 stores in, I believe two cities Istanbul and Ankara and you have plans for expansion there as well. What are your plans for Turkey and the region in general?

Schultz: I must say, I had never been to Turkey before and I visited your country a year ago, and actually I brought my daughter with me and we had an extraordinary visit. The warmth and hospitality of the people... I love the food, and I was taken with what I believe to be a much larger opportunity for Starbucks than I think we originally thought. So, at this point given the reception that we have, there will be many more stores throughout the country in multiple cities over the next few years and I can't say how many

passion n.
热情，激情

appropriately adv.
确切地，适当地

elaborate v.
阐述，描述

entrepreneurial adj.
企业家的，创业者的

incredible adj.
难以置信的，惊人的

expansion n.
扩张，膨胀

extraordinary adj.
特别的，临时的

hospitality n.
殷勤，好客

multiple adj.
多个，多样的

星巴克注重客户体验

有效学习十分钟

记者： 今晚我们的客人是星巴克咖啡公司的董事长，霍华德·
舒尔茨。他用自己对咖啡的热情创造了价值数十亿的
全球生意，在全世界一万多个地方经营咖啡店，包括
土耳其在内。

舒尔茨： 是的。

记者： 欢迎您的到来，舒尔茨。

舒尔茨： 很高兴来这里，谢谢。

记者： 我想我们的观众[1]会对您早期的生活很感兴趣，星巴克是如何进入您的生活
的？或者更确切地说，在上世纪80年代初期，您是如何开始星巴克生活的？
您可以说说吗？

舒尔茨： 当然。其实我最开始是做星巴克的雇员，是在1982年的秋天。我刚加入公司
的时候，我们有3家店，正在打算开第4家。这家公司吸引我的地方在于它可
以提供成为企业家的机会，咖啡的质量很好，并且那个时候，星巴克正在向
西雅图所有的人解释什么才是好咖啡。那个时候我做梦都没想过这家公司有
一天会属于我，也没想过有一天我们会在全世界范围内拥有如你所说的1万
多家星巴克店，这对我们来说是一场令人难以置信的[2]旅程。

记者： 事实上，现在您在土耳其也开店了，并且我知道，您计划大约3年内在伊斯
坦布尔和安卡拉这两座城市开大约20多家店，并且还有扩张的打算。您在土
耳其这个地区大致的计划是怎样的？

舒尔茨： 我必须要说的是，之前我从没有来过土耳其，一年前我带着我的女儿一起来
过你们的国家，那是一段极好的旅程。土耳其人民热情[3]好客[4]。我很喜欢这
里的食物，我看到了这里有比我们原来想象的要大得多的开星巴克店的机
会。因此，根据我们收到的反馈情况，我们将在未来几年内在土耳其全国大
城市中开更多的咖啡店，我们现在还不能确定数量，因为我们可能会低估这
个数量，但是我们很兴奋，也感觉自己很幸运[5]，在如此短的时间内，我们开

1. viewer n.

2. incredible adj.

3. warmth n.

4. hospitality n.

5. fortunate adj.

we would have because I think I might put too low of a number on it. But we are very excited, very enthused and feel very fortunate that in such a short period of time the stores that we have opened have done extremely well; we give a lot of credit to our local team there.

Reporter: Did they make you taste Turkish coffee?

Schultz: Yes, well, I have had Turkish coffee before and I think the funny story about this is when we were getting ready to open up in Turkey, many of our own people as well as friends of the company said: we had to make sure we had traditional authentic Turkish coffee and Turkish coffee preparations in the store. So we did that. But the truth is that not many Turkish people are ordering Turkish coffee. They want traditional Starbucks coffee or frappuchino. And it's so funny that we have tried to be as respectful as possible but most Turkish people are not drinking it.

Reporter: It's true but I think it is a good addition to the menu even though I heard the same thing in Turkey and I was surprised because the Turks are such coffee drinkers of their own coffee as well.

Schultz: Well, I think that having the traditional Turkish coffee in our stores is really emblematic of what we have tried to do around the world and that is to be extremely respectful of the history of the culture and tradition of different countries' understanding and sensitivity around coffee and the coffee experience, and whenever possible demonstrate our respect by bringing to them the way they have learned to drink coffee. And this is a perfect example.

Reporter: You are operating in so many different markets in terms of cultural differences, like think of France or China or Jordan or many other countries around the world. How do you deal with these cultural differences? Do you do a lot of marketing research before? Do you team up with a lot of local people? What is your strategy?

Schultz: I've never been a big believer in market research personally. So we haven't done a lot of that over the years. The benefit that we have had in countries like Turkey and around the world is that we have fantastic local partners. Who I guess I would say, I would loosely describe as we co-author the strategy with them and leave the execution to them. And, Turkey is operated by the Alshia Group, which is our partner throughout the Middle East. We have a great team led by a fantastic woman Icek whom I think you know. And they have allowed us I think to bring the Starbucks experience into Turkey and slightly refine it for the local market. The interesting thing about what we've been able to do in almost every single country that we've entered is that the local customer wants and demands the authentic Starbucks experience and does not want it watered down for their local markets. So the stores you see in Turkey are very similar to the ones we have right there in Seattle.

Reporter: That's true actually and they are all over the town in Seattle. Every other

enthuse *v.*
感兴趣，热情

authentic *adj.*
正宗的，真正的

addition *n.*
添加物，添加

emblematic *adj.*
象征的，可当标志的

sensitivity *n.*
敏感，过敏

demonstrate *v.*
证明，展示

strategy *n.*
战略，策略

loosely *adv.*
松散地，宽松地

execution *n.*
实施，执行

throughout *prep.*
遍布，贯穿

refine *v.*
改善，提炼

actually *adv.*
实际上，事实上

的店都经营得很好，这主要归功于我们当地的经营管理团队。

记者：　他们让您尝过[6]土耳其咖啡了吗？

舒尔茨：是的，嗯，我以前就喝过土耳其咖啡。我觉得有趣的是，我们准备在土耳其开业的时候，很多人也包括我们公司的朋友说，我们必须保证店里有传统的正宗[7]土耳其咖啡及其配料[8]。所以我们就这样做了。但是事实上，并没有很多土耳其人点[9]土耳其咖啡。他们通常想要传统的星巴克咖啡或者法布奇诺[10]。所以我觉得很有趣，我们尽量尊重[11]当地的饮食习惯，但是多数的土耳其人却并不买账。

记者：　是的，但是我想这也是对原有菜单的丰富[12]，即使在土耳其听到同样的事情我也会大吃一惊，因为他们太喜欢喝自己的咖啡了。

舒尔茨：嗯，我认为在我们的咖啡店里经营传统土耳其咖啡确实代表着我们正努力在全球范围内做的事情。我们要尊重各国不同地区的历史和文化传统，尊重不同国籍的人对咖啡不同的理解和感受。我们通过他们习惯的方式来为他们提供服务，这就是我们表达[13]尊重的一个很好的例子。

记者：　你们的生意涉及很多不同文化氛围的销售市场，比如法国、中国、约旦和世界上许多其他国家。你们怎样处理这些文化差异[14]呢？会在开店之前做很多市场调查[15]吗？会在当地招聘组织经营管理团队吗？你们的战略[16]是怎样的呢？

舒尔茨：从个人角度来讲[17]，我从来不相信市场调查。所以这些年来，我们并没有做很多这一类的市场调查。不论是在土耳其还是在世界其他地方，我们的优势在于，我们有很出色的[18]当地合作伙伴。我想我应该说，我们是松散的[19]合作关系，是我们合作制订出了战略计划，并由他们来开展工作。土耳其的店是由Alshia集团在经营，它是我们在整个中东地区的合作伙伴。我想你们应该认识伊塞克，这位女士是我们一位很出色的领导者。我认为是他们允许我们把星巴克的经验带入土耳其，并根据当地的特色稍作[20]完善，使之更适合当地的市场。几乎我们去的每个国家都会有这样有趣的事情，人们想要正宗的星巴克的体验，并不想让星巴克去到他们的国家之后被稀释[21]。因此，土耳其的星巴克咖啡店和我们现在在西雅图看到的其实是差不多的。

6. taste v.
7. authentic adj.
8. preparation n.
9. order v.
10. frappuchino n.
11. respectful adj.
12. addition n.
13. demonstrate v.
14. cultural difference
15. marketing research
16. strategy n.
17. personally adv.
18. fantastic adj.
19. loosely adv.
20. slightly adv.
21. water down

corner. You can't ask "Where's Starbucks?" because there's another one. That's right. I've wanted to ask you, your company has been a high growth company for so many years now and you're going into different markets, differentiating your product mixture, even going into music, and we'll get to that shortly. How is it, does it, how does a company that is so successful so consistently outdo itself. Is it kind of more difficult when you are so successful so consistently because of expectations?

Schultz: Well, I appreciate the compliment of being so successful. I'm not sure that's true but I think that the cultures and values of the company are steeped in an ongoing commitment to try and create long-term value for our shareholders while integrating a social conscience in everything we do. The culture is also built. I think on a commitment to under promise and over deliver. And we are not a group or company that celebrates a great deal. We want to celebrate the customer and the customer experience. But for many many years we opened many stores around the world and have been able to think especially in terms of the stock market to demonstrate to our shareholders, a company that really does meet its commitments. And as a result of that we have been rewarded in the marketplace. But I would also say that we have taken a very long view of the opportunity despite the fact that we've grown this significantly and these are still the very early stages for growth and development of the company and we want to emerge as one of the most recognized and respected brands in the world and we have a long way to go to ultimately accomplish that.

Reporter: I recently read somewhere that you are envisioning a store number of 30 thousand over the next several years. What is the time horizon that you have and what would be the mix of domestic US stores and international stores in your vision?

Schultz: Well, we're sitting now with 10 thousand or so stores in North America and outside of North America. We've said publicly one day we will have close to 30 thousand stores or so. I think ultimately it's probably 50-50 between international and North America. But I also believe given the success we have had in the emerging markets that appear to be right for Starbucks, 30 thousand stores may turn out to be too low. I also believe that we have a very powerful opportunity to create other products like bottled frappichino, whole bean coffee, our ice cream, music and things that are also part of the growth and development of the company outside of our stores and that will occur around the world. We just recently introduced ready to drink coffee like bottled frappichino here in the US, Japan and Taiwan, and other markets for that.

Reporter: I know that you are very keen on China as a market and you are traveling there a lot. What are some of the other hot spots and what in, what in particular about in China? People, when you think of China you think of

differentiate v.
区分化

consistently adv.
一贯地

compliment n.
称赞，问候

integrate v.
使成为一体，使完整

marketplace n.
市场，商场

emerge v.
显示，出现

envision v.
想象，预想

domestic adj.
国内的

ultimately adv.
最后

bottled adj.
瓶装的

spot n.
斑点，地点

particular adj.
特别，尤其

记者： 确实是这样的，而且星巴克咖啡遍布西雅图。每个角落都有。你无法问"星巴克在哪儿？"因为有很多个星巴克。是的。我想问您，这些年来您的公司一直保持高速的发展，您也正在进入不同的市场，将产品进行差异化[22]组合，甚至涉及到了音乐领域，我们一会儿谈一下这个。一家如此成功如此持久的公司如何自我超越[23]呢？当预期[24]的前景很成功的时候，自我超越是不是更难实现呢？

舒尔茨： 嗯，感谢你对我们成功的称赞。我不知道是不是正确，但是我认为公司的文化和价值观沉浸[25]在一种长期持久的[26]承诺和奉献精神中。我们在做每一件事情的时候都考虑到社会责任心[27]，同时，我们正努力为股东创造长期的价值。我认为，这种文化也建立在信守承诺和提供超值服务的基础之上。我们并不是为了一笔大生意而庆祝的集团或者公司。我们关注的是顾客和他们的体验。多年来我们在世界各地开了很多家星巴克店，我想，尤其是在股票市场上，我们有能力向我们的股东[28]证实我们是守诚信的。我们也因此在市场上得到了回报[29]。但同时我得说，我们十分看重发展机会的长远性。虽然我们现在发展很快，但是这还只是一家公司发展的初级阶段。我们希望成为世界上最出名和最受欢迎的品牌，要做到这一点，我们还有很长的路要走。

记者： 最近我看到你们打算在未来几年内发展到3万家星巴克店的规模。时间上的具体计划[30]是怎样的？在您看来美国国内和国外会怎样分配呢？

舒尔茨： 嗯，我们现在有1万左右家店，在北美和北美以外的地方。我们公开说过将来有一天我们会开到3万家店。我想在北美和其他地区的比例应该差不多是一半一半[31]的。当然我也相信从目前星巴克已开店的成功经验来看，3万家店可能有点太少了。同时我也相信，我们很有实力开发类似于瓶装[32]法布奇诺、全豆[33]咖啡、冰激凌、音乐及其他产品，作为咖啡店以外的公司成长和发展的一部分，这也将在全世界范围内实现。我们现在已经在美国、日本和中国台湾推出了瓶装法布奇诺这样的即饮咖啡[34]，同时正在开发其他市场。

记者： 我知道您很想开拓中国的市场，并去了那里很多次。中国有什么其他的热点和特殊之处？当人们想到中国的时候，就会想到茶和饮茶文化[35]。这和你差不多也算同行了。

舒尔茨： 我刚刚结束了一段为期两个星期的亚洲旅程。我在中国待了一个星期。我不得不说，中

22. differentiate *v.*
23. outdo *v.*
24. expectation *n.*
25. be steeped in
26. ongoing *adj.*
27. social conscience
28. shareholder *n.*
29. reward *n.*
30. time horizon
31. 50-50
32. bottled *adj.*
33. whole bean
34. ready to drink coffee
35. tea drinking culture

tea and tea drinking culture. That kind of works with you as well.

Schultz: I just returned from a two-week trip to Asia and a week in China and I must say I was stunned and overwhelmed with the growth and development and the significance of the cultural change in China, in terms of the people and what's happening there. We have appropriately 170 stores in mainland China and 70 in Hong Kong and 150 or so in Taiwan and we believe that ultimately China will be the second largest market in the world for Starbucks after the US. But if I look at the Middle East and your own country, I don't think we ever imagined that Starbucks could so quickly demonstrate such relevancy in the market in so many of the countries in Middle East. As a result of that, we are looking at how big those markets could be and have significantly underestimated the number of stores.

国文化重大的改变与发展令我惊奇，那里的人们和那里发生的一切都令我折服。我们在中国大陆大概有170家星巴克咖啡店，在中国香港有70家，在中国台湾地区有150家左右。我相信最终中国将成为美国之外星巴克的全球第二大市场。但是如果看看中东地区和你们国家，我不敢相信星巴克会发展得如此之快，并且相应地发展到很多中东地区的许多国家。因此，我们在考虑这个市场究竟会有多大，我们远远低估[36]了这个市场的潜力。

---

stunned *adj.* 受惊的

overwhelmed *adj.* 彻底制服的

relevancy *n.* 关联，恰当

underestimate *v.* 低估，看轻

36. underestimate *v.*

自由输出十分钟

1. 前缀multi–表示"多……的"，例如：multifunctional（多功能的），multidisciplinary（有关各种学问的），multi–dimension（多维度）等。

2. 表示与过去事实相反的虚拟语气，从句为：if+主语+had+done；主句为：主语+should/would/could/might+have done。例如：If I had got there earlier, I should/could have met her.（如果我早点到那儿，我就会见到她。）

3. "秋天"的表达方式有两种，一种是autumn（英式），另一种是fall（美式）。例如：In the fall of 1988, I was born.（在1988年的秋天，我出生了。）

4. whenever表示no matter when，意思是"无论什么时候"，例如：He asked about our health whenever he met me.= He asked about our health no matter when he met me.（他每次碰到我，都问我们的健康情况。）

5. 过去分词做定语可以前置，例如：The injured workers are now being taken good care of in the hospital.（受伤的工人现正在医院接受良好的照料。）

6. 词组draw one's attention意为"吸引某人的注意力"，例如：The views on campus draw my attention.（校园的景色吸引了我的注意力。）

7. "大量的"的表达方式有：a great deal of/ a large number of/a mass of/ plenty of 等。例如：The poll found a great deal of concern about geo–location services which pinpoint someone's whereabouts.（调查发现，很多人对于能够确定某人所在位置的地理定位服务感到担忧。）

8. 前缀in–可以表示否定的意义，例如：infertile（不能生育的），inapt（不恰当的），inappreciation（不欣赏）等。

9. 词组turn out的意思是"证明是……"，例如：It may turn out, however, that some differences both between and within groups are quite marked.（然而，也可能证明：两个种群之间和种群内部的一些差异是相当明显的。）

18.2 Drinking Coffee While Enjoying Music

轻松输入十分钟

Reporter: One of the segments that really interested me in reading about your company is the music angle that seems to be. That's good. The entertainment aspect actually kind of goes with the original strategy of the third place and you're explaining it a lot in your interviews. And you made an acquisition of a music company and a lot of big name stars have started to release albums through you. Can you talk a little bit about this dimension?

Schultz: I think this is a great example where the entrepreneurial spirit of the company is alive and well. Despite the fact that we have grown to be a large company, we've always played music in our stores and has always acted as an opportunity to create a mood in our stores. And customers started asking, "What song are you playing and can I buy that?" And we said "No." And that was kind of the catalyst for beginning to look at music. We started out with our own compilations and after the success of that, we had the courage to say, "Let's produce our own record." And the first record was with Ray Charles before he unfortunately passed away. The result was that Starbucks won multiple Grammy's and Album of the Year and we sold 4 million copies of that record. We've just replicated that success with Herbie Hancock in which we currently reproduced his record and now we have that in our stores around the world. I don't know if it's in Turkey or not. I'll give you a copy. It's a fantastic record and so we believe that on a global level in all our stores eventually we're going to have music and other forms of entertainment and I think what it says more about the company is that our customers have given us the permission. Because of the trust they have perhaps in the editorial voice or the quality of our company, the sensitivity that we have about things. To extend the Starbucks experience beyond coffee, the challenge, and I think, the art is not to take that too far to in any way we do not want to dilute the trust the customers have by doing something that they would view as something not appropriate for Starbucks. But we are very excited and very bullish about music and other forms of entertainment.

Reporter: Another thing I was reading which caught my attention was for maybe younger customers. You are going to have some facilities in some of your stores or have already?

segment *n.*
部分，段

entertainment *n.*
娱乐，消遣

acquisition *n.* 收购，获得

dimension *n.* 方面

entrepreneurial *adj.* 企业家的

catalyst *n.*
催化剂，刺激因素

compilation *n.*
唱片，编辑

replicate *v.*
复制，折叠

fantastic *adj.*
极好的

permission *n.*
许可，允许

editorial *adj.*
编辑的

dilute *v.*
削弱，稀释

bullish *adj.*
看涨的，上扬的

facility *n.*
设备，灵巧

边喝咖啡边享受音乐

有效学习十分钟

记者： 有一点让我很感兴趣的是你们的公司似乎是在向音乐方面发展。这很好。事实上，娱乐方面的发展与你们最初的<u>第三方战略</u>[1]相配，您在很多访谈中都对此做了大量解释。您<u>收购</u>[2]了一家音乐公司，很多<u>音乐巨星</u>[3]都开始通过你们发布<u>唱片</u>[4]。您能谈谈这方面的事情吗？

舒尔茨： 我想这很好地证明了企业精神的活力和良好状态。排除我们已经发展成为了一家大公司这一点，我们经常在店里播放音乐，把这当作一个在我们的店里<u>营造</u>[5]<u>心情</u>[6]的机会。顾客会问：你们播放的是什么歌？我能买到吗？我们则回答："不能。"这就是我们发展音乐的<u>催化剂</u>[7]。我们先是自己制作，成功之后我们就有勇气说："让我们出属于自己的唱片吧。"第一张唱片是与雷·查尔斯合作的，在他不幸<u>逝世</u>[8]之前。结果星巴克获得了<u>格莱美奖</u>[9]和年度最佳唱片奖[10]，我们的唱片销量达到400万张。我们用同样的方法与赫比·汉考克合作，最近我们刚刚又制作了一批他的唱片，在世界各地的星巴克咖啡店里都可以找到。我不知道是不是在土耳其的店里也有。我会给你一张。这张<u>专辑</u>[11]很好。我相信今后在我们的店里会有很多国际水准的音乐或其他形式的娱乐。我想，是我们的顾客给了我们这样的机会，是出于他们对<u>编辑</u>[12]声音、公司<u>品质</u>[13]以及我们对事物敏感度的信任。要为星巴克<u>拓展</u>[14]咖啡以外的生意，我们面临的挑战是，艺术不会以任何形式走得太远，因为我们不想让顾客觉得这些创新与星巴克的整体风格不合适，从而降低他们对星巴克的信任。但是我们很<u>看好</u>[15]音乐和其他娱乐形式，我们对此充满热情。

记者： 另一件吸引我注意的事情是关于年轻顾客的。你们会引进一些设施，还是你们已经有一些在店里了？

舒尔茨： 好的。我们已经在洛杉矶开了一家店，并且今年秋天将在佛罗里达州的迈阿密和得克萨斯州的圣安东尼奥各开一家店。顾客来到店里之后，不像他们使用iPod或者iTunes一样，他们可以<u>下载</u>[16]歌曲，

1. the third place
2. acquisition n.
3. big name star
4. album n.
5. create v.
6. mood n.
7. catalyst n.
8. pass away
9. mutiple Grammy's
10. Album of the Year
11. record n.
12. editorial adj.
13. quality n.
14. extend v.
15. bullish adj.
16. download v.

Schultz: Okay. We have opened one store in Los Angeles and two are opening this fall in Miami Florida and San Antonio Texas, where the customer can come into the store and not unlike what they do with their iPod, or iTunes, they can download music digitally and physically print and take home a physical CD from the Starbucks store. And so we are looking more and more at creating those kinds of opportunities for our customers.

Reporter: And is it true also that you are allied or have invested in a radio channel or you are affiliated with one?

Schultz: Well, one of the new aspects of technology has been satellite radio. And satellite radio in America has just taken off where it's commercial free, and there is a company called XM radio and Starbucks has its own channel on XM radio in which we program and you can hear all the music we play in our stores on a separate channel. And so we have a partnership with XM and that satellite radio is in cars, and in places that Starbucks music can't live naturally. And so it's another way to extend the brand.

Reporter: You talk a lot about the human connection in your interviews and your books. In fact, you kind of talk about customers and then shareholders and then employees as a continuum. How in a way we tend to think of big business, we mean around the world, as kind of harsh and cold and make corporate decisions, sometimes they may not be too humane and on the other hand we see a lot in your work that you're talking about the warmth and the retention and the bean stock issue when you gave away to the company people way back when in the early days. Can you be a kind businessman and also be a successful businessman?

Schultz: Well, this is a subject that I have spoken about for the better part of 20 years and I give speeches and conversations like this around the world to sensitize people that Starbucks is a living breathing example of the act that being a company that has a sense of humanity and a sense of benevolence and a social conscience is just good business. And what I mean by that specifically is that I feel strongly that if you look at the 14-year history of Starbucks as a public company, our stock price has gone from a market cap of 200 million dollars from June of 1992 to over 20 billion dollars today. Over 4,000 percent and one of the driving forces of that value creation has been in the relationship we have had with our customers, the community, and most importantly our people. And the long term value creation is directly linked to giving back and so when people ask the direct question, "Can you be a benevolent company and make a profit?" I feel so strongly that we wouldn't be as successful as we are today if we did not demonstrate this level of sensitivity to what other people call the soft side of business. I don't think it's the soft side, it's the right side. And in view of that, I thank that every consumer brand, mostly consumer brands that have a relationship with the customer are going to succeed at a higher level if the customer has a level of trust, in not only what the product stand for, but what the ethics and values of the company stand for.

digitally *adv.*
数字式的

ally *v.*
联合，结盟

affiliate *v.*
加入，参加

partnership *n.*
合作关系，合伙

continuum *n.*
连续体

humane *adj.*
仁慈的

retention *n.*
保留

sensitize *v.*
使敏感

benevolence *n.*
仁慈，善行

specifically *adv.*
特别地，明确地

benevolent *adj.*
仁慈的，慈善的

demonstrate *v.*
证明，展示

ethics *n.*
道德标准，伦理观

刻录[17]并可以从星巴克带一张实体[18]CD回家。因此，我们正在寻找更多的机会为顾客提供这样的服务。

记者：　你们与一个电台频道进行了合作，还是投资？或者你们附属[19]于哪一个电台？

舒尔茨：嗯，现在的一项新技术是卫星[20]电台。卫星电台在美国刚刚起步，是免费提供商业服务的。有一个叫做XM的电台，星巴克在那里有属于自己的频道，你可以在一个独立的频道里收听到星巴克店里放的所有音乐。因此，我们与XM合作，卫星电台可以在车上或者一些其他本收听不到星巴克音乐的地方收听到。因此，这也是另外一种品牌[21]宣传模式。

记者：　您在访谈中和您的书中提到了很多人际关系的话题。事实上，您似乎是把星巴克的顾客、股东和员工作为一个连续的统一体[22]在谈论。我们应该怎样去看待大的生意？作为全球性的生意，有时您要冷酷无情地做出企业决定，不能太过于仁慈[23]，另一方面，我们看到您在早期的很多工作中都谈到了温暖、为公司员工保留[24]和存货[25]等方面的事情。您可以同时做一位善良并且成功的商人吗？

舒尔茨：嗯，这是我讲述20年成功部分的主题[26]。我经常在全世界发表演讲或接受访问时谈论这件事情。我向人们讲述有人道主义[27]、慈善心[28]和社会道德的公司才是好公司，星巴克就是一个活生生的例子。我想表达的具体意思是如果看看星巴克这14年的发展历史，这种感觉就会更加强烈。作为一家公众公司，我们的股票从1992年6月的2亿美元上升到今天的200亿美元。40倍的增长，其中的一个推动力就是我们与客户之间、社区之间的关系，最重要的就是与我们的工作人员之间建立的关系。长久价值的创造直接与回报相关联，所以，人们会问比较直接的问题："作为一家慈善公司你们能同时营利吗？"我感觉，如果我们没有显示出对所谓的经济柔软方面的敏感度，就不会有今天这样的成功。我并不认为这是柔软的方面，这是正确的方面。这样来看，我感谢每一个顾客品牌，如果顾客的信任不仅仅建立在产品上，还建立在公司的道德[29]和价值观[30]上的话，建立在顾客关系上的顾客价值往往会将成功提上一个新的高度。

记者：　所以我们之前谈到过这个问题，那么你们最喜欢哪些慈善团体？你们与之合作最多的慈善团体有哪些？

舒尔茨：嗯，首先，你需要整合公司的社会责任心，以占有一席之地。所以，必须将它战略性地[31]融入我们的生意中。不仅仅是在管理桌上，在董事会里也是一样，人们明白这正是公司所代表的。但是我们相信，我们必须在咖啡店周边

17. print *v.*
18. physical *adj.*
19. affiliate *v.*
20. satellite *n.*
21. brand *n.*
22. continuum *n.*
23. humane *adj.*
24. retention *n.*
25. stock *n.*
26. subject *n.*
27. humanity *n.*
28. benevolence *n.*
29. ethics *n.*
30. value *n.*
31. tactically *adv.*

Reporter: So we touched upon it previously but what are some of your favorite charities; what are some of the top charities you are associated with?

Schultz: Well, first of all, you have to integrate corporate social responsibility to have a seat at the table. So it's integrated tactically and strategically into the business. And not only at the management table but in the boardroom, where people understand that this is what the company stands for. But our belief is that we should be very active in the local communities where we have stores. We have always felt strongly that we want to be active in charities that involve children that either have been left behind or disenfranchised. We have opened stores in under served communities across America to provide employment opportunities and other opportunities for people who have been left behind. Most recently, this is an example, we are very active in the relief in Tsunami. We've been very active in Katrina relief, and we've tried to do things locally around the world that demonstrate to our customers that this is not a press release but this is a way of life. And we also want our own people to volunteer in the communities. The most significant aspect of that is what we've done around children's literacy efforts. To make sure that every child understands how to read and write and has a level of self-esteem that gives him opportunities later in life.

Reporter: When there's a choice to do corporate social responsibility in, internationally do you leave, is that decision taken in conjunction with here or do they make the suggestion or do you make the suggestion in terms of topics?

Schultz: More often than not, decisions are locally based where Isik Imhertem and Mohammed Alshaya are doing things locally that they believe are compatible with the Starbucks way of doing business and they have already done that.

Reporter: How often are you traveling? How many days can you sleep at home?

Schultz: When I look back at the year, it appears that it's one week a month. And more often than not, maybe more than a half of that on an annualized basis is international. But clearly our responsibility is to be in the marketplace with our people not sitting in our office in Seattle. And so I want to be as available and accessible to our people and our customers around the world as possible. But you can't travel everyday. I'd say about a week a month.

Reporter: What's the next challenge for you as SCHULTZ, Schultz?

Schultz: Well, the challenge I think is to stay highly focused on our core business and the need that our people have. And not to allow the success of our company and the blessings that have, that has provided us to anyway to give us a sense of entitlement. I've seen all too often companies and management teams that have achieved success become this arrogant group of people and they either lose their way or they lose what they were once about. And I think it is not necessarily a challenge as it is a watch out to make sure we stay as humble and as sensitive and as hungry as we were when we were starting the company. And I think that's my responsibility to share that with our 100 thousand people who work for the company and my responsibility is to do everything I can to support them.

previously adv.
以前，预先

charity n.
慈善团体

tactically adv.
战术性地，策略
高明地

disenfranchise v.
剥夺公民权，使
失去投票权

release n.
发布

significant adj.
有意义的，有效
的

conjunction n.
结合，同时发生

compatible adj.
能共处的，兼容
的

annualized adj.
按年计算的，年
度的

accessible adj.
能接近的，可进
入的

blessing n.
福气，祝福

entitlement n.
权利，津贴

humble adj.
谦恭的，恭顺的

地区表现得非常活跃。我们经常强烈地感觉到我们愿意在慈善事业中表现得非常活跃，帮助被抛弃和失去公民权利的孩子们。我们在美国一些未得到政府足够重视和支持的社区开店，为那些落后的人提供就业机会和其他机会。最近，有一个例子，我们在海啸救援[32]中表现得非常积极。我们在卡特里娜救援中表现得很积极。我们在当地做了很多事情，向我们的顾客证明这不是一场发布会[33]，而是一种生活方式。我们还鼓励员工做社区的志愿者。最有意义的是我们为提高孩子的文化水平做出了贡献。确保他们都学会读写，有一定的自尊心[34]，这些在今后的生活中会给他们带来更多的机会。

记者： 当你们决定如何表现企业的社会责任的时候，你们如何做出决定？是他们提议还是您根据主题来提议？

舒尔茨：多数时候是由地方自己决定的。只要他们认为这些行为与星巴克的做事方式相一致就可以，伊斯克·伊姆赫特穆和默哈默德·阿尔沙亚已经这样做了。

记者： 您出差的频率高吗？能在家住多少天？

舒尔茨：回顾[35]一下今年的经历，大概每个月有一个星期吧。一年算来，通常有超过半年的时间是在国外。但是很明显，我们的责任是在市场上与我们的员工一起奋斗，而不是坐在西雅图的办公室里。因此，我希望只要是我们的员工或者顾客需要我的时候，我都能够尽量出现。但是你不能每天都出差。差不多每个月有一个星期出差。

记者： 对您——舒尔茨来说下一个挑战会是什么？

舒尔茨：嗯，我想接下来的挑战是要把精力高度集中在我们的核心生意[36]和员工的需求上。我们不能因为公司的成功和福气就感觉自己有了某些权利。我看过太多成功的公司和管理团队变成了一个傲慢的[37]团体，失去了最初的道路和样子。我想如果我们像最初建立公司时一样谦逊、善解人意、渴望成功的话，这就不是一个挑战。我想我有责任与我们的10万员工分享这一点，我的责任是力所能及地为他们提供一切支持。

32. relief *n.*
33. press release
34. self-esteem *n.*
35. look back
36. core business
37. arrogant *adj.*

1. a little bit的意思是"有点，有几分"，例如：So tell me a little bit about yourself, where do you come from?（那么告诉我一点关于你的事吧，你从哪里来？）

2. dimension一词有多重意思，用起来也比较灵活，常见的有"部分，内容"的意思，例如：We should not forget that education has an important spiritual dimension.（我们不应该忘记精神教育是教育的一个重要方面。）

3. 平行结构是指连词连接两个对等的词和对等的结构，例如：Your semester grade is based not only on how well you do on each test, but also on how you participate in class. 在这句话中，not only...but also...是平行结构的连接词。

4. pass away是die的一种委婉的表达法，例如：Most people don't like to think about death. It hurts when friends or family pass away.（大多数人并不喜欢去想跟死有关的事，当朋友或家人去世时人们会感到难过。）

5. 前缀re-表示"重复，再一次"的意思，例如：replicate（复制），reproduce（再生产），reborn（重生的）等。通过添加词缀构成的新词为派生词。

6. 由连接词if或unless引导的状语从句叫做条件状语从句。在英文中，条件是指某一件事情实现之后（状语从句中的动作），其他事情（主句中的动作）才能发生，通常译作"假如"。例如：If you ask him, he will help you.（如果你请他帮忙，他会帮你的。）

7. 仿拟（parody）是一种模仿名言、警句、谚语，改动其中的部分词语，从而使其产生新意的修辞。例如：Rome was not built in a day, nor in a year.（罗马不是一天建成的，也不是一年建成的。）这句话中添加了"nor in a year"这一部分。

8. 词组can't help doing sth.的意思是"忍不住做某事"，例如：I can't help laughing.（我忍不住大笑起来。）

9. 表示"实际上"的副词或短语有：in fact /actually/ in practice/ as a matter of fact 等，例如：Actually there is no need to upstaff.（实际上没有必要增加员工。）

10. 英语中的破折号可以用来表示犹豫或迟疑，例如：I-I-I rather think–maybe–Amy has taken it.（我——我——我想——也许——是艾米拿了吧。）

思科公司首席执行官：
约翰·钱伯斯
CEO of Cisco: John Chambers

　　约翰·钱伯斯（John Chambers），1944年8月23日出生于美国西弗吉尼亚州的查尔斯顿，父母都是医生，曾获得商业管理学士、法律学士、金融和管理MBA三种文凭。1976年，他加盟IBM并工作了七年。1983年，他加盟王安公司，负责亚洲区的销售，后来就任副总裁。1991年思科董事长摩哥里奇以自己继承人的身份让钱伯斯加盟思科。进入公司后，钱伯斯为思科带来了新的发展思路，参与了公司一系列重大决策的制定。1994年，钱伯斯被提升为执行副总裁。1995年1月担任思科公司总裁兼首席执行官。

　　钱伯斯是当今世界最出色的企业经理人之一。美国硅谷的《Upside》杂志将其评为"数字世界之父"；美国《商业周刊》也在短短4年间3次将他评为全球前25位高级企业总裁之一。

19.1 Cisco Expected To Change the Lifestyles of People all Over the World

轻松输入十分钟

Reporter: What are the most important leadership lessons you've learned?

Chambers: People think of us as a product of our successes. I'd actually argue that we're a product of the challenges we faced in life. And how we handled those challenges probably had more to do with what we accomplish in life. I had an issue with dyslexia before they understood what dyslexia was. One of my teachers, Mrs. Anderson, taught me to look at it like a curveball. The ball breaks the same way every time. Once you get used to it, you can handle it pretty well. So I went from almost being embarrassed reading in front of a class to the point where I knew I could overcome challenges. I think it also taught me sensitivity toward others. I learned another lesson from Jack Welch. It was in 1998, and at that time we were one of the most valuable companies in the world. I said, "Jack, what does it take to have a great company?" And he said, "It takes major setbacks and overcoming those." I hesitated for a minute, and I said, "Well, we did that in '93 and then we did it again in '97 with the Asian financial crisis." And he said, "No, John. I mean a near-death experience." I didn't understand exactly what he meant. Then, in 2001, we had a near-death experience. We went from the most valuable company in the world to a company where they questioned the leadership. And in 2003, he called me up and said, "John, you now have a great company." I said, "Jack, it doesn't feel like it." But he was right.

Reporter: How has your leadership style evolved over time?

Chambers: I'm a command-and-control person. I like being able to say turn right, and we truly have 67,000 people turn right. But that's the style of the past. Today's world requires a different leadership style—more collaboration and teamwork, including using Web 2.0 technologies.

Reporter: Did you need to be pushed?

Chambers: I thought I was very leading-edge in terms of how I communicated. My team just kept pushing, and I finally said, "Why do you want me to do

---

handle *v.*
处理，操作

dyslexia *n.*
失读症，阅读障碍

curveball *n.*
曲线球

embarrass *v.*
阻碍，使困窘

sensitivity *n.*
敏感，过敏

setback *n.*
挫折，退步

hesitate *v.*
踌躇，犹豫

valuable *adj.*
有价值的，贵重的

evolve *v.*
发展，进化

collaboration *n.*
合作，勾结

communicate *v.*
沟通，传达

思科希望改变全世界人的生活方式

有效学习十分钟

记者：　您所学过的有关领导方面的最重要的内容是什么呢？

钱伯斯：人们认为，我们是由不断的成功累积而成的；事实上，我想说的是，我们是由生活中所面临的各种挑战而磨砺成的。我们所取得的成就都是与我们在生活中所遇到并解决的那些挑战相关联的。我以前在他们还不明白什么是<u>失读症</u>[1]时，就有这方面的问题。安德森夫人，我的一位老师，教我把那个问题看成是一个<u>曲线球</u>[2]，因为曲线球每次总是以相同的方式突然出现。当你习惯了之后，你就能很好地处理那个问题。所以，我从一开始在班级同学面前朗读会感到窘迫，变到对自己有信心，能够<u>克服</u>[3]困难。那也教会了我对别人的行为有一定的敏感性。我还从杰克·韦尔奇身上学到了一些东西。1998年，那时我们是世界上最有价值的公司之一。我问他说："杰克，怎样才能使公司变成一家伟大的公司呢？"他回答说："主要是依靠遭遇<u>挫折</u>[4]并解决挫折。"我犹豫了一会儿，然后说："我们在1993年的时候遭遇并解决过问题，1997年由于<u>亚洲金融危机</u>[5]我们又经历了一回。"他说："约翰，不是这样的，我的意思是一次<u>濒死</u>[6]状态的经历。"那时候，我并不理解他所指的是什么。之后在2001年，我们经历了一次濒死的状况。我们从世界上最有价值的公司沦落为大家都<u>质疑</u>[7]我们领导阶层的公司。2003年的时候他给我打电话，并且说："约翰，你现在有一家大的公司了。"我说："杰克，这感觉不像是一家大的公司。"但是其实他是正确的。

记者：　随着时间的推移，您的领导方式发生了怎样的变化呢？

钱伯斯：我是一个善于领导和控制的人。我希望我说"向右转"的时候，我们的6.7万名员工就都能够向右转，但是那是过去的领导方式。当今的世界需要一种不同的领导方式，更多的是进行<u>协作</u>[8]和<u>团队合作</u>[9]，包括共同运用Web2.0技术等等。

记者：　您需要其他一些因素来<u>推动</u>[10]您前进吗？

钱伯斯：我认为，在我与他人进行交流的方面我是处于<u>最前沿</u>[11]的。我的团队总是在推动我进步，然后我问他们："为什么你们希望我这样做呢？"他们说："约翰，

1. dyslexia *n.*
2. curveball *n.*
3. overcome *v.*
4. setback *n.*
5. Asian financial crisis
6. near-death
7. question *v.*
8. collaboration *n.*
9. teamwork *n.*
10. push *v.*
11. leading-edge

this?" And they said: "John, if you don't do it, our company won't learn how to do this. It won't be built into our DNA for the way we interface with customers, our employees. The top has to walk the talk." I was expecting text blogging and we did video blogging.

Reporter: What's that about?

Chambers: The first one was a little bit uncomfortable, because it's very unprofessional. You just basically put a camera there, and then you go. By the second one, I realized this was going to transform communications—not just for the CEO, but also it would change how we do business.

Reporter: You mentioned Jack Welch. Who else do you rely on for advice?

Chambers: My wife. She has a way of picking me up when I get knocked on my tail. But also if I get a little bit overconfident, she brings me back to earth. The other day, I was practicing a concept with her and saying, "You know, there are two major mistakes that I make and Cisco makes repeatedly." She looked at me and she said, "Only two?" My mistakes are always around moving too slow, or moving too fast without process behind it. And it's something that, if we're not careful, we'll repeat again and again.

Reporter: How do you hire?

Chambers: First thing I want to ask you about: tell me about your results. I never get hard work confused with success. So I'd walk you through the successes, and what you did do right. I'd also ask you to tell me about your failures. And that's something people make a tremendous mistake on. First, all of us have had mistakes and failures. And it's surprising how many people say, "Well, I can't think of one." That immediately loses credibility. It's the ability to be very candid on what mistakes you've made, and then the question is, what would you do differently this time? Then I ask them who are the best people they recruited and developed, and where are they today? Third, I try to figure out if they're really oriented around the customer. Are they driven by the customer, or is the customer just somebody who gets in the way? And I look at their communication skills, and one of the largest parts of communications is ... what?

Reporter: Listening?

Chambers: You betcha. Seeing how they listen, and are they willing to challenge you? And then I look at their knowledge in industry segments, especially the area I'm interested in.

Reporter: What's changed in the last few years?

Chambers: Big time, the importance of collaboration. Big time, people who have teamwork skills, and their use of technology. If they're not collaborative, if they aren't naturally inclined toward collaboration and teamwork, if they

---

interface v.
打交道，接触

blogging n.
博客，网志

unprofessional adj.
非专业的，非职业性的

overconfident adj.
过于自信的，自负的

concept n.
观念，概念

repeatedly adv.
反复地，再三地

tremendous adj.
极大的，巨大的

immediately adv.
立即，立刻

credibility n.
可信性，确实性

candid adj.
公正的，坦白的

recruit v.
招募，聘用

segment n.
部分，段

collaborative adj.
合作的，协作的

incline v.
倾向，倾斜

如果你不那样做的话，我们的公司就不会去学习怎样做，那么它就不会深入到我们与顾客、与员工之间的交流合作方式中，因为公司的领导是要主持整个谈话的。"我期望我们使用的是文本[12]博客，但是我们使用的是视频博客。

记者：　那是关于什么的呢？

钱伯斯：第一种方式人们用起来会感觉不太舒服，因为它不太专业。你只是把一个摄影机[13]摆在那里，然后你就可以开始了。但是我意识到，第二种方式能够改变人们交流[14]的方式，不仅仅是首席执行官，它也会改变我们做生意的方式。

记者：　您刚才提到了杰克·韦尔奇，那么除了他之外，您还听从[15]谁的建议呢？

钱伯斯：我的妻子。当我遇到挫折的时候，她总是有办法使我振作[16]起来。但是当我有些过于自信[17]的时候，她也会使我以平常心来对待。几天之前，我在跟她一起练习一个概念[18]时跟她说："你知道吗？我有两个主要的错误，思科也在一直不断地重复那两个错误。"她看着我，然后说："只有两个吗？"我所犯的错误总是关于公司运行得太快或者是太慢，而如果我们不注意这些错误的话，我们会一直反复地犯下去。

记者：　公司雇用员工方面，您是怎样做的呢？

钱伯斯：首先我会问你：请告诉我你所取得的成就。我从来不会将"努力工作"和"成功"混为一谈[19]。所以我想要知道你所取得的成绩是什么，你做过的正确的事是什么。我也会问你曾经遭遇的失败有什么，这也是很多人经常犯错误的地方。首先，我们所有人都会犯错和经历失败，但是令我们感到惊讶的是，很多人都会回答说：我记不起来了。那立刻就使你失去了可信度。这是一种能够坦率[20]面对自己所犯错误的能力。然后接下来的问题就是，如果还有一次机会的话，你会怎样做？然后我会问他们：你们所招聘和培训的人员当中，谁是最优秀的，他们现在在哪里工作。第三，我会弄清楚[21]他们在客户之间是否真的会发挥导向[22]作用。他们是会被顾客牵着走还是客户只是阻碍[23]他们的人。我还会看他们的交流技巧。关于交流方面最重要的一点是什么呢？

记者：　是倾听吗？

钱伯斯：是的。要看他们怎样听你说话，他们是否愿意挑战你的问题，然后看他们在专业领域方面的知识水平，尤其是在我所感兴趣的领域。

记者：　在最近这几年中，什么事情发生了改变？

钱伯斯：改变比较大的是，协作[24]的重要性，人们开始有集体合作意识，并且能够使用科技了。如果人们不具备协作的精神，如果他们不能自然地倾向于参加集体

12. text *n.*
13. camera *n.*
14. communication *n.*
15. rely on
16. pick up
17. overconfident *adj.*
18. concept *n.*
19. confuse with
20. candid *adj.*
21. figure out
22. oriented *adj.*
23. get in the way
24. collaboration *n.*

are uncomfortable with using technology to make that happen both within Cisco and in their own life, they're probably not going to fit in here.

Reporter: You invest a lot in R and D about three point five billion dollars, that's the figure I read, on a revenue of about twenty five billion dollars. This is a huge amount. We know that you have research centers not only in the US, other places around the world. What are your other top research centers, which ones are they? And going back to Turkey, do you anticipate at any point that you will make a R and D investment in Turkey? How do you decide the physical locations for the research centers?

Chambers: We tend to make R and D investments where we see start-ups. And so where we see very aggressive start-ups, whether it's Scientific Atlanta in Atlanta, in the US, or investments in Bangalore, or in Shanghai, which are two of our other major investment centers around the world, we tend to go where the start-ups are. That's because the start-ups may bring in benefits for us. And we tend to go next to the universities who train the people. So we try to attract the best and the brightest of a country wherever they are in the world. Some of them will be in physical location such as Bangalore or Shanghai, or Raleigh, or San Hose, or Boston, or Texas, or elsewhere. This would be virtually around the world where we attract the best and the brightest, perhaps they work in Turkey, or we attract them to work in one of our other centers around the world. So our goal is to attract the best and the brightest and get them to be a part of Cisco. I believe, that is quite important for Cisco.

Reporter: OK, I see your point. My next question is, in the coming years of development, what is your vision for Cisco?

Chambers: My vision for Cisco has not changed in fifteen years. I view that Cisco can play... if we are effective and if we do what is right... the leading role in changing the way the world works, lives, learns and plays through the Internet. And we would like to be the company that helps that happen, both from a success on the financial side, but also a success on the corporate/social responsibility side. There can be no higher goal in life than changing people's lives on a global basis, and I believe the Internet is that equaliser along with education. So that is our dream for Cisco. Time will tell whether we can achieve that or not. We hope that Cisco can play quite an important role in people's lives.

Reporter: Well, on that note, I want to thank you very much for this candid interview, and for your time. We appreciate it very much.

Chambers: In fact it's a pleasure. Thank you for allowing me to share my views.

revenue *n.*
收入，税收

anticipate *v.*
期望，预期

aggressive *adj.*
好斗的，侵略性的

investment *n.*
投资，投入

virtually *adv.*
事实上

vision *n.*
愿景

effective *adj.*
有效的，起作用的

corporate *adj.*
共同的，法人的

equaliser *n.*
均衡器，平衡装置

活动进行协作，如果在思科公司内部和他们的日常生活中，他们不能够使用科技的话，那么他们可能就不适合待在思科。

记者：　我曾经读到过一组数据[25]，上面写道，思科的财政收入[26]为250亿美元，而其在研发[27]方面的投入很多，大约有35亿美元，这是一笔不小的数目。我们知道，思科不仅在美国有研究中心，在世界上的很多其他国家也有。思科在美国以外的重要研究中心有哪些呢？我们回到土耳其，您准备在那里进行研发方面的投资吗？对于研究中心的物理位置[28]，您是通过怎样的方式确定的呢？

钱伯斯：任何一个有始创公司[29]的地方我们都会进行研发投资，无论是在美国亚特兰大的"科学亚特兰大"，还是在班加罗尔和上海，这两个地方是我们在世界上的主要[30]投资地。我们试图[31]进入那些新发展起来的地方，因为他们可能会为我们带来收益。接下来我们也试图走进培养人才的大学，吸收[32]世界上最优秀、最聪明[33]的人才，他们中的一些人可能会在班加罗尔、上海、纳罗利、圣荷西、波士顿或者德克萨斯等地。事实上[34]，我们将从世界范围内寻找那些聪明的人才，有可能他们在土耳其工作，或者我们吸引他们到我们其他地方的研发中心去工作。所以我们的目标[35]就是，要争取引进世界上最出类拔萃、最聪明的人才，使他们成为思科的一分子[36]。我相信，那对思科的发展是很重要的。

记者：　好的，我已经明白[37]您的意思了。我的下一个问题是，在接下来的几年里，您希望思科有怎样的发展呢？

钱伯斯：我对思科未来的发展规划已经15年没有发生变化了。如果我们能够进行有效的[38]工作，做正确的事情，我希望思科能够通过因特网，在改变全世界的工作、生活、学习、娱乐方式[39]等方面发挥领导作用。我们希望能够成为一个促进上述改变实现的公司，无论是从金融方面，还是从社会责任方面来说我们都可以获得成功。再也没有比改变全世界人民的生活方式更高的目标了，我相信因特网能够与教育一样，成为一个均衡器[40]。所以那就是我们对于思科未来发展的梦想，时间会告诉我们是否能够做到那样。我们希望，思科能够在人们的生活中发挥重要作用。

记者：　嗯，基于此[41]，我非常感谢您能够抽出时间来接受这次坦率的采访，我们感激不尽！

钱伯斯：事实上我也很高兴来到这里，也谢谢你们给我这个机会来分享我的一些观点。

25. figure *n.*
26. revenue *n.*
27. R and D
28. physical location
29. start-up
30. major *adj.*
31. tend to
32. attract *v.*
33. brightest *adj.*
34. virtually *adv.*
35. goal *n.*
36. a part of
37. see *v.*
38. effective *adj.*
39. play *n.*
40. equaliser *n.*
41. on that note

10 min

自由输出十分钟

1. 思科系统公司（Cisco Systems, Inc.），是互联网解决方案的领先提供者，其设备和软件产品主要用于连接计算机网络系统。1984年12月，思科系统公司在美国成立，创始人是斯坦福大学的一对教师夫妇，莱昂纳德·波萨克（Leonard Bosack）和桑蒂·勒纳（Sandy Lerner），夫妇二人设计了叫做"多协议路由器"的联网设备，用于斯坦福校园网络（SUNet），将校园内不兼容的计算机局域网整合在一起，形成一个统一的网络。这个联网设备被认为是联网时代真正到来的标志。约翰·钱伯斯于1991年加入思科。1996年，钱伯斯执掌思科帅印，把思科变成了一代王朝。

2. "I can't agree with you more." 的意思是"我非常同意你的观点。"而不是"我一点都不同意你。"这是一种固定的表达方法，切不可断章取义。

3. front一词除了常见的"前面"之意外，还有"非法或秘密活动掩盖者"的意思，例如：The travel company is just a front for drug trafficking.（这家旅行社不过是毒品交易的掩护场所。）

4. 杰克·韦尔奇（Jack Welch）是原通用电气（GE）董事长兼CEO，1935年11月19日出生于马萨诸塞州塞勒姆市；1960年加入通用电气塑胶事业部；1981年4月，他成为通用电气历史上最年轻的董事长和CEO。他所推行的"六西格玛"标准、全球化和电子商务，几乎重新定义了现代企业。他于2001年9月退休，被誉为"最受尊敬的CEO"、"全球第一CEO"、"美国当代最成功最伟大的企业家"。

5. 表示"挫折"的词汇有：setback, frustration, failure等，例如：It's easy to be thankful for the good things, while a life of rich fulfillment comes to those who are also thankful for the setbacks.（对美好的事物感恩很容易；精彩的人生属于那些对挫折也心存感激的人。）

6. 英语中，前缀"inter-"表示"在……之间，互相"，例如：international（国际的），interaction（互动），Internet（互联网）等。

7. 一般来说，to后面应跟do，但如果to是介词，则应跟doing，例如：How much of its output should a society wish to devote to fending off once in 50 or 100-year crises.（一个社会应拿出总产值的多少来抵挡50年或100年一遇的危机？）

8. 词组rely on的意思是"依赖"，例如：If she were to become head of the organization, she would have to rely on the advice of those around her.（如果她成为总裁，届时将不得不依赖周围人的建议。）

9. advice意为"建议"，是不可数名词，而其同义词suggestion是可数名词。例如：They give advice for people with HIV and AIDS.（他们向艾滋病病毒携带者和艾滋病患者提供建议。）；Can I make a suggestion?（我可以提个建议吗？）

10. big time有"（活动，职业等的）顶峰"的意思，例如：He hit the big time with films such as *Ghost* and *Dirty Dancing*.（他因《人鬼情未了》和《热舞》两部影片而达到了事业的顶峰。）

19.2

Internet Can Promote the Development of Productivity

因特网可促进生产力的发展

 轻松输入十分钟

Reporter: Our guest today is John Chambers who is the President and CEO of Cisco Systems. Welcome to the show.

Chambers: It's an honor to be here, and if you'd call me John, I'd be honored as well.

Reporter: OK. John, we're sitting here at the heart of the Silicon Valley which is very much related to the Internet, and the fortunes of the Internet, and so is also Cisco's path, and the path of the Internet. How is your feeling now about the pace of the growth of the Internet sector, and whether governments and companies and even individuals, are we able to keep up with this increase?

Chambers: Well, I think technology will not be the limiting factor on how quickly we can apply the technology of the Internet to change education or healthcare,

有效学习十分钟

记者： 我们今天请到的嘉宾[1]是思科集团的主席兼首席执行官——约翰·钱伯斯，欢迎来到我们的节目。

钱伯斯： 很荣幸能够来到这里。如果你称呼我约翰，我也会感到荣幸的。

记者： 好的，约翰。我们现在是在硅谷的核心[2]地带，这里是一个与因特网及其创造的财富有密切关系的地方，思科集团从事的也是跟因特网有关系的事业。您现在对于互联网行业的发展速度[3]有怎样的感受呢？无论对于政府、公司还是个人来说，我们能够跟得上它发展的速度吗？

钱伯斯： 嗯，我想，对于我们能够以

---

fortune *n.* 财富

sector *n.* 行业，部门

healthcare *n.* 医疗保健，健康护理

1. guest *n.*
2. at the heart of
3. pace *n.*

or even government. I think it's more how we learn how to change our underlying business process; our governmental process; our healthcare process, that will be the key limiting factor on how fast we grow. In terms of the Internet, I think it will merely drive a level of productivity for the next, probably, two to three decades. You almost want to think about it like a highway system of the past, where how well your railroads or your highway systems were, your airports, your harbors, determined the large part of the economic strength of your country. I would say your infrastructure in terms of your high-tech will do this the same.

Reporter: And when you look at emerging markets, emerging countries such as Turkey, and many other countries, we see that technology and the Internet are actually great opportunities to foster growth, and maybe catch up. So in your opinion, I know that Turkey you have chosen as one of your most eminent emerging countries, how is Turkey keeping up with this pace, and what can be done to turn it into more of a competitive advantage?

Chambers: When we look at successful countries, in terms of future direction, we often see leadership at the top being very very key. Your Prime Minister truly understands the capability of the Internet brings to the country. We also see the focus on education, the willingness to say how you raise the standard of living for all the citizens of a country. So if you look at what occurs to many of the countries around the world, in the past, a company made its growth in its business profits, if you will, from the top ten countries around the world.

Reporter: What do you mean actually?

Chambers: Now you see the world as truly becoming flat, and I believe progressive companies will focus as much on the emerging countries as they do, quote, "on the established countries". How well that country builds up its infrastructure in terms of broadband, the ability really to change an education system, or healthcare system, would determine its economic future. Do the top leaders of government really understand that? Do you have a Prime Minister who truly understands what the power of the Internet can be? And how do you say—not only in government, but also in education, healthcare and for the general standards of living of the citizens. So I'm very optimistic about the role that emerging countries will play in the future growth of the Internet. I think it's not like the past, where emerging countries will follow the quote "developed countries", I think emerging countries will often lead: whether they're in China, or in India, or in Turkey, or in other parts of Eastern Europe.

Reporter: When you look at Turkey, we have over seventy million people, and a very

怎样的速度将因特网技术应用于教育、卫生保健[4]甚至政府等方面来说，技术并不是一个限制性[5]因素。我认为，更重要的是我们要学习怎样改变现存的商业过程[6]、政府的进程和卫生保健的发展进程，那些将是决定我们发展速度的限制性因素。至于因特网，我想它只能够在接下来的10年、20年或者是30年的时间里有效地促进生产力[7]的发展。你总是认为它就像是过去的公路[8]系统一样，铁路、公路、机场和海港的发展状况，从很大程度上决定了一个国家的经济实力[9]。我想说的是，高科技领域的基础设施[10]的建设和发展也能够起到同样的作用。

记者：　当您看发展中的市场、发展中的国家，比如土耳其及许多其他国家的时候，我们可以发现，科技和因特网实际是促进增长，并可能赶上[11]发达国家的很好机会。我知道您已经选择土耳其作为一个很有潜力的发展市场，所以在您看来，土耳其如何能够跟上科技的快速发展，我们能够做什么来增加它的竞争优势[12]呢？

钱伯斯：当我们去看一些有良好的未来发展方向的国家时，我们能够看到，国家顶层的领导起着非常非常重要的作用。贵国的总理能够真正地体会到因特网给这个国家带来的实力。我们还可以看到贵国对于教育的重视程度，以及在提高人民生活水平方面所做出的努力。所以如果我们来回望一下过去，世界上很多国家的企业创造的利益大都是从世界前10强[13]国家中获得的。

记者：　您指的是什么呢？

钱伯斯：现在你也看到世界确实变得扁平[14]了。我相信先进的[15]企业会在发展中国家投入与发达国家同样多的精力。一个国家以宽带为代表的基础设施的建设情况，改变教育体系[16]和医疗卫生保健体系的真正能力，都决定[17]了国家的经济未来。国家的领导人了解这些情况吗？一个国家的总理是否真正了解因特网的力量呢？政府的情况、教育、卫生保健和广大公民[18]的生活水平[19]是怎样的呢？所以我对于发展中国家在因特网的未来发展方面所发挥的作用是持乐观[20]态度的。我认为现在并不像是过去那样，发展中国家要追随[21]着发达国家的脚步，发展中国家也会经常发挥领导的作用，无论是在中国、印度、土耳其还是东欧的其他一些国家。

记者：　我们来看一下土耳其这个国家的情况，这是一个拥有7000万人口的国家，并且年轻

4. healthcare *n.*
5. limiting *adj.*
6. process *n.*
7. productivity *n.*
8. highway *n.*
9. economic strength
10. infrastructure *n.*
11. catch up
12. competitive advantage
13. top ten
14. flat *adj.*
15. progressive *adj.*
16. system *n.*
17. determine *v.*
18. citizen *n.*
19. standard of living
20. optimistic *adj.*
21. follow *v.*

young population, but at the same time the Internet usage is about five million people, about 1.7 million of them is broadband. In your opinion, when you look at a country at our growth level, at our penetration level, what are the potentials? What is the potential for this?

Chambers: Well, I think the potential is for every citizen of every major country around the world having access to the Internet. And I think that when that occurs you'll suddenly be able to train people faster, you'll be able to do job creation. The jobs will go where the best educated work-force is, to the best infrastructure, that creates an environment of innovation and supportive government. And so I think this opens up a way that countries can participate in economic growth in a way, perhaps, it would not have been capable of in the past. So I'm clearly, in many ways, the champion of the Internet, and very proud to be known as that, and I'm the optimist for what it can do for all members of society. So I really believe it can change the standard of living, productivity, education systems, in ways that people are just beginning to imagine. And I actually view the fact that Internet penetration is just on a rapid uptake in Turkey, in a very positive way. It means that we can build up a structure for the future, in terms of capabilities, as opposed to build up a structure for the past. Much like dirt highways versus the modern four-lane highways. I think Turkey has the opportunity to build a four-lane highway system that will benefit the majority of its citizens, government, and businesses as a whole.

Reporter: When you look at globalization, several years back the word "digital divide" was very much in use. And some people argued that globalization, and the advance of technology, is helping poorer nations or developing nations, and others argue that actually the divide is just getting larger. I know that Cisco has many initiatives having to do with education and other issues. How to make the best of technological advances, who is further: poorer countries, or developing countries?

Chambers: I think if you use India as an example of where a country has taken perhaps a generation of young people that were behind on the global economics scale, and suddenly by putting in these new highways, if you will, suddenly started to participate in a much more rapid phase. It is clearly a country in transition with a standard of living and a GDP growth occurring very rapidly. I see Turkey in the same scenario. I see the chance to suddenly participate in ways that were not capable before.

Reporter: Can you make some explanations?

Chambers: We have a terminology in high-tech field which is called Moore's Law, which is a very nice way of saying that the capability of a product doubles

---

usage *n.*
使用，用法

penetration *n.*
洞察力

potential *n.*
潜能，可能性

innovation *n.*
创新，革新

participate *v.*
参与，参加

capable *adj.*
能胜任的，能干的

champion *n.*
拥护者

uptake *n.*
摄取

oppose *v.*
反对，对抗

versus *prep.*
对，与……相对

digital *adj.*
数字的

initiative *n.*
举措，方案

transition *n.*
过渡

scenario *n.*
方案，情节

terminology *n.*
术语，术语学

人很多，但是同时，因特网使用数量只有500万，而其中170万用户使用的是宽带。在您看来，如果一个国家拥有像我们这样的发展速度和洞察力[22]的话，他们的发展潜力是怎样的呢？他们在因特网方面的潜力如何呢？

钱伯斯：嗯，我想，潜力就是世界上每一个主要国家的每一个公民都能够用上因特网。到那时候你会发现，培训员工的速度会提高，你也有能力创造更多的工作机会。工作当然都会提供给那些受过良好教育的人，提供给拥有最好的基础设施的地方，因为只有那样，才能够创造出创新环境，政府才能够给予相应的支持。我想，这从某种方式上，为国家能够参与到经济发展中提供了一个途径[23]，这在过去可能是行不通的。所以我从很多方面来说，是因特网的拥护者[24]，并且为我所做的事情感到骄傲，而且对于它能够为每一位社会成员所带来的益处持有乐观的态度。所以我真的相信它能够有效地提高人民的生活水平和生产力[25]，很好地改善教育体系，就像人们想象中的那样。而且我发现，因特网正在以很快的速度、以一种很积极的[26]方式普及到土耳其人民的生活中。这就意味着在能力方面，我们能够为未来而不是过去建造网络系统。这就像是泥泞的公路和现代化的四车道[27]的公路之间进行的对比。我认为，土耳其能够建立一个那样的"四车道的公路系统"，以使其国家的大多数公民、政府和商业作为一个整体而受益。

记者：　有关于全球化的问题。几年前，"数字鸿沟[28]"是一个很常用的词。有人说，全球化和科技的进步能够给予贫困国家和发展中国家以帮助，而有人说，那只会使两者之间的差距越来越大。我知道，思科集团有很多与教育和其他问题相关的目标。那么应该如何充分地利用科技的进步呢？主要是在贫困国家还是在发展中国家进行发展呢？

钱伯斯：我想我们可以以印度为例。印度的一代年轻人原本落后于全球经济发展，但是在引入[29]这些新的"高速公路"之后，它开始以很快的速度和状态[30]参与到经济全球化的活动中。现在在印度，人民的生活标准很显然处于过渡阶段[31]，GDP也增长得非常快。土耳其也是同样的一个发展模式[32]。从中我看到了进行突然参与的机会，这在以前是不可能的。

记者：　您能给我们作一些解释吗？

钱伯斯：在高科技领域我们有一个术语[33]叫做"摩尔定律[34]"，它向我们很好地说明：产品的效能较过去增加了一倍，而产品的价格每18个月就降低一半。那也就

22. penetration *n.*
23. way *n.*
24. champion *n.*
25. productivity *n.*
26. positive *adj.*
27. four-lane
28. divide *n.*
29. put in
30. phase *n.*
31. transition *n.*
32. scenario *n.*
33. terminology *n.*
34. Moore's Law

in performance, or the price gets cut in half every eighteen months. That's also a very nice way of saying something that cost ten times too much five years ago is completely affordable today. And so I'm the optimist of what this means for the average citizen around the world. I think we'll be able to participate whether it's as simple as phone calls over the Internet, or as complex in terms of how we would do education, or healthcare or entertainment over the Internet for the majority of the world's citizens. So I'm the optimist here. I think there is a challenge in terms of global interdependencies, if you will, I think it will benefit most countries, and most people, as opposed to be a negative. That's really what I want to make sense.

Reporter: In 2005 you accepted a prestigious prize from the State Department, and this was linked to Cisco's involvement in the Jordan Education Initiative. I know that you prize this highly and you talk about your involvement with Jordan, and with King Abdullah as well and his involvement with this project. Can you give our audience a sense of what the mission of this project was and how it has progressed?

Chambers: Well, we were honored this last year to receive the State Department's Corporate Citizenship Award. We also won the top award as a large company for American business CEOs: in terms of which company was doing the best job on giving back on a global basis. What was really exciting about that is that when you have a government leader who really gets it—and King Abdullah in Jordan. They understand that this really offers an opportunity for the future in terms of where markets are going. They understood that it's about not only education, but also venture capital, job creation, and how do you change a country. And in a very challenging environment, their GDP is growing at seven percent.

Reporter: It's our pleasure to have you here. We really appreciate your time and effort. Thank you very much, Mr. John.

Chambers: Glad to be here. Thank you.

affordable *adj.*
负担得起的

average *adj.*
普通的

optimist *n.*
乐观主义者，乐天派

prestigious *adj.*
有名望的，享有声望的

involvement *n.*
牵连，包含

mission *n.*
使命，任务

award *n.*
奖品，判决

venture *v.*
冒险

appreciate *v.*
欣赏，感激

很好地说明了，5年前价格是现如今10倍的产品，现在大家都能够负担得起了。对全世界普通公民来说，这意味着什么，所以对此我持乐观态度。我想我们都能够参与到其中，无论它是像在网络上打电话一样简单，还是像我们怎样通过  网络解决大多数公民的教育、卫生保健或娱乐等问题一样复杂，我都是持乐观态度的。我认为，在全球相互依赖[35]方面存在有很大的挑战，如果我们能够克服这一挑战，那么大多数国家、大多数人民都能够从中受益，而不是受到损害。这是我真正想要说明的。

记者：2005年，您在美国国务院被授予了一个享有声望的大奖，这与思科参与到约旦教育行动的活动中有关。我知道您非常珍视这个奖项，您谈论了与约旦以及阿卜杜拉国王之间的合作，并且也谈论了他与这项活动的关系。您能跟我们的听众朋友们说一下，这项计划的任务是什么？它是如何发展的？

钱伯斯：嗯，我们去年因此而受到嘉奖，得到国务院授予的企业公民奖[36]。作为一家大公司，我们也赢得了为美国商业界的首席执行官们设立的奖项中的头等奖，这个奖项是依据公司为全球化进程所做出的努力而颁发的。真正让人感到高兴的就是一个政府的领导人能够理解到这一点的重要性，就像是在那项约旦计划中，阿卜杜拉国王所做到的那样。他们明白，那为市场的未来提供了很好的发展方向；他们明白，那不仅仅与教育，还与风险资金[37]、工作机会，以及如何改善一个国家的情况有关。在一个充满挑战的环境中，他们的GDP正以7%的速度增长着。

记者：很高兴您今天能够抽出时间来接受我们的采访，非常感谢您，约翰先生。

钱伯斯：很高兴来到这里，谢谢！

35. interdependency *n.*
36. Corporate Citizenship Award
37. venture capital

10 min
自由输出十分钟

1. as well表示"也"的意思，通常放在句末，例如：Most of the artists have had little exposure outside of Australia, however, making the show a way of raising their profiles as well.（大多数艺术家都没有走出过澳大利亚，因此此次巡回展也成了他们提高知名度的一个途径。）

2. 词组keep up with的意思是"跟上，不落后"，例如：In Egypt, the bread crisis is a symptom of a larger problem—one of stagnant wages that have failed to keep up with the cost of living.（在埃及，面包危机只是一个深层问题——埃及停滞的工资水平没有跟上生活开支的增速——的表象而已。）

3. 合成法是英语中重要的构词方法之一，构成了英语中大量的合成词，例如：healthcare（医疗保障），setback（挫折），feedback（反馈），highway（高速公路）等。

4. 英语中表示"重要的，关键的"意思的词汇有：key，important，significant，vital，essential等。例如：It is not easy to talk about the role of the mass media in this overwhelmingly significant phase in European history.（在欧洲历史上这个绝对重要的时期讨论大众媒体的作用并不是很容易的事情。）

5. 在英语中，后缀-ology/-logy表示"学科"的意思，例如：biology（生物学），sociology（社会学），genealogy（宗谱学）等。

6. 词组put aside可以表示"留作……用"的意思，例如：Encourage children to put aside some of their allowance to buy Christmas presents.（鼓励孩子们留下部分零用钱来买圣诞礼物。）

7. 在英语中，turkey是"火鸡"的意思，如果将首字母大写，Turkey则是国家"土耳其"的意思；同样的词还有china（瓷器），China（中国）。

8. 当虚拟条件句的谓语动词含有were，should，had时，if可以省略，这时条件从句要用倒装语序，即把were，should，had等词置于句首，多用于书面语。例如：Had he learnt about computers, we would have hired him to work here.（如果他懂一些电脑知识的话，我们已经聘用他来这里工作了。）

9. 词组set out可以表示"启程，出发"的意思，例如：When setting out on a long walk, always wear suitable boots.（出发进行长距离徒步时，一定要穿上合适的靴子。）

20 卡夫食品首席执行官：
艾琳·罗森菲尔德
CEO of Kraft Foods:
Irene Rosenfeld

　　艾琳·罗森菲尔德1953年5月3日出生于纽约郊外韦斯特伯里镇的一个犹太家庭。她毕业于美国康奈尔大学，拥有工商管理博士、工商管理硕士（MBA）、艺术和心理学学士学位。她曾担任杂货制造商协会和美国康奈尔大学董事会的董事。2004年，艾琳·罗森菲尔德成为百事快餐分公司菲多利北美的总负责人，具体负责健康产品的前期推广工作。2006年6月，艾琳·罗森菲尔德被任命为卡夫食品CEO。2007年3月，她成为卡夫食品董事长。

　　2008年，她入选华尔街日报评选的"50 Women to Watch"名单。2009年，她被《财富》杂志评选为全美最有影响力的50位商界女性的第二名。美国《福布斯》杂志在2010年10月6日公布了"最有权势女性"年度榜单，美国"第一夫人"米歇尔·奥巴马荣膺榜首，艾琳·罗森菲尔德位列第二。

20.1 / We've Got to Get 1.3 Billion Chinese Eating Oreo's

轻松输入十分钟

Reporter: Irene Rosenfeld, good to have you with us.

Rosenfeld: Glad to be here.

Reporter: Notwithstanding the fact that people have to eat no matter what the economy is, is this a good time to be in the food business?

Rosenfeld: Oh, I'll tell you I think it's a fabulous time to be in the food business. As you say, people have to eat and I think that certainly helps our industry in general but I think it's a particularly good time to be a Kraft. We make a number of the foods that people love. What we're seeing in response to the difficult economic environment, we are seeing a lot more people that are eating at home. And when they eat at home, they come home to Kraft. I think that's been very helpful to our business and I think it will serve us well as we continue into 2009.

Reporter: How do you continue that though when the economy is most likely not getting any better any time soon and people are really going to have to watch what they are spending on?

Rosenfeld: Well, I think we have a variety of offerings that play well in the current economic environment. We have products like DiGiorno frozen pizza, that are very viable substitutes for some of the foods that they might have bought at quick serve restaurants—and then we have a number of value oriented products like Kraft Macaroni and Cheese, Kool-Aid, Jell-O that offer a great value in the current economic environments. I think that we are well positioned to continue to grow in this very difficult environment.

Reporter: How do you—not restructure—but how do you reframe this company to make it more attractive when people are really watching their pocketbooks?

Rosenfeld: I think the biggest thing we have done is to ensure that the message about our iconic brands is focused on the value that they offer. So we talk for example in Kool-Aid, we talk about offering more smiles per gallon. The fact that you can get five times as many pitchers of Kool-Aid as you can

---

notwithstanding *conj.*
不论，尽管

fabulous *adj.*
极好的，极妙的

in general 总之

particularly *adv.*
尤其，特别地

response *n.*
应对，反应

variety *n.*
多样，种类

substitute *n.*
代替品，代用品

oriented *adj.*
导向的，以……为方向的

reframe *v.*
重组，再构造

pocketbook *n.*
钱包，笔记本

iconic *adj.*
标志性的，图标的

gallon *n.*
加仑

pitcher *n.*
大水罐

我们想让中国的13亿人口 都吃奥利奥产品

有效学习十分钟

记者：　艾琳·罗森菲尔德，欢迎来到我们的节目。

罗森菲尔德：很高兴能够来到这里。

记者：　不论经济怎样，人们总得吃，有了这一事实，您认为当前对于食品产业的发展是一个不错的时期吗？

罗森菲尔德：哦，我认为现在对于食品产业来说，正是一个非常好的时期。正如你所说的，人们必须要吃东西，这一点就促进了我们整个产业的发展，但是我想说现在对于卡夫集团来说，是一个非常好的机遇。我们生产了很多人们喜欢吃的食品。从现在困难的经济环境中，我们看到的是越来越多的人选择在家里吃东西，而当他们在家吃的时候，他们就会选择卡夫食品。我认为这对我们的产业发展是很有帮助的，而且当我们跨入2009年的时候，那也同样会给我们带来很大的帮助。

记者：　在经济很可能不会很快好转的时候，人们在消费时都会非常小心谨慎，在这种情况下，您如何继续保持产业的进步发展呢？

罗森菲尔德：嗯，在现在的经济环境下，我们给顾客提供了很多产品。我们有DiGiorno冷冻[1]比萨，这些可以作为人们以往在快餐店[2]购买的东西的替代品[3]。我们也有很多以价值为导向的[4]产品，比如卡夫通心粉[5]和奶酪、酷爱、果冻等，这些在现存的经济环境中都给我们带来了很大的价值。我想在这个困难的时期，我们也会继续发展。

记者：　当人们对自己的钱包看得很紧的时候，您怎样对公司进行重组[6]，以使其对消费者更具吸引力呢？

罗森菲尔德：我想，我们所做的最重要的事情就是确保向顾客们传达这样的信息即我们的标志性[7]品牌地位是在与产品的价值紧密相连的基础上建立起来的。所以比如说我们会谈论"酷爱[8]"产品，谈论我们能让每加仑多一些微笑。我们会为顾客提供是2升汽水[9]瓶容量的5倍的产品；我们也会谈论我们的一人份通心粉或者奶酪的花费是40美分。这些都是一些非常有价值的信息。事实是，如果你吃我们公司生产的奶酪和咸饼干[10]的话，你一

1. frozen *adj.*
2. quick serve restaurant
3. substitute *n.*
4. oriented *adj.*
5. Macaroni *n.*
6. reframe *v.*
7. iconic *adj.*
8. Kool-Aid
9. soda pop
10. cracker *n.*

get with a two-liter bottle of soda pop. We talk about the fact that our macaroni and cheese costs 40 cents a serving. Those are very strong value messages—the fact that when you eat some of our cheese and crackers, it's less than a dollar a serving. And so we are trying hard to help consumers understand the value of the products that we are offering and we're shifting a lot of spending this year to that kind of messaging.

Reporter: Let me ask you about that—that messaging—or marketing is another phrase. Do you find it to be a cost effective thing to get all that advertising out there when there's first of all, a lot of value messaging out there from other companies, but also consumers really watching what they spend?

Rosenfeld: Very much so. There's no question that we have well recognized, beloved brands and to the extent that we can tell those brands' stories in a way that is relevant to consumers in the current economic environment. I think that we will be successful in the future. So we are actually finding that the value of investing in those kinds of messages today is much more important than ever.

Reporter: You say beloved brands, others would say, "oldish". I mean, Kraft cheese, Oreo's, I mean they're not the most sparkling brand new kids on the block. What do you think about this kind of issue?

Rosenfeld: I feel awfully proud of what our team has accomplished as they have reframed these beloved, age-old brands to be increasingly relevant to consumers in the current environment. So if you look at the packaging that you see for a number of our products, I think that you see much more of a contemporary feel. I think if you look at what we've done to the ingredients—salad dressing for example, we've taken out the preservatives; we've added fiber to a number of our biscuit products—across the board we are working very hard to ensure that we are upgrading these age-old products that consumers grew up with and love that we are upgrading these products to address contemporary consumer needs.

Reporter: Let me pick up on that for a second. My kids for some reason, and maybe this is because of my wife and I, I don't know—but I grew up with Kraft Singles, I mean that was just a staple around my house. But my kids have just sort of discovered them. How do you get something as iconic as Kraft Singles out into the marketplace so more consumers do it? What do you do as a marketer?

Rosenfeld: What you do is you pick up on the fact that it is the number one cheese used in making grilled cheese, which is one of America's favorite foods. And so we are finding again, in this difficult economic environment, there is nothing more exciting to a consumer than grilled cheese and a bowl of soup. And so we are able to benefit greatly from people's desire to return

---

macaroni *n.*
通心粉，通心面条

cracker *n.*
饼干

messaging *n.*
消息传送

recognize *v.*
认可

extent *n.*
程度，范围

be relevant to
和……相关

oldish *adj.*
稍旧的，稍老的

sparkling *adj.*
闪闪发光的，闪烁的

awfully *adv.*
非常，十分

accomplish *v.*
完成，实现

contemporary *adj.*
当代的，同时代的

ingredient *n.*
原料，要素

preservative *n.*
防腐剂，保存剂

biscuit *n.*
饼干

upgrade *v.*
升级

staple *n.*
主食

grill *v.*
烤，烧

consumer *n.*
消费者

次只需花费不到1美元。所以我们尽全力帮助顾客们了解我们产品的价值，我们也将一些花费转移[11]到了这种信息的宣传上面。

记者：　　　让我来问一下您有关市场方面的问题。您认为当有很多其他公司的价值信息存在并且消费者对钱包看得很紧的时候，不用为产品做广告是否是一件很节省开支的事情呢？

罗森菲尔德：是这样的。我们现在拥有被广泛认可[12]、为顾客所喜爱[13]的品牌，对于每一个品牌，我们都能够讲出一个在当前[14]经济环境下与消费者相关的小故事。我认为未来我们会取得成功。所以我们发现，今天对于价值信息的投资[15]是非常重要的，比以往都要重要。

记者：　　　您说你们的品牌是"为顾客所喜爱的品牌"，有人可能会说这些品牌"有点古老"。我的意思是，卡夫食品中的奶酪、奥利奥并不是出售产品中最突出[16]的全新品牌。您对这个问题是如何看待的呢？

罗森菲尔德：我为我们的团队所取得的成绩感到非常[17]骄傲，他们对那些曾经受顾客喜爱的但是比较古老的品牌产品进行重构，使它们在现在的经济环境逐渐与消费者产生联系。所以如果你去看一下我们很多产品的包装的话，你会发现，我们的产品都给人一种很现代的[18]感觉。如果你去看一下我们对于产品配料[19]所作的调整，比如说色拉味调料[20]等，你就会发现，里面并没有防腐剂[21]；我们向很多饼干产品中添加了纤维素[22]。我们所有的工作人员都非常努力地工作，以确保我们可以对那些顾客从小就喜爱的古老的[23]产品进行升级，并且这些升过级的产品可以满足[24]当代消费者的需求。

记者：　　　这一点让我觉得很熟悉[25]。我的孩子就喜欢吃卡夫芝士片，可能是因为我和我妻子的原因，我不知道，但我是吃着卡夫芝士长大的，我的意思是那是我家里的主食[26]，我们的孩子也很喜欢。您是怎样做使你们诸如此类的传统产品更好地打入市场呢？作为商人，你们是怎样做的呢？

罗森菲尔德：我们在烤[27]奶酪时用的是最好的奶酪，那也是美国人民都最喜欢吃的一种食品。所以在现在的经济困难时期，我们再次发现，对于消费者来说，没有什么比烤奶酪和一碗汤更让人感到高兴的了。所以从人们希望返回到节俭又可口的饮食方式中，我们获得了一些益处。

记者：　　　我懂得一些有关市场营销[28]的内容，但是为什么说没有什么比烤奶酪和一碗汤更让人感到高兴的呢？

罗森菲尔德：你午饭准备吃什么呢？如果我告诉你，我可以为你提供烤奶酪和一碗

11. shift *v.*
12. recognized *v.*
13. beloved *adj.*
14. current *adj.*
15. invest *v.*
16. sparkling *adj.*
17. awfully *adv.*
18. contemporary *adj.*
19. ingredient *n.*
20. salad dressing
21. preservative *n.*
22. fiber *n.*
23. age-old
24. address *v.*
25. pick up on
26. staple *n.*
27. grilled *adj.*
28. marketing *n.*

to economical, delicious alternatives.

Reporter: I understand marketing but, nothing more exciting than grilled cheese and a bowl of soup?

Rosenfeld: What are you going to have for lunch? If I told you I could serve you grilled cheese and a bowl of soup, wouldn't you be happy?

Reporter: I love a good grilled cheese sandwich and a bowl of soup, but if I'm packing lunch for the kids in the morning, it's really tough to pack a grilled cheese sandwich for lunch for kids seven hours later.

Rosenfeld: No, it works just fine. You stick it right in the microwave and it tastes just delicious.

Reporter: Tell me about Chinese Oreo's.

Rosenfeld: Oreo's in China, you mean?

Reporter: Oreo's in China, right and that's sort of the root of the question. I mean you guys have this iconic brand—Oreo's—and amazing success story in this country, a billion dollar brand for you. You try to grow it internationally, you take it overseas and it doesn't really work out. So you reinvent them into something that, in this country anyway wouldn't be recognizable as an Oreo cookie. Tell us the story of how you went to China and said, "listen, we've got to get 1.3 billion Chinese eating Oreo's".

Rosenfeld: Well, it starts with the fact that we began by giving the responsibility of making some of those decisions back to our local managers. In the past, we would have mandated what an Oreo looked like around the world from Northfield, Illinois. And that wasn't necessarily consistent with what consumers in the local markets were eating. So what we found was sandwich cookies as a format is just not appealing to Chinese consumers but wafer formats are what they are eating. We know we have to make a shift. And so all we did was taking the flavoring and the strong cocoa taste of our Oreo together with some of the fabulous marketing that we've done around the world and brought it to the Chinese consumer. And we are pleased to see that it is the fastest growing biscuit in China right now.

Reporter: You stopped planting flags, so you are not looking to expand into other countries, you're going to grow where you are.

Rosenfeld: Well, we're in 150 countries, so it's less a question of going to new countries, but we have chosen to focus our resources on those ten countries that we think are most important to our future. Of the ten countries, half of them are developing markets where we've continued to have significant double digit growth, and I think we will continue to see strong growth into the future. The other half are solid markets like what we see in Western Europe that have been strong markets for our brands.

alternative n.
供选择的办法，选择性的事物

microwave n.
微波炉

brand n.
商标，牌子

reinvent v.
重新使用，彻底改造

mandate v.
授权，托管

format n.
版式，格式

appeal v.
吸引，迎合

flavoring n.
调味品

expand v.
扩张，发展

汤，难道你不会感到很高兴吗？

记者：　　我喜欢烤奶酪三明治外加一碗汤，但是如果我要在早上为孩子们准备打包午饭的话，我想给他们准备一个烤奶酪三明治作为7个小时以后的午餐会很困难吧！

罗森菲尔德：不会的，到时你把它放在微波炉[29]里热一下，仍然会美味可口。

记者：　　请跟我们说一下中国的奥利奥[30]。

罗森菲尔德：你的意思是指，我们在中国的奥利奥产品吗？

记者：　　是的，在中国的奥利奥产品，就是要问这个。我的意思是你们的这个传统品牌，奥利奥在中国取得了很大的成功，你们从中赚取了10亿美元。所以你们想要这个产品国际化，把它引进到其他一些海外国家中，但是它并没有获得成功。然后你们对它进行重新改造，使得在其他国家，消费者并不把它当作是一种奥利奥曲奇[31]饼干。请跟我们说一下您是怎样打入中国市场的，并且说"我们要让中国的13亿人口都吃奥利奥产品"的。

29. microwave *n.*
30. Oreo's
31. cookie *n.*
32. wafer *n.*
33. strong *adj.*
34. double digit
35. solid *adj.*

罗森菲尔德：嗯，这开始于我们将做决定的责任分配给当地的经理人这一事实。在过去，我们将决定奥利奥品牌在世界上如何发展的权利都给了伊利诺伊州的北地市，但是那有时候与当地顾客习惯吃的食品有很大出入。所以后来我们发现，三明治曲奇对中国消费者并没有吸引力，他们喜欢吃的是薄脆饼[32]。因而我们知道我们必须要进行一些调整。所以我们就将调味料和奥利奥浓郁的[33]可可粉味道结合到一起，并将产品以我们在世界上采用过的优秀市场营销方式带给中国的消费者。我们很高兴地看到，我们的产品是中国饼干发展最快的一个品牌。

记者：　　你们现在并没有将业务继续打入其他的国家，你们是要在已有的业务基础上继续不断发展吗？

罗森菲尔德：嗯，我们的企业在150个国家都有分支，所以对于我们来说继续将业务拓展到一些新的国家并不是什么问题。但是我们最终选择将我们的重心放在有利于我们未来发展的那10个国家，其中一半是发展中国家，在那里我们的业务将会有两位数[34]的增长，我认为我们未来将会有更好的发展。剩下的一半是稳定的[35]市场，比如说我们在西欧的市场，我们的品牌在那里有牢固的市场。

10 min 自由输出十分钟

1. 常春藤联盟（The Ivy League）是指由美国东北部八所院校组成的体育赛事联盟。这八所院校包括：布朗大学、哥伦比亚大学、康奈尔大学、达特茅斯学院、哈佛大学、宾夕法尼亚大学、普林斯顿大学及耶鲁大学。美国八所常春藤盟校都是私立大学，和公立大学一样，它们同时接受联邦政府资助和私人捐赠用于学术研究。由于美国公立大学享有联邦政府的巨额拨款，私立大学的财政支出和研究经费要低于公立大学。

2. 犹太人，其祖先为希伯来人，是起源于阿拉伯半岛的游牧民族，属于闪米特人的一支，原始血缘上与阿拉伯人相近，主要信仰犹太教。以色列的《回归法》界定犹太人的身份是按母系相传为标准，凡是母亲是犹太人的，其子女都会被以色列承认为犹太人，有权移民以色列。

3. address一词可表示"解决"的意思，例如：Mr. Obama has repeatedly said he would not support a temporary deal because it would not address the nation's fiscal issues.（奥巴马已多次表示，他不会支持一个临时性的协议，因为这解决不了政府面临的财政问题。）

4. 《福布斯》（Forbes）是福布斯先生经营的世界上最著名的财经杂志名称，因前瞻性强、有不妥协精神、观点鲜明、简明扼要而闻名于世。90年来，《福布斯》杂志一直以"关注实践和实践者"为口号，倡导企业家精神和创新意识。正是由于其明确的定位和独特的深度报道，使《福布斯》成为今天美国主要商业杂志中惟一保持10年连续增长的刊物，其受众群在商业杂志中占据魁首。

5. food一词本身是个集合名称，表示"食物"，其单复数形式一样，但当后面加s时，表示不同种类的食物，例如：You are in a new country, you may want to try new foods but you need to be careful about how much you eat.（你在一个新的国家，你也许想要尝尝新的食物，但你吃多少需要小心。）

6. pocketbook可以表示"（个人或国家的）财政状况"，例如：Many foreign goods are too expensive for American pocketbooks.（许多外国货都太贵，与一般美国人的财力都不符。）

7. 英语中破折号可以表示在说话时有意地中断了一下，以便强调或引起别人注意破折号后面要说的话，例如：In a word, the spirit of the whole country may be described as—self-reliance and arduous struggle.（总而言之，整个国家的精神可以说是——自力更生，艰苦奋斗。）

8. 一些我们常见的饮料的名称，例如：可口可乐，Coca Cola，简称Coke；百事，Pepsi；健怡可乐，Diet coke；雪碧，Sprite；芬达，Fanta；七喜，7up；红牛，Red Bull等。

9. 词组take over的意思是"接管"，例如：It would be up to them to decide who should take over, or whether they should let an outsider run the company.（届时将由他们决定谁来接管，或是否应让外人参与管理公司。）

10. kid一词做动词时表示"戏弄，开玩笑"，通常用于进行时，例如：I thought he was kidding when he said he was going out with a rock star.（他说他在与一位摇滚乐歌星谈恋爱，我还以为他在开玩笑。）

21

麦当劳创始人：
雷·克洛克
Founder of Mcdonald's: Ray Kroc

　　雷·克洛克(Ray Kroc)，麦当劳之父，快餐巨人。他于1902年出生在美国洛杉矶橡树园。1922年，他开始正式为莉莉特利普制杯公司做推销工作，而后被一种新型的奶昔搅拌器所吸引，用所有积蓄取得了独家代理权并穿越美国全境进行推销，就这样他经历了30年的推销生涯。

　　1961年，克洛克说服麦当劳兄弟将餐馆转让给自己，此后麦当劳进入了克洛克时代。他坚信整洁是餐饮业的核心，并从各个细节开始整顿。在严格的制度管理下，5年后，克洛克旗下的麦当劳发展到1000家店铺，到1978年达到5000家的规模。经过40余年的发展，目前麦当劳已有近3万家店铺，遍布全球114个国家和地区，成为和万宝路、可口可乐齐名的三大品牌之一。

21.1 To Have Success, You Should Be Daring, First and Different

轻松输入十分钟

Reporter: Thank you very much for letting me interview you. I realize you just got out of the hospital.

Ray Kroc: Well, seeing America as a winner again is the most important thing in the world to me. If I weren't at the end of my road, this magazine is what I would want to do.

Reporter: I wish you could get involved.

Ray Kroc: Like I said, I would but what I need to do now is get my affairs in order, take care of my family before I go. But I am impressed with you and the positive attitude you are presenting through your *Winners* Magazine. You are taking Teddy Roosevelt's "Man in the Arena" and making it work. *Winners* Magazine may be the avenue for standing and cheering for the Achiever, the Doer, the Leader, the Winner. I think you have got something that can help America be number one again.

Reporter: How important is it for Americans to regard themselves as?

Ray Kroc: You know, I think that's terribly important. In the automobile business, in any business. You're either accomplished, you're either number one or you're not. Hell, we're number one at McDonald's and I couldn't stand it if we weren't. There are lots of people in the fast food business and they can't all be. But I'd rather be number one than anything else. We're the oldest and, so, if we can't be, there must be some reason. But we are! We do the biggest volume. We do the best job. My interest in McDonald's is so they don't fall behind. So they stay ahead of competition. I'm the old-fashioned guy in competition—I'll kill the son of a bitch.

Reporter: Anything goes?

Ray Kroc: Sure. Business is business.

Reporter: So you subscribe to cutthroat?

Ray Kroc: I'm only surfacing how I feel. I wouldn't really kill them but that's the way I feel.

Reporter: The Padres, unlike McDonald's, are not number one. Do you love baseball

affair *n.*
事情，私事

attitude *n.*
态度，看法

avenue *n.*
林荫大道，大街

terribly *adv.*
非常，可怕地

accomplished *adj.*
熟练的，完成的

volume *n.*
量，体积

competition *n.*
竞争，比赛

cutthroat *n.*
杀手，谋杀者

surface *v.*
揭露，浮出水面

baseball *n.*
棒球，棒球运动

要想成功，必须要有胆量、率先行动和与众不同

有效学习十分钟

记者：　非常感谢能有幸采访您，我知道您刚出院。

雷·克洛克：没事，对于我来说，世界上最重要的事就是再次看到美国成为赢家。如果我不是走到了尽头的话，我是想做这个杂志的。

记者：　我希望您能介入[1]。

雷·克洛克：正如我曾经说过的那样，我将做并且现在必须要做的是有条不紊地安排我的事情，在我离开之前照顾我的家庭。但你和你们的《赢家》杂志所展现[2]的积极的态度给我留下了很深的印象。你们引用了泰迪·罗斯福的"竞技场[3]上的人"，并且使其行之有效。《赢家》杂志就像是一条林荫大道[4]，供我们停留，为成功者[5]、实干家[6]、领导者和赢家欢呼雀跃。我想你们有方法能够促使美国再次成为第一。

记者：　美国人把自身视为第一有多重要？

雷·克洛克：我认为是非常重要的。在汽车[7]行业或者是任何行业，你要么是很熟练，位居第一，要么不是。我们的麦当劳就是位居第一，如果它不是第一，我会无法忍受。还有许多人在快餐[8]行业，他们都不是第一。但我只想当第一，我们是做得最久的，如果成为不了第一，那肯定有原因。但我们就是第一，我们的销售额是最大的，做的是最好的。我对麦当劳的兴趣就是这样，所以它不会落后，一直领先于竞争。在竞争中，我是一个守旧的[9]人，讨厌混账卑鄙的人。

记者：　任何事情都可能发生吗？

雷·克洛克：当然，商业就是这样。

记者：　所以你会聘请杀手[10]吗？

雷·克洛克：我只是表现我所想的，虽然我会这么想，但是不会真正地去杀他们。

记者：　教士队棒球不像麦当劳，它就不是第一。您爱棒球胜过生命吗？

1. involved *adj.*
2. present *v.*
3. arena *n.*
4. avenue *n.*
5. achiever *n.*
6. doer *n.*
7. automobile *n.*
8. fast food
9. old-fashioned
10. cutthroat *n.*

more than you love being?

Ray Kroc: I lost $2,700,000 on the Padres last year and I'm not going to lose it this year. If I do, I'm going to get rid of them.

Reporter: What about your background? Have you come a long way in achieving your success as a winner or were you born into a healthy head start?

Ray Kroc: Oh no, no, no, no. I came from a poor family. You know, relatively poor. Not POOR. Not destitute. Not in the general sense. BUT they had trouble making their payments. We struggled and we were just lucky we accomplished.

Reporter: Luck is a big part of success?

Ray Kroc: Yeah. Luck and perseverance. I never had a penny until I was—a penny? I meant a nickel—until I was 60 years old.

Reporter: What's the worst point in your life? When were you most down and out?

Ray Kroc: When I went to Florida to sell real estate. That was in 1925.

Reporter: How close did you come to giving up?

Ray Kroc: Well, I didn't consider giving up because I was a professional piano player and I can always make a damn good living through playing the piano. Vice presidents of banks couldn't get $25 a week and I could play the piano and make $125.

Reporter: So you had another profession to fall back on?

Ray Kroc: I always have that to fall back on.

Reporter: Then what made your Florida experience the worst point in your life?

Ray Kroc: I was married. I had a little baby. I got married when I was 20 years old—I was about 22 then—I didn't have any money. I made $125 a week and that was a lot of money in 1925. But you must understand the unique harshness of the Florida economy at that time. Everything was very expensive. Milk was $0.40 a quart! So I had problems. But I didn't give up.

Reporter: Have you ever felt like giving up?

Ray Kroc: No.

Reporter: It never occurs to you?

Ray Kroc: No. I'm impatient as hell, but, when it comes to this sort of thing, well, I exercise a lot of patience. Perseverance.

Reporter: Besides perseverance, what other attributes have helped you succeed?

Ray Kroc: I have a sign in my office. It says, "To Be a Success in Business—Be Daring. Be First. Be Different." Most important, however, is the fact I have never worked for money. I like the convenience of money, but I have never worked for it. I'll pay my men a lot of money but I don't want it. If you work for money, you're limited in what you can achieve because

---

achieve v.
实现，达到

destitute adj.
穷困的，缺乏的

struggle v.
努力，奋斗

perseverance n.
坚持不懈，不屈不挠

nickel n.
镍币，镍

estate n.
房地产，财产

professional adj.
专业的，职业的

harshness n.
严肃，刺耳

quart n.
夸脱，一夸脱的容器

impatient adj.
不耐心的，焦躁的

attribute n.
特质，属性

convenience n.
便利

雷·克洛克：我去年在那里损失了270万美元，今年不会了。如果还继续亏的话，我就会卖掉他们。

记者：　　您的背景如何？您在实现成功成为赢家的过程中花了很长时间吗？或者是您一出生就抢占了先机？

雷·克洛克：哦，不是的。我来自一个贫困的家庭，应该说是相对穷的家庭，没到一贫如洗的程度，也不是一般意义上那种穷。但是支付[11]花费还是有些困难，我们很努力，幸运的是，最后我们做到了。

记者：　　幸运占成功很大一部分吗？

雷·克洛克：是的，幸运和坚持[12]。在我六十岁之前，我一直身无分文，应该说没有半分钱。

记者：　　你生命中最糟糕时是什么时候？什么时候您最潦倒？

雷·克洛克：在1925年，我去佛罗里达出售房地产的时候。

记者：　　您当时是不是差点就放弃[13]了？

雷·克洛克：没，我没有想过放弃。因为我是一个专业的钢琴弹奏者，所以我总能通过弹奏钢琴过一个好的生活。银行的副总裁一周25美元都赚不到，而我凭借弹钢琴能赚取125美元。

记者：　　所以您还有另一个职业可依赖？

雷·克洛克：我一直能依赖它。

记者：　　那么是什么使得佛罗里达成为您生命中最糟糕的经历？

雷·克洛克：我那时候已经结婚了，有了一个小孩。我20岁的时候结的婚。在22岁那年，我没什么钱，每个月挣125美元，这在1925年算多了。但是你知道当时佛罗里达的经济尤其艰苦，什么东西都贵，每一夸脱[14]的牛奶要0.4美元。所以我遇到了困难，但是没有放弃。

记者：　　您有想过放弃吗？

雷·克洛克：没有。

记者：　　从来没有想过？

雷·克洛克：对。我遇到低谷，就会没有耐心。但是遇到这种事情的时候，我会拿出很大的耐心去坚持。

记者：　　除了坚持以外，还有什么素质帮助您成功？

雷·克洛克：我办公室里有一个标牌，写到"要想在生意上成功，你必须有胆量[15]、率先行动和与众不同。"最重要的是，我从来不是为了钱而奋斗。我喜欢钱带来的便捷，但是从来不是为了它而奋斗。我付给我的员工很多钱，但自

11. payment n.
12. perseverance n.
13. give up
14. quart n.
15. daring n.

when you have enough money, for practical reasons, you don't have the urge to make any more. I work for satisfaction. A man's work is his whole life. You know? If you don't like the work you do, get away from it, do something else or you're a goddam bum! My salary as Chairman of the Board of McDonald's—and I'm the founder of a $7 billion a year business—is only $175,000 a year. I pay an 80% tax rate on my stock dividends. 80%! I have a foundation for arthritis, diabetes, multiple sclerosis—they give away approximately four to six million dollars per year. I do not work for money.

Reporter: You say you pay your men a lot of money, yet, the Padres has lost valuable talents who didn't think you were paying enough.

Ray Kroc: We pay our players good wages and if they demand too much, I'll let them go. You see, baseball has changed. It used to be a game and now the players are trying to retire in 2 or 3 years. It used to be a player would say, "Look, I had a pretty good year. I did this. I think I ought to have $3000, $5000, $8000 more. And the boss would look it over and say "yes" or "no". Now rookies come in and want a No Trade Contract and a big bonus. If they sign up with a new team, they want a $500,000~$1 million signing bonus. A signing bonus! For their right to play baseball! Why it's ridiculous. We are no longer dealing with players, we're dealing with corporations. The player has a manager and a lawyer and you deal with them, not with him. It's not a close relationship. Baseball has changed. There is no loyalty between the owners and the players. It's dog eat dog. Everybody's acting in their own selfish interests, and that's unfortunate because you can't have a good business with that kind of basis.

Reporter: Regarding competition, you said you'd "kill the son of a bitch". Don't you subscribe to "dog eat dog"?

Ray Kroc: No, no, I don't. There is a difference. I believe in the man sticking with something that he respects and honors to the point he gives it his life instead of being a whore and selling out for the largest amount. Like Kemp of the Tigers. The Tigers are a real fine people yet an arbitrator who has no experience in baseball awards a $600,000 contract. So if he has a good year now, what will they give him next year? $800,000 or $1 million?!

Reporter: What about the players' attitude that they've only got 10 years to earn big money, so, therefore, they should go for broke since they may not get the chance to earn that kind of money after they leave baseball?

Ray Kroc: That's a lot of crap. The players are all college educated and not a damn

---

satisfaction n.
满意，满足

dividend n.
股息，奖金

arthritis n.
关节炎

sclerosis n.
硬化症，硬化

approximately adv.
将近，大约

ought v.
应该，大概

rooky n.
新手

ridiculous adj.
荒谬的，可笑的

corporation n.
公司，社团

selfish adj.
自私的，利己主义的

subscribe v.
认购，赞成

stick v.
坚持，粘贴

arbitrator n.
仲裁人，公断人

crap n.
废话，废物

己并不渴望钱。如果你是为了钱而奋斗，你所实现的东西就会受到限制。因为当你有钱的时候，你会变得实际，不会渴望去赚取更多。我是为了满足而奋斗。一个人的工作是他的整个生命。你知道吗？如果你不喜欢你做的工作，那就别做了，去做其他的，否则只能说明你是一个讨厌鬼。我所创立的这家公司每年盈利70亿美元，我作为麦当劳的董事会主席，一年的工资只有17.5万美元。我还要缴纳80%的股息[16]，80%啊！我为关节炎[17]、糖尿病[18]、多发性硬化病患者创建了一个基金会[19]，每年大约花费400万到600万。所以，我不是为了钱而工作。

记者：　您说您付给员工许多钱。但是教士棒球俱乐部丧失了很多人才，他们认为您没有支付多少钱。

雷·克洛克：我会付给运动员高工资，但是如果他们要求得过多，我会让他们走人。你知道，棒球已经发生了变化。它以前是一项比赛，而现在的运动员在2至3年间就会退休[20]。在以前，运动员会说，我今年表现得很好，应该赚3000美元、5000美元、8000美元或者是更多。我的老板会审查，然后说是或否。现在，新秀们参与进来，他们希望在不签订贸易合同下获取丰厚红利。如果他们要和一支新的队签约，他们希望得到50万～100万的签约金。这只是请他们打球的签约金啊！太荒谬[21]了！我们不再和运动员洽谈，转向跟公司洽谈。运动员有经理或者是律师，我们可以和他们洽谈，而不是和运动员本人，关系也就没那么近。棒球已经发生了变化。主办方和运动员双方彼此间不再忠诚[22]，就像是"狗吃狗"，每个人都在为个人自私的[23]利益而工作。这个是很不幸的，因为在这种基础上，没法做好。

记者：　提及竞争的时候，您说您想杀了那些卑鄙的混账东西，那么您会想杀了这些"狗吃狗"的人吗？

雷·克洛克：没有，这个是不同的。我信赖那些付出生命来坚持[24]自己所尊重的东西的人，而不是像妓女一样，为了大笔的钱出卖自己。例如猛虎队的坎普，猛虎队非常好，但是它的仲裁人[25]在棒球方面没有经验，仅以60万美元签订了合同。如果它表现好的话，明年将会获得多少钱呢？80万或者100万美元。

记者：　运动员只有十年的时间赚大量的钱，他们的态度是怎样的？由于他们离开棒球后，可能就失去赚这么多钱的机会，因此，他们是否孤注一掷呢？

雷·克洛克：这纯粹是胡扯[26]。运动员都是在大学受过教育的人，每个人都是有素质

16. stock dividend
17. arthritis *n.*
18. diabetes *n.*
19. foundation *n.*
20. retire *v.*
21. ridiculous *adj.*
22. loyalty *n.*
23. selfish *adj.*
24. stick with
25. arbitrator *n.*

one of them—barely any of them—do any work in the off-season. They've got 10 years to appreciate investments in the bond market or whatever they want to stick with. That way, there'd be something for them when they're through with baseball. But they don't! They don't do a damn thing and then when they're through playing they wonder why nobody will give them a job. You've got to learn the business. If they want to be a baker or whatever, they have to apprentice in it and they should do so while they're being paid a lot of money and have the free time. But they don't provide for anything and that 10 years is their responsibility.

Reporter: What would you say to an athlete that says, "Why shouldn't I ask for more money? Look at all the money Ray Kroc makes?"

Ray Kroc: You're probably talking about a youngster, 20 years old, maybe 23... (pause while he computes) Hell, there 60 years difference in our ages! Man alive! If you're halfway to my point in life, I'll reason with you. But not when you're only 20 years old.

Reporter: Okay, Ray, one last question: you're a man successful in a couple of fields. What would we say your Art is? Making an excellent hamburger, or building an efficient, quality oriented business, or –

Ray Kroc: Providing other people with goals that are satisfying.

Reporter: Helping other people to achieve those goals?

Ray Kroc: If they gloat over money, I won't help them at all. But if they use money to good intentions, to help other people, to provide opportunities for young people, I'll help them. That's what I do: I help other fellows to become millionaires.

off-season n.
淡季

damn adj.
可恶的，讨厌的

apprentice v.
当学徒

responsibility n.
责任，义务

orient v.
适应，确定方向

millionaire n.
百万富翁，大富豪

的。他们当中几乎没有人在淡季[27]的时候做过任何工作。十年的时间可以让他们在证券市场[28]的投资升值，或者是可以做任何他们想坚持的事。那样的话，他们在打棒球期间，还有其他的事情可做。但是他们没有，什么事情都不做，他们在打球期间，疑惑为什么没人给他们一份工作。他们必须要了解商业。如果想要成为一名面包师的话，就应该去当学徒[29]，并且要在挣大钱和闲暇的这段期间就去这么做。但是他们什么都不提供，十年时间就像是在履行职责。

记者：　　有一位运动员说，"看看雷·克洛克赚的钱有多少啊，为什么我不能要求更多钱？"，您对这个有什么要说的？

雷·克洛克：你说的可能是一个20岁或者23岁的年轻人[30]（他一边计算，停顿了一下），我们的年龄相差60岁啊！对于一个活人，如果你活到了我生命的一半，我可能跟你评理，但是你只有20岁，我绝对不会跟你理论。

记者：　　好的，最后一个问题。您在很多领域都很成功，像是制作一个精良的汉堡，成立一个有效率、有质量的公司，又或是其他，您成功的艺术是什么？

雷·克洛克：为别人提供满意的目标。

记者：　　帮助别人实现这些目标？

雷·克洛克：如果他们对钱沾沾自喜的话，那么我是不会帮助他们的。但如果他们把钱用在好的意图[31]上，去帮助别人，为年轻人提供机会，我就会帮助他们。这就是我做的：帮助其他的伙伴们成为百万富翁[32]。

26. crap *n.*
27. off-season
28. bond market
29. apprentice *n.*
30. youngster *n.*
31. intention *n.*
32. millionaire *n.*

1. suggest一词意为"建议"时用虚拟语气，意为"暗示"时则不用。例如：His face suggests that he looks worried.（他的表情暗含着他很担心。）；I suggest that you should finish you homework seriously.（我建议你应该认真做完作业。）

2. 注意affect和effect两个词做动词的区别：affect做动词时表示"影响某事/某人"，例如：Does television affect children's behaviour?（电视对孩子的行为有影响吗？）；"effect"做动词时一般用于正式场合，表示"实现，产生"，例如：They hope to effect a reconciliation.（他们希望实现和解。）

3. 介词词组in order的意思是"整齐，井然有序"，例如：I would have soon found the one I wanted if the books had kept in order.（如果书籍摆放整齐了，我本可以很快就找到我想要的那本书的。）

4. 平行结构（parallelism）是把两个或两个以上结构大体相同或相似、意思相关、语气一致的短语、句子排列成串，形成一个整体。例如：No one can be perfectly free till all are free; no one can be perfectly moral till all are moral; no one can be perfectly happy till all are happy.

5. sb. can (not) help doing sth.表示"某人忍不住做某事"，例如：I can't help thinking he knows more than he has told us.（我总觉得他没有把他知道的事情全告诉我们。）

6. dog eat dog是一种比喻的说法，字面意思是"狗吃狗"，但其真正意思是"残酷无情地竞争，自相残杀"，例如：I'm afraid in this line of work is a case of dog eat dog.（恐怕在这种行业中竞争是残酷无情的。）

7. 英语中，动词不定式可以做主语，但如果主语过长，则用形式主语it代替，真正的主语置后。例如：To learn a foreign language well is not easy. 这句话可以改写成：It is not easy to learn a foreign language well.

8. 词组fall back的意思是"退回，后退"。例如：In panic mode, we fall back into our old habits.（在恐慌状态中，我们又回到了我们的老习惯。）

9. damn一词平时多用于表示失望的情况，但还可以表示"十足的，完全的"，用来加强语气，例如：What a damn shame!（真是太遗憾了！）

22 耐克公司创始人之一：
菲尔·奈特
Co-founder of Nike: Phil Knight

　　菲尔·奈特(Phil Knight)，耐克的传奇领袖，是财富500强公司里最古怪的领导人之一。他出生于1938年2月24日。青少年时，他就十分热爱体育运动，并在高中校报上刊登有关体育的采访文章。1959年毕业于俄勒冈大学，获得了工商行政管理学学士学位，并于1962年在斯坦福大学获得工商管理学硕士学位。

　　1964年，奈特与他在大学时的长跑教练比尔·鲍尔曼各自出资500美元创立了耐克的前身蓝带公司。1971年，奈特以希腊胜利女神的名字将公司命名为耐克（NIKE）公司。耐克也是第一个采取名人代言方式打响知名度的厂商，它的广告更屡屡成为广告史上的经典之作。2012年4月，菲尔·奈特因其创立的耐克公司对于篮球运动的杰出贡献入选2012年奈·史密斯篮球名人堂。

22.1 / The Growing History of Nike

轻松输入十分钟

HBR: Nike transformed the athletic shoe industry with technological innovations, but today many people know the company by its flashy ads and sports celebrities. Is Nike a technology company or a marketing company?

Phil Knight: I'd answer that question very differently today than I would have ten years ago. For years, we thought of ourselves as a production-oriented company, meaning we put all our emphasis on designing and manufacturing the product. But now we understand that the most important thing we do is marketing the product. We've come around to saying that Nike is a marketing-oriented company, and the product is our most important marketing tool. What I mean is that marketing knits the whole organization together. The design elements and functional characteristics of the product itself are just part of the overall marketing process. We used to think that everything started in the lab. Now we realize that everything spins off the consumer. And while technology is still important, the consumer has to lead innovation. We have to innovate for a specific reason, and that reason comes from the market. Otherwise, we'll end up making museum pieces.

HBR: What made you think the product was everything?

Phil Knight: Our success. In the early days, anybody with a glue pot and a pair of scissors could get into the shoe business, so the way to stay ahead was through product innovation. We happened to be great at it. Bill Bowerman, my former track coach at the University of Oregon and cofounder of the company that became Nike, had always customized off-the-shelf shoes for his runners. Over the years, he and some other employees came up with lots of great ideas that we incorporated. One of Bowerman's more legendary innovations is the Waffle outsole, which he discovered by pouring rubber into a waffle iron. The Waffle Trainer later became the best-selling training shoe in the United States. We were also good at keeping our manufacturing costs down. The big, established players like Puma and Adidas were still manufacturing in high-wage European countries. But we knew that wages were lower in Asia, and we knew how to get around in that environment, so we funneled all our most promising managers there to supervise production.

HBR: Didn't you do any marketing?

---

flashy *adj.*
华丽的，瞬间的

celebrity *n.*
名人

manufacture *v.*
制造，加工

overall *adj.*
总的，全体的

innovate *v.*
创新，改革

scissors *n.*
剪刀

customize *v.*
定制，定做

legendary *adj.*
传奇的，传说的

pour *v.*
倒，倾泻

established *adj.*
知名的，已制定的

funnel *v.*
调动

supervise *v.*
监督，指导

耐克公司的成长史

有效学习十分钟

哈佛商业评论：耐克通过技术创新转变为一家运动鞋[1]公司，但现在很多人都是通过其华丽的广告和体育界名人[2]而知道这家公司的，那么耐克到底是一家技术公司还是一家营销公司呢？

菲尔·奈特：我今天要与十年前完全不同地回答这个问题。这些年来，我们把自己的公司视为以生产为导向的[3]公司，这就意味着我们要把重点放在产品设计和生产上面。但是我们现在明白我们做的最重要的事是产品营销。

可以说耐克是一个以市场营销为导向的[4]公司，产品是我们最重要的营销工具。我的意思是说，营销能把整个组织结合在一起，产品的设计元素和功能特点只是整个营销过程的一部分。我们以前认为一切都是始于实验室的，但现在我们意识到一切都是由顾客生产的。技术仍然重要，消费者会引导创新。我们必须要为一个具体理由而创新，这个理由就是市场。否则[5]的话，我们最终的产品便是博物馆藏品（卖不出去）。

哈佛商业评论：是什么使您认为产品意味着一切？

菲尔·奈特：我们的成功。早前，任何人只要他有一个熬胶锅和一把剪刀就能步入制鞋这个行业，因此要向前行，只能通过创新。而我们恰巧擅长这个。我在俄勒冈州的前任田径教练[6]比尔·鲍尔曼———耐克公司的共同创办人[7]，他总是为跑步者定制[8]现成的鞋子。这些年来，他和其他员工想出了很多供我们吸收采纳的好点子。鲍尔曼的一项传奇性[9]创新是华夫鞋跟[10]，这是他在一次把橡胶倒进烙铁时发现的。华夫跑鞋后来成为美国最畅销的跑鞋。我们也很擅长降低制造成本。像一些大的、知名的公司，例如彪马和阿迪达斯仍在欧洲的一些工资水平高的[11]国家制造。但是我们清楚亚洲的工资更低些，我们知道如何应对这个环境，因此，我们把最有前途的[12]经理们都集中调去那里监督[13]生产。

1. athletic shoe
2. celebrity *n.*
3. production-oriented
4. marketing-oriented
5. otherwise *adv.*
6. track coach
7. cofounder *n.*
8. customize *v.*
9. legendary *adj.*
10. outsole *n.*
11. high-wage
12. promising *adj.*
13. supervise *v.*

formally *adv.* 正式地，形式上	
contract *n.* 合同	
revolve *v.* 旋转	
formula *n.* 准则，公式	
dominate *v.* 占领，支配	
aerobics *n.* 有氧运动，增氧健身	
miscalculate *v.* 失算，算错	
clunky *adj.* 沉重的，笨拙的	
leather *n.* 皮革，皮革制品	
momentum *n.* 势头，动力	
disastrous *adj.* 灾难性的，损失惨重的	
casual *adj.* 随便的，临时的	
grocery *n.* 食品杂货店	
signal *n.* 信号，标志	
profitable *adj.* 盈利的，赚钱的	
trimming *n.* 调整	
blank *n.* 空白，空虚	

Phil Knight: Not formally. We just tried to get our shoes on the feet of runners. And we were able to get a lot of great ones under contract—people like Steve Prefontaine and Alberto Salazar—because we spent a lot of time at track events and had relationships with the runners, but mostly because we were doing interesting things with our shoes. Naturally, we thought the world stopped and started in the lab and everything revolved around the product.

HBR: When did your thinking change?

Phil Knight: When the formulas that got Nike up to $1 billion in sales—being good at innovation and production and being able to sign great athletes—stopped working and we faced a series of problems. For one thing, Reebok came out of nowhere to dominate the aerobics market, which we completely miscalculated. We made an aerobics shoe that was functionally superior to Reebok's, but we missed the styling. Reebok's shoe was sleek and attractive, while ours was sturdy and clunky. We also decided against using garment leather, as Reebok had done, because it wasn't durable. By the time we developed a leather that was both strong and soft, Reebok had established a brand, won a huge chunk of sales, and gained the momentum to go right by us. We were also having management problems at that time because we really hadn't adjusted to being a big company. And on top of that, we made a disastrous move into casual shoes.

HBR: What was the problem with casual shoes?

Phil Knight: Practically the same as what happened in aerobics, and at about the same time. We went into casual shoes in the early 1980s when we saw that the running shoe business, which was about one-third of our revenues at the time, was slowing down. We knew that a lot of people were buying our shoes and wearing them to the grocery store and for walking to and from work. Since we happened to be good at shoes, we thought we could be successful with casual shoes. But we got our brains beat out. We came out with a functional shoe we thought the world needed, but it was funny looking and the buying public didn't want it. By the mid-1980s, the financial signals were coming through loud and clear. Nike had been profitable throughout the 1970s. Then all of a sudden in fiscal year 1985, the company was in the red for two quarters. In fiscal 1987, sales dropped by $200 million and profits headed south again. We were forced to fire 280 people that year—our second layoff ever and a very painful one because it wasn't just an adjustment and trimming of fat. We lost some very good people that year.

HBR: How did you know that marketing would solve the problems?

Phil Knight: We reasoned it out. The problems forced us to take a hard look at what we were doing, what was going wrong, what we were good at, and where we wanted to go. When we did that, we came to see that focusing solely on the product was a great way for a brand to start, but it just wasn't enough. We had to fill in the blanks. We had to learn to do well all the things involved in getting to the consumer, starting with understanding who the consumer is and what the brand represents.

HBR: Didn't Nike understand the consumer right from the start?

哈佛商业评论：您没有做过任何市场营销吗？

菲尔·奈特：没有正式地做过。我们只是试着把鞋子穿在跑步者的脚上，通过签订合同，我们能把它们穿在一些名人脚上，例如史蒂芬·普雷方丹和萨拉扎尔。这是因为我们在田径赛事和与跑步运动员建立关系上面花了很多时间，更多的是由于我们一直在做关于鞋的趣事。自然而然，我们认为世界在实验室里停止和开始，一切都是围绕产品运转的。

哈佛商业评论：您的思维是什么时候转变的？

菲尔·奈特：是在促使耐克销售额上升到10亿的准则[14]即要善于创新、做好产品、能够与伟大的运动员[15]签约不再有效且我们面临一系列的[16]问题的时候。一方面，锐步突然占领了有氧运动[17]市场，这是我们完全失算的。我们制造的有氧运动鞋在功能上要比锐步好，但是在款式[18]上是失败的。锐步的鞋光滑[19]而吸引人，我们的则是结实[20]而沉重[21]的。我们决定不使用锐步使用过的衣服革，因为很不耐用[22]。等我们制出了既牢固又柔软的皮革时，锐步已经建立了它的品牌，获得了巨大的销售额，赢得了本来向我们走去的势头[23]。那时我们还有管理问题，因为我们还未真正调整成为一家大公司。除此以外，我们还有一个灾难性的举措就是进入了休闲鞋[24]领域。

哈佛商业评论：休闲鞋的问题是什么呢？

菲尔·奈特：实际上，与同期的有氧运动鞋是一样的。在20世纪80年代初期，跑鞋占我们盈利额的三分之一，由于跑鞋利润增长减缓了，我们就开始进入休闲鞋领域。我们知道，有很多人购买我们的鞋子，走去上班或者是下班，而且穿着我们的鞋子去食品杂货店[25]。因为我们的跑鞋做得好，便认为在休闲鞋领域也会好。但是我们想错了，最后生产了我们认为市场需要的功能鞋，功能鞋看起来很滑稽，购买的人们并不喜欢。到20世纪80年代中期，财务问题信号[26]越来越响亮而清楚。耐克在20世纪70年代一直是盈利的，突然[27]在1985财政年[28]连续两个季度亏损[29]。在1987财政年，销售额下降了2亿元，并且利润还在不断下降。我们不得不在那一年解雇280人，这是我们有史以来第二次裁员，也是很痛心的一次，因为这不仅仅是人员的调整和削减，也让我们在那一年丧失了一些很好的员工。

哈佛商业评论：您是如何知道市场营销可以解决所有问题的？

菲尔·奈特：我们推理[30]得出的。这些问题迫使我们冷眼看待我们所做的，什么做错了，什么是我们擅长的以及我们想达到的。这样做以后，我们便明白单单集中在产品上面虽然是品牌建立的一个良好途径，但是远远不够。我们必

14. formula n.
15. athlete n.
16. a series of
17. aerobics n.
18. styling n.
19. sleek adj.
20. sturdy adj.
21. clunky adj.
22. durable adj.
23. momentum n.
24. casual shoes
25. grocery store
26. signal n.
27. all of a sudden
28. fiscal year
29. in the red
30. reason v.

Phil Knight: In the early days, when we were just a running shoe company and almost all our employees were runners, we understood the consumer very well. There is no shoe school, so where do you recruit people for a company that develops and markets running shoes? The running track. It made sense, and it worked. We and the consumer were one and the same. When we started making shoes for basketball, tennis and football, we did essentially the same thing we had done in running. We got to know the players at the top of the game and did everything we could to understand what they needed, both from a technological and a design perspective. Our engineers and designers spent a lot of time talking to the athletes about what they needed both functionally and aesthetically. It was effective—to a point. But we were missing something. Despite great products and great ad campaigns, sales just stayed flat.

HBR: Where did your understanding fall short?

Phil Knight: We were missing an immense group. We understood our "core consumers", the athletes who were performing at the highest level of the sport. We saw them as being at the top of a pyramid, with weekend jocks in the middle of the pyramid, and everybody else who wore athletic shoes at the bottom. Even though about 60% of our product is bought by people who don't use it for the actual sport, everything we did was aimed at the top. We said, if we get the people at the top, we'll get the others because they'll know that the shoe can perform. But that was an oversimplification. Sure, it's important to get the top of the pyramid, but you've also got to speak to the people all the way down. Just take something simple like the color of the shoe. We used to say we don't care what the color is. If a top player like Michael Jordan liked some kind of yellow and orange, that's what we made—even if nobody else really wanted yellow and orange. One of our great racing shoes, the Sock Racer, failed for exactly that reason: we made it bright bumble-bee yellow, and it turned everybody off.

HBR: What's different now?

Phil Knight: Whether you're talking about the core consumer or the person on the street, the principle is the same: you have to come up with what the consumer wants, and you need a vehicle to understand it. To understand the rest of the pyramid, we do a lot of work at the grass-roots level. We go to amateur sports events and spend time at gyms and tennis courts talking to people. We make sure that the product is the same functionally whether it's for Michael Jordan or Joe American Public. We don't just say Michael Jordan is going to wear it so therefore Joe American Public is going to wear it. We have people who tell us what colors are going to be in for 1993, for instance, and we incorporate them. Beyond that, we do some fairly typical kinds of market research, but lots of it—spending time in stores and watching what happens across the counter, getting reports from dealers, doing focus groups, tracking responses to our ads. We just sort of factor all that information into the computer between the ears and come up with conclusions.

recruit *v.*
招募，聘用

essentially *adv.*
本来，本质上

perspective *n.*
远景，观点

aesthetically *adv.*
审美地，美学观点上地

immense *adj.*
巨大的，广大的

pyramid *n.*
金字塔

oversimplification *n.*
过分简单化，过度单纯化

bumble-bee *n.*
大黄蜂

vehicle *n.*
工具，媒介

amateur *adj.*
业余的

dealer *n.*
经销商，商人

须填补空白，做好涉及消费者的一切事情。我们开始了解谁是消费者以及品牌代表[31]的是什么。

哈佛商业评论：耐克不是从一开始就正确理解消费者的吗？

菲尔·奈特：在早期我们只是一家跑鞋公司，几乎所有的雇员都是跑步者的时候，我们对消费者理解得很好。那时没有制鞋学校，去哪儿为公司招募[32]人手来研发和营销跑鞋呢？田径场。这个想法行得通并且很奏效。我们和消费者是相似的，甚至是一体的。当我们开始为篮球、网球和足球制鞋的时候，我们从根本上来说与制跑鞋时做一样的事。我们去认识顶级比赛的运动员并尽力了解他们在工艺[33]和设计方面的需求。我们的工程师和设计师花了很多时间去和运动员交谈，了解他们在功能和审美上的需求。在某点上来说，这很有效，但是我们也丢失了一些东西。尽管有很好的产品和广告做宣传，但我们的销量平平。

哈佛商业评论：您的理解哪儿不足呢？

菲尔·奈特：我们失去了一个很大的[34]群体。我们理解核心的消费者，即在最高水平的运动员。我们把他们放在金字塔[35]的顶端，把那些周末运动的人放在金字塔的中间，把其他穿运动鞋的所有人放在底端。尽管60%的产品都是不参加真正运动的人购买的，我们所做的都是瞄准顶端。我们曾说，只要能让顶层的人购买，就能让其他的人购买，因为他们会知道这种鞋很好。但这过分简单化[36]了。当然，金字塔顶端很重要，但是还要与下面的人交谈。拿鞋的颜色举个简单的例子，我们经常说不在乎鞋的颜色，如果一个顶级运动员，像迈克尔•乔丹喜欢黄色和橙色，我们就制造那种颜色的鞋，即使其他人几乎没有喜欢黄色和橙色的。我们的一种跑鞋——袜子赛车手，就是因为那个原因失败的。它是明亮的黄蜂[37]颜色，不是每个人对其都有兴趣。

哈佛商业评论：现在有什么不同吗？

菲尔•奈特：不管你说的是核心消费者还是街上的行人，有一个原则是一样的：你必须要知道消费者想要的，并且需要一个了解这个的工具[38]。为了了解金字塔的其他部分，我们对草根阶层[39]做了很多工作。我们去业余的[40]体育赛事，在体育馆[41]和网球场与人们交谈。我们确信的是，不管是对于迈克尔•乔丹，还是美国大众，产品在功能上是一样的。我们不会说，正是因为迈克尔•乔丹穿了这种鞋，所以美国大众也会穿。例如，我们会问人们1993年流行的颜色是什么，并且采纳[42]。除了这个，我们还做一些有代表性的市场调查。大多数时间都是在商店观察柜台边发生的事，从经销商那里获取报告，进行小组讨论，跟踪我们广告的反响。我们只是把听到的信息要素归类到电脑里，然后得出结论。

31. represent *v.*
32. recruit *v.*
33. technology *n.*
34. immense *adj.*
35. pyramid *n.*
36. oversimplification *n.*
37. bumble-bee *n.*
38. vehicle *n.*
39. grass-roots level
40. amateur *adj.*
41. gym *n.*
42. incorporate *v.*

1. 词组come around to是"觉悟，醒悟"的意思，后接动名词形式，例如：Most vendors have come around to recognizing that this is the most reasonable approach.（大部分厂商已经觉悟过来，认识到这是最合理的途径。）

2. 注意词组used to do与be used to doing的区别，前者表示"过去惯常做某事，而现在不做了"，例如：I used to smoke, but I gave up a couple of years ago.（我以前抽烟，但几年前就戒掉了。）；而后者表示"习惯于，适应于"，例如：We're used to getting up early.（我们习惯早起。）

3. 英语中，破折号可用来补充说明，特别是在非正式文字中。例如：We'll be arriving on Monday morning—at least, I think so.（我们将在星期一上午抵达——至少我是这样想的。）

4. 词组spin off可以表示"使脱离（原组织）而独立"的意思，例如：He rescued the company and later spun off its textile division into a separate entity.（他挽救了该公司，后来又把它的纺织部脱离出来组建成一个独立实体。）

5. 在英语中，动名词可作主语，往往表示经常性、习惯性的动作，在口语中也可以表示具体的动作。例如：Working with you is a pleasure.（和你一起工作是一种乐趣。）

6. 英语中有众多词缀，大多具有一定的意义，例如前缀dis-表示否定，如：disregard（漠视），discard（扔弃），disburden（减轻负担），disagree（不同意）等。

7. 词组beat out有"弄明白"的意思，例如：We must beat out the sense of every phrasal verb.（我们必须搞懂每个短语动词的含义。）

8. 词组fall short的意思是"没有达到目标或要求"，例如：She took careful aim, but her arrow fell short.（她仔细瞄准，但箭没有击中目标。）

9. 后缀-age构成名词，表示集合，身份，费用，活动，动作等，例如：mileage（里程），pupilage（学生时期），postage（邮资），breakage（破损）等。

23

长江实业集团创始人：

李嘉诚

Founder of Yangtze Industrial Corporation: Li Ka-shing

　　李嘉诚，汉族，现任长江实业集团有限公司董事局主席兼总经理。1928年出生于广东潮州，1940年为躲避日本侵略者的压迫，全家逃难到香港。1958年，李嘉诚开始投资地产市场。1979年，"长江"购入老牌英资商行——"和记黄埔"，李嘉诚因而成为首位收购英资商行的华人。

　　此后他获得了多项荣誉，如1981年被选为"香港风云人物"，1989年获英国女皇颁发的CBE勋衔，1992年被聘为港事顾问，被评为1993年香港年度"风云人物"及1999年亚洲首富等。2011年，据《福布斯》中文版杂志的统计，李嘉诚的总资产达260亿美元，蝉联全球华人首富。

23.1 Maintaining Stability While Advancing, Advancing While Maintaining Stability

轻松输入十分钟

Forbes: We wanted to start by exploring your arrival in Hong Kong, your background. You're obviously influenced by your father, a teacher. He instilled in you a deep thirst for reading and knowledge. It sounds as if, despite the difficulties of your early career, you are an optimist about the future. Would you classify yourself as an optimist?

Li: First of all, I am an optimist. When you study hard and work hard, your knowledge grows, and it gives you confidence. The more you know, the more confidence you gain. When I was 10 years old, I lost my schooling, but I still had plenty of hope to return to school. When we came to Hong Kong, the family had no choice, and I had to work. I was facing life for the first time. I was 12 years old, but I felt like a 20-year-old. I knew then what life was. My father had tuberculosis, which was as a devastating disease as cancer today. If you were rich and could afford proper care, you might have a better chance. We had no choice. I needed to be strong, and needed to find some way to secure a future.

Forbes: And as long as you have that preparation, that confidence, you have the general belief that things will work out?

Li: During the Japanese occupation, besides working, I also needed to get plenty of fresh air to remain healthy, because at that time, I also had TB. But at the same time, I also needed to study and work. These gave me confidence. I got my first break right after the Second World War. My boss needed a letter writer. He had a secretary who wrote his letters for him, but he was on sick leave. When he asked around the office to see who could take his place temporarily, my colleagues recommended me. My boss said that my letters were quick and nice, and I got his meaning. He was happy with my work, and I was promoted to head a small department. I always believe that knowledge can change life. It was a case of knowledge changing my life.

Forbes: Do you think that in the circumstance at that time, you could have been in any business?

Li: After my promotion, I requested that I be reassigned as a wholesale salesman.

---

explore *v.*
探索，探测

instill *v.*
灌输

optimist *n.*
乐观主义者，乐天派

confidence *n.*
信心，信任

tuberculosis *n.*
肺结核，结核病

devastating *adj.*
致命的

secure *v.*
保证

preparation *n.*
准备，预备

occupation *n.*
占领

secretary *n.*
秘书，书记

temporarily *adv.*
临时地

recommend *v.*
推荐，介绍

circumstance *n.*
情况，环境

reassign *v.*
重新任命，再指定

wholesale *adj.*
批发的，大规模的

在前进中保持稳定，
在保持稳定中前进

有效学习十分钟

福布斯：首先，我们谈谈您初来香港的情形以及您的背景[1]。
毫无疑问，您深受您父亲的影响，您父亲是一位老
师。在他的灌输[2]下，您对阅读和知识十分渴望。据
说，貌似不管您早期事业遇到多少困难，您对于未
来都是个乐观主义者[3]。您会把自己归类为一名乐观
主义者吗？

李嘉诚：首先，我是个乐观主义者。当你努力学习和工作时，你的知识会增长，这会
给予你信心。你知道得越多，信心就会不断增加。我十岁的时候失学了，但
我对重归校园仍抱有很大的希望。当我们来香港时，我的家人没有选择，我
必须去工作。这是我第一次面对生活，那时只有12岁，我却觉得自己有20岁
了，之后我便明白了生活是什么。我父亲患有肺结核[4]，这和今天的癌症一
样，是一种致命的[5]病。如果你富裕，能够接受正规的治疗，治愈的机会就越
大。我们没有选择，我只有变得强大，才能找到途径保证[6]能有一个未来。

1. background *n.*
2. instill *v.*
3. optimist *n.*
4. tuberculosis *n.*
5. devastating *adj.*
6. secure *v.*
7. on sick leave
8. temporarily *adv.*
9. circumstance *n.*
10. promotion *n.*

福布斯：那么您认为只要您做好准备，拥有信心，就基本能确定事情会解决吗？

李嘉诚：在日本占领期间，我工作之余，还会呼吸充足的新鲜空气来保持健康，因为
那时候我也患有肺结核。同时，我还需要学习和工作，它们给了我信心。二
战后，我获得了第一次休假。我的老板需要一个写信的人，他本来有一个替
他写信的秘书，但那时秘书正休病假[7]。当他在办公室里询问是否有人可以暂
时[8]接替他秘书的工作时，我的同事们推荐了我。我老板说我的信写得既快又
好，我便明白了他的意思。他对我的工作很满意，我之后便升职去主管一个
小部门。我一直相信知识能改变生活，这便是一个例子。

福布斯：那么您认为在当时的那个环境[9]，您能从事商业吗？

李嘉诚：在我升职[10]后，我请求希望自己能被重新任命为批发销售员。这其实是一个

This was actually a more difficult job, but the prospects were better. At the time, our company had seven other salesmen. On New Year's Day, the boss announced that the bonus that year would be based on sales. At the end of the year, my sales figure was seven times higher than the second best. If they paid my bonus based on my sales, my bonus would have been higher than the general manager's. The other salesmen were already jealous. So I said to my boss, "Just pay me the same as the second best salesman; it would make everyone happy." As a result, I became a manager when I was 17 going on 18. I was second in command only to the boss. At 19, I became the general manager of the factory. I was already keeping an eye on the political developments within China, and I also had a firm grasp on economics, industry, management and the latest development and production of the plastics industry. I knew that plastics had a great future, because so many products can be made from plastic. Not many people in Hong Kong at that time (after the Second World War) were aware of the potential. It was still quite new in Hong Kong and China. As the civil war and political situation in China developed, I knew that with 90% of our sales going to mainland China, our business would fall off tremendously if the Chinese leadership changed. Sure enough, our business dropped 90% in 1949, which was worse than I expected. But the company did not suffer much, because I didn't keep too much stock or order too much raw materials. The boss told me that I would become the general manager of the head office. I was confident about the bright prospects of the plastics industry, and I told him that I would like to start my own business. Before doing so, however, I would help my boss sell the remaining stock and wind up the company's business in an orderly manner. That was 1949. I started my business in 1950 and named it Cheung Kong.

Forbes: So instead of restructuring the company, you chose to start your own business?

Li: My boss wanted to close down the business and become partners with me, but I wanted to start the business small on my own. I already knew a lot about the plastics business, including the technology, the market and sales. I knew everything including the accounting. The first year, as I didn't have much capital, I did everything by myself, including the first set of account books. I needed to go to the Inland Revenue Department, and I asked my auditor if my accounts were correct, since I had no experience in doing accounting. He said that it was complete and that I could take this to the government. I had no experience, but I learned by reading books on accounting. When you want to understand the balance sheet, you needed to know a little bit about accounting. I did so many things by myself, which kept my overhead low. I have made a profit every year since 1950. I have

bonus *n.*
红利，额外津贴

jealous *adj.*
妒忌的

grasp *n.*
领会

plastic *n.*
塑料

aware *adj.*
意识到的，知道的

tremendously *adv.*
可怕地，惊人地

raw *adj.*
未加工的，生的

prospect *n.*
前途，预期

restructure *v.*
重建，调整

auditor *n.*
审计员，听者

overhead *n.*
经费，天花板

难度更大的工作，但是前景[11]也更好。那时，我们公司还有其他7名销售员。在新年那天，我们老板说这年的红利[12]要基于我们的销售额。年末，我的销售额是第二名的七倍。如果他们真按销售额来支付红利的话，那我的红利就比总

经理的都要高。其他的销售员都很嫉妒[13]，所以我对老板说，"只要付给我与销售额第二的人一样的红利就行了，这样每个人都会开心。"结果，我成了经理，那年我已满17岁，还未满18岁。我是仅次于老板的领导人。19岁那年，我成了整个工厂的总经理[14]。我一直在关注中国的政治发展，紧盯经济、工业、管理以及塑料[15]工业最新的[16]发展和生产。我知道塑料的前景非常好，因为塑料可以制造很多产品。那时（二战后），在香港，意识到这个潜力[17]的人不多，塑料在香港和中国内地还是一个很新的东西。伴随着中国国内战争和政治形势的发展，我们90%的销售额都是流向中国内地[18]的，我知道一旦领导阶层更换，我们的业务会大幅度下降。果然，在1949年，我们的业绩下降了90%，比我想象的还要糟糕。但是公司受的打击并不大，因为我没有保留太多的库存[19]、订单[20]和原材料[21]。我的老板告诉我，我将成为主管部门的总经理。我对塑料工业的前景十分有信心，因此，我告诉老板说，我要自己创业。但是在此之前，我会帮助老板销售完剩下的库存，并有序地结束了自己的公司业务交接。那时是1949年。1950年，我创立了自己的公司，名为长江集团。

福布斯：所以您没有重组[22]公司，而是选择自己创业？

李嘉诚：我的老板想关闭公司，成为我的合伙人，但是我想独自一人创业。我对塑料行业已经了解很多，包括技术、市场和销售额等，还包括会计[23]。第一年的时候，由于我没有充足的资金[24]，所有的事情都由我一个人做，包括创立第一本账簿。我需要去内地税局，由于我在会计方面没有经验，我需要向审计员[25]询问我的账簿是否正确。他说已经很完整了，我可以把它交给政府。我没有经验，但是我通过阅读书籍学习会计。如果你要了解资产债务表[26]，那么你就需要了解一点会计知识。这些都是我一个人做的，开销就降低了。自1950年开始，我就盈利[27]了，我从没在任何一年亏过本。

11. prospect n.
12. bonus n.
13. jealous adj.
14. general manager
15. plastic n.
16. latest adj.
17. potential adj.
18. mainland n.
19. stock n.
20. order n.
21. raw material
22. restructure v.
23. accounting n.
24. capital n.
25. auditor n.
26. balance sheet
27. make a profit

never lost a penny in any year.

Forbes: You also learned about finance in that early business?

Li: I started from the bottom up and went through so many different levels, doing different jobs. Like a mechanical watch, if one gear breaks down, the watch doesn't work. In manufacturing in particular, you must be well versed not only with the market, but also with productivity and quality. I had worked at every level, doing different tasks. I was very careful. I had no debt (actually, I was not qualified for a bank loan at the time), but I knew my company's finances like the back of my hand, and I could answer any question that anybody asked. In 1956 to 1958, I was already buying properties. I bought my first property with a partner. By 1958 or 1959, I owned my factory site as well as other real estates. By 1960, we were the biggest manufacturer in Hong Kong in terms of dollar value export. I started working in 1940, I started a business in 1950, and by 1960, I was the biggest manufacturer. I am very prudent financially because of those hard times I went through. During the Japanese occupation of Hong Kong, which lasted three years and eight months, I sent 90% of my salary to my mother. I spent nothing. I had a haircut every three months. I shaved my head like a monk. Nor did I go to see a movie during this period. Seeing a movie was very cheap at the time, but I needed to save every penny. My father was hospitalized at the beginning of the Japanese occupation. The hospital fee was not much, but you had to pay for the medicine. I had always wanted to go back to school. My father was a schoolmaster, though not at the same school as mine. But I knew that he would be upset if my exam results were bad. I was always among the top students in class, though not the first, as I liked to play. If the Japanese had invaded just one year later, I am sure I would have been first in class. I entered Form One when I was 10. We came from a scholarly family. During the late Ching Dynasty, my father's two elder brothers studied for Ph.D.s at Tokyo University (known as Imperial University then). Every generation of my family took education very seriously. During my father's time, our family finances were deteriorating. My uncles did not make any contribution to the family after they came back from Tokyo. I always had a fighting heart. I only had a small amount of capital when I started my own business. That's why I am always conservative. I never forget to maintain stability while advancing, and I never forget to advance while maintaining stability. Stability and advancement must always be in balance.

Forbes: So even when you have knowledge and confidence, you still want to be cautious?

Li: I have not had any personal debts in many years. Even now, if I have a debt, I could repay the loan within 24 hours if the bank calls me. Or maybe 72 hours,

bottom *n.*
底层，末端

versed *adj.*
精通的，熟练的

qualified *adj.*
合格的，有资格的

estate *n.*
房地产，财产

prudent *adj.*
谨慎的，节俭的

haircut *n.*
理发，发型

hospitalize *v.*
住院，就医

upset *adj.*
心烦的，混乱的

invade *v.*
侵占，侵略

deteriorate *v.*
恶化，变坏

conservative *adj.*
保守的

stability *n.*
稳定性，坚定

debt *n.*
债务，借款

福布斯：您在早期的商务中，也学习过财务吗？

李嘉诚：我从最底层²⁸做起，经过不同的层次，做过不同的工作。就像机械²⁹手表一样，如果一个齿轮³⁰坏掉，手表就无法运转。尤其是在制造业，你不仅要精通市场，还要精通生产力³¹和质量。我每一个级别都做过，不同的工作都做过，我十分谨慎，也没欠过债（实际上，我那时没有向银行贷款³²的资格）。但是我对公司的财务了如指掌，我能回答任何人提出的任何问题。在1956年至1958年间，我已经购买房产，我与一个合伙人购买了第一套房产。到1958或1959年，我拥有了我的厂房和其他房地产³³。到1960年，就美元价值出口而言，我们是香港最大的制造商。我在1940年开始工作，1950年开始创业，到1960年成为了最大的制造商。由于过去我经历的困难，我在财务方面十分谨慎³⁴。在日本占领香港的3年8个月间，我把我90%的工资寄给了母亲，我自己一分没花，我三个月剪一次头，把头剃³⁵成和尚³⁶那样。那期间我从来没看过一次电影，那时候看电影很便宜，但是我要把每分钱存起来。在日本占领初期，我父亲住院了，医院费用不多，但必须要支付药费。我一直想重归校园。我父亲是一位校长，虽然他不是跟我一所学校，但我知道如果我考试成绩差的话，他会生气。我在班级一直是尖子生，尽管不是第一，因为我爱玩。如果日本迟一年侵占的话，那我坚信我会是班上的第一名。我在10岁那年就上中学一年级³⁷了。我来自一个书香门第，在清朝后期时，我父亲的两个哥哥就都在东京大学读哲学博士（那时该学校以"帝国大学"著称）。我们家里每一代都很重视教育，到我父亲这一代的时候，我们家里的经济情况恶化。我的伯伯们从东京回来后，并没有对家里贡献多少。我总有一颗好斗的心。在刚创业的时候，我只有一小笔资金，所以我总是很保守³⁸。我从来没有忘记要在前进中保持稳定³⁹，还要在保持稳定中前进。稳定和前进⁴⁰必须总要保持平衡。

福布斯：所以，即使您有了知识和信心，您仍要谨慎？

李嘉诚：我已经很多年没有过个人债务。即使是现在，如果我欠债的话，只要银行致

28. bottom *n.*
29. mechanical *adj.*
30. gear *n.*
31. productivity *n.*
32. bank loan
33. real estate
34. prudent *adj.*
35. shave *v.*
36. monk *n.*
37. Form One
38. conservative *adj.*
39. stability *n.*
40. advancement *n.*

to be more conservative. I am talking about personal loans, not for Hutchison Whampoa. Hutchison is also very conservative. Many of Hutchison's assets are stated at cost on the balance sheet. When these assets are disposed of for commercial reasons, the company can make a handsome profit. Many events have occurred over the past 50 years, from the 1950s until now, that have had an adverse impact on Hong Kong. But how many times have you heard that Cheung Kong's finances were in trouble over the last 50 years? Never. The reason is, we are always prepared for the worst. That is my policy.

Forbes: When you first started investing in properties in 1958, that is a business historically built on debt?

Li: No, for me, all cash. In my case, I bought land with my own cash. If somebody invites me to be a partner, and I take only 15% to 20% as a minority stakeholder, they would perhaps get a loan from the bank. But I had no personal debt. At that time, when Cheung Kong went public in 1972, the company had almost no debt. Even if the company had to borrow from the bank, we would have alternative arrangements, such as buying government bonds equivalent to the bank loan amount, to ensure that we can readily cash out at any time. The interest income would continue to accumulate, while interest expense on the loan would be repaid monthly. So you see, our corporate finance is very conservative and prudent. Actually, I don't think I am a good "businessman". There are two reasons. First, I don't like to entertain. When I was still in the manufacturing business, my clients who accounted for 90% of my production came to see me twice a year, and each time they placed a six-month order. I would have a quiet dinner with them, but we didn't go to nightclubs or ballrooms. I just tried to do a good job. Second, I am extremely trustworthy. I always make good on my promises. But perhaps times have changed. Nowadays, many people don't honor their promises, and even a signed contract can be voided.

电给我，我能在24小时内还清，或者保守地说，在72小时内还清。我现在说的是个人债务，不是"和记黄埔"（"和记黄埔"为一个公司的名字）。"和记黄埔"也很保守，它的许多资产都是按照资产负债表上的成本来计算的。如果这些资产由于商业原因需要处理[41]的话，该公司可以获得一笔相当大的收入。从1950年到现在这五十年间发生了许多事情，对香港产生了负面影响[42]。但是你有多少次听说"长江"集团陷入财务问题呢？从来没有。原因是我们一直对最坏的情况做好准备，这就是我的政策。

福布斯：您在1958年投资房产时，是建立在债务基础上的吗？

李嘉诚：不是，我用的是现金。对于我来说，我都是用自己的现金购买土地的。如果有谁邀请我当合伙人，作为一位小股东，我只控股15%至20%。他们可能会向银行贷款，但是我没有个人债务。当长江集团在1972年上市时，公司几乎没有欠债。即使公司必须向银行借贷，我们也有其他可供选择的[43]安排，例如购买与银行贷款等值的[44]政府债券，从而保证我们能随时支付现金。利息收入会不断积累[45]，我们会每月支付银行的贷款利息。因此，你可以看出，我们公司的财务是十分保守和谨慎的。实际上，我认为我不是一个好的"生意人"。原因有两个：首先，我不喜欢娱乐[46]。当我还在制造行业时，占总产值90%的客户每年来看我两次，每次确定六个月的订单。我只是和他们安静地共进晚餐，不去夜总会[47]或者是舞厅[48]。我只是想好好做实事。第二，我十分可靠[49]，总是会信守我的承诺。但时代可能已经变了。现在，许多人不信守承诺，甚至是签订的合同也可以无效[50]。

41. dispose *v.*
42. adverse impact
43. alternative *adj.*
44. equivalent *adj.*
45. accumulate *v.*
46. entertain *v.*
47. nightclub *n.*
48. ballroom *n.*
49. trustworthy *adj.*
50. voided *adj.*

自由输出十分钟

1. 与汉语中的名词动词化相同，英语中的一些名词也可以被用作动词，例如：I friend him in Facebook.（我在脸谱网加他好友了。），将friend用作动词"加为好友"。这种用法多用于口语、报纸杂志等非正式场合。

2. 英语中后缀很多，且大多具有实意。例如后缀–ist表示"……者，……人"，如：artist（艺术家），communist（共产主义者），socialist（社会主义家），capitalist（资本主义家）等。

3. 英语中有许多专业词汇是我们不常见的，但是在文章中却常常遇到，例如一些表示疾病的词汇：tuberculosis（肺结核），diabetes（糖尿病），diphtheria（白喉），headache（头痛），indigestion（消化不良），leukemia（白血病）等。

4. 英语中合成词的意思一般为用来合成的词的意思的结合，例如：wholesale（批发的），overhead（天花板，在头顶上），rainfall（降雨，降雨量）等，这些词都是由两个单词形成的合成词，其新词的词意也为两个词的意思合成。

5. state与condition都有"情况，状况"的意思，但是前者指特定时间的状况，可不加形容词；而后者尤指人与事物的外观、品质或工作状况。例如：the present state of medical knowledge（医学知识的现状）；The car is in excellent condition.（这辆汽车的状况好极了。）

6. 词组keep an eye on的意思是"注视，密切关注"，例如：I'm going to keep an eye on this website because it is in its early days, but good to see a brand as big as Samsung jumping into the fun.（我将对这个网站继续保持关注，因为它只是在初期，但是我看好像三星这么大的品牌能够跨入新媒体中。）

7. real estate意为"不动产"，Inland Revenue意为"国内税务，税务局"，balance sheet意为"资产负债表"。

8. 由no matter how，however和how引导的状语从句要求部分倒装，因为形容词或副词通常紧跟在这三个引导词后面，然后才是主语和谓语，形成形式上的部分倒装句。例如：I know nothing about this river, neither how long, how wide nor how deep it is.（我一点也不了解这条河，不知道它有多长、多宽或多深。）

9. 英语中，一些名词前加of可以作为相应的形容词使用，例如：It's great of importance for you to search for your dream and the longing in your mind.（追寻你的梦想和心中的憧憬非常重要。）这句话也可以改写成：It's greatly important for you to search for your dream and the longing in your mind.

10. 移就（transferred epithet）也可以称为转移修饰，是文学作品中常用的一种修辞格，指甲乙两项相关联，就把原属于形容甲的修饰语转移到修饰乙事物上。例如：The big man crashed down on a protesting chair.（这个大个子一屁股坐了下来，椅子发出抗议声。）用修饰人的protesting修饰了物chair。

24 惠普公司首席执行官：
马克·赫德
CEO of HP Corp.: Mark Hurd

　　马克·赫德，原惠普CEO、董事会主席。1957年出生于纽约市，曾就读于美国得克萨斯州贝勒大学，于1979年获得商业管理学学士学位。大学期间，赫德曾是学校的网球队队员，并且成为该校网球队排名第一的队员。赫德在大学毕业企图进入职业网球界失败之后，于1980年进入了俄亥俄州Dayton的美国著名的收银机公司NCR，先后在管理、运营、销售和营销等领域担任不同职务，并于2003年3月担任NCR公司的CEO兼总裁。他于2005年4月加入惠普公司，出任总裁兼CEO，2006年成为董事会主席，并领导惠普超越IBM，使之成为全球最大的IT企业。2010年8月，赫德辞去惠普CEO、董事会主席的职务。

24.1 / I Don't Think Compensation Is the Only Thing that Drives Behavior

轻松输入十分钟

Reporter: From an attach-rate issue, the argument out there has always been that you have to be competitive. I can put the HP peripherals or anything I want to attach to it, but if it puts me in a position where I'm trying to deliver a solution and it's not price-competitive…

Hurd: Then shame on us, because our job is to have our products competitive as point products and competitive as bundles. And frankly we want to put more energy behind that attach. Let's say we're going to put this economic hook in place so that you represent these poorly positioned products to the marketplace. Our objective is to say, we think we've got great products, and we want to put incentives for aligning those products together to put a better configuration, a better basket of goods if you will, in front of the end customer.

Reporter: Can you talk a little bit about when you first came here, and you were looking at the direct vs. the indirect. What were the metrics you were looking at? And I'll just give you an example: A number of years ago, IBM (NYSE:IBM) did a very in-depth analysis on direct vs. indirect, just in the PC space, because everyone said direct was absolutely more profitable. And they went out and did little things like, OK, if that ad in that newspaper is really driven to get somebody to buy direct, then we'd better assign that cost to the direct side of the business. So when they did all of that, in the PC space, they found it was less than one percentage point difference. Obviously, you did this over a much larger product set. Are there places where you say, as you really look at the data, that the channel is more profitable for us and are there places where direct is more profitable?

Hurd: You can find data to support any thesis. You've got to be careful to normalize the data. For example, it would be unfair for us to say our cost of an order direct is more expensive than the cost of an order indirect if we didn't normalize the volume. Today, the cost of an order for us indirect is actually less expensive than the cost of an order direct. But the bulk of our business is not direct. So you have to go normalize it and say, listen, in a normalized state what would the two look like? So for example we get tremendous cash-flow turns by dealing with our partners. It's different when you go direct because you actually have to have more people shipping and packing more orders. So when I sell you a PC one at a time, I have to go collect for that PC. When I sell you a thousand PCs and

peripheral n.
外部环境，外围设备

frankly adv.
坦白地，率直地

objective n.
目标，目的

incentive n.
动机，刺激

configuration n.
配置，结构

metric n.
度量标准

absolutely adv.
绝对地，完全地

assign v.
分配，指定

channel n.
通道，频道

normalize v.
使标准化，使正常化

volume n.
体积，量

tremendous adj.
巨大的，极大的

ship v.
搬运，运送

我认为报酬不是唯一驱动行为的力量

有效学习十分钟

记者：对于附加比例[1]这一问题来说，社会上普遍认为企业需要具有自己的竞争力。我拿惠普的外部环境或者其他事情来举个例子，如果把我放在一个提供[2]解决方案的位置上，我认为，保证竞争力的绝不仅仅是价格……

赫德：我们很惭愧[3]。我们的任务正好是让我们的产品成为不仅是具有竞争力的尖端[4]产品也是具有竞争力的捆绑[5]产品。老实讲，我们还想投入更多的精力加强这方面的附加值[6]。让我们假设，如果我们把这个经济杠杆[7]运用得当，那么公司的那些未能很好定位的产品也能够成功地推向市场。我们的目标是，我认为我们的产品很棒，我们要将这些产品更好地排列组合，使产品更加令顾客满意，将最佳组合的产品呈现给我们的终端客户[8]。

记者：您能具体谈一下当您初次进入这个市场，看到直销[9]与分销[10]两种销售模式时的感想吗？当时您是依据什么标准来衡量[11]的呢？我来举一个例子：几年前，IBM 在个人电脑[12]领域中作了一次非常深入的[13]直销相对于分销模式的分析，因为当时大家都说直销绝对会比分销模式利润更高。如果报纸上的广告真的能让人们选择直销方式购买，那么我们将这笔广告费归到直销成本里。所以当 IBM 在个人电脑领域作了这样的分析后，他们发现直销和分销之间的差别不到1%。显然，这个分析是基于[14]更加广泛的产品范围。看到数据后，您就会知道有哪些行业适合渠道销售以赚取更多利润，您认为有哪些行业采用直销业绩更好呢？

赫德：你能够找到数据来支持任何理论。不过你要很小心地将这个数据推广。比如说，如果我们在没有考虑订单多少的前提下，就说接受直销模式订单的成本要比分销订单的成本更加高昂，这是非常不公平的。如今，分销模式订单的成本要小于直销模式。但是我们的整体业务不是直销模式。所以你必须将它普遍化，也就是在一个规范化状态[15]的基础上，比较两种模式的差异有哪些。比如说我们从合作伙伴那里得到大量的资金周转[16]。若采取直销模式是非常不同的，因为直销模式中，你需要更多的人力来进行搬运和装货等工作。所以当我每次只

1. attach-rate
2. deliver v.
3. shame n.
4. point n.
5. bundle v.
6. attach n.
7. hook n.
8. end customer
9. direct adj.
10. indirect adj.
11. metric n.
12. PC (personal computer)
13. in-depth adj.
14. over v.
15. normalized state
16. turn n.

then you sell them one at a time, I'm going to send you one bill for a thousand PCs. I've lowered my administrative overhead, so you've got to get through all that process and understand what is the true infrastructure overhead that you've got to serve customer or partner. We somehow had ourselves convinced that a person deployed in the marketplace had to sell direct as opposed to creating demand for Hewlett-Packard. We want people in the marketplace creating demand for Hewlett-Packard. Then we can decide what the appropriate route is to get that demand fulfilled. But in the end, we need to make sure we've got the marketplace covered, so that the buying points on the planet that make sense for HP have some sort of demand-creation expertise.

Reporter: Well, that's kind of an interesting point, because one of the things you will hear out there is that some solution providers will tell you that HP (NYSE: HPQ) doesn't have as many people on the street as some others to help them sell. But what you're really saying is if you have someone out there just creating demand, you actually get a bigger benefit out of that than having somebody just dedicated to creating demand for channel or creating demand for direct sales.

Hurd: I agree at a macro level, very generalized without any specifics, I agree with that view, that we have too few people out in the marketplace with a Hewlett-Packard badge creating demand for HP products. And we're going to go fix that. So we're investing in sales people today. That said, I don't want that message to be perceived that we're trying to eliminate the channel as we put people out there. We're trying to create more demand for HP. And as I explain in individual partner meetings, I get partners who say, "This is great!" But sometimes it's interpreted as we're trying to be in conflict with our partners. That's not the case. If we're in conflict with a partner, it'll be a different issue from this.

Reporter: So are there some markets where it makes more sense to go direct for you than it does through an indirect model?

Hurd: I don't know that I would define it as markets. I think it's better if we define it a bit more by customer. Clearly in SMB, you're going to see us very, very reliant on the channel.

Reporter: What do you mean when you say SMB? Because everybody's got a different explanation.

Hurd: All but the biggest 2,000 accounts. We're going to be almost exclusively channel-oriented through that market. I mean, if a customer said, you've absolutely got to do this direct or they're going to go to *HP.com* or something, that's fine. We want to put multiple distribution methods so the customer can choose. We're not going to dictate in entirety how they do it. But our predominant view is going to be to leverage the channel. I think when you get into the big accounts, we're actually going to put more energy into those big accounts and we're going to try to do account plans for those accounts that map partners into those accounts. So I think you're going to find more—I think the right word for it is more specificity by account the roles those partners play in those accounts, whereas SMB is probably going to be more market-oriented. We really have to have those partners driving

administrative *adj.*
管理的，行政的

infrastructure *n.*
公共建设，基础建设

fulfill *v.*
满足，实现

expertise *n.*
专门知识，专门技术

dedicate *v.*
致力于，奉献

generalized *adj.*
普遍的，广义的

perceive *v.*
察觉，意识到

eliminate *v.*
排除，忽视

interpret *v.*
解释，翻译

reliant *adj.*
依赖的，可靠的

exclusively *adv.*
专门地，独占地

predominant *adj.*
主要的，占优势的

energy *n.*
精力，能量

specificity *n.*
具体性，专一性

卖一台个人电脑时，我需要去收取一台电脑的钱。而我销售1000台个人电脑，然后你一次性将这1000台电脑卖出去，那么只需开一张1000台电脑的账单[17]即可。所以我降低了我的管理成本[18]。这下你明白这些过程都是怎么回事，以及拥有一个客户或者一个合作商真正的基础成本了吧。出于某种原因我们要劝服自己，派人在市场上直销而不是为惠普创造需求。我们希望市场上的人们为惠普创造需求。那么我们就能决定采取哪种方式来满足需求。但是最后我们需要确保我们能够覆盖所有市场，这样惠普就持有创造需求的主动权了。

记者：嗯，这是很有意思的观点，因为其中一点就是，您将听到一些方案提供商告诉您，惠普并没有那么多销售人员站在街上卖惠普产品。但是如果有人真的能创造需求，那么您认为真的能从这些渠道中获得比专门渠道销售或是直销方式更多的利润吗？

赫德：从宏观[19]上我表示赞同。如果笼统地说，排除特殊情况的话，我同意这样的观点。在市场上佩戴惠普公司的徽章[20]为惠普产品创造需求的人手太少。我们将解决这个问题。所以我们正在投资培训销售人员。我并不希望因此被误解为我们正在试图取消渠道[21]销售。我们正在试图为惠普公司创造更多的需求。正如我在每个合作商会议上解释的那样，我会让合作商说，"这太棒了！"，但是有时会被曲解成我们试图与合作商闹矛盾。实际上并不是。如果我们与合作商真的有矛盾的话，事情就不会是现在发展的这样了。

记者：那么，您是否认为一些市场真的适宜惠普进行直销而取消过去的分销模式？

赫德：我并不知道那是否可以定义为一个市场。我认为如果我们将其定义为客户会更好。明显地在中小型业务[22]里，你将看到我们非常依赖渠道销售。

记者：您如何解释中小型业务？因为大家对此都有不同的解释。

赫德：除了2000位最大的客户，其他都是中小型业务。我们在这个市场上将完全采用渠道销售模式。我的意思是，如果一个客户说，你一定要做直销要不他们就上HP.com购买惠普产品，那也无所谓。我们希望能够采用多种营销[23]方式，以便客户能够选择。我们不会规定他们全部的做法。但是我们主要的观点是这种做法将很好地平衡[24]补充渠道销售。我认为当你卷入这个大账户时，我们实际上会投入更多的精力。我们试图想出更多的账户计划使我们的合作伙伴参与到账户之中。因此，我想你会发现更多，确切地说是那些合作伙伴在这些账目中所扮演的角色更加专一，而中小型业务可能会更加市场导向化[25]。我们真的是不得不让那些合作商从事中小型业务。由于我们从微观市场[26]这一角度定义它，那么这就是个很广泛的定义——从1到10个一直到前2000个，或者3000个账户。这对

17. bill *n.*
18. overhead *n.*
19. macro *n.*
20. badge *n.*
21. channel *n.*
22. SMB:Small and Medium Business
23. multiple distribution
24. leverage *n.*
25. market-oriented
26. micro business

on that small and medium business. It becomes a pretty broad definition because we can define it from a micro business—that one to ten seats all the way up to something that falls below the actual top 2,000 or top 3,000 accounts. And that's a ton of business for Hewlett-Packard. A ton of our business sits in that raw definition of SMB.

Reporter: Talk a little bit about compensation. This new channel program to me is really a compensation program ultimately. And compensation drives behavior. It drives behavior with a direct sales force; it drives behavior with an indirect sales force. And this is pretty innovative from what I see.

Hurd: I don't think compensation is the only thing that drives behavior. If you went into your own employees, you could ask the question. And I look at the majority of the partners as a very direct extension of Hewlett-Packard (NYSE:HPQ). And compensation isn't the No. 1 thing that drives our employees. Sometimes they say it is, but in the end it's being part of a winning team. When you're part of a winning team, we all know, go look at an analogy of a sports team. There are plenty of examples of people who take a cut in pay so they can be on a team that wins the Superbowl. Why do they do that? They like to win. So you can't show up with just a compensation plan. You've got to show up with winning products. You've got to show up with a winning environment, where partners feel like they can go to the marketplace and they can win. So one of the real risks you have when you go through the channel —there's very few of these, but we actually have a few bad actors. If they use our brand as the lead, fill it up with non-HP product, so they can get more margin, but what sits in front of that consumer is the HP brand, then what happens is a huge failure rate in that product. We take a lot of accountability for that. So one dimension that gets some of the direct mania that you see out there is better control structure over all that. I have better control structure over the elements of the solution that go to the customer, I have better control over the support that goes to the customer, and I can align that behavior directly. When you're indirect, you're a little bit more removed. You've got to bank on your partners doing the right thing, and most of ours do.

Reporter: Obviously, there's nothing wrong with any company wanting its solution provider partners to sell more of its product. I mean that's kind of a basic tenet of business. But what do you say about somebody who's doing maybe $100 million or more in HP but has large practices in some of your competitors? Is it any different for them than for anyone who might be 100 percent-dedicated to HP and maybe smaller?

Hurd: Well, we think it's easier if you're 100 percent dedicated to HP. But the world isn't 100 percent HP. We'd like it to be. But I think it's not an objective for at least my tenure. But yeah, we have to deal with a world that's mixed but partners have to decide. To get back to your earlier point, our compensation program in isolation isn't going to drive anybody to buy, by definition, more HP. It's got to be because our products and solutions and our support are compelling. So in the end that's what's going to be the primary driver. I think all the compensation program tries to do is to get them more engaged with HP.

account n.
账单，说明

compensation n.
补偿，赔偿

extension n.
伸展，延长

analogy n.
类比，相似

margin n.
利润，极限

accountability n.
有责任，有义务

dimension n.
方面，尺寸

tenet n.
原则，教义

tenure n.
任期，占有期

compelling adj.
吸引人的，引人注目的

于惠普来说是一大批生意。而这些业务很多都得
益于中小型业务这一最初的想法。

记者：请谈一谈关于报酬。新渠道项目对于我来说其实
是报酬项目。报酬驱动行为。报酬驱动直销力
量；报酬驱动分销力量。这是我看到的非常有意
义的创新。

赫德：我不认为报酬是惟一驱动行为的力量。如果你调
查自己的员工，你可以问他们。我把大多数合作商看作惠普直销的延伸。报酬
并不是驱动[27]我们的员工的首要事宜。有时他们说是的，但是最终报酬只是作为
一部分制胜的驱动因素。当你作为一个想要夺冠的小组成员时，我们知道，就
像一个体育团队一样。有很多例子关于人们为加入赢得超级杯的团队而自愿减
薪。他们为什么要这么做呢？他们喜欢赢的感觉。所以你不能仅仅拿出一个薪
酬方案[28]。你应该拿出一个必胜的产品。你必须营造一个胜利的气氛[29]，让合作
商认为进入市场后他们能够赢。所以渠道销售的一个真正的风险就是——虽然
非常少，但确实有表现很差的人员。如果他们使用我们的品牌作为招牌[30]，然
后填入一些不是惠普的产品，这样他们虽然会得到更高的利润，但是摆在客户
面前的是惠普品牌，最后这些产品会导致大的失败。我们要为此负责任。所以
直销模式中令人狂热的一个方面就是我们能够更好地控制产品质量。我能够更
好地控制每一个提供给客户的解决方案的元素，能更好地控制提供给客户的支
持，并且我能直接校准行为。当采用分销模式时，你将更加被动。你必须依靠
合作商，希望他们能够尽责，而我们的大多数合作伙伴也都做得很好。

记者：显然，对于公司想要方案提供商卖掉自己更多产品的想法是没有什么错的。我
是说这是做生意的基本规则。但是如果有人可能卖掉惠普1亿美元或者更多的
产品，而同时也在为您的竞争者们大量销售产品，您是如何看待这个的？他们
较之于销售额较小的惠普专属[31]分销商有什么区别？

赫德：我们认为如果你是惠普专卖分销商，问题会比较容易解决。但是世界不可能专
属于惠普。当然，我们希望是这样。但是我认为客观上至少在我任职期间是不
会出现的。但是，我们必须处理与那些同时承包其他品牌产品的合作商的关
系。回到你早些时候提出的观点，孤立[32]的报酬项目不能驱动任何人购买，很明
显[33]，卖出越多产品的合作商能得到的报酬就相应越多。由于我们的产品和技术
相对来讲是有一定吸引力的，所以我们能够卖出更多的产品，这应该是主要动力
[34]。我认为所有报酬项目都是致力于让合作商能够更多地参与到[35]惠普品牌中。

27. drive v.
28. compensation plan
29. environment n.
30. lead n.
31. 100 percent-dedicated
32. in isolation
33. by definition
34. driver n.
35. engage v.

10 min

自由输出十分钟

1. 惠普研发有限合伙公司（Hewlett-Packard Development Company, L.P.）（简称HP）（NYSE：HPQ）位于美国加州的帕罗奥多，是美国电子工业企业，世界IT巨头。公司成立于1954年，创始人是威廉·休利特和大卫·帕卡德。当时他们的"公司"只是设在一个汽车库里。这就是著名的"博士＋车库＝惠普"的出处。

2. 英语中，动词不定式可以做表语，实际上就是主语补足语，即对主语进行补充说明。例如：His job is to clean the house.（他的工作就是打扫屋子。）to clean the house是对主语job的补充说明。

3. 前缀in-和im-具有否定的意义，例如：inevitable（不可避免的），impossible（不可能的），informal（不正式的）等。

4. 词组make sense的意思是"讲得通，有意义"，例如：And as it approached, a gale of social media messages swirled, as New Yorkers "flocked" together, trying to make sense of events.（此外，当风暴逼近时，社交媒体上也刮起一阵信息旋风——纽约人纷纷"聚集"到一起，试图弄明白事态的发展。）

5. though和although可以引导让步状语从句，表示"虽然，纵然"的意思。这两个连词意思大致相同，在一般情况下可以互换使用。在口语中，though较常使用，although比though正式，两者都可与yet, still或nevertheless连用，但不能与but连用。例如：Although/Though he was exhausted, (still) he kept on working.（虽然他已经精疲力竭了，但仍然继续工作。）

6. 词组dedicate oneself to的意思是"投身于……"，例如：For the next few years, she dedicated herself to her work.（随后的几年里，她全身心地投入工作。）

7. issue在表示"问题"的时候，多指意见能达成一致的问题，但要通过争论或讨论解决，常见于政治、经济和社会问题。例如：We should raise the issue of discrimination with the council.（我们应该向委员会提出讨论歧视问题。）

8. 一般情况下，动词后加-or可以变成相应的名词形式，表示人或物，例如：actor（演员），inventor（发明家），accelerator（加速器），accumulator（蓄电池，存储器），collector（收集者）等。

9. 隐喻（metaphor）是缩减了的明喻，是将某一事物的名称用于另一事物，通过比较形成。例如：Hope is a good breakfast, but it is a bad supper. 这句话就是将hope比喻成了早餐和晚餐。

24.2

Active Data Warehousing Is the Vision For the Future of Decision Support

动态数据存储是对未来决策支持模式的预见

轻松输入十分钟

Reporter: We've noticed at TDWI and other shows lately that your booths have a new look featuring the Teradata name. Can you tell us about this shift in branding?

Hurd: NCR has decided to give even greater focus to its data warehousing and CRM business. In July 2000, NCR created two operating divisions within the company, with all data warehousing and analytical solutions under the Teradata Division. Then, earlier this year, we pushed the emphasis further by implementing a new branding approach for this business. Following extensive research and analysis with customers, we decided to create a new brand icon featuring the Teradata name and began identifying ourselves as "Teradata , a division of NCR Corporation". This will be the lead brand to promote our data warehousing and analytical solutions, projecting a technology-savvy, passionate, confident organization.

10 min 有效学习十分钟

记者： 最近我们注意到在TDWI以及之后的其他节目中，您的展台[1]前面换了个新面孔——Teradata（用于世界上最大的商用数据库的关系数据库管理系统）。您能跟我们谈一谈这个品牌的转变吗？

赫德： NCR更加关注数据库[2]和CRM项目。在2000年7月，NCR开设了两个事业部，Teradata事业部下属主要做数据存储和分析解决方案[3]。之后在今年早些时候，我们通过开设新品牌名称来推动这个项目的发展。通过与客户一起进行大量研究和分析，我们决定再设一个品牌Teradata并确立"NCR公司分支[4]Teradata"。这

---

booth *n.* 展台，货摊
warehousing *n.* 储仓，周转性短期贷款
division *n.* 分部，分开
analytical *adj.* 解析的，分析的
icon *n.* 形象，符号
passionate *adj.* 有活力的，热情的

1. booth *n.*　　　　　　　　2. data warehousing
3. analytical solution　　　　4. division *n.*

Reporter: Give us your view of the data warehousing market. What factors are driving your division's growth in this space?

Hurd: If you take a look at the volatility in the marketplace today, where business cycles are compressing at an accelerated rate and investors are demanding growth, an executive's biggest challenge is making better decisions—faster and more efficiently. Executives are also desperate to push decision-making deeper in the organization in order to win and keep customers in today's frenetic competitive pace. There's no room for mistakes. Teradata's strength lies in helping companies grow their business by enabling this "instant" decision-making environment. We accomplish this by first delivering powerful data warehousing and analytical solutions that offer a single view of the business across the enterprise. An integrated view is an extremely important first step, because all questions, no matter how complex, will result in more accurate decisions if they are analyzed against a single consistent view of the data. The next step is to deliver power to the people—providing analysis capabilities throughout the organization that delivers quick, fact-based answers. Giving people the ability to take action based on facts, balancing very costly, sometimes sensitive issues is critical to nimble business performance. Finally, for those companies ready for the new competitive frontier, Teradata solutions are ready to link the results of analysis with other business applications, automatically updating systems with new information that affects pricing, processes, logistics, and service. That's our vision for how business and decision making will quickly evolve to succeed in the networked economy. The enabling technology environment is something we call active data warehousing.

Reporter: Tell us about the new data warehousing and CRM products and solutions we can expect to see coming from Teradata Division in the near future.

Hurd: This spring we have a number of promising enhancements and additions to our solutions. In March we announced the availability of Teradata CRM Version 4.0. This product integrates NCR's Relationship Optimizer product line with the analytics and campaign management products of Ceres, a company NCR acquired in April 2000. This new CRM product suite takes full advantage of the valuable customer information in a company's data warehouse, presenting marketers with analysis, action, evaluation and learning from within one tool. In early April we launched the newest version of Teradata E-Business Analytics, which enhances BroadVision's suite of e-business applications. This product will allow businesses to tap into the information they gather from click stream analysis and transactions to provide personalized offers online. Also in April we announced Teradata Warehouse 6.1, which includes our new Teradata Miner data mining software. This release provides additional capabilities for businesses to develop active data warehouses. Active data warehousing is a new trend in decision support; it involves making the insights from the data warehouse available in real time to thousands of users.

Reporter: Tell us more about active data warehousing.

Hurd: Active data warehousing is our vision for the future of decision support. We see a trend in data warehousing away from using these systems just to generate reports for top management. The future of data warehousing

---

volatility *n.*
活跃，反复无常

accelerated *adj.*
加速的，加快的

executive *n.*
经理，执行者

frenetic *adj.*
狂热的，发狂的

integrate *v.*
综合，使成整体

accurate *adj.*
准确的，精确的

capability *n.*
能力，功能

nimble *adj.*
敏捷的，精明的

frontier *n.*
先锋，边境

logistics *n.*
物流，后勤学

enhancement *n.*
提高，增强

availability *n.*
可用性，有效性

evaluation *n.*
评估，估价

transaction *n.*
交易；事务

mine *v.*
采集，开采

insight *n.*
洞察力，洞悉

generate *v.*
产生，发生

个品牌将引领数据存储和分析解决方案等领域的发展，并且未来将成为一个精通技术、充满活力和自信的、精通技术[5]的组织。

记者：您能谈一谈对数据存储市场的看法吗？在这个领域中，是什么因素推动您的事业部发展的呢？

赫德：如果你看一下当今的市场活跃程度，就知道商业周期[6]正在加速发展，投资需求高涨。作为一位总经理最大的挑战就是如何更快更高效地做出决策。经理们同样渴望进一步在企业中推进计划的执行，以便在当今极快的竞争速度下更好地赢得并保留客户。这不允许出任何差错。Teradata的优势在于通过加强这种即时决策[7]环境，帮助公司增长业务。我们首先通过传输强有力的数据存储和分析解决方案来达到这个目的，这将为整个企业提供独特的发展计划。首先整合观点是关键的一步，这是因为所有问题，无论多么复杂，如果从一个持续的数据角度分析它们，都将得到更加精确的决策。下一步就是给人们授权——使整个企业都有分析能力，使他们能够基于事实快速地得出答案。赋予[8]人们从实际出发的行动力，平衡有时甚至对灵活的商业表现来说也是非常棘手的敏感问题。最后，对于那些准备成为新的有竞争力的先锋[9]的企业，Teradata解决方案准备将其他商业应用软件的分析结果连接在一起，自动更新[10]可能具有影响定价、流程[11]、物流[12]和服务的新信息系统。经营和决策制定如何迅速发展，以至在网络经济中获得成功是我们的愿景[13]。有利的技术环境，就是我们所说的动态[14]数据存储。

记者：请谈一谈近阶段我们能够看到的有关新型的数据存储和CRM产品的解决方案有哪些？

赫德：今年春天我们将一些非常有希望的增强和新增[15]功能添加到了我们的解决方案中。3月份我们推出Teradata CRM 4.0版。这个产品整合了NCR的Relationship Optimizer产品线、克瑞斯分析和活动管理产品。克瑞斯是NCR在2000年4月收购的公司。这个CRM新产品充分利用了企业数据存储中的宝贵的客户信息，为营销者提供分析、行动、评估[16]并利用同一工具互相学习等功能。在4月初，我们推出最新版Teradata电子商务[17]分析工具，加强了BroadVision电子商务应用程序。这个产品将使企业搜集客户公司数据分析和交易，向企业提供在线定制化服务。同样在4月，我们推出了Teradata存储6.1版，其包括最新的Teradata Miner数据采集[18]软件。这次推出的产品加强了企业开发动态数据库的能力。动态数据存储在决策支持中是一种新趋势[19]；涉及将现实中数据库中的建议提供给成千上万的用户使用。

记者：请多谈一谈动态数据存储。

赫德：动态数据存储是我们对于未来决策支持[20]模式的预见。除了仅仅使用这些系统数据库存储功能为高层管理者提供报告之外，我们还看到一个趋势，数据存储的

5. technology-savvy
6. business cycle
7. decision-making
8. give v.
9. frontier n.
10. update v.
11. process n.
12. logistics n.
13. vision n.
14. active adj.
15. addition n.
16. evaluation n.
17. e-business
18. data mining
19. trend n.
20. decision support

involves not only using the system for strategic decision-making but putting the company's data in the hands of front line employees, allowing them to make quick and informed decisions. To accomplish this, companies require a data warehouse that can load data quickly and handle thousands of complex queries coming from thousands of users. Today we are helping customers implement data warehouses with these characteristics.

Reporter: Tell us about your customers? What industries do you target?

Hurd: We've had a great deal of success with major global retailers, but we also have customers who are leading the banking, airline, telecommunications, insurance, manufacturing, energy, and entertainment industries, plus several of the most successful e-businesses. Our customers include six of the top seven airlines, six of the top ten retailers, six of the top nine communications companies, more than 40% of the largest US manufacturers and the world's leading banks. These customers include Royal Bank of Canada, Delta Air Lines, Qantas, SBC, UnumProvident, Samsung Life Insurance, Edison Mission Energy, Harrah's Entertainment, Federal Express, Shanghai Stock Exchange, Travelocity, ETRADE and MatchLogic.

Reporter: Do you consider IBM and Oracle as your main competitors? How do you stack up against them?

Hurd: We do consider IBM and Oracle as our main data warehousing competitors, although we don't compete with them in every product area. We feel we compare very favorably to these two competitors, especially when it comes to the ability to grow without boundaries. We are often brought in by companies to replace systems that were originally built on IBM or Oracle technology. Also, we feel we have an advantage in our specialization on data warehousing and decision support. Our competition doesn't have the same focus, evidenced by the fact they promote online transaction processing systems, which can't really handle the data loads or process the complexity of queries our database can. We're especially proud of the industry recognition we've gained in the past year with our customers. The world's largest commercial Teradata user, SBC Communications, led five out of six categories in a recent database scalability survey by analyst firm Winter Corporation. The Data Warehousing Institute recognized Teradata customer Harrah's Entertainment as its 2000 Leadership in Data Warehousing Award winner.

Reporter: How would you summarize the benefits you bring to customers?

Hurd: We help them drive growth. And we make them smarter with better decision-making.

Reporter: If you're going to drive one message to your channel partners, what do you really want to say to them? What are you trying to do here?

Hurd: We need you. We can't get to every buying point. And even when we get to every buying point, we can't bring every solution. So we need help. We look at the channel as a strategic advantage and not as a strategic problem. The issue for us, though, is to make sure we get as aligned as we possibly can with our channel so that we eventually go and scale our business together in a way that's not only profitable for both of us but leaves a bunch of doggone happy customers at the end that are going to wind up doing more business with us.

---

strategic *adj.*
战略上的，战略的

implement *v.*
实施，执行

retailer *n.*
零售商，传播的人

telecommunication *n.*
远程通信，无线电通讯

manufacturer *n.*
制造商，厂商

stack *v.*
堆积，堆叠

boundary *n.*
界限，范围

originally *adv.*
最初，本来

process *v.*
加工，处理

recognition *n.*
识别，承认

category *n.*
种类，范畴

summarize *v.*
总结，概述

partner *n.*
伙伴，合伙人

align *v.*
使结盟，匹配

doggone *adv.*
非常地，极端地

未来不仅涉及[21]使用系统做出战略决策，而且能把该公司的资料显示给一线员工，使他们能够做出迅速和明智[22]的决定。为实现这一目标，公司需要一个数据存储库，可以快速加载数据并且处理来自数以千计的用户的复杂查询[23]。如今我们正在帮助客户完成数据库的这些功能。

记者：您能谈一谈您的客户吗？什么行业是您的目标客户？

赫德：我们与全球很多零售商[24]都有过很成功的合作，但是我们同样拥有很多领导银行业、航空业、通信业[25]、保险业、制造业、能源业和娱乐业的客户，还有几个非常成功的电子商务客户。我们的客户包括世界七大航空公司中的6家、前10家零售商中的6家、前9家通信公司中的6家、40%以上的美国最大生产制造商以及全球各大著名银行。这些客户包括加拿大皇家银行、达美航空公司、澳大利亚坎塔斯航空公司、瑞士银行公司、UnumProvident、三星人寿保险、爱迪生使命能源公司、哈拉斯娱乐公司、联邦快递、上海证交所、Travelocity、ETRADE（美国著名网络公司）和美其罗吉克公司等等。

记者：您是否认为IBM和甲骨文[26]是您的主要竞争对手？您如何与他们竞争？

赫德：尽管我们没有在每个产品领域[27]都与之竞争，但我们确实认为IBM和甲骨文是惠普数据存储事业部的主要竞争对手。我们认为自己的实力优于这两家公司，特别是发展能力。我们的产品经常被公司引进来代替原先安装的基于IBM或者甲骨文技术的系统。此外，我们认为我们在专业化[28]数据存储和决策支持方面有优势。我们的竞争并不在同一个点上，他们促进在线交易处理系统[29]，不能处理数据加载或者特殊情况，而我们的数据库是可以做这些事情的。我们特别自豪于过去几年中与客户建立起来的产业认知度[30]。近来在分析公司Winter Corporation（一家独立的权威的评测机构）做的有关数据库拓展性[31]调查中，世界最大的商业Teradata用户SBC传媒公司在六个选项中，五项选择了Teradata。数据库研究所将Teradata客户哈拉斯娱乐公司认定为2000年数据库奖获得者。

记者：您认为客户从您的产品中可以获得哪些好处？

赫德：我们促使[32]他们增长。我们使他们能够更好地进行决策。

记者：如果您要给渠道[33]合作商一个信息，您要跟他们说什么？您要做哪些事情？

赫德：我们需要你们。我们不能到达每一个买入点。即使我们能够覆盖到每一个买入

点，我们也不能提供每一个解决方案。所以我们需要帮助。我们将渠道看成是一种战略[34]优势，而不是战略问题。然而，对于我们来说，确保我们能够更多地与渠道合作，最终扩大[35]我们的业务范围，不仅是我们还有合作商都会从中盈利，而且客户也会得到最满意的服务，从而愿意在今后与我们做更多的生意。

21. involve v.
22. informed adj.
23. query n.
24. retailer n.
25. telecommunication n.
26. Oracle n.
27. area n.
28. specialization n.
29. online transaction processing system
30. recognition n.
31. scalability n.
32. drive v.
33. channel n.
34. strategic adj.
35. scale v.

1. Teradata Corporation——天睿资讯，是全球企业级数据仓库解决方案领导厂商。其致力于：协助客户制定更明智、更有效的决策，赋予企业不断增长的原动力。在CMP出版集团旗下《智能企业》杂志（*Intelligent Enterprise*）的编辑推荐奖（Editors' Choice Awards）中，Teradata被评为2008年值得关注的全球最具影响力的前十二大杰出企业之一。

2. 英语中的破折号可用来概括前面列举的若干事物。例如：New houses, larger schools, more sheep, more pigs and chickens, more horses and donkeys—everywhere we saw signs of the village's prosperity.（新房子，扩建的学校，更多的羊、猪、鸡、马和驴，到处我们都可以看到这个村庄的繁荣景象。）

3. 在 suggestion，proposal，idea，plan，order，advice等名词后的表语从句、同位语从句中要用虚拟语气，即should+动词原形或只用动词原形。例如：Our suggestion is that you should be the first to go.（我们建议你第一个去。）

4. 动词词组可以通过添加-变成相应的形容词，例如：make decision——decision-making（决策的），face south——south-facing（朝南的）等。

5. business一词的用法非常灵活，例如 "Business is business." 这句话的字面意思是 "生意是生意。" 但其实际意义则引申为 "公事公办。" 例如：Harry may be a friend but business is business, and he's not the best man for the job.（哈里也许是朋友，但公事公办，他不是这项工作的最佳人选。）

6. 可用来做总结的短语或词汇有：to sum up，to put it in a nutshell，in conclusion，in short，in brief等，都表示 "总之" 的意思。例如：We should, in brief, invest heavily in digital systems.（简而言之，我们应该对数字化系统大量投资。）

7. express一词做名词时有 "邮件快递服务" 的意思，例如：Federal Express（联邦快递），Send these books by express.（把这些书用快递寄出去。）

8. e-也是一个有实际意义的前缀，是electronic的缩写，表示 "电子的"，例如：e-businesses（电子商务），e-mail（电子邮件）。

9. 英语中不定式可表示计划做某事，例如：He is to clean the house.（他将要打扫屋子。）这句话中不定式不是做表语用来补充说明主语的，而是表示一种将来的动作。